T0334614

Microeconomic Theory

Microeconomic Theory: A Heterodox Approach develops a heterodox economic theory that explains the economy as the social provisioning process at the micro level. Heterodox microeconomics explores the economy with a focus on its constituent parts and their reproduction and recurrence, their integration qua interdependency by non-market and market arrangements and institutions, and how the system works as a whole.

This book deals with three theoretical concerns. Due to the significance of the price mechanism to mainstream economics, a theoretical concern of the book is the business enterprise, markets, demand, and pricing. Also, since heterodox economists see private investment, consumption, and government expenditures as the principal directors and drivers of economic activity, a second theoretical concern is business decision-making processes regarding investment and production, government expenditure decisions, the financing of investment, the profit mark-up and the wage rate, and taxes. Finally, the third theoretical concern of the book is the delineation of a non-equilibrium disaggregated price-output model of the social provisioning process.

This book explores the integration of these various theories with a theoretical model of the economy and how this forms a theory that can be identified as heterodox microeconomics. It will be of interest to both postgraduates and researchers.

Frederic S. Lee was Professor of Economics at the University of Missouri-Kansas City, USA until he died in 2014. He played an essential role in developing heterodox microeconomic theory and in building a global community of heterodox economists over his thirty-year professional career. He was the founding editor of *Heterodox Economics Newsletter* (2004–2009) and the editor of *American Journal of Economics and Sociology* (2009–2013). Lee published over 172 journal articles, book chapters, and books, including *Post Keynesian Price Theory* (1998), *A History of Heterodox Economics* (2009), and *Handbook of Research Methods and Applications in Heterodox Economics* (2016).

Tae-Hee Jo is Associate Professor of Economics at the State University of New York – Buffalo State, USA.

Routledge Advances in Heterodox Economics

Edited by Mark Setterfield
The New School for Social Research, USA
and
Peter Kriesler
University of New South Wales, Australia

Over the past two decades, the intellectual agendas of heterodox economists have taken a decidedly pluralist turn. Leading thinkers have begun to move beyond the established paradigms of Austrian, feminist, Institutional-evolutionary, Marxian, Post Keynesian, radical, social, and Sraffian economics – opening up new lines of analysis, criticism, and dialogue among dissenting schools of thought. This cross-fertilization of ideas is creating a new generation of scholarship in which novel combinations of heterodox ideas are being brought to bear on important contemporary and historical problems.

Routledge Advances in Heterodox Economics aims to promote this new scholarship by publishing innovative books in heterodox economic theory, policy, philosophy, intellectual history, institutional history, and pedagogy. Syntheses or critical engagement of two or more heterodox traditions are especially encouraged.

For a full list of titles in this series, please visit www.routledge.com/series/RAHE

Microeconomic Theory

A Heterodox Approach

Frederic S. Lee
Edited by Tae-Hee Jo

Routledge
Taylor & Francis Group

LONDON AND NEW YORK

First published 2018
by Routledge

2 Park Square, Milton Park, Abingdon, Oxfordshire OX14 4RN
52 Vanderbilt Avenue, New York, NY 10017

Routledge is an imprint of the Taylor & Francis Group, an informa business

First issued in paperback 2019

British Library *Cataloguing-in-Publication Data*
A catalogue record for this book is available from the British Library

Library of Congress Cataloging-in-Publication Data
Names: Lee, Frederic S., 1949–2014, author. | Jo, Tae-Hee, 1973– editor.
Title: Microeconomic theory : a heterodox approach / authored by Frederic
    S. Lee ; edited by Tae-Hee Jo.
Description: 1 Edition. | New York : Routledge, 2018. | Series: Routledge
    advances in heterodox economics | Includes bibliographical references
    and index.
Identifiers: LCCN 2017034723 (print) | LCCN 2017036297 (ebook) |
    ISBN 9781351265287 (Ebook) | ISBN 9780415247313 (hardback :
    alk. paper)
Subjects: LCSH: Microeconomics.
Classification: LCC HB172 (ebook) | LCC HB172 .L434 2018 (print) |
    DDC 338.501—dc23
LC record available at https://lccn.loc.gov/2017034723

ISBN: 978-0-415-24731-3 (hbk)
ISBN: 978-0-367-35684-2 (pbk)

Typeset in Times New Roman
by Apex CoVantage, LLC

Contents

Figures

Tables

Preface

The origin of this book can be traced back to my graduate days at Rutgers University (1978–1981) when I thought about writing my dissertation on Post Keynesian microeconomics. This grandiose project was quickly reduced to writing a historical and comparative analysis of the administered, normal cost, and mark-up price doctrines; and even this project was further reduced so that my eventual dissertation was on 'Full Cost Pricing: An Historical and Theoretical Analysis' (1983). After completing it, I spent the next fifteen years working on the administered and mark-up price doctrines; my price doctrines project was published in 1998 as *Post Keynesian Price Theory*. However, I never gave up on my grandiose project of writing a book that would set out Post Keynesian microeconomics much in the same way that neoclassical microeconomics is delineated in advanced textbooks and scholarly monographs. In particular, I envisioned Post Keynesian microeconomic theory as a complete alternative to neoclassical microeconomics. My first attempt at such a book was a set of lecture notes I wrote for a course on the introduction to microeconomics that I taught in 1979–1980 while still a graduate student at Rutgers. The notes dealt with production, cost, and pricing of the business enterprise, the determination of market prices, input-output framework of the economy, Sraffian price equations, convergence of market prices to long-period prices, distribution, and the wage-profit frontier. The distinction between Post Keynesian and Sraffian economics, which much is made of today, simply did not exist for me or for those few others, such as the late Alfred Eichner (who was my dissertation advisor and mentor), working in Post Keynesian microeconomics. In particular, at this time Eichner had begun working on his ultimately unfinished text, *The Macrodynamics of Advanced Market Economies* (1987), in which the microeconomics was an infinitely more developed but conceptually not much different than my notes.

While Eichner maintained this particular Post Keynesian-Sraffian vision of microeconomics, I started deviating from it while still at Rutgers. As I was energetically discussing the convergence of market prices to long-period prices one day with Nina Shapiro (also on my dissertation committee), she calmly asked me, "How do I know that they will converge?" as she was unconvinced by the mathematical argument I was putting forth. With the question posed, the genie was out of the bottle, at least for me, for if convergence means anything in this context, it must mean the movement of actual market prices in historical time to long-period prices. But in historical time, anything can happen and generally does. Hence, there is no necessary reason for convergence, which in turn means that long-period positions have no connection to real world economic activity and, therefore, cannot theoretically contribute to explaining it. Consequently, I rejected long-period positions and, to be consistent, short-period positions as well. Moreover, my concurrent research on full cost/normal cost pricing led me to reject the concept of market clearing and to replace it with the concept of a non-clearing market where, in the context of a circular production economy, there are continuous market transactions in historical time so the market is never cleared. Stuck in historical time, I began articulating a microeconomic theory without equilibrium, long- and short-period positions, market clearing, and any notion of certainty (see Lee 1984; 1985; 1994; 1996; 1998). But this did not mean that I rejected all of the Sraffian contributions: the disaggregated input-output representation of production and the economy, circular production and the commodity residual, interdependent price equations, and the possibility of prices being determined independent of supply and demand curves remain important components of my work on microeconomic theory. For example, my work on production and costs of the business enterprise (Lee 1986) was designed to be compatible with input-output models.

Influenced by Paul Davidson and Jan Kregel (both of whom I took courses from while at Rutgers) combined with my research on Gardiner Means meant that I had almost no choice but to explicitly embed my microeconomic theory in a monetary production framework. While this dissolves the wage-profit frontier of a non-monetary Sraffian model, it does not do away with the issue of how the surplus goods and services get produced and then divided up between the various classes. However, adopting the view that a capitalist economy is a non-ergodic, historically grounded, monetary, circular, and surplus production economy generated two major interrelated theoretical issues blocking my quest to produce an alternative microeconomic theory. The absence of demand curves and the principle that markets clear implied that prices do not coordinate economic activity or allocate inputs among productive activities – so I was faced with questions: What do prices do? What are markets? How are market transactions regulated? And what does coordinate economic activity? Drawing on my dissertation and early work (Lee 1984; 1985), the answer I came up with to the first question is that prices reproduce the business enterprise which quickly led me to adopt the Marxian view and notation of M-C-M' as part of its characterization and then later adding to it the institutionalists' notion of the going concern. The answers to the next two questions – markets are social institutions and transactions are regulated by cooperation among business enterprises – came over a fifteen-year period as I examined business histories of trade associations and enterprises, became engrossed in the workings of the US gunpowder market and trade association for the period of 1865 to 1890, and stumbled upon the economic sociology literature concerning markets as social structures and business networks. What became apparent to me is that my evolving views of markets and transactions were old hat to institutionalists and in fact almost indistinguishable from long-established institutionalist arguments. If only the Rutgers economics department had a Walton Hamilton or at least a Bill Dugger! The answer to the last question was, as my Post Keynesian background would suggest, the production of the surplus in the form of investment, consumption, and government goods and services. It is business production, investment decisions, and government expenditure decisions that create and coordinate economic activity, and these decisions are reached largely independent of concerns about prices, rates of profit, or interest rates (which imply that cost minimization, profit maximization, and production-cost duality have no meaning).

The second related issue concerned the theoretical implications of production as a circular and surplus producing process. The first and most significant implication is that the neoclassical concept of scarcity had no definitional, organizing, or other meaningful role in the microeconomic theory I was building. This fundamental theoretical rejection of neoclassical theory, while common among heterodox economists of the 1970s who took the time to examine Sraffa, is unfortunately ignored today by younger heterodox economists. Without scarcity defining and grounding the method used to explain the social provisioning process, then prices are no longer scarcity indexes and, most importantly, the economics of the social provisioning process ceases to be the study of the allocation of scarce resources among competing ends. Instead, as elegantly argued by David Levine (1978) and Heinrich Bortis (1997), production and distribution are social activities, and the study of social provisioning involves the study of social relationships, not theoretically non-existent scarce resources. Consequently, human activity and agency in the guise of acting persons (drawn from social economics) underpin all economic activity and social relationships, social organizations, and established patterns of social activity (or institutions as institutionalists would say) dictate the particular forms economic activity takes. That enterprise and market activities of buying, selling, hiring, firing, producing, investing, and innovating are clearly social activities – that is, combinations of social relationships and agency in action – do not, however, mean that there is only one possible way to delineate them, such as Marxian value theory. Brought up on the Classical-Dobbian-Sraffian view of the labor theory of value, I dismissed it (but not the Marxian concern with the social) and decided to stay in the 'objective' world of commodities. This decision was reinforced by my Post Keynesian background in which investment and government expenditures generate profits (not the exploitation of labor) as well as coordinate economic activity. But this world of commodities was a by-product of social activities and this I felt was both the central organizational and defining feature of the microeconomic theory I wanted to develop. Yet, how to develop such a theory was, for a long time, a puzzle to me.

Dismissing short- and long-period positions, equilibrium, optimality, minimization, maximization, scarcity, and traditional value theory as central organizing features for the theory, what I wanted to develop was, in hindsight, a drawn-out debate I was having with myself over its appropriate methodological foundations (although for a long time I viewed it strictly in terms of theoretical rejection). When I moved to the United Kingdom in 1990, the British Marxists and Post

Keynesians were engaged in methodological discussion over critical realism that simply did not exist in the United States at that time. Not being terribly interested in methodology or understanding much of the debate in any case, I just ignored it. But then Paul Downward wrote a critique of my work on pricing (Downward and Reynolds 1996) using fancy words, such as open-system theorizing and process-truth, that I did not understand. But I knew our work on pricing was compatible and therefore was greatly puzzled by his comments. Then one day I got in an extended discussion with Steve Fleetwood (my colleague at De Montfort University) over history versus critical realism; and in the end, he convinced me that methodology was important and that critical realism was the appropriate onto-logical basis of the microeconomic theory I wished to write. This led me to do further research on the methodology of theory creation and the end result was the adoption of the research strategy of the grounded theory method. With the critical realism-grounded theory approach, it was now possible to delineate a microeco-nomic theory organized around social activities and which clearly contributed to explaining the social provisioning process of a capitalist economy.

The diverse heterodox influences on my thinking and theorizing since my first lecture notes on microeconomics has transformed what initially was a Post Keynesian approach into a heterodox one. Marxian, institutional, and Sraffian influences combined with Post Keynesianism, critical realism, and social econom-ics mean that the microeconomic theory delineated in this book has gone through a transformational synthesis that makes it an emergent heterodox theory, albeit only a provisional one. This has two implications. The first is that the integrative approach produces arguments that do not include or are critical of theoretical concepts and arguments that are cherished by many heterodox economists. Con-sequently, when some of the material in the book, such as the heterodox theory production and costs for the business enterprise, was submitted to heterodox jour-nals for publication, the referees quickly condemned and dismissed it. Of course the critics never actually produce an alternative heterodox theory of production and costs but continue to rely on neoclassical production and cost theory. Sec-ondly, the microeconomic theory presented in the following pages is incomplete because the possible contributions of ecological and feminist economics as well as other heterodox approaches are largely absent, and because not all subject areas are covered, most notably distribution of income and workplace control. Their absence in the book is not due to unimportance or irrelevance on their part, but to recognition by me that my grandiose project is indeed too grandiose for me to complete. The omissions I hope will attract brash heterodox economists to com-plete what I started if not dramatically develop and extend it. For the success of my book is not to be measured in the number of copies sold or the number of cita-tions in journal articles, but in how quickly it gets superseded. As Eichner made quite clear to me through his own actions, it is not so much what I write that is important, but that what I write opens opportunities for other economists to make contributions to the development of heterodox economics.

In addition to the above named economists, there are many others whose comments and support have made this thirty-five year journey possible: Steve Dunn, Peter Earl, Stephanie Kelton, John King, Marc Lavoie, Warren Samuels, Andrew Trigg, my graduate students at the University of California-Riverside who kindly let me learn Sraffa while I taught it to them, and my students at De Montfort University and University of Missouri-Kansas City who have suffered through my lectures which are the basis for this book. Taking the road less traveled is an intellectually and emotionally difficult journey. With the support of my wife, Ruth, the journey was possible; without her there would have been no journey at all.

Lastly, earlier versions of several chapters have been published in academic journals and books. They have been amended or updated for the present book.

Chapter 1 includes material that originally appeared in Lee, F. S. (2002), "Theory Creation and the Methodological Foundation of Post Keynesian Economics," *Cambridge Journal of Economics* 26 (6): 789–804; and Lee, F. S. (2016), "Critical Realism, Method of Grounded Theory, and Theory Construction" and "Modeling as a Research Method in Heterodox Economics," in *Handbook of Research Methods and Applications in Heterodox Economics*, edited by F. S. Lee and B. Cronin, 35–53, 272–285, Cheltenham: Edward Elgar.

Chapter 2 includes material that originally appeared in Lee, F. S. (2011), "Modeling the Economy as a Whole: An Integrative Approach," *American Journal of Economics and Sociology* 70 (5): 1282–1314; and Lee, F. S. and T.-H. Jo (2011), "Social Surplus Approach and Heterodox Economics," *Journal of Economic Issues* 45 (4): 857–875.

Chapter 4 includes material that originally appeared in Gu, G. C. and F. S. Lee (2012), "Pricing and Prices," in *Elgar Companion to Post Keynesian Economics*, 2nd edn, edited by J. E. King, 456–462, Cheltenham: Edward Elgar.

Chapter 6 includes material that originally appeared in Lee, F. S. (2012), "Competition, Going Enterprise, and Economic Activity," in *Alternative Theories of Competition: Challenges to the Orthodoxy*, edited by J. K. Moudud, C. Bina, and P. L. Mason, 160–173, London: Routledge; and Lee, F. S. (2013), "Post-Keynesian Price Theory: From Pricing to Market Governance to the Economy as a Whole," in *The Oxford Handbook of Post-Keynesian Economics,* Vol. 1, edited by G. C. Harcourt and P. Kriesler, 467–484, Oxford: Oxford University Press.

Chapter 7 includes material that originally appeared in Lee, F. S. (2012), "Heterodox Surplus Approach: Production, Prices, and Value Theory," *Bulletin of Political Economy* 6 (2): 65–105.

Frederic S. Lee

August 2014

***

As Fred Lee mentioned in his preface, this book has a long history which goes back to his graduate days at Rutgers University (1978–1981) where he studied with Alfred Eichner, Nina Shapiro, Paul Davidson, and Jan Kregel – the most important figures in the formation and development of Post Keynesian economics in the United States. In particular, it was Fred's "discovery of Alfred Eichner" in 1977 that is "the most important in my entire academic career" (Lee 2015, 318). Fred recalled in his tribute to Eichner that "he was the first economist I met who really encouraged me in my work on pricing and thought that I was not a complete fool" (Lee 1991, 26). The relationship between Fred Lee and Alfred Eichner parallels the relationship between Eichner and Joan Robinson, as Eichner dedicated his last book, *The Macrodynamics of Advanced Market Economies* (1987), to her: "To Joan Robinson who, by first putting together into a coherent whole the alternative post-Keynesian paradigm, showed us the path out of the Valley of Darkness that is the neoclassical theory." Were he alive today, Fred would have dedicated the present book to Eichner.

This book, *Microeconomic Theory: A Heterodox Approach*, is Fred's 'grandiose' project which took about forty years to come to its fruition. If he were an ordinary economist, he could have finished it in 2003 (which is the initial deadline of the manuscript under contract with Routledge, and we know that Fred was a most responsible person). Unlike most self-interested economists, he put this book aside and engaged in other works that were, he thought, more important than his own research – just to mention a few, his work on ranking journals and departments and on Research Assessment Exercise in the UK (both of which became part of his 2009 book, *A History of Heterodox Economics*), creating and editing *Heterodox Economics Newsletter*, editing *American Journal of Economics and Sociology*, managing a heterodox doctoral program at the University of Missouri-Kansas City, organizing conferences and seminars, and supervising doctoral dissertations. He undertook all these activities because he believed that there would be no demand for heterodox economists, no opportunity for students to learn heterodox economics, and hence no future of heterodox economics, if heterodox economists did not carry out what's required for the survival and reproduction of heterodox economics. Certainly, he showed through his actions and writings that neoclassical economics in which people are always self-interested and the world is self-adjusting is nothing but a fairy tale.

Until I took Fred's microeconomics course in 2003, I had no idea of what heterodox microeconomics was. Like most students then and now I was interested in macro, money, and financial crises (it was partly because I witnessed the Asian crisis in 1997 when I was a student in Korea, as those students who are now interested in macro-financial issues went through the 2007–2008 crisis and the following recession). To my surprise, for the first time in my study of economics, I found that microeconomic theory made sense to me because he provided theoretical frameworks to analyze the real world and real people that we have contact with every day, as well as how the economy is structured and managed by acting persons and organizations. More importantly, his lectures and a body of literature therein enlightened me that it is possible to develop a historically-grounded heterodox microeconomic theory that is assumed to be impossible or non-existent.

The reason I am talking about my own experience is that the primary purpose of this book is precisely to show both heterodox and mainstream economists that heterodox microeconomic theory is possible, although it is in the process of developing like any other theory, and it offers novel explanations derived from actual history as to how the business enterprise, the state, the household, and market governance organizations make decisions and carry out deliberate actions in the uncertain and transmutable world; how those 'micro' decisions and actions are intertwined with 'macro' outcomes; and, eventually, how we analyze the capitalist economic system and its provisioning process. Fred had never claimed that his theory was "the" theory. Rather, he wanted other heterodox economists to develop a better heterodox theory by way of his own work. He would have been happy to see that his theory is criticized and improved by younger heterodox economists.

Let me describe what I have done as the editor of this book. In January 2015, I was able to see the unfinished manuscript. The first three chapters were complete. However, the following four chapters were either partly completed or roughly drafted with notes and outlines. For those incomplete chapters I utilized already published articles and book chapters of Fred's and edited them for the sake of this book. Those reproduced materials are listed at the end of Fred's own preface. For Chapter 8, I added the edited transcript of Fred's last microeconomics lecture delivered at the University of Missouri-Kansas City, instead of writing the conclusion in my own words or leaving the book without a conclusion. Except for Chapter 8, all the chapters are what Fred initially planned, although I have made some minor changes and corrected obvious errors in each chapter. In addition, I have recreated or updated all the figures and tables, edited mathematical symbols and equations in order to make sure that they are used consistently throughout the book, and added an "Editor's note" where an explanation regarding the text is necessary. I have also added two appendixes. Appendix 1 is Fred's heterodox microeconomics course syllabus with a list of readings (last updated in 2013), and Appendix 2 is the problem set for the course. These two appendixes would help develop a heterodox microeconomics course if one wishes to do so.

Lastly, I wish to thank Ruth Lee for allowing me to edit the book and John F. Henry for correcting my errors in an early version of Chapter 8. I am grateful to Andy Humphries, Elanor Best, and Anna Cuthbert at Routledge for being patient and supportive throughout the editing process.

Tae-Hee Jo
July 2017

Notations and abbreviations

Notes: Scalars in *italic*, vectors in **bold**, matrices in UPPERCASE roman, variables in *italic*, abbreviated words in UPPERCASE or lowercase roman.

a	Vector of direct intermediate input technical coefficients
a*	Vector of intermediate input production coefficients
a$_{ee}$	Vector of enterprise intermediate input technical coefficients for the accounting period
å$_k$	Vector of the amounts of intermediate inputs needed to produce the maximum flow rate of output of the k-th plant
å$_k^*$	Vector of intermediate production coefficients at q_e flow rate of output
a$_{se}$	Vector of managerial intermediate input technical coefficients in absolute amounts for the accounting period
a$_{sek}$	Vector of managerial intermediate input technical coefficients for the k-th plant in absolute amount for the accounting period
a$_{sef}^*$	Vector of shop intermediate input production coefficients for the f-th production period at q_e flow rate of output
a$_{sekf}^*$	Vector of plant managerial intermediate production coefficients for the f-th production period and q flow rate of output
ACSTP	Average shop technique of production
AEE	Average enterprise expenses
AOHC	Average overhead costs
APMTP	Average plant's managerial technique of production
ASE	Average shop expenses
ASP	Average structure of production
ASTP	Average shop technique of production
B$_5$	Amount of banking sector liabilities paid off by ruling class households (LB$_{HRC}$) and the working and dependent class households (LB$_{HWDC}$)
B$_{f1}^t$	Portion of profits of the f-th production period in the t-th accounting period set aside for use as working capital in the next accounting period

B^t_{f2}	Portion of profits of the f-th production period in the t-th accounting period set aside for expanding capacity in the next accounting period
$c_{it\text{-}1}$	Reduction in NEATC in the t-th accounting period due to the technically new plants introduced in the previous accounting period, $t-1$
CETP	Cost of the enterprise technique of production
CSTP	Cost of the shop technique of production
d_i	Depreciation pricing coefficient
d	Vector of depreciation pricing coefficients
D_E	Depreciation of the economy
e	Sum vector
EADC	Enterprise average direct costs
$EADC_B$	Enterprise average direct costs at the budgeted flow rate of output
EADLC	Enterprise average direct labor costs
EADMC	Enterprise average direct intermediate costs
EADSP	Enterprise average direct inputs structure of production
EALC	Enterprise average labor costs
EAMC	Enterprise average intermediate costs
EATC	Enterprise average total costs
$EATC_B$	Enterprise average total costs at the budgeted flow rate of output
$EATC^a_{it}$	Actual EATC of the i-th enterprise in the t-th production period
EE	Enterprise expenses
EPADC	Emergent plant average direct costs
EPDCP	Emergent plant direct costs of production
ETP	Enterprise technique of production
FA_{SRC}	Amount of government bonds purchased by ruling class households
FA_{BE}	Amount of government bonds purchased by bank and non-bank enterprises
$\mathbf{FA_{S1}}$	Vector of FA_{SGB1} and FA_{SDD1}
$\mathbf{FA_{S2}}$	Vector of FA_{SGB2} and FA_{SDD2}
FA_{S2}	Stock of financial assets-government bonds associated with the production of bank loans $(\mathbf{Q_{3L}})$
FA_{S5}	Stock of financial assets-government bonds associated with household activities
FA_{SBL3}	Stock of bank loans
FA_{SDD1}	Stock of demand deposits associated with the production of $\mathbf{Q_1}$
FA_{SDD2}	Stock of demand deposits associated with the production of $\mathbf{Q_2}$
FA_{SDD5}	Stock of demand deposits associated with household activities
FA_{SGB1}	Stock of financial assets-government bonds associated with the production of $\mathbf{Q_1}$
FA_{SGB2}	Stock of financial assets-government bonds associated with the production of $\mathbf{Q_2}$
FA_{SGB3}	Stock of financial assets-government bonds associated with the production of bank loans $(\mathbf{Q_{3L}})$

FA_{SGB5}	Stock of financial assets-government bonds associated with household activities
g	Flow rate (or amount) of output per production period
g^a	Actual market growth rate
g^a_a	Actual market growth rate after the change
g^a_b	Actual market growth rate before the change
g^*_a	Steady market growth rate after the change
g^*_b	Steady market growth rate before the change
G	Matrix of intermediate inputs consisting of produced resources, goods, and services
G^*	Augmented G matrix
$\mathbf{G}_i$	Vector of intermediate inputs used in the production of the i-th output (Q_i)
G_{11}	Matrix of intermediate inputs used in the production of $\mathbf{Q}_1$
G_{21}	Matrix of intermediate inputs used in the production of $\mathbf{Q}_2$
$\mathbf{G}_{31}$	Vector of intermediate inputs used in the production of bank loans
$\mathbf{G}\mathbf{p}_1$	Value of the intermediate inputs by product used in the production of the social product
GOV_E	Total government expenditures
GP	Amount of government payments
GP_d	Government income payments to the dependent class
GP_E	Government interest payments to business enterprises (GP_{ib}) and banks (GP_{iB})
GP_{ib}	Government interest payments to business enterprises
GP_{iB}	Government interest payments to banks
GP_{ih}	Government interest payments to households
$\mathbf{h}_i$	Vector of labor pricing coefficients at normal capacity utilization
H	Matrix of labor pricing coefficients that are invariant with respect to short-term variations in output
HII	Household interest income
HPADC	Hybrid plant average direct costs
HPDCP	Hybrid plant direct costs of production
i_B	Rate of interest on current bank loans
i_{Bp}	Rate of interest on past bank loans
$i_{Bp}FAH_{SBL3}$	Interest income made on loans to the household sector
$i_{Bp}FA_{SBL3}$	Interest income from bank loans
i_D	Rate of interest on demand deposits set by the banking sector
$i_D FA_{SDD5}$	Interest income from demand deposits
$i_D LBH_{S3}$	Interest payments made on household demand deposits
$i_D LB_{S3}$	Interest costs of demand deposits to the banking sector
i_G	Rate of interest on government bonds
$i_G FA_{SGB3}$	Interest income from government bonds
k	Mark-up for overhead costs and profits
k_{mu}	Degree of capacity utilization

$\tilde{k}_{mu}$	Full capacity utilization of the plant
k_{mue}	Degree of capacity utilization of the product line where $\tilde{q}_e$ is the enterprise's maximum flow rate of output when all plants are used and producing at full capacity
$\mathbf{k}$	Vector of fixed investment goods associated with PS
$\mathbf{k}_d$	Vector of fixed investment goods across all plants that are 'directly' used in the production of the product line
$\mathbf{k}_{hp}$	Vector of fixed investment goods associated with the hybrid plant
$\mathbf{k}_{se}$	Vector of fixed investment goods associated with STP
$\mathbf{k}_{spk}, \mathbf{k}_{epk}, \mathbf{k}_{hpk}$	Vectors of fixed investment goods for the segmented plant, emergent plant, and hybrid plant
$\mathbf{K}_{F4}$	Vector of the flow of government fixed investment goods into $\mathbf{K}_{S4}$
K_{S1}	Matrix of the basic goods sector stock of fixed investment goods used in the production of $\mathbf{Q}_1$
K_{S2}	Matrix of the surplus goods sector stock of fixed investment goods used in the production of $\mathbf{Q}_2$
$\mathbf{K}_{S3}$	Vector of the stock of fixed investment goods used in the production of bank loans
$\mathbf{K}_{S4}$	Vector of the stock of government fixed investment goods used in providing government services
$\mathbf{l}$	Vector of direct labor input technical coefficients
$\mathbf{l}^*$	Vector of labor production coefficients
$\mathbf{l}_{ee}$	Vector of enterprise labor technical coefficients for the accounting period
$\mathbf{l}_{se}$	Vector of managerial labor input technical coefficients in absolute amounts for the accounting period
$\tilde{\mathbf{l}}_k$	Vector of the amount of the labor inputs needed to produce the maximum flow rate of output of the k-th plant
$\tilde{\mathbf{l}}_k^*$	Vector labor input production coefficients at q_e
$\mathbf{l}_{sef}^*$	Vector of shop labor input production coefficients for the f-th production period when the flow rate of output is q_e
$\mathbf{l}_{sekf}^*$	Vector of plant managerial labor input coefficients for the f-th production period and q flow rate of output
L	Matrix of labor skills
L*	Vector of all the labor skills
L	Vector of total labor skills employed in the private sector
L*	Vector of total labor skills employed in the economy
L_{11}	Matrix of labor skills used in the production of $\mathbf{Q}_1$
L_{21}	Matrix of labor skills used in the production of $\mathbf{Q}_2$
$\mathbf{L}_{31}$	Vector of labor skills employed in the banking sector
$\mathbf{L}_{41}$	Vector of labor skills used in providing government services

L_w	Wage bill by product incurred in the production of the social product
L^*_w	Total wage bill of the economy
$\mathbf{L}_{31}\mathbf{w}$	Wage bill by product incurred in the production of the bank loans
$\mathbf{L}_{41}\mathbf{w}$	Government's wage bill
LB_{BE}	Amount of liabilities ($LB_{S1,2}$) paid off by non-bank enterprises.
$\mathbf{LB}_{S1}$ (LB_{S1})	Vector (scalar) of the stock of liabilities-bank loans associated with the production of $\mathbf{Q}_1$
$\mathbf{LB}_{S2}$ (LB_{S2})	Vector (scalar) of the stock of liabilities-bank loans associated with the production of $\mathbf{Q}_2$
LB_{S3}	Stock of financial liabilities-deposit accounts of business enterprises and households
LB_{S4}	Stock of financial liabilities (national debt) associated with providing government services (GS)
LB_{S5}	Stock of liabilities-bank loans associated with household activities
M	Matrix of material pricing coefficients that are invariant with respect to short-term variations in output
$\mathbf{m}_i$	Vector of material pricing coefficients at normal capacity utilization
M_{wc}	Cash advanced in the form of working capital
NEATC	Normal enterprise average total cots (or EATC at the normal flow rate of output)
$NEATC_d$	Normal enterprise average total costs of the dominant enterprise in the market
$NEATC_f$	Normal enterprise average total costs of the price following enterprise in the market
$NEATC_{i0}$	NEATC for the *i*-th enterprise in the initial accounting period
$NEATC_{it}$	NEATC for the *i*-th enterprise in the *t*-th accounting period
OHC	Overhead costs
p	Price of product or of a single product line
p_{ej}	Enterprise price of the *j*-th good
p_e^H	Price charged by the high cost enterprise
p_{it+1}	Actual market price for the *i*-th good at time $t+1$
p_m	Market price
p_{mj}	Market price of the *j*-th good
p_t	Price of *j*-th good in the *t*-th accounting period
$\mathbf{p}$	Vector of state money prices of all resources, goods, and services
$\mathbf{p}_1$	Vector of prices of intermediate inputs
$\mathbf{p}_2$	Vector of prices of surplus goods and services
$\mathbf{p}_{1t}$	Vector of input prices at time t
$\mathbf{p}_{ee}$	Vector of enterprise intermediate input prices
$\mathbf{p}_{se}$	Vector of managerial intermediate input prices
P_B	Production at budgeted output

P_n	Production at the normal flow rate of output
PADC	Plant average direct costs
PADLC	Plant average direct labor costs
PADMC	Plant average direct intermediate costs
PMTP	Plant's managerial technique of production
PS	Plant segment
PSDCP	Plant segment direct costs of production of a product line
q	Flow rate of output
q_B	Budgeted output
q^*	Steady state market growth rate
$\tilde{q}$	Plant's practical maximum flow rate of output when all PSs are utilized
q_e	Enterprise's flow rate of output for k plants with each plant producing at full capacity
$\tilde{q}_e$	Enterprise's maximum flow rate of output when all plants are used and producing at full capacity
$\tilde{q}_k$	Maximum flow rate of output of the k-th plant
q_{jkf}	Enterprise's market share (or share of flow rate of output) in the f-th production period
$\tilde{q}_{jkf}$	Enterprise's maximum flow rate of output for producing the j-th good
q_{jnf}^t	Normal flow rate of output (j-th good) for the f-th production period in the t-th accounting period
q_m	Market flow rate of output
q_{m0}	Initial market flow rate of output
q_{mt}^a	Actual market flow rate of output
q_{mt}^*	Steady market flow rate of output
Q_i	i-th product
Q_d	Diagonal matrix of the total social product
Q_1	Vector of intermediate resources, goods, and services
Q_2	Vector of final goods and services for consumption, investment, and government use
Q_{2C}	Vector of consumption goods
Q_{2G}	Vector of government goods
Q_{2I}	Vector of investment goods
Q_{3L}	Amount of bank loans made to enterprises and households
$Q^T p$	Total value of the total social product
$Q_1^T p_1$	Total value of the intermediate inputs
$Q_2^T p_2$	Total value of the social surplus
$Q_{2I}^T p_2$	Total value of investment goods
$Q_{2G}^T p_2$	Total value of government goods and services
$Q_{2C}^T p_2$	Total value of consumption goods and services
r	Profit mark-up
r_d	Profit mark-up of the dominant enterprise

r_f	Profit mark-up of the price following enterprise
r_i	Profit mark-up for the i-th good
R_d	Diagonal matrix of profit mark-ups
rr_{ij}	Amount of the j-th resource reserve available for the production of Q_i
rr	Vector of resource reserves associated with PS
$\mathbf{rr}_d$	Vector of resource reserves across all plants that are 'directly' used in the production of the product line
$\mathbf{rr}_{hp}$	Vector of resource reserves associated with the hybrid plant
$\mathbf{rr}_{se}$	Vector of resource reserves associated with STP
$\mathbf{rr}_{spk},\ \mathbf{rr}_{epk},\ \mathbf{rr}_{hpk}$	Vectors of resource reserves available for the segmented plant, emergent plant, and hybrid plant
$\mathbf{RR}_{F4}$	Vector of the flow of government resource reserves into $\mathbf{RR}_{S4}$
RR_{S1}	Matrix of the amount of resource reserves available for the production of $\mathbf{Q}_1$
RR_{S2}	Matrix of the amount of resource reserves available for the production of $\mathbf{Q}_2$
$\mathbf{RR}_{S3}$	Stock of resource reserves used in the production of bank loans
$\mathbf{RR}_{S4}$	Vector of government resource reserves available for providing government services
$\mathbf{s}_{ee}$	Vector of enterprise yearly salaries
S	Vector of surplus goods and services
SALC	Shop average labor power costs
SAMC	Shop average intermediate costs
SP	Segmented plant
SPADC	Segmented plant average direct costs
STP	Shop technique of production
TC	Total costs
TC_B	Total costs at budgeted output
TC_n	Total costs at the normal flow rate of output
TR	Total revenue
TR_3	Total interest income of the banking sector
TR_B	Total revenue at budgeted output
TR_n	Total revenue at the normal flow rate of output
TRR	Target rate of return on capital assets
VCA	Value of the capital assets
w	Vector of state money wage rates
$\mathbf{w}_{se}$	Vector of managerial labor salaries
x_i	Mark-up to cover an allocated part of i-th overhead cost
z	Mark-up for overhead costs
z_i	Overhead mark-up for the i-th good
z_{it}	Percentage change in EATC due solely to a change in the i-th enterprise's level of output in the t-th production period
Z_d	Diagonal matrix of overhead mark-ups

Greek and other symbols

θ	Targeted profit mark-up
π_t	Target profits
Π	Total gross profits of the economy
Π^*	Total profits after taxes
Π'	Total net profits of the economy
Π_1	Total gross profits of the basic goods sector
$\mathbf{\Pi}_1$	Vector of profits for each intermediate input
Π_2	Total gross profits of the surplus goods sector
$\mathbf{\Pi}_2$	Vector of profits for each surplus product
Π_3	Total gross profits of the banking sector
Π_D	Gross dividends
Π_D^*	Dividends after taxes
Π_R	Gross retained earnings
Π_R^*	Retained earnings after taxes
τ_i	Income tax rate
τ_p	Profit tax rate
$\oplus$	"combined with"
$:$	"given"

1 The making of heterodox microeconomics

Economics is the science of the social provisioning process

Economics as a discipline is a specialized, scientific, factual body of knowledge that endeavors to develop theoretical explanations of real economic activities that connect acting persons qua households with the flow of goods and services needed to sustain their existence and promote their well-being over time. Thus economic activities are enmeshed with others to form an interdependent, intertwined system of production and consumption. Similarly, acting persons are not isolated, but are enmeshed in various social relationships that cannot be stripped away. Together they imply that the economy is an emergent system of social-economic activities that generate an array of surplus goods and services (over what is used up in production) needed to sustain households and their social relationships, and thus society as a whole – in short, the economy is about social provisioning. Consequently, economics is about developing theoretical explanations of the process by which the economy provides social provisioning – that is, *economics is defined as the science of the social provisioning process*. For any factual field of inquiry or scientific research field to exist, it must have a research community whose members exist in a society that at least tolerates, if not supports, their research activities. Moreover, its object of study must be real (as opposed to fictitious or non-existent) and relate to the problems and issues that are the focus of the research community. Finally, the methods used by the researchers to study the objects and address the problems and issues need to be grounded in the real world. Economics as a research field has a research community, albeit one divided between mainstream and heterodox economists, that is located within a society that supports it more (for mainstream economics) or less (for heterodox economics). The two sub-fields of economics, mainstream and heterodox economics, have some overlapping objects of study and problems and issues to address, but much less overlapping of research approaches and methods used to study the objects and issues, which ultimately generate quite distinct theoretical and hence rival explanations of the social provisioning process. What makes mainstream and heterodox economics distinctly different is that the former, at a fundamental level, is not capable of developing coherent theoretical explanations of the social provisioning process that are grounded in the real world.[1]

This claim merits further but brief discussion. First, the objects of study of mainstream economics, such as preferences-utility, marginal products, demand curves, rationality, relative scarcity, and homogeneous agents, are ill-defined, have no real world existence, and, where relevant, are non-quantifiable and non-measurable.[2] Consequently, the issues and problems for which the objects are relevant, such as competitive markets, efficiency, and constrained optimality, are either fictitious in that they are unrelated to the real world or, if the issues and problems are clearly located in the real world, such as prices and unemployment, the objects have no bearing on their existence. Secondly, the methods used by mainstream economists to develop theoretical explanations addressing the issues and problems, such as deductive methodology and ontological and methodological individualism, generally include fictitious objects and utilize concepts that have no grounding and hence no meaning in the real world. Together, they clearly suggest that it is not possible for mainstream economists to conjure up any theoretical explanations relevant to the provisioning process that takes place in the real world. In addition, the mainstream theory of the provisioning process that is the core area of study of mainstream economics (Hirshleifer 1985, 53) and is itself also quite problematical. The core propositions of the theory, such as scarcity, preferences and utility functions, technology and production functions, rationality, maximization/optimization, market clearing, equilibrium, ontological and methodological individualism, heterogeneous agents, and positivist and deductivist methodology, have all been subject to intensive heterodox critiques; and in many cases there are multiple, overlapping heterodox critiques of core propositions.[3] But even if these critiques are ignored, it is well-known that it is not possible to generate internally coherent explanations or stories or parables of market activity (such as the pervasive urban legend of the market as a self-adjusting mechanism) at either the micro or macro level; even if particular stories (represented in terms of models) of market activities are accepted, such as general equilibrium, game theory, or IS-LM, they have been shown, on their own terms, to be theoretically incoherent and empirically unsupported. The combination of critiques and incoherence means that none of the mainstream theoretical concepts or, more generally, its theoretical language and narrative story can be transferred to heterodox economics (Rizvi 1994; Lawson 1997a; Keen 2001; Ackerman and Nadal 2004; Lee and Keen 2004; Petri 2004; White 2004; Palacio-Vera 2005).

The above arguments suggest that mainstream theory lacks truth and value and contributes nothing (not even terms such as equilibrium, demand curve, or short period) to explaining the social provisioning process in a capitalist economy. Hence, it is not surprising that mainstream theory has become increasingly separated from its subject matter and progressively engaged in articulating properties of worlds within the model that have no connection to the real world. Nor is it surprising that its method of evaluating its fictional theories is to compare the projected fictional outcomes of a fictional model to actual data as if this had any meaning. Finally, it is not surprising that mainstream economists are increasingly defining economics as a particular method of inquiry without factual content. Given the fictitious nature of mainstream theory, it arguably represents bogus, false, or pseudo-knowledge because "it refers to non-existents or because it represents existents in an utterly false manner" (Bunge 1983, 195). Thus, mainstream theory is not a rival scientific theory to heterodox theory because it is not 'scientific,' although it remains a non-scientific rival much like Creationism is a non-scientific rival of the theory of evolution.[4] The fact that it is considered part of the research field of economics indicates the extent to which economics is a highly contested discipline where non-scientific aims and attitudes still play a significant role. Therefore, economics is perhaps a proto-science or semi-science with heterodox economics representing pockets of an almost mature science (Bunge 1983; 1985; 1998; Mahner 2007; Lee 2013a).

Heterodox economics

As stated above, economics is the science of the social provisioning process, and that scientific endeavor is best carried out by heterodox economists. Heterodox economics refers to a specific group of theories aimed at explaining it, to economic policy recommendations predicated on the theories, and to a community of economists engaged in this theoretical and applied scientific activity. Heterodox economic theory specifically focuses on human agency in a cultural context and social processes in historical time affecting and directing resources and their usage, consumption patterns, production and reproduction, and the meaning (or ideology) of economic activities engaged in social provisioning utilizing empirically grounded concepts and a critical realist-grounded theory methodology. However, for the occurrence of such scientific activity, there must exist a research community of heterodox economists and its existence must be, to some degree, supported by society at large.

Community of heterodox economists

The scientific research community of heterodox economists is grounded in a social system of work that produces scientific or economic knowledge that contributes to the understanding of the economy as the social provisioning process. Moreover, this system of work is largely embedded in educational systems and their employment markets. So, although economic research and employment can be found in a variety of non-educational institutions, such as governments, private or public research institutes, trade unions, and advocacy organizations, the reproduction and expansion of the community is primarily tied to the academy. This means that the social system of work for heterodox economists is (as for mainstream economists) located in university economics departments. In particular, the department is the local employment market, establishes the career structure, is the organizational locale for teaching students and training future heterodox economists, and is the site for the production of heterodox scientific knowledge that must be publishable in referred journals, books, and other reputable outlets.[5] In addition to university departments, there are other organizations that support and compliment the social system of work and support and promote the development of heterodox economic theory, including journals, book publishers, professional associations, and informal groups. Their importance is that they help sustain through their material property, financial support, and organizational activities the various heterodox departments within the heterodox community. In turn, the departments, connected by various social networks, provide the positive critical rivalry necessary for intellectual creativity within the community.

The social network of heterodox economists consists of direct and indirect social relationships between heterodox economists. The relationships or social ties include correspondence; intellectual and social interactions at conferences, in seminars, or with students, such as teacher-student relationship; and belonging to the same mailing lists, subscribing to and publishing in the same journals, attending the same conferences and seminars, and supporting a common course of action. Thus, a social network produces a connected and integrated body of specialized individuals who develop a common set of arguments, are concerned with a common set of questions and topics, and develop common standards for judging the arguments, answers, and discourse. In other words, the network acts as a chain of intellectual discourses where intellectual interaction through face-to-face situations at seminars, in conferences, or over dinner brings together the intellectual community; focuses members' attention on and builds up vested interest in their own theoretical, historical, applied, and empirical topics and problems; and ties together written texts and lectures that are the long-term life of the community and gives it distinctiveness. The concatenated discourse that emerges from the face-to-face interaction keeps up the consciousness of the community's agenda and purpose by transcending all particular occasions of the interactions – that is, the discourse that emerges ensures that the community's purpose and agenda continue to be advocated independently of any individual member of the community or any specific face-to-face interaction. The discourse also has another impact in that it is the communicative process that creates thinkers within the community (Lee 2009a).

Heterodox economic theory

The intellectual and theoretical roots of heterodox economics are located in heterodox traditions of Post Keynesian-Sraffian, Marxist-radical, Institutional-evolutionary, social, feminist, and ecological economics, all of which emphasize the social surplus; accumulation; justice; social relationships in terms of class, gender, and race; full employment; and economic and social reproduction.[6] Hence, as a scientific research field, heterodox economics is concerned with explaining, proposing, and advocating changes in the historical provisioning process of producing the social surplus that provides the flow of goods and services required by society to meet the reoccurring needs and promote the well-being of those who participate in its activities. That is, *heterodox economics is a historical science of the social provisioning process*, and this is the general research agenda of heterodox economists. Drawing from all heterodox approaches, its explanation involves human agency qua acting persons embedded in a transmutable and, hence, inherently uncertain world with fallible knowledge and expectations and in a cultural context, as well as social processes in historical time affecting resources, consumption patterns, production and reproduction, and the meaning (or ideology) of market, state, and non-market/state activities engaged in social provisioning. This implies that agency can only take place in an interdependent social context which emphasizes the social and deemphasizes the isolated nature of individual decision-making; and that the organization of social provisioning is determined outside of markets, although the provisioning process itself in part takes place through capitalist markets. Thus, heterodox economic theory is a theoretical explanation of the historical process of social provisioning within the context of a capitalist economy; hence, it is also a historically contextualized explanation. It is, therefore, concerned with explaining those factors that are part of the process of social provisioning, including the structure and use of resources; the structure and change of social wants and corresponding consumption patterns; the structure of production and the reproduction of the business enterprise, household, state, and other relevant institutions and organizations; and the distribution of income among households. In addition, heterodox economists extend their theory to examining issues associated with the process of social provisioning, such as racism, gender, ideologies, and myths.

Because heterodox economics involves issues of ethical values, social philosophy, and the historical aspects of human existence, heterodox economists feel that it is also their duty to make *heterodox economic policy* recommendations to improve human dignity – that is, recommending ameliorative and/or radical social and economic policies to improve the social provisioning for all members of society and especially the disadvantaged members. Moreover, they adopt the view that their economic policy recommendations must be based on an accurate historical and theoretical picture of how the economy actually works – a picture that includes class and hierarchical domination, inequalities, social-economic discontent, and conflict. The distinction between theory and policy is not the same as the positive-normative distinction found in mainstream economics. Heterodox theory is an explanation of how the social provisioning process *actually* operates, not how it is supposed to operate under 'ideal conditions' while heterodox policy aims at altering the actual process to achieve a particular historically contingent outcome. Thus, the ethos embedded in heterodox economic theory is that the social provisioning process is to be accurately explained so that it can be changed – an accurate explanation is not the same thing as a value neutral explanation, which implies that derivative economic policy is not value or ethically neutral (Polanyi 1968; Foster 1981; Gruchy 1987; Stevenson 1987; Dugger 1996; Bortis 1997; Hodgson 2001; Power 2004).

Theoretical core

Since the economy is an emergent system with various sub-systems, the heterodox theory of the social provisioning process is also an emergent theoretical system with various theoretical sub-systems. This implies that it cannot be divided into disjointed sub-systems of microeconomics and macroeconomics, which in turn are based on quite different theoretical arguments. In particular, the core theoretical elements generate a three-component structure-organization-agency heterodox economic theory that culminates in an economic model of the economy as a whole and hence, the social provisioning process.[7] The first component of the theory consists of the productive and monetary schemata of the social provisioning process, and together they are the schema of the structure of a real capitalist economy. The former represents the circuit of production as an inherent circular process in that the production of goods and services requires goods and services to be used as inputs. Hence, with regard to production, the overall economy (which includes both market and non-market production) is represented as an input-output schema of resources, material goods, and services combined with different types of labor skills to produce an array of resources, goods, and services as outputs. Many of the outputs replace the resources, goods, and services used up in production, and the rest constitute a surplus to be used for social provisioning – that is, for consumption, private investment, government usage, and exports. The latter is a schema of the structural relationships between the wages of workers, profits of enterprises, and taxes of government and expenditures on consumption, investment, and government goods as well as non-market social provisioning activities which are facilitated by a flow of funds or state money accompanying the production and exchange of the goods and services. Together the two schemas produce a monetary input-output model of the social provisioning process where transactions in each market are state-money transactions; where a change in the price of a good or in the method by which a good is produced in any one market will have an indirect or direct impact on many different markets throughout the economy; and where the amount of private investment, government expenditure on real goods and services, and the excess of exports over imports determines the amount of market and non-market economic activities, the level of market employment and non-market laboring activities, and consumer expenditures on market and non-market goods and services.

The second component of heterodox theory consists of three categories of acting organizations and institutions that are embedded in the monetary input-output structural model of the economy. The first category is particular to a set of markets and products and consists of the business enterprise, private and public market organizations (such as trade associations and government marketing boards) that manage competition in resource, good, and service markets; and the organizations (such as trade unions) and institutions (such as minimum wage laws) that regulate the wages of workers. The second category are organizations that are spread across markets and products or not particular to any market or product and includes the state and various subsidiary organizations as well as particular financial organizations – that is, those organizations (such as Congress and the central bank) which make decisions about government expenditures and taxation, and determine the interest rate. Finally, the third category consists of non-market organizations and institutions that promote social reproduction and includes households and the state.[8] The significance of organizations is that they are where agency qua the acting person, the third component of heterodox theory, is located. That is, agency, which consists of decisions made by acting persons, concerning the social provisioning process and social well-being takes place through these organizations. And because the organizations are embedded in both instrumental and ceremonial institutions, such as gender, class, ethnicity, justice, marriage, ideology, and hierarchy as authority, an agency acting through organizations (that is acting organizations) affect both positively and negatively (but never optimally) the social provisioning process. The integration of the structural and agency components produces a descriptive economic model of the social provisioning process; and then placing the model within a historical-social framework creates a historically, grounded schema of the economy as a whole.

Heterodox microeconomics

As argued above, the position adopted in this book is that heterodox economic theory is an emergent whole, and the economy is conceived as a disaggregated interdependent system.[9] This starting point sidesteps much of the debate regarding the microfoundations of macroeconomics or the macrofoundations of microeconomics. At the same time, it rejects the possibility that economic activity of the economy as a whole can be understood independently of the real acting persons qua organizations and institutions, and of their actions that generate the economy-wide economic activity, and that the whole can be completely reduced to the individual acting person. With their embeddedness in a socially and activity-wide interdependent economy, it is not possible to 'understand' the decisions and actions of individual acting persons isolated from other acting persons and from the rest of the economy.[10] This has the consequence that acting persons join together to form emergent acting organizations and institutions, such as business enterprises, the state, households, trade associations, and trade unions, which can neither be aggregated upwards or disaggregated downwards. What this means is that heterodox microeconomics is not about explaining individual behavior regarding decisions and choices.

To theorize about the social provisioning process in terms of a disaggregated, interdependent economy, it is necessary to delineate and explain its constituent parts and their reproduction and recurrence, their integration qua interdependency by non-market and market arrangements and institutions, and how the system works as a whole. This implies examining how changes in one part of the economy produces changes in other parts as well as the economy as a whole. Heterodox microeconomics is thus concerned with delineating and explaining the constituent parts or sub-systems of the economy and their interdependencies, while heterodox macroeconomics is concerned with the economy as a whole and changes that occur as a result of changes in various parts of the economy. As a result, the macro outcomes, such as variations in output and employment and differential access to social provisioning, are grounded in and hence compatible with the micro sub-systems that connect the economy into a whole. More significantly, this means that all economic activity is simultaneously a micro-macro activity.

Thus, dealing with the business enterprise and changes in antitrust laws is not *per se* microeconomics and dealing with government expenditure decisions and fiscal policy is not *per se* macroeconomics, which means that fiscal policy in principle is of no more or less important than antitrust policy; rather, they are differently important.[11]

The sub-systems include the business enterprise and other private business organizations, such as trade and employer associations, the household, trade unions, and state-public organizations, while the interdependencies include technological-production relationships between enterprises, private investment-government expenditures and profit-employment, wages-capitalist income and workers-capitalist consumption patterns, state expenditures and taxes-financial assets. Heterodox microeconomic theory thus involves working with the sub-systems and interdependencies to develop analytical narratives – that is, theoretical explanations that contribute to understanding the social provisioning process. In principle, heterodox microeconomics consists of a wide range of theories, such as the business enterprise, the household, the state, markets, and urban development, and social welfare. For this book, however, the scope will be limited to theorizing about the more traditional sub-systems and interdependencies. Because of the significance of the price mechanism to mainstream economics, one theoretical concern of the book is the business enterprise, markets, demand, and pricing. Also, since heterodox economists see private investment, consumption, and government expenditures as the principle directors and drivers of economic activity, a second theoretical concern is business decision-making regarding investment, production and employment, government expenditure decisions, the financing of investment, the profit mark-up and the wage rate, and taxes. Finally, the third theoretical concern of the book is to complement the schema of the economy as a whole with a historically grounded model of a going economy as a whole, which includes the economic model of the social provisioning process, a price model, and an output-employment model. The integration of the 'micro' theories of the business enterprise, markets, demand, investment, finance, and the state with the economic model of the going economy forms a nexus of what can be identified as heterodox economic theory of the social provisioning process.

There are also some emergent theoretical issues in the heterodox microeconomic explanations of the social provisioning process – that is, the origins of the social surplus (or the questions of the origins of profits, wages, and rents) and access to the provisioning process (or the question of producing and distributing the surplus). Through dealing with these issues, the theoretical narrative of the provisioning process is transformed into a theory of value. That is, a theory of value is a narrative that is linked to a quantitative analysis (usually a schema and a model or a concatenated set of models) that succinctly explains why and how the particular goods and services that constitute the social provisioning process get produced and the households, business enterprises, and the state get access to them.

As shall be developed in the following chapters (in particular, Chapter 7), the ruling class determines the surplus goods and services they want and hire the surplus labor to produce them; the production of surplus goods and services for workers are an unintended by-product. That is to say, the production decisions are controlled by the ruling class. This means that the capitalists' decision to produce consumption goods and services for workers governs the workers' access to the social provisioning process by simultaneously creating the wage rate as an income category. In a similar manner, the capitalists' and state's decisions to produce fixed investment and consumption goods and services for the capitalists and for the state govern the capitalists' and the state's access to the social provisioning process by simultaneously creating the profit mark-up and state money as income categories. In short, because the capitalist class and the state determine the production of the surplus along with wage rates, profit mark-ups, and state money, they govern the real direction of the capitalist economy, control the volume of and access to the social provisioning process (while the price system plays a secondary role of governing the access of particular capitalists and workers to social provisioning and ensuring the reproduction of the business enterprise), and maintain the capitalist (dominate)-worker (subordinate) social relationships necessary for capitalism to exist. What this clearly implies is that the creation and distribution of the surplus is effectuated through the social relationships that sustain the ruling class, while the trappings of market forces are a veil that obscures them; more strongly put, it is social relationships coupled with social agency that are the primary movers of economic activity and the provisioning process while the role of markets and the price system play both a secondary role and an obscuring role. Heterodox microeconomics pierces this veil and reveals what is hidden and obscured; in doing so, it makes it clear that heterodox economics is shunting economics to the classical-Marxian track that has been advanced, developed, and changed by Institutional, Post Keynesian, social, and other heterodox contributions.

Methodology of heterodox economics

Heterodox economic theory is not a pre-existing doctrine to be applied to an invariant economic reality. Rather, there are many heterodox theoretical arguments that appear to contribute to its construction, but there is no reason why they should command blind acceptance; in any case, they fall short of making a comprehensive theory. Consequently, new theories are needed to fill the gaps and omissions. In either case, there needs to be a basis for accepting the theories as reasonable scientific theoretical contributions to explaining the social provisioning process. This suggests that the development of heterodox theory requires theory creation and theory evaluation. Scientific theory creation requires a philosophical foundation on which a research strategy for theory creation and evaluation is based. Such a combination is, however, either not recognized by many heterodox economists or, when recognized, underdeveloped, as in the case of critical realism and abduction. Moreover, issues about research methods are, with the exception of analytical statistics (such as econometrics), generally minimized while the historical nature and the role of the historical narrative in heterodox theories are ignored all together. The objective of this section is to delineate a particular integration of a realist philosophical foundation centered on critical realism with the well-known research strategy that is usually associated with qualitative theorizing and the method of grounded theory to produce a critical realist-grounded theory approach to theory creation and evaluation that directly engages with a variety of research methods (such as data triangulation, case study, analytical statistics, and modeling) and historical theorization.

Philosophical foundation

Being both participants in and observers of the social and economic activity around them, heterodox economists approach their study of economics with a common sense understanding of the world. By common sense, it is meant a complex set of beliefs and propositions (many of which are historically grounded) about fundamental features of the world that individuals assume in whatever they do in ordinary life. Thus, they take particular features, characteristics, institutions, and human actors of economic activity as real, obvious, and practical initial starting points for further research. To be real, obvious, and practical means that various features, institutions, and actors qua acting persons[12] exist; they are ingrained everyday properties of the world of economic activity, and they are encountered when observing or participating in ongoing economic activity. In particular, heterodox economists can, as observers, see them in action in the economy, or they can directly experience them as participants in economic activity. In short, they interact with what they study. By being a participant-observer, they are able to be close to the real, concrete form of the economy. Consequently, their common sense beliefs and propositions provide the background against which they carry out their research. Hence, this common sense understanding of economic activity informs the methods which heterodox economists actually use to examine economic activity, particularly with regard to the way it is explained – it is impossible for any heterodox economist, or indeed any researcher, to approach the study of economics with a 'blank mind' (Mäki 1989; 1996; 1998a; 1998b; Coates 1996; Dow 1999; 2001).

Heterodox economists characterize their common sense propositions by stating that the real (actual) economy is a non-ergodic, independent system with agency and economic-social-political structures and institutions embedded in a historical process located in historical time. Other accepted and articulated propositions that support and clarify the above include: the actual economy and the society in which it is embedded is real and exists independently of the heterodox economist; the economy is transmutable, hence its future is uncertain and unknowable; ends are neither entirely knowable nor independent of the means to achieve them; economic outcomes come about through acting persons interacting with social, political, and economic structures, and hence are ethical and political outcomes as well; and a capitalist society is a class society and the economy is permeated with hierarchical power derived in part from it. The final common sense proposition is that the study of a particular economic activity cannot be done independently of the whole economy or from the social system in which it is embedded. Mutually shared among heterodox economists, these common sense propositions provide the basis for its ontological realist foundation (Wilber and Harrison 1978; Gruchy 1987; Lawson 1994; 1999; Arestis 1996; Davidson 1996; Dow 1999; 2001; Downward 1999; Rotheim 1999).

From the common sense propositions, heterodox economists conclude that the economy works in terms of causal-historical processes. Moreover, because they accept the ontological constraint implicit in this, a specific form of realism, *critical realism*, is the ontological basis of heterodox economics. Not only do they posit that economic phenomena are real, heterodox economists also argue that their explanations or theories have real components, refer to real things, represent real entities, are judged good or bad, true or false by virtue of the way the economy works, and are causal explanations – in short, heterodox theories are factual theories.[13] As a causal explanation, heterodox theory provides an account of the process as a sequence of economic events and depicts the causes that propel one event to another in a sequence. In addition, while accepting that theories are evaluated on the accuracy of their explanations, heterodox economists also accept *epistemological relativism*, which is that explanations of economic events are historically contingent. That is, accuracy and historical contingency are not separate in heterodox theory. Finally, to ensure that their theories are causal explanations of real things, the *method of grounded theory* is utilized as a research strategy to create and evaluate economic theories (Ellis 1985; Mäki 1989; 1992a; 1996; 1998a; 1998b; 2001).

Critical realism

Critical realism (CR) starts with an account of what the economic world must be like for economic analysis to be possible. Thus its fundamental claim is that the economic world is causally structured, which means that economic theories are historical and narratively structured. CR begins with four propositions, the first being that the economic world consists not only of events and our experiences, but also of underlying *structures* and *causal mechanisms* that are, in principle, observable and knowable. Second, it is argued that economic events, structures, and causal mechanisms exist independently of their identification. Third is the argument that all economic events are produced by an underlying set of causal mechanisms and structures. Finally, as an *a posteriori* observation, it is commonly noted that the social world is open in that economic events are typically produced as a result of interactions of numerous, often counteracting structures and contingently related causal mechanisms. Consequently, there is a three-tier view of economic reality. The first two tiers are the 'empirical' events of experience and impression and the actual events underlying them. Understanding the former depends on the explanations of the 'actual' events that are derived from causal mechanisms and economic structures, which constitute the third tier of economic reality. The causal mechanisms and structures together are the ontological core of heterodox economics in that when they are identified and understood, the empirical and actual events are jointly understood. Moreover, because causal historical processes are knowable and observable, so are the causal mechanisms and structures. Thus for heterodox economists, identifying structures and causal mechanisms and describing their way of influencing or acting on specific events in the open economic world are their scientific undertaking – they put critical realism into practice, thereby making the unknown knowable and the unseen observable, although it will not be perfect.[14]

A causal mechanism in the context of heterodox economics is irreducible. It has a relatively constant internal organization whose components are intentionally, not mechanistically, related. It is real, observable, and underlies (and hence governs or produces) actual events. It acts transfactually – that is, it has effects even when it does not generate discernible actual events.[15] Being 'irreducible' means that the form and organization cannot be disaggregated into its constituent components and still function as a causal mechanism. In this sense, a causal mechanism is an emergent entity in that its properties and powers cannot be completely traced to its individual components. To have a constant form and organization means that the mechanism can be empirically identified by stable patterns of behavior and organizational format, and hence empirically observed and delineated. Furthermore, the ability to act means that the mechanism has the power to generate qualitative and/ or quantitative outcomes; the triggering of the mechanism comes from agency, human intentionality via the acting person, which is embedded in, yet distinct from, the form and organization that constitute the mechanism. This means that the causal mechanism cannot be thought of as a machine or 'mechanistic' – that is, not completely structurally determined. Thus, economic actors qua acting persons have independent power to initiate actions (and so make the system open), thereby setting in motion causal mechanisms that generate outcomes that underlie, and hence govern, actual economic events. Because the causal mechanism utilizes the same processes when producing results, the same results are repeatedly produced; conversely, a causal mechanism does not produce accidental, random, or transitory results.[16] To say that a causal mechanism acts transfactually to produce the same results is also to say that its form, internal organization, and agency are constant, thereby making it a relatively enduring entity (meaning that it can be slowly transformed over time). Hence, if the same causal mechanism operates in different situations, it will produce the same, or transfactual, results each time it is in operation; but the empirical and actual events need not be regular or repeatable, as other contingently related causal mechanisms may be affecting them. So, in a system with multiple independent causal mechanisms, a single causal mechanism only has the tendency to produce regular, repeatable, qualitative or quantitative actual economic events denoted as 'demi-regularities.'

A structure is different from a causal mechanism in that the former does not include agency; hence it can only help shape or govern the actual event. Otherwise, it is similar to a causal mechanism in that it is real, observable, relatively enduring in form and organization, irreducible, and governed transfactually. The structures of an economy have two additional properties: (1) being sustained, reproduced, and slowly transformed by economic and social events that are caused by acting persons through their causal mechanisms; and (2) their form and organization have a historical character. Moreover, all economic structures are social structures in that they represent and delineate recurrent and pattern interactions between acting persons or between acting persons and technology and resources. Economic structures include economic and social norms; practices and conventions; social networks such as associational networks or interlocking directorates; technological networks such as the production and cost structures of a business enterprise or the input-output structure of an economy; and economic, political, and social institutions such as markets or the legal system. As distinct entities, neither causal mechanisms nor structures can separately cause and govern actual economic events. Rather, they must work jointly where the structures provide the medium or the conditions through which causal mechanisms act. So, as long as they remain enduring, there will be a tendency for regular and repeatable actual economic events to occur. In fact, in a transmutable world where the future is not completely knowable, acting persons are only possible if causal mechanisms and structures are relatively enduring so that they can connect their acts to outcomes; for if acting persons could not see themselves producing transfactual results, they would not act[17] (Mäki 1989; 1998b; Lovering 1990; Kanth 1992; Sayer 1992; Lloyd 1993; Lawson 1994; 1997a; 1997b; 1998a; 1998b; 1998c; Lawson, Peacock, and Pratten 1996; Ingham 1996; Wellman and Berkowitz 1997; Hodgson 1998; 2000; Joseph 1998; Dow 1999; Downward 1999; Rotheim 1999; Fleetwood 2001a; 2001b).

Epistemological relativism

Epistemological relativism is the view that knowledge of economic events is historically contingent. That is, because the social and economic activities of interest to heterodox economists change over time, knowledge and understanding of them is historically contingent; hence, there are no eternal 'truths,' and knowledge is always in the process of being created, even for past events. Consequently, what is known about actual economic events of the past need not be knowledge about current or future economic events. As a result, heterodox economists are continually engaged in creating new knowledge, new explanations to take the place of those that cease to refer to real things, represent real entities, and explain actual economic events. Thus, CR explanations or theories are historically conditioned and hence historically contingent, which implies that, for heterodox economists, there are no ahistorical economic laws or regularities. Moreover, it is not possible to make ahistorical, general statements with absolute certainty beyond the historical data and context in which the statements are embedded. Another implication is that theories must be, in some sense, grounded in historical data in order to tell historical stories explaining historical economic events. A third implication is that the difference between good and not-so-good, between true and simply plain wrong theories is how well their explanations correspond to, if not 'embody,' the historically contingent economic events being explained. Finally, epistemological relativism implies that the continual creation of knowledge is a social act carried out by informed actors – that is, by heterodox economists – in a socially, historically contingent context (Sayer 1992; Pratt 1995; Lawson 1997a; Yeung 1997).

Research strategy: method of grounded theory

To develop a critical realist empirically grounded theory that analytically explains causally related, historically contingent economic events, the critical realist heterodox economist needs to identify and delineate the structures, causal mechanisms, and causal processes producing them. The research strategy for creating causally explanatory theories that is also consistent with realism, critical realism, and epistemological relativism is the *method of grounded theory*.

The grounded theory method (GTM) is a process by which researchers create their theory 'directly' from data (which is defined below), and in which data collection, theoretical analysis, and theory building proceed simultaneously (see Figure 1.1). The use of the method begins with the economist becoming familiar with, but not dogmatically committed to, the relevant theoretical, empirical, and historical literature that might assist them in approaching, understanding, and evaluating the data relevant to their research interest. Then, one engages in fieldwork by collecting comparable data from economic events from which a number of specific categories or analytical qua theoretical concepts and their associated properties are isolated and the relationships between them identified. With the theoretical concepts and relationships empirically grounded in detail and hence empirically justified, the economist then develops a theory in the form of a complex analytical explanation based on the data's core concepts. A theory is thus a conceptual system that accurately and correctly describes the items and objects that constitute economic events, and then the economist uses these concepts to fashion an analytical explanation of the events (Brown 2001). The essential property of such a theory is that it explains why and how the sequence of economic events represented in the data took place. Hence, the economist does not attempt to construct a simplified or realistically deformed empirically grounded theory by ignoring or rejecting particular data. Rather, the economist endeavors to capture the complexity of the data by establishing many different secondary concepts and relationships and weaving them together with the core concepts into structures and causal mechanisms. This ensures that the resulting theory is conceptually dense as well as having causal explanatory power. The process of selecting the central theoretical concepts and developing the theory brings to light secondary concepts and relationships that also need further empirical grounding, as well as suggesting purely analytical concepts and relationships which need empirical grounding if they are to be integrated into the theory. After the theory is developed, the economist evaluates it by seeing how it explains actual economic events. Let us now consider aspects of the GTM in more detail.

Pre-existing ideas and concepts

Any researcher undertaking a project of economic theory creation is already aware, to one degree or another, of various 'competing' economic theories. So the question is: how aware should they be of the 'local' research frontier of the project as well as what lies behind it? To use the GTM fruitfully, the heterodox economist must be familiar with the contemporary heterodox and mainstream theoretical and

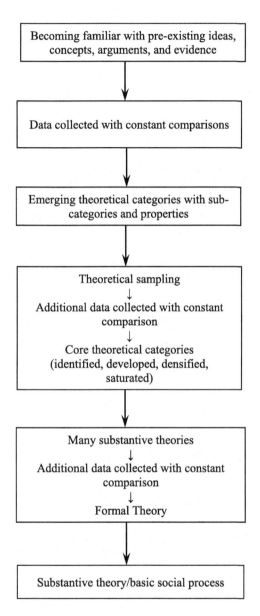

Figure 1.1 Schema of grounded theory method

non-theoretical literature, the controversies between economists, and the relevant literature from the history of economic thought. In particular, they need to make a detailed and critical investigation of the pre-existing heterodox ideas and concepts to see which might lend themselves to empirical grounding. The economist also needs to be familiar with some of the empirical literature as well as with the relevant literature from economic history. By acquiring a critical awareness of the pre-existing economic theories and empirical findings, they attain a theoretical sensitivity regarding the data and theoretical concepts they will be examining, comparing, and empirically grounding. As a result, the economist will have the ability to recognize what might be important in the data and to give it meaning as well as recognizing when the data do not support a pre-existing theoretical concept or category, hence requiring a large or small transformation of the pre-existing concept or category, or 'produce' a new category. Thus, the GTM not only recognizes that observations, data, and descriptions are conceptually qua theory laden, it also reinforces the latter by demanding that all economists enter into theory creation as theoretically knowledgeable and aware individuals, as well as with the conviction that the creation of a new substantive economic theory will most likely require them to set aside forever some of that acquired knowledge. Consequently, the economist can still pursue the GTM even though they may favor particular non-grounded concepts and theories. Hence, the grounded theory economist is not a neutral observer sifting through given 'facts' that present them, through some sort of immaculate conception, with a theory without a moment of forethought; rather, the economist is actively and reflectively engaged with it and is aware of the possibility of 'observer bias' (Olsen 2012, 65–71). By acknowledging the issue of conceptually-laden observations while at the same time demanding that the economist be skeptical of all pre-existing theory, the grounded theory method is a highly self-conscious, engaging, and open-minded approach to economic research, data creation-collection, and theory building and evaluation.

Data, constant comparisons, and theoretical categories

The development of theoretical categories is a complex task that starts using various research methods to collect analytically and theoretically unembedded different kinds of quantitative, qualitative, and historical information that is believed to be relevant for the task at hand. Information is obtained from interviews, surveys, and other types of questionnaires, oral histories, historical and current documents, videos, images, ethnographic investigations, and other forms of participant observations, experiments, and site visits. Through comparing, analyzing, and interpreting the information while simultaneously organizing it into generalized categories qua theoretical concepts, information is transformed into data. This has three implications: the first being that data is created rather than pre-existing, which means that the economist has direct and reflective relation to it. Secondly, not all information gets transformed into data. Through critical evaluation of it, some information may be deemed not relevant, while other information may be found as inaccurately reflecting reality relevant to the task at hand. The third implication is that data is not restricted to just sense experience. For example, historical documents or field reports contain data that cannot be verified by the reader's sense experience. The same can also be said for oral histories that deal with past events. On the other hand, non-written data, such as informal rules, hierarchical power, and expectations inside the business enterprise, are not unobservable in that they can be verbally articulated and hence written down, filmed and then identified at a later point in time, or observed as institutions – that is, as observable patterns of behavior, hence capable of being recorded. Thus all data is observable, although the sources and medium in which they exist vary; to be unobservable in this sense is not to be real and hence to be no data at all. Hence, the theoretical categories that emerge come from the information qua data, not after they are all collected, but in the process of collecting them. Consequently, each category is tied to or empirically grounded in its data; since the data is real, observable, and measurable, so is the theoretical category. Moreover, since the data lie in time and history, each theoretical category is anchored in a particular historical setting. In short, a grounded theory category is theoretical and actual, grounded in real time, and historically specific (Olsen and Morgan 2005; Olsen 2012).

The purpose of constant comparison of the data is to see whether they support and continue to support emerging categories.[18] Thus, each theoretical category that becomes established is repeatedly present in very many comparable pieces of data derived from multi-sources; in other words, a category represents a 'pattern' that the researcher recognizes in the data generated by replicatory or comparable studies. Consequently, categories are created by the researcher rather than 'discovered' in the data; hence, categories are conceptual outcomes that arise from the researcher's immersion in the data. It is in this sense that categories emerge from the data (Dey 2007). In this way, datum that would not be significant on its own obtains a collective, emergent significance. The categories that emerge are of two types: one that is derived directly from the data and the other that is formulated by the economist. The former tends to denote data self-description and actual processes and behavior while the latter tends to denote explanations. In either case, the language used to describe the categories may be quite different from the existing theoretical language. As a result, the building of a grounded theory may require the creation of a new language and discarding old words and their meanings. On the other hand, the language used may come directly from the data collected and/ or from commonly used language (which is generally not theoretical language) (Konecki 1989; Coates 1996). Finally, each category has properties also derived from data in the same manner – that is, by using constant comparisons. The more properties a category has, the denser and hence the more realistic it is. A grounded theory category does not ignore the complexity of reality; rather it embraces it.

Theoretical sampling and saturation

In the process of collecting data, the economist may feel that what is being collected is not revealing additional properties of a specific kind that they believe, owing to their familiarity with the relevant theoretical, empirical, and historical literature, might exist. As a result, they engage in theoretical sampling. This involves sampling or collecting data that are expected to increase the density of a specific category by producing more properties, as well as increasing the number of pieces of data supporting each of the properties, hence making it more definitive and analytically useful.[19] Theoretical sampling and collection of data for a single category, as well as for a range of categories, continues until theoretical saturation is reached – that is, when no new data regarding a category and the relationships between the categories continue to emerge. A saturated category is not a function of the number of pieces of data, as it may become saturated after only a small portion of the available data has been analyzed. The significance of this empirical grounding process is that the theoretical categories cannot be unrealistic, hence false, since they are derived from the data. If the data collection and theoretical sampling is incomplete, then the categories are not adequately dense, as relevant properties are missing; thus such categories are incompletely realistic. On the other hand, if future data emerge which the empirical grounding process shows do not fall into a previously existing category, then that category is not relevant, but it is not empirically false.

Structures, causal mechanisms, demi-regularities, and grounded theories

Once the real, observable theoretical categories are delineated and grounded, the economist, perceiving a pattern of relationships among them, puts critical realism into practice by classifying some directly as economic and social structures and others as components of them. Continuing the practice, other categories that center on acting persons' motivation and action and a set of outcomes are woven together into a causal mechanism; and finally, some categories are identified as demi-regularities. The resulting structures, causal mechanisms, and demi-regularities are real and observable as opposed to unreal, metaphoric, and hidden. So, to observe a structure or causal mechanism is to observe the working together of its observed concrete components. Hence structures, causal mechanisms, and demi-regularities are real and observable precisely because their categories are real and observable.

Given their research interest, the economist selects from the causal mechanisms identified, one as the central causal mechanism around which the structures and secondary causal mechanisms and their outcomes are arranged. Criteria for selecting the central causal mechanism from among a number of possible causal mechanisms include its frequency in the data as a cause of the outcomes, its implications for a more general theory, and its allowance for increasing the number of interrelationships between the structures and causal mechanisms. Thus the causal mechanism is central to the narrative being analytically developed in conjunction with the economic structures and secondary causal mechanisms. More specifically, the narrative is not a description of the present or a recounting of past unique and/or demi-regular economic events, although both techniques of presenting empirical and actual economic events are included in the narrative. Rather, it is a complex analytical explanation of those described or recounted events. Even when the basic narrative is decided upon, its development will involve further theoretical sampling and collecting of data as new properties for and interrelationships between the existing structures and causal mechanisms emerge. Consequently, the narrative evolves into an economic theory while at the same time becoming increasingly denser (in terms of the increasing number of interrelationships between the structures and causal mechanisms).

The critical realist-grounded theory (CR-GT) that eventually emerges is an intrinsically complete or closed (but 'externally' open via its causal mechanism) analytical explanation (which is inclusive of but not reduced to models, graphs, and other forms of representations of the data) or interpretation of the actual economic events represented in the data. Thus the theory is not a generalization from the data, but of the data; more specifically, a grounded theory does not go beyond the data on which it is based – it does not claim universality or the status of an empirical-theoretical law. This means that the GTM is not the same as induction. That is, the GTM establishes (or creates) structures and causal mechanisms (which must exist for scientific research to be possible according to CR) from the data with the point of arguing that the relevant economic events, assuming that the structures and causal mechanisms remain relatively enduring, remain relatively ongoing as well. Consequently, the CR-GT approach is also not a deductivist research strategy, with the implication that it cannot be evaluated or judged in terms of logical coherence of a deductivist kind. Rather, the coherence of a CR-GT is evaluated and judged on how rigorously – that is, strictly exact or accurate – its explanation corresponds to the actual historically contingent economic events (Sarre 1987; Sayer 1992).

Since the theory is a clear theoretical account of empirical and actual events that occur in historical time, the critical realist's three-tier view of economic reality collapses into a single integrated tier for the CR-GT heterodox economist. In other words, reality is built into the theory (as opposed to having a non-grounded theory representing reality). With the grounded theory in hand, the heterodox economist can directly 'see' the causal mechanisms and structures and 'hear' the acting persons determining the empirical and actual events – the mysterious, random, and unintelligible is replaced by clear explanation. Moreover, being a weave of a central causal mechanism, secondary causal mechanisms, and economic and social structures designed to explain actual economic events in historical time, the theory also consists of realistic (as opposed to stylized, fictionalized, or idealized) descriptions of economic events and accurate narratives of sequences of economic events. As a result, the grounded economic theory is an emergent entity, a concatenated theory that cannot be disassembled into separate parts that compose it.

Economic theory centered on a single central causal mechanism is classified as a substantive economic theory since it is an explanation of a single basic economic process that occurs widely in the economy. From a number of substantive theories, a more holistic or macro economic theory is developed in a concatenated manner where the relationship or pattern among the substantive theories is its analytical explanation. That is, the holistic theory is built up from substantive theories; it has no prior existence. As in the process of grounding the substantive economic theory, the holistic theory also has to be grounded. In particular, the relationships between the substantive theories that constitute the macro theory need to be grounded in data assisted and directed by theoretical sampling. Consequently, the macro economic theory is grounded, historically contingent, and its analytical explanations are not empirical extrapolations. Moreover, it is no more (or less) abstract than a substantive grounded theory. Because a grounded theory must at all times be grounded, it cannot be an abstract theory where the modifier denotes some degree of non-groundness, such as the use of fictional categories or the elimination of data. Hence, grounded theories cannot be differentiated according to the levels of abstraction.

Evaluating grounded theories

Since the categories and their relationships that constitute the theory are intimately linked with the data, the grounded theory itself cannot be falsified. More specifically, because a grounded theory is developed with the data rather than prior to it, it does not stand independently of the data. Thus, it is not possible to test for the truth or falsity of a grounded theory by checking it against the data from which it is constructed. But a grounded theory is evaluated by how well it explains actual economic events – that is, how well it identifies empirically and weaves together the causal mechanisms, structures, and descriptions into a narrative of the economic events being explained. In short, a grounded theory refers to real things, represents real entities, and is evaluated on how well it rigorously accounts for the causal manner in which the economy actually operates. The evaluation process takes place within a community of scholars where delineating tentative drafts of the theory are presented to colleagues at conferences and seminars for critical comments; more refined presentations of the theory are published where colleagues have the opportunity to point out inadequacies. Through this cooperative process the community of heterodox economists arrives at, hopefully but not necessarily, adequate theories (and therefore, this process illustrates the social nature of knowledge construction). Consequently, a grounded theory as socially constructed knowledge is, in the first instance, only as good as its theoretical categories. If the data selected do not cover all aspects of the economic event(s) under investigation; if the economist compiles categories and properties from only part of the data collected or forces data into pre-determined categories; if the density of the categories is small or the relationships between categories are not identified or under-grounded due to incomplete data collected; if the economist chooses the 'wrong' central causal mechanism; and/or if the narrative is static, terse, unable to fully integrate structures and central/secondary causal mechanisms, and relatively un-complex, then the commentary of critics will make it clear that the economic theory is poor, ill-developed, and hence to a greater or lesser extent less-realistic and unable to provide a comprehensive and convincing explanation of actual economic events. That is to say, all grounded theories are realistic in that they are grounded in every detail in data. A grounded theory may be relatively complete or a much incomplete explanation of an economic event; but in both cases they are entirely realistic. To be unrealistic from a grounded theory perspective is to include non-grounded concepts in the theory, but then it would not be grounded.

A second way to evaluate a grounded economic theory is to see how well it deals with new data: data are taken seriously and the continued validity of previously developed knowledge is always questioned. The relatively enduring structures, causal mechanisms, and their outcomes of a grounded theory are based on data collected in a specific time period. So, it is possible to evaluate whether they have remained enduring outside the time period by confronting them with 'new' data derived from replicating studies, especially data from actual events that at first glance appear to fall outside existing categories and not to support demi-regularities and expected transfactual results. If the new data fall within the existing categories and conform to the transfactual results – that is, the pattern of data and the narrative of the new data match that of the existing theory – then the structures and causal mechanisms have been relatively enduring (Wilber and Harrison 1978; Yin 1981a; 1981b). On the other hand, if the new data fall outside the existing categories and not supporting the transfactual results – that is, the pattern of the data and narrative do not match the existing theory – then at least some of the structures and causal mechanisms have changed. Consequently, the existing grounded economic theory needs to be modified or replaced by a completely new one. Therefore, theory evaluation is designed to check the continual correspondence of the theory with the real causes of ongoing unique and demi-regular economic events. Hence, it is essentially a positive way of promoting theory development and reconstruction as well as new theory creation when the correspondence between theory and events breaks down.

The fact that good or poor research practices lead to better or worse grounded economic theories indicates that choices made by economists do affect the final outcome. Therefore, within the GTM it is possible, although not likely, to have good but different substantive and macro economic theories for the same economic events. Given the same theoretical categories, a different choice of a central causal mechanism produces a different theory; or if the same central causal mechanism is used but integrated with different structures and secondary causal mechanisms, a different theory will also be produced. However, since heterodox economists are critical realists, and their theories concern causal historical events, they do not accept the possibility that there are multiple valid grounded theories explaining the same economic events; hence, they reject the possibility that there is no empirical evidence that could distinguish between two incompatible grounded theories. Thus, following the same procedures as above, the way forward for the grounded theorist is to collect new data to see which of the two theories they support supplemented by critical commentary from colleagues. Hence, although the procedures used are the same and the data collected are, in principle, the same, checking the continual explanatory adequacy of a grounded theory is a different activity from choosing between two different grounded theories, for the former produces a historically linked sequence of grounded theories, while the latter concludes that one of the two theories is not an explanation after all (Glaser and Strauss 1967; Diesing 1971; Conrad 1978; Wilber and Harrison 1978; Fusfeld 1980; Turner 1981; 1983; Charmaz 1983; Ellis 1985; Gruchy 1987; Strauss 1987; Konecki 1989; Megill 1989; Corbin and Strauss 1990; Mäki 1990; 2001;

Strauss and Corbin 1990; 1994; Tosh 1991; Wisman and Rozansky 1991; Glaser 1992; 2007; Sayer 1992; Bigus, Hadden, and Glaser 1994; Hunt 1994; Boylan and O'Gorman 1995; Annells 1996; Atkinson and Oleson 1996; Emigh 1997; Runde 1998; Dey 1999; 2007; Finch 1999; 2002; Lewis and Grimes 1999; Pentland 1999; Tsang and Kwan 1999; McCullagh 2000).

Summary of the critical realist-grounded theory approach

The CR-GT approach to theory creation and evaluation overcomes the perceived shortcomings of CR and the GTM: the former has little to say about theory, while the latter lacks the ontological foundation and so appears to be little more than an inductive research strategy. However, CR provides the ontological realist foundation for the GTM and identifies its objects for empirical grounding – structures and causal mechanisms, while the GTM provides the research strategy by which they are empirically grounded. The theory resulting from the CR-GT approach is a conceptually dense analytical explanation of the actual events represented in the data; its relatively enduring capability in this regard can be evaluated by confronting it with new data. Hence the CR-GT approach is not based on deductive or inductive logic, but on a reflective form of scientific knowledge creation data that is interactively fused with the creation of theory. So the theory is of the data, not separate from it; if new data support the theory, the former become part of the latter; while if the new data do not support it, then those data become part of a new theory with different structures, causal mechanisms, and perhaps demi-regularities.

Issues of research methods

The GTM of theory creation effectively dismisses not only the traditional issue of the 'realisticness' of assumptions, but also the role of assumptions in theory creation and development. The reason is that assumptions are by definition not grounded in the real world, so their use for theory creation cannot be part of the GTM. Consequently, the degree of their realisticness or their adequacy as a logical axiomatic foundation for theory is not a concern. This implies that logical coherence is irrelevant for evaluating grounded theories. Moreover, because the role of theoretical isolation (such as partial analysis) in traditional theory building and theorizing is dependent on assumptions (such as *ceteris paribus*), their absence in the GTM means that grounded theories are not isolated theories that exclude possible influencing factors. The combination of CR, with its relatively enduring structures and causal mechanisms, and epistemological relativism, and the GTM produces theories that include all the relevant factors and influences, are historically contingent, and exist in 'real' space and time. To deliberately exclude some factors would leave the mechanisms, structures, and theories insufficiently grounded; to claim to establish laws and certain (timeless) knowledge would remove the mechanisms, structures, and theories from the real world economic events they are to explain. Thus, the integration of critical realism and grounded theory results in theories and theorizing fundamentally different from the traditional mode. In particular, it means that heterodox economic theory is not an axiomatic-based approach to theory creation, does not use deductivist methods to create theory, and rejects every research strategy of theory creation that is not empirically grounded. On the other hand, their integration invites the utilization of many different research methods (rather than just econometrics) and types of data.[20] This, however, raises some methods and data issues centering on using mixed research methods and data triangulation, on using of the case study method in theory creation, on using analytical statistics, and on using schemas, models, and mathematics (Spiethoff 1953; Mäki 1989; 1992a; 1992b; 1998b).

Mixed research methods and data triangulation

A CR-GT consists of a heterogeneous array of structures, a primary and some secondary causal mechanisms. Various research methods are needed to collect the various kinds of data. The diversity in terms of research method and data is inevitable, since some structures are based on statistical data while others are based on social-relational data; the causal mechanisms require some data that clearly reveals intentionality qua decision-making. The use of different kinds of data derived from using different research methods to construct a CR-GT is called *mixed research methods and data triangulation*. More specifically, the CR-GT approach requires the use of mixed methods and data triangulation, since no one type of research method-data is sufficient for theory construction.

For example, to construct a critical realist-grounded explanation of a particular set of past and present economic events, such as pricing and price stability, the use of historical and quantitative methods to examine existing written, recorded, physical, and quantitative records and artifacts is warranted. Since these methods and data sources might very well prove insufficient for the task at hand, it is necessary to use other research methods – such as surveys, interviews and oral histories, industrial archaeology investigations, mapping, direct observation, participation in activities, fieldwork, and statistical analysis – to create new data. In this context, subjective evaluations and interpretations of future possibilities constitute a particular kind of data that require particular research methods to observe and record. When it is important to explain how and why particular pricing decisions are made and who made them, the economist needs to create narrative accounts of relevant lived-historical experiences embedded within the cultural milieu of particular business enterprises. Thus the economist needs to examine letters and other written documents, undertake interviews and other oral documentation, and possibly engage in participant observation in which the economist may directly engage with, for example, the enterprise in the process of collecting data that is used in the pricing decision. So what constitutes appropriate research methods and data depends on the object of inquiry. Consequently, real, observable, and measurable theoretical categories, hence real, observable, and measurable economic structures and causal mechanisms that constitute the CR-GT, are grounded in the data via different research methods obtained from various sources (Thurmond 2001; Goulding 2002; Olsen 2003; Downward and Mearman 2007).

Case study

The theoretical categories that make up grounded theories are based on an array of comparable data generated by case studies. A case study is defined as an in-depth, multifaceted investigation of a particular object or theme where the object or theme is ontologically real and gives it its unity. The object or theme can be historical or a current real-life event and the study may use several kinds of data sources. For example, the theme of a case study may be the pricing procedures used by business enterprises; consequently, the case study will involve the collection, comparison, categorization, and tabulation of pricing procedures obtained from various empirical pricing studies along with a critical narrative that examines and integrates the data. Thus, the case study approach is the principle method of data collection and comparison used to develop categories, structures, and causal mechanisms. Moreover, by providing information from a number of different data sources over a period of time, the case study permits a more holistic study of structures and causal mechanisms.

A case study does not stand alone and cannot be considered alone. It must always be considered within a family of comparable case studies. If the economist is faced with a shortage of case studies, the response is not to generalize from them but to undertake more case studies. Moreover, theoretical sampling is specifically carried out through case studies in that the economist makes a conscious decision to undertake a particular case study in order to increase the empirical grounding of particular theoretical categories.[21] Thus a case study may be of, for example, an individual business enterprise, and the theme of the study may be to delineate the complex sets of decisions regarding pricing, production, and investment and to recount their effects over time. On the other hand, a case study may be concerned with a particular theoretical point, such as pricing, examined across many different case studies of different enterprises. The different case studies provide not only comparable data for comparisons, but also descriptions of structures and causal mechanisms and a narrative of the causal mechanism in action over time. A third type of the case study is a narrative that explains a historical or current event. The narrative includes structures and causal mechanisms which, when combined with the history or facts of the event, explains how and why it took place. Hence, this type of the case study is both a historical and theoretical narrative, an integration of theory with the event. Consequently, it provides a way to check how good a CR-GT is and, at the same time, contributes to its further grounding and extension. A robust substantive CR-GT is one that is based on an array of case studies of historical and current events (George 1979; Yin 1981a; 1981b; 1994; Eisenhardt 1989; Orum, Feagin, and Sjoberg 1991; Sayer 1992; Vaughan 1992; Wieviorka 1992; Smith 1998; Stake 1998; Finch 1999; 2002; Scheibl and Wood 2005).

Analytical statistics

Analytical statistics (as opposed to descriptive statistics) is the use of statistical methods to examine various types of quantitative and qualitative data for the purpose of assisting in delineating structures, causal mechanisms, transfactual outcomes, and demi-regularities; in evaluating CR-GTs for their accuracy in explaining past and present economic events; and in evaluating claims in the historical literature regarding causal mechanisms, transfactual outcomes, and demi-regularities. Analytical statistics includes various forms of regression analysis qua econometrics (for example, average economic regression and vector autoregression) and factor analysis (for example, cluster analysis and qualitative comparative analysis). Constrained to a critical realist causally-related world of structures and causal mechanisms and the GTM insistence of not making inferences beyond the existing data, the use of analytical statistics, especially econometrics, is restrained. For example, in the process of transforming categories into an economic theory, the heterodox economist provisionally identifies and associates structures and causal mechanisms with particular transfactual outcomes. In so doing, the economist subjects the causal mechanism and its outcomes to econometric evaluation or testing. The econometric model used includes components for the quantitative representation of structures as well as components for the causal mechanism; its particular statistical form is determined by the causal mechanism. As a result, the model is provisionally intrinsically closed. If the econometric tests of the given data support the existence of the causal mechanism's transfactual outcomes, then the empirical grounding of the causal mechanism is enhanced. A failure of the tests would, on the other hand, indicate that the causal mechanism and its associated structures are inadequately developed and needed further development. Assuming the testing a success and in light of the other empirical support, the economist can provisionally identify the causal mechanism and its transfactual outcomes. At this stage, they can engage in further theoretical sampling to see if additional qualitative and quantitative evidence supports it; econometric testing can again be utilized in this context. Thus, in the CR-GT approach, econometric testing is about understanding the relationship between the causal mechanism and its transfactual outcomes (given structures) and not about future prediction or about making inferences beyond the data to a larger population from which it was 'drawn' – that is, it is about significance testing. If econometric testing of new data fails to support the causal mechanism and its outcomes, then the implication is that the structures and causal mechanisms have changed; it then becomes necessary to re-ground them.

Econometrics can also be used to evaluate grounded theories that are associated with demi-regularities. In this case, the economic theory is econometrically modeled so as to include all the structures, the primary causal mechanism, and the secondary causal mechanisms. If the evaluation is a success, then it can be more strongly argued that there exists a demi-regularity associated with the primary causal mechanism of the theory. But if the examination is not successful, then all that can be said is that it is less likely that the theory has a demi-regularity. Hence, econometric testing provides a way to evaluate the continual correspondence of the theory with the real causes of ongoing economic events. By doing so, it contributes to the promotion of new theory building when the empirical connection between theory and events breaks down (Lawson 1989; Yeung 1997; Downward 1999; 2003; Downward and Mearman 2002; Olsen and Morgan 2005).

Schemas, modeling, and mathematics

From a critical realist perspective, the real economic world is a structural-causal analytical narrative; because of this, it is also a historical analytical narrative. As part of the overall narrative there can be a schema or a model that represents some structures in terms of quantitative-mathematical relationships and includes causal mechanisms and agency. In this regard, because the real world consists of structures and causal mechanisms, it contains schemas and models or there are models in the world. Consequently, to engage in modeling, it is necessary to create the world in the model that is empirically grounded from the real world in that it has the same structures, causal mechanisms, and agency that exist in the real world. Therefore, through the use of the method of grounded theory, the model in the world becomes the world in the model. So heterodox economists work with CR-GT models where the real world 'constrains' the model; that is to say, heterodox economists require their CR-GT along with abstractly-directly representing models to abstractly-directly represent the actual structures and causal mechanisms with their agency of the phenomenon under analysis to generate outcomes that are part of the real world. In this manner, a heterodox CR-GT, abstract-direct-representation (ADR) modeler aims to create a model that is a complete real-world representation of the phenomenon under analysis, which contains no fictitious components.[22] Such an approach to modeling is quite distinct from the approach used by mainstream economists (Weisberg 2007).

Representing by a schema or modeling a subject matter is a distinct yet hierarchical activity. A schema takes the form of an analytical, abstract diagram that focuses primary attention on the quantitative relationships of the core concrete structures that clarify the complex relationships associated with the subject matter. Being empirically grounded, a schema establishes relationships between quantities that in turn facilitate the modeling and theorizing of the subject matter. What is significant about a schema is its claim to abstractly, directly represent the relatively enduring structural relationships among the quantities under investigation, thus restricting the kind of modeling and theorizing that is possible. In short, a schema establishes, from the beginning, the analytical limits of how the subject matter can be understood, and theorized about.

Within the CR-GT-ADR approach, the schema represents the ontological vision and the substantive nature or relatively enduring relationships of the economic event under examination. Thus, it provides the empirical foundation of the model that the latter cannot exceed. Models represent mathematical relationships between quantities; thus they are associated with schemas that represent only structures, but they can be integrated into schemas that have causal mechanisms and agency so the latter become part of the model. Consequently, the model is open and hence need not have a solution based solely on structures. Once created, the model is capable of being 'manipulated' by the modeler or the agents associated with the model via the subject matter under investigation. In this manner, the narrative explanation of the subject matter is worked out in conjunction with the model and its underlying schema. As a result the subject matter is directly embedded in the schema-model and the schema-model is in the subject matter – that is, the world in the model and the model in the world.

Models have a dual role in heterodox theory. First, a model is used to assist in developing the narrative of the heterodox theory. In this case, the model is an analytical exploratory tool that starts with empirically grounded structures and causal mechanisms and ends with rigorous outcomes. For example, if the empirical data that is being used to develop the theoretical narrative suggests a particular quantitative relationship between a set of variables, then attempting to model and hence evaluate the relationship is one way to help develop the narrative. Thus heterodox models are integral to the construction of heterodox theory. The outcome is that models are directly embedded in the theoretical narrative rather than having a narrative of their own. Secondly, once the models and narrative are developed, they can be used to evaluate new data or explore the robustness of the narrative under different hypothetical conditions. In this case, heterodox models contribute to the filling out of the narrative as well as assisting it to adapt to new data and slowly changing structures and causal mechanisms. A CR-GT-ADR model also has a role in examining and evaluating theoretical propositions associated with different heterodox theories. Hence, a proposition, which is articulated in a manner that can be modeled and that is asserted to be true, can be examined by an empirically grounded model. The outcome of such a 'modeling examination' provides support or not for the proposition.

As noted above (and also discussed in the next section), the method of grounded theory compacts the scale of reality and therefore the degree of detail and specificity required of the narrative. When applied to model-construction, the world in the model is also compact as well as empirically grounded. Consequently, the model is small enough to examine the issue at hand while maintaining the diversity of structures and its manipulability through the agency embedded in the causal mechanisms by the modeler.

The starting point of building a model is the array of structural relationships and causal mechanisms to be examined relative to particular outcomes. The next step is to determine what real world structures should be used to frame the model and what causal mechanisms with particular types of agency need to be included. Moreover, the empirically grounded structures must be relatively enduring, and the agency via the acting person working through the causal mechanism must also be relatively enduring and make the decisions that generate the rigorous outcomes emanating from the model. The result is a model that abstractly and directly represents the real world under examination, rather than being similar to, a surrogate of, an imitation of, analogous to, mimic of, or an outright falsification of the real world. Because of the acting person who can make a great variety of decisions, the model is open to different rigorous outcomes, as opposed to a single deterministic outcome. Hence, it is possible for the modeler to develop different analytical narratives for different decisions as a way to examine the structural properties of the model.

With the world built into the model, the evaluation of the model consists of two distinct components, the model itself and its output. The former concerns how closely the internal structures and causal mechanisms of the model matches those in the real world – that is to say, how close the model's ADR of the real world is to the actual real world. This means that it is possible to reject a model based on what it is – that is, on its empirical grounding and ADR – prior to any evaluation of its output.[23] The latter involves evaluating the differences between the rigorous outcomes that are grounded in the real world with the actual real world outcomes.

Working the CR-GT-ADR model is a form of theoretical exploration, or, more specifically, a research method for developing and extending heterodox economic theory. This is done in a number of ways. Starting with the empirically grounded model that has been developed and its relatively enduring structures and causal mechanisms, the working of this 'core' model consists of focusing on agency within the primary and secondary causal mechanisms because it can make decisions. In this manner, it is possible to see the different kinds of rigorous outcomes that are produced through the structures and causal mechanisms of the model. While appearing as a form of comparative statics, it is not because it does not involve changes in the structures and causal mechanisms (that is, the 'givens' of the model) but only changes in agency decisions that are consistent with their embeddedness in their causal mechanisms.[24] Thus, the variations in the core model's rigorous outcomes do represent plausible outcomes in the real world if the same decisions are made. Hence, we have reasoning within the model and through the model to the real world. The modeler could, upon reflecting on different theoretical arguments, also institute specific demands on the model to see what the rigorous outcomes would be relative to the core model. This could involve imposing uniform decisions on the agents or emphasizing the agency of a secondary causal mechanism over the agency of the primary causal mechanism. In both cases, the outcomes will provide the modeler with a better theoretical understanding of the core model and its contribution to the development of heterodox theory.

Historical change takes place through the interactive changes in structures and causal mechanisms, which implies changes in how agency is carried out. To explore the world of historical change and begin thinking of different possible analytical ways of narrating it, the core model can be explored and manipulated to provide different possible outcomes and hence narratives that can be compared to the core model's output and its narrative. This can be done by varying the structures and causal mechanisms independently or both together. The core model's variations include emphasizing secondary structures or causal mechanisms over the primary ones, reducing the causal mechanisms to a single one, altering structures and causal mechanisms, having agency decisions affect structures, having the changing structures affect causal mechanisms and hence agency decisions, all of which affect the outcomes which can be compared and analyzed relative to the core outcomes. In all cases, the variations must be empirically plausible if not to some degree empirically grounded, as opposed to outright empirical fictions. Through the variations and the subsequent comparing of the outcomes with the outcomes of the core model, it is possible to determine which structures and causal mechanisms of the core CR-GR-ADR model are the ones that give it its essential properties and hence its theoretical identity and the ones that contribute little or may even contradict its essential properties. This helps the modeler to strengthen the core model and the analytical narrative that goes along with it as well as providing an insight to identify historical change when it is occurring.

The heterodox CR-GT-ADR modeling approach has the world in the model grounded in the real world. Hence, the mathematics in the model is constrained by the real world. That is, model building involves converting the relevant empirically grounded structures and causal mechanisms (which embody accurate measurements and observations) in the real world into a system of mathematical equations and language. As a result, the mathematical form of the model is determined and constrained by the empirically grounded structures (such as the input structures of an input-output model) and causal mechanisms (such as investment decisions by business enterprises), and hence is isomorphic with its empirical data (as well as the theory), which means it is intrinsically closed but externally open via the causal mechanism. The requirement that the mathematics be constrained by the real world means that only certain types of mathematics, such as arithmetic and linear-matrix algebra (especially when used in an arithmetical mode), can be used and that the measurable and observable outcomes of the model are determined, constrained, and real (as in the real world).[25] Hence, the model generates non-logical, empirically grounded outcomes that are in the real world, although not necessarily equivalent with the actual outcomes of the real world; that is because the mathematics of the model is of the world itself. When this is the case, the model and its outcomes are characterized as rigorous and non-deductive. This is similar to the late nineteenth century view that mathematical rigor is established by basing the mathematics on physical reasoning resulting in physical models. However, the difference for heterodox modeling is that rigor results when the mathematical model is based on social reasoning represented by the CR-GT-ADR approach (Burchardt 1931, 528–532; 1932; 2013, 5–11; Israel 1981; 1991; Weintraub 1998a; 1998b; 2001; 2002; Boumans 2005, 21–23; Morgan 2012; Martins 2014).

Historical character of heterodox economic theories

The common sense propositions combined with critical realism exclude, as part of heterodox theorizing, ahistorical, atemporal entities and theoretical concepts; atemporal diagrams, given known ends independent of means or processes to attain them; models and other forms of analysis unaccompanied by temporal-historical analysis; and the utilization of ahistorical first principles or primary causes. Being outside of history, historical time, and an unknowable transmutable future, these ahistorical entities and concepts are also rejected by the GTM as fictitious since they do not emerge as categories in the historical data. Consequently, ahistorical theories with their ahistorical concepts are not connected to the range of economic events they intend to explain and hence are not capable of explaining them. In contrast, the concatenated integration of the common sense propositions and critical realism with the grounded theory method – that is, the CR-GT approach – prescribes that heterodox theorizing include the delineation of historically grounded structures of the economy and the development of historically grounded emergent causal mechanisms. Consequently, CR-GT theories are *historical theories* in that they are historical narratives that explain the present or past internal workings of historical economic processes and events connected to the social provisioning process in the context of relatively stable causal mechanisms (whose actions and outcomes can be temporally different) and structures. So, the simultaneous operation of primary and secondary causal mechanisms with different time dimensions ensures the existence of historical economic processes that are being explained. But even when the primary causal mechanism concludes its activity, the historical processes do not come to an end for the secondary, and other causal mechanisms can also have an impact on the structures so that the slowly transforming structures (and their impact on causal mechanisms) maintain the processes.

Historical processes are organized and directed by multiple independent structures and causal mechanisms and are what constitutes historical time. Since those same structures and causal mechanisms also change slowly, historical processes change as well, implying that there are no end points, 'constants' to which the processes tend or lock-in, evolutionary pathways that must be followed irrespective of agency, or cyclical 'movements.' In short, historical change is non-teleological, non-historicist, non-cyclical, and, hence, can just only be change. With historical process and historical change as intrinsic properties of historical theories, such outside-of-history concepts and methods as equilibrium, optimization-maximization-minimization, short-period/long-period positions, centers of gravitation, market clearing, states of rest, or comparative statics *cannot be utilized to organize and direct economic inquiry and to narrate economic events.* These concepts are sometimes theoretically justified in the context of a layered view of reality and economic events, since it allows some structures and mechanisms to exist essentially outside of time and historical process. At other times, they are justified in terms of slow moving variables (structures and causal mechanisms) and fast moving variables (outcomes) where the latter do not have an impact upon the former. However, the interplay and linkages between structures, causal mechanisms, and outcomes means that the distinction between the two kinds of variables is not sustainable and that, consequently, historical outcomes are not based on accidental, random, or autonomous factors; hence no structures, causal mechanisms, and outcomes are independent of historical processes. In short, it is not possible to start with a static theory and dynamize it into a theory that explains historical processes – no amendments to an outside-of-history theory can transform it into a historical theory.

Historical economic theories are possible because, as noted under critical realism, all historical events are, due to the existence of structures and causal mechanisms, narratively structured. There are no accidental or uncaused events – that is, events without a narrative. Hence, heterodox economists do not impose narratives on actual economic events to make sense of them, but derive them from the events via the GTM. Moreover, as long as historical events are narratively structured, subjectivity, uncertainty, and expectations do not introduce indeterminacy into heterodox theories. In addition, being a narrative, theories have a plot with a beginning, middle, and end centered on a central causal mechanism and set within structures and other causal mechanisms. Therefore, antedated events prompt the causal mechanisms to initiate activity to generate particular results and hence start the narrative; and it comes to an end when the causal mechanisms conclude their activity. Finally, the storyteller of the narrative is the heterodox economist whose objective is to help the audience – which include fellow economists, students, politicians, and the general public – understand theoretically how and why the actual economic events transpired[26] (McCullagh 1984; Carr 1986; Norman 1991; Appleby, Hunt, and Jacob 1994, Chs. 7, 8; Dey 1999; Pentland 1999).

As narratives linked with critical realism and centered on causal mechanisms and structures, CR-GTs as historical heterodox theories are not completely aggregated or disaggregated, nor are they devoid of explicit human intentionality and activity. That is, because causal mechanisms embody data from many case studies, they aggregate economic reality or, put differently, compact the scale of reality and therefore the degree of detail and specificity required of the narrative. However, the degree of aggregation is limited because of the existence of structures and causal mechanisms that cannot be aggregated or disaggregated and human intentionality and activity that are both differentiated and specific. As a result, for the CR-GT approach, heterodox economic theories are neither an aggregate theory where the differentiation among the causal mechanisms with agency and structures disappear, nor such a disaggregated theory so that causal mechanisms with its agency and structures are individual-event specific and hence of little interest.[27] The impossibility of aggregating emergent entities to produce representational aggregate entities – that is, aggregate entities with the same properties and behavior as the individual entities – means that heterodox economic theory must consist of linked causal mechanisms and structures. Thus, heterodox theories tell quasi-aggregated narratives explaining the many and overlapping actual economic events occurring in a differentiated economy.[28] The fact that the narrative is embedded in the events as opposed to mimicking them (as is the nature of non-CR-GTs) is perhaps the most compelling reason to use the CR-GT approach for theory creation.

The making of heterodox microeconomic theory

Heterodox economic theory is an encompassing theoretical explanation of the social provisioning process within the context of a capitalist economy and therefore is concerned with explaining those factors that are part of the process;

heterodox microeconomic theory is one component of the whole. To use the CR-GT approach to develop a microeconomic theory means first delineating the empirically grounded causal mechanisms and structures that make up the constituent parts of the economy and their interdependencies; and secondly developing theories or analytical narratives of how they contribute to explaining the social provisioning process. Thus, the research and referencing requirements for developing an empirically grounded microeconomic theory are significant; in some instances, the necessary empirical evidence does not yet exist. Consequently, the microeconomic theory presented in the subsequent chapters will only be partially empirically grounded, leaving further work for heterodox economists to do. But what will become apparent is that the empirical stipulation of the structures and causal mechanisms has a significant impact on a number of theoretical issues and arguments in heterodox economics. That is to say, the use of grounded theory only 'permits' specific structures and causal mechanisms to emerge, which in turn limits the range of theoretical models, arguments, and narratives that can contribute to understanding the social provisioning process in actual capitalist economies. This means that various arguments, models, and theories that had a historical explanatory role in heterodox economics are to be put to the side. This will inevitably generate misgivings among heterodox economists as they may well ask 'what theory, friends, is this?' It needs to be recognized that all knowledge is contestable and that even respected arguments and theories by great heterodox economists are not immune to questioning and being discarded.

To start the process of theory creation, the next chapter delineates a theoretical picture of a capitalist economy that will serve as the foundation for developing an empirically grounded microeconomic theory of the social provisioning process as well as an empirically grounded model of a going economy as a whole. This involves delineating the core structures of a capitalist economy relevant to the social provisioning process and locating within them the organizations, institutions, and agency that direct, engage in, or facilitate the economic events that result in social provisioning. And the economic events of specific interest are those that affect the production, pricing, demand, and distribution of goods and services. The structures help shape and govern economic events while the organizations and social institutions (that are located in the structures) house the causal mechanisms in which agency through the acting person is embedded. What these structures, organizations, and agency determine is the kind of heterodox microeconomic theory that is developed. The core structures include the productive structures and the structure of the linkages between incomes and the surplus, which together make for the monetary structure of the social provisioning process, while the core acting organizations and social institutions relevant to the social provisioning process and embedded in the structures are the business enterprise, the state, the household, and market governance organizations such as trade associations, cartels, employers' associations, and trade unions. Together, the structures and causal mechanisms qua agency produce the core economic model of the provisioning process.

The subsequent chapters represent four of the central components of the theory – the business enterprise, the business enterprise and the market, market governance, and the economy qua social provisioning process as a disaggregated, interdependent whole. More specifically, the first three core areas concentrate on delineating 'micro' structures and causal mechanisms and developing substantive and macro or holistic theories of the business enterprise (Chapters 3 and 4), of market demand (Chapter 5), and of market governance (Chapter 6). With the structures, causal mechanisms, and substantive theories in place, the final step is to develop a holistic heterodox microeconomic theory (Chapter 7) that brings together the constituent parts of the economy and their interdependencies. This will involve integrating the economic model of the social provisioning process, the causal mechanism with agency-based price model, and the causal mechanism with agency-based output-employment model into a model of a going economy as a whole. Then it will be possible to develop analytical narratives of the social provisioning process. In particular, the theory and the model together will then be used to delineate the impact of the 'micro' – that is, prices, profit mark-ups, finance, and the surplus – on the overall level of economic activity and hence on social provisioning.

Notes

1 There is a debate within heterodox economics on whether heterodox and mainstream economics are really different or to some degree compatible and commensurable (Lee 2011b; 2011c; 2013a). Those who advocate the latter position discount the theoretical critiques and ignore the clearly articulated statements by various heterodox economists, especially Marxists, radical institutionalists, and Post Keynesian-Sraffians, who claim the former position.

2 In some cases, concepts and their derivative symbols are presented in such a way so as to look like they are quantifiable, such as the utility function and 'U' for total amount of utility. However, 'U' is not well-defined, has no dimensions, and its units of measurement are not stated. This is a case of *pseudo-quantitation* (Bunge 1998; Mahner 2007).

3 To illustrate, consider the heterodox critiques of the mainstream concept of scarcity. The Post Keynesians argue that produced means of production within a circular production process cannot be characterized as scarce and that production is a social process (Bortis 1997); the Institutionalists view that natural resources are socially created to enter into the production process (De Gregori 1987); and the Marxists argue that the scarcity concept is a mystification and misspecification of the economic problem (Matthaei 1984) – that is, it is not the relation of the individual to given resources, but the social relationships that underpin the social provisioning process. The three critiques are complementary and integrative and generate the common conclusion that the concept of scarcity must be rejected, as well as the mainstream approach to the study of the social provisioning process in terms of the allocation of scarce resources among competing ends in light of unlimited wants. This is the basis of the popular statement that the only thing heterodox approaches have in common with each other is their opposition to mainstream economics. But if they have similar and overlapping critiques, then there is a good possibility that their positive analyses of the social provisioning process are also similar and integrative to some extent. This is, after all, the basis for heterodox economics.

4 Other characteristics of a scientific research field include intimate relations (as opposed to imperialistic relations) with other research fields, direction of scientific activity determined internally to the research field as opposed to accommodating to government, ecclesiastical, or business demands, and an ethos of free search for truth rather than an ethos of ideological faith, a quest for power or consensus, or an enforced blindness of the research community to alternative theories. Mainstream economics falls short on all three accounts, most notably in countries subject to national research assessment exercises and where state power is used to legitimate particular approaches in a research field (Bunge 1998; Mahner 2007; Lee 2009a; Lee, Pham, and Gu 2013).

5 This suggests that heterodox economists are relatively indistinguishable from their mainstream brethren except for their scientific output. There is, however, a difference. Being theoretically different often brings the individual heterodox economist under attack if he/she works in a predominately mainstream department. It also brings heterodox departments under attack by university administrators (and often times supported by mainstream economists) who are concerned about department rankings and the production and teaching of 'improper' or low-value knowledge. For a detailed history of such incidents, see Lee (2009a) and Lee, Pham, and Gu (2013).

6 Since its beginnings in the 1960s and particularly since 1990, heterodox economists have been melding together various aspects of different heterodox approaches (see Lee 2009a; 2010a).

7 A number of elements constitute the theoretical core of heterodox theory. Some elements are clearly associated with particular heterodox approaches as noted by Phillip O'Hara:

> The main thing that social economists bring to the study [of heterodox economics] is an emphasis on ethics, morals and justice situated in an institutional setting. Institutionalists bring a pragmatic approach with a series of concepts of change and normative theory of progress, along with a commitment to policy. Marxists bring a set of theories of class and the economic surplus. Feminists bring a holistic account of the ongoing relationships between gender, class, and ethnicity in a context of difference. . . . And post-Keynesians contribute through an analysis of institutions set in real time, with the emphasis on effective demand, uncertainty and a monetary theory of production linked closely with policy recommendations.
>
> (O'Hara 2002, 611)

   However, other core theoretical elements – such as the socially embedded economy, the economy as an emergent system comprised of sub-systems, circular production, and cumulative change – emerge from a synthesis of arguments that are associated only in part with particular heterodox approaches. For a more detailed discussion of heterodox 'metaparadigm' theory building, see Lee (2009a; 2010a); also see Gioia and Pitre (1990) and Lewis and Grimes (1999).

8 To simplify the representation and modeling of the economy as a whole, religious and secular private non-market organizations – such as charities that contribute to and support the household, while important in many capitalist economies where the state does not support households, especially poor households – are not included.

9 This position has a long lineage reflecting the influence of Karl Marx, Michał Kalecki, and Piero Sraffa; since 1970 a number of heterodox economists have contributed to this tradition, including Kregel (1975), Pasinetti (1981; 1993), Eichner (1987a), and Bortis, (1997; 2003). As a result, much of what is covered in this book can also be found in the works of these authors. This is particularly the case for Alfred Eichner's work.

10 This implies that the problem of the fallacy of composition does not haunt heterodox economics.

11 The position adopted here to bridge the micro-macro divide is similar to some of the pre-1970 attempts to ground macroeconomics on appropriate neoclassical microfoundations. One difference is that neoclassical microeconomics is theoretically incoherent, so that the overall project of building microfoundations of macroeconomics is more or less doomed to fail (Hoover 2012).

12 As will be further discussed in the next chapter, the acting person is a theoretical conceptualization and representation of decision-making and implementation by a going concern organization, such as a business enterprise or institution, such as a household. It has an ongoing, repeated pattern of culturally particular, ethically informed social relationships. Moreover, the acting person is reflexive in terms of its decisions and thus visualizes the possible impact of its actions. Finally, it can determine the extent to which its decisions qua actions achieve the desired outcomes.

13 The contrast to a factual theory is a theory that is concerned exclusively with conceptual objects (such as scarcity) that have no connection to the real world or with theoretical objects (such as utility functions) that are explicitly divorced from the real world.

14 This implies that the acting person qua decision-making is an objective activity as opposed to a purely subjective one, as found in the work of radical subjectivist Austrian economists and in variants of mainstream economics. Hence, preference for 'subjective' structures over 'objective' agency and causal mechanisms in modeling and theorizing by some heterodox economists is rejected (Sraffa 1960; Pasinetti 1981; 1993; Kurz and Salvadori 1995; 2005; Lewis 2005).

15 Because its components are intentionally related, a causal mechanism cannot be thought of as a machine or 'mechanistic' – see Cartwright (1995) and Dupré (2001) on machines and economic thinking.

16 This property of causal mechanisms obviates the need for an inductivist approach for theory creation (Sayer 1992).

17 The Sraffian-classical long period methodology is also based on slowly changing structures; however, it does not include 'slowly changing' agency and the interaction between agency and structures. As a result, the theoretical entities determined by the structures are distinct from the actual entities that are determined by agency, such as long period prices and actual market prices. The critical realist structure-agency methodology eliminates this distinction so that the entities are both theoretical and actual. This means that actual market prices are 'structurally' stable but also change slowly over time.

18 Constant comparison can also involve exact replicating previous studies to see how robust they are.

19 The point of theoretical sampling is specifically to find data to make categories denser and more complex. Since the aim of the grounded theory method is to build theories based on data collected, the issue of generalizing in a statistical sense is not relevant (Glaser and Strauss 1967; Corbin and Strauss 1990).

20 For a survey of research methods and their application for heterodox economics, see Lee and Cronin (2016).

21 It is important to realize that a case study that involves the replication and re-evaluation of a previous case study is theoretical sampling. In this instance, the researcher is re-examining an existing case study to see how robust its data and results are.

22 'Abstract,' in this context, means to 'summarize' or directly represent the actual structures and causal mechanisms in the real world, much like an abstract of a book or article. This is in contrast to the use of abstracts by mainstream economists. They use it as a way to remove the real world from the model so as to be able to introduce fictional concepts into it. In order to differentiate the two uses of abstract, I am using 'direct representation' to denote the former meaning of abstract.

23 Many modelers find this mode of evaluation unacceptable because it prevents them from using their outcomes to legitimize the model that produced them.

24 For a similar form of modeling, see Setterfield (2003).

25 Other types of mathematics could be used if the structures and causal mechanisms warrant it.

26 The historical character of heterodox economic theories is closely aligned with the view of economic theories espoused by the German Historical School (Spiethoff 1952; 1953; Betz 1988).

27 The outcome of a grounded theory approach to constructing causal mechanisms is a rejection of methodological individualism. While acting persons make decisions based on subjective and objective evaluations of a somewhat uncertain future and generate outcomes, for theoretical purposes their decisions and outcomes are aggregated and embedded in a causal mechanism. Hence, the empirically grounded role of the subjective and the uncertainty in the causal mechanism is observable, persistent, and systematic.

28 See Dopfer and Potts (2008, 21–26) for a similar argument regarding meso and macro.

2 Structure, agency, and modeling the economy

The social provisioning process

People have social, caring lives; they have households, parents, children, friends, colleagues, and a history; and they need to be fed, housed, clothed, married, schooled, and socially engaged. The needed and desired surplus goods and services are produced to sustain their socially constructed, caring lifestyle.[1] Thus the social provisioning process is a continuous, non-accidental series of production-based, production-derived economic activities through historical time that provide 'needy' households goods and services necessary to carry out their sequential reoccurring and changing social activities through time. This means that the social provisioning process is embedded in a production-with-a-social surplus 'paradigm' (a point further delineated below).[2] Hence, as a particular kind of social activity, economic activities cannot be disembedded or separated from society, and similarly the economy cannot be separated from society. Rather, the economy and its economic activities are linked with the society's social fabric that consists of a matrix of cultural values, norms, societal institutions, social joint-stock of knowledge (which includes technology), and the ecological system. The social fabric affects the organization of economic activities delivering the goods and services that make the social activities possible: it gives this delivery mechanism or the social provisioning process its meaning and its value.[3] Moreover, the components of the social fabric change slowly relative to the structures, organizations, institutions, and agency that specifically mold and direct economic activity and affect access to and delivery of social provisioning (Hayden 1982; 2006; 2011; Lee and Jo 2011). Since the aim of this chapter is to delineate the latter, the components of the social fabric are treated as 'social parameters.'

Social activities are socially created as opposed to being naturally or arbitrarily given. Thus, there is no limitation on what the activities can be or how diverse they are. This means that the goods and services relevant for the activities are diverse and socially specified. This has four implications. The first is that differentiated social activities require differentiated goods and services which in turn require differentiated production processes (that include different labor skills); so it is the differentiated social activities that bring into existence the division of labor and technical variation and change and not the reverse. A second implication is that the production processes, which include produced means of production,[4] differentiated labor, and technology, are also socially specified. In particular, the means of production are not limited by the natural properties of the resources used in their construction; specific types of labor are not genetically determined; and technology is not a natural transformation process that turns nature and natural labor into natural goods for 'social' utilization. Rather, they are social entities and hence are not naturally but technically specified via the social joint-stock of knowledge to be combined together to produce goods and services – without the 'intervention' of the social joint-stock of knowledge there would be no production at all (Veblen 1908, 518; 1914, 103). This means that production is socially determined and production activities are social activities. As a result, there exists an array of social relationships qua social structures within the production process that are endemic to capitalist societies, including class, hierarchy and dominance, gender, and race; it is through these social structures combined with the agency of *acting persons* that the production-economic activities underpinning the social provisioning process are conducted, coordinated, and given meaning and value.

The third implication is that since the means of production are not homogeneous so as to consist of a single all-purpose good, labor is not homogeneous, and technology is not homogeneous; that is, it is not conceptually or analytically possible to reduce economic activity as a whole to a single homogeneous non-monetary substance, whether it be nature, labor, a single all-purpose good, corn, or even utility.[5] Moreover, the non-homogeneity of labor suggests that the skills of an individual are insufficient by themselves for survival. The final implication is that all goods, services, and resources used in production and for social provisioning – that is, all inputs and outputs – have socially distinct, determined uses that are well defined within an array of social practices and customs. Consequently, their uses are socially and objectively determined; thus, they are intrinsic to them and are illuminated by their name(s).[6] Hence, the combination of differentiated social activities and labor means that economic activity must form an interdependent network for social provisioning to continually take place and individuals qua households to survive not just physically but also socially through maintaining a socially caring, meaningful lifestyle. This pursuit of social needs in turn provides the impetus for a further multiplication of economic activity. In short, to understand how the economy continuously generates its socially determined economic activities, it is necessary to treat the economy as a technically and socially differentiated but integrated whole – that is, as a going concern (Bortis 1997; 2003; Levine 1998; Danby 2010).

The concept of the 'going concern,' which first appeared in accounting literature in the late 1800s, refers to business enterprises with continuity of economic activity and an indefinite life span (as opposed to a terminal venture or an enterprise in the process of liquidation). For such an enterprise, it is necessary to keep its productive capabilities intact and to reckon its costs, revenues, and income in a manner that does not disrupt its productive capabilities. Thus the accounting profession uses the concept to base their understanding of productive assets or fixed investment goods, depreciation, and business income. The concept was further developed and differentiated into a 'going plant,' or productive capabilities, and a 'going business,' which refers to the activities associated with transactions, such as pricing and marketing, and their continuation over time. Moreover, for the going plant and the going business to work together to ensure a flow of actual and expected transactions, there must be working rules (formal ways of doing things) and routines (informal practices) within the going concern that make it happen; and also an external array of working rules which ensure that the flow of transactions in the marketplace occurs in a manner which enables the going concern to continue with its flow of transactions. Thus, a *going business enterprise* has the productive capabilities, managerial capabilities, and the working rules and routines that enable it to have expectations of a future.[7]

For the enterprise to exist as a going concern, the economy itself also has to be a going concern – that is, its circuit of production must be inherently circular. For this to happen, the going economy must have the productive capabilities, 'managerial' capabilities, and the working rules and routines that enable it to have expectations of a future, by which is meant that the social provisioning process is sustainable. One way to depict a *going concern economy* is the Sraffian social surplus approach; but it has no room for the agency of acting persons.

A second way is the heterodox social surplus approach in which agency (hence change) is present. In both approaches, the economy is productive in that it produces a social surplus and is viable in that the working class is sustained as a whole (but not necessarily the individual worker or the household) and so are the social relationships that sustain the working and ruling classes. However, the Sraffian approach assumes a self-replacing (or simple reproduction) economy and a given total social product or normal capacity utilization. The heterodox approach, in contrast, includes structural conditions of ruling class and (to a lesser extent) working class viability, assumes a non-self-replacing economy, and assumes agency qua acting person, which determines the social surplus that in turn determines the total social product and its composition. Hence, the going concern economy is consistent with the heterodox social surplus approach. So changes in goods and services that comprise the viable social provisioning process in a going concern economy are due to changes (but not fundamental changes) in the social relationships. If fundamental changes in class relationships occur, however, then the economy and its social provisioning process cease to be viable and cease to be a going economy from the perspective of the ruling class, even though it still retains the productive capabilities to produce the social surplus (Veblen 1904; Commons 1957; Storey 1959; Sterling 1968; Chatfield 1974; Chiodi 1992; 1998; 2008; 2010; Ramstad 2001; Kaufman 2006; Lee and Jo 2011).

As a theoretical concept and methodological approach, the economy as a going concern is abstracted from its historical origins and conceptually situated in a circular circuit of production. That is, it represents a 'currently' functioning working capitalist economy complete with structures and causal mechanisms with agency. Hence, the structures that give the economy its form, the organizations and institutions that structurally organize and coordinate economic activity, and the causal mechanisms that initiate and direct economic activity operating interdependently and contemporarily, although not necessarily synchronically. So while the structures, organizations, and institutions provide the framework for the economy to be a going concern and to continuously generate economic activities, it is acting persons (agency) at the center of the causal mechanisms that make economic activity happen or not – the economy does nothing on its own accord.[8]

Thus, the aim of this chapter is to theoretically delineate a capitalist economy as a going concern that will serve as the foundation for developing an empirically grounded microeconomic theory of the social provisioning process as well as an empirically grounded model of the economy. The first step in this process is to establish the core structures of a capitalist economy relevant to the social provisioning process and then, secondly, to locate within them the acting organizations and institutions that direct, engage in, or facilitate the economic events that result in social provisioning. And the economic events of specific interest are those that affect the demand for, production of, and access to the social surplus, that deal with the determination of prices, and that concern market governance. The structures help shape and govern the provisioning process while the organizations and social institutions (that are located in the structures) house the causal mechanisms in which agency is embedded. Because the social provisioning process is founded on the production of goods and services, the structure of production and the social surplus and the structure of the linkages between the social surplus and incomes are represented and modeled in the next two sections. In the third section, the central organizations and social institutions relevant to the social provisioning process are delineated and located in the structures; the acting person whose agency or decisions, which take place through the core organizations and institutions, direct and sustain the social provisioning process are identified and delineated. The final section draws upon the previous three sections to delineate the core structure-agency economic model of the social provisioning process. The economic model is then integrated with the social fabric and historically situated to create a historically grounded model of the economy as a whole. This model provides the overarching framework in which heterodox microeconomic theory is situated.

Representing and modeling the productive structure of the economy and the surplus

Since the social provisioning process is founded on the social and interdependent production of goods and services, one aspect of the organization of economic activity is its organization of production at the level of the circuit of production of the economy as a whole, of the production schema of the economy or the system of production of the economy, and of the production schema for a specific good or service. The *circular circuit of production* represents the economy reproducing itself (but not exactly) through time. For the circuit to be possible, the economy itself must have a circular production schema. The schema is represented as an input-output table of resources, material goods, and services combined with different types of labor skills to produce an array of resources, goods, and services as outputs. Many of the outputs replace the resources, goods, and services used up in production, while the rest constitutes the social surplus to be used for consumption, private investment, and government services that underpins the social provisioning process and sustains social activities. At the elementary level of the individual good, the production schema is represented in terms of a flow of produced resources, goods, and services and different types of labor skills as inputs in a technically required sequence for the production of a specific good or service.[9] For example:

$$\text{cloth} \oplus \text{thread} \oplus \text{seamstress} \rightarrow \text{dress} \tag{2.1}$$

which reads as cloth combined ($\oplus$) with thread combined with a seamstress produces a dress. The *elementary production schema* is different from the *circular production schema of the economy* in that, by itself, it is not engaged in circular production; circular production, rather, is a property of the production schema of the economy as a whole (Lee 2014).

Circular production

The individual elementary production schema depicts the flow of resources, goods, and services and labor needed to produce a specific resource, good, or service, and together with the other schemas depict the circular nature of production, technical differentiation of resources, goods, and services and labor, and the surplus of goods and services that are not used up in production. Specifically, the economy circular production schema is empirically represented in terms of a product-by-product input-output table (or matrix) and a labor skills-by-product table.[10] The table shows n resources, goods, and services (or intermediate) inputs and z labor skills inputs are used in the production of m resources, goods, and services, where $m > n$ and $z > m$. Thus, letting g_{ij} represent the amount of the j-th product (resource, good, or service) and L_{iz} represent the amount of the z-th labor skill needed to produce Q_i amount of the i-th product, the elementary production schema is represented by:

$$[g_{i1}, \ldots, g_{in} \oplus L_{i1}, \ldots, L_{iz}] \rightarrow Q_i$$
$$[\mathbf{G}_i \oplus \mathbf{L}_i] \rightarrow Q_i \tag{2.2}$$

where $\mathbf{G}_i = (g_{i1}, \ldots, g_{in})$ is a row vector of n intermediate inputs, and $\mathbf{L}_i = (L_{i1}, \ldots, L_{iz})$ is a row vector of z labor skills inputs.

Hence, the economy production schema takes the following form:

$$\begin{bmatrix} \mathbf{G}_1 \oplus \mathbf{L}_1 \\ \vdots \\ \mathbf{G}_m \oplus \mathbf{L}_m \end{bmatrix} \rightarrow \begin{bmatrix} Q_1 \\ \vdots \\ Q_m \end{bmatrix} \tag{2.3}$$

Representing the array of $(\mathbf{G}_1, \ldots, \mathbf{G}_m)$ as G a product-by-product input-output matrix, the array of $(\mathbf{L}_1, \ldots, \mathbf{L}_m)$ as L a labor skills-by-product matrix, and the total quantity produced of each product as $\mathbf{Q}$, the production schema of the economy of 2.3 is be depicted as:

$$G \oplus L \rightarrow Q \tag{2.4}$$

or

$$\begin{bmatrix} G_{11} \\ G_{21} \end{bmatrix} \oplus \begin{bmatrix} L_{11} \\ L_{21} \end{bmatrix} \rightarrow \begin{bmatrix} Q_1 \\ Q_2 \end{bmatrix} \tag{2.5}$$

where G is a non-negative $m \times n$ flow matrix of intermediate inputs consisting of produced resources, goods, and services; L is a non-negative $m \times z$ flow matrix of labor skills; $\mathbf{Q}$ is a strictly positive $m \times 1$ column vector of output or the total social product; G_{11} is a non-negative square $n \times n$ matrix of intermediate inputs used in the production of $\mathbf{Q}_1$ a strictly positive $n \times 1$ column vector of intermediate resources, goods, and services; G_{21} is a non-negative $(m - n) \times n$ matrix of intermediate inputs used in the production of $\mathbf{Q}_2$ a strictly positive $(m - n) \times 1$ column vector of final goods and services for consumption, investment, and government use; L_{11} is a non-negative $n \times z$ matrix of labor skills used in the production of $\mathbf{Q}_1$; L_{21} is a non-negative $(m - n) \times z$ matrix of labor skills used in the production of $\mathbf{Q}_2$; and $\oplus$ means both intermediate and labor inputs are used to produce the output.

One feature of the production schema is that the production of Q_i involves the utilization of many distinct resources, goods, and services $(\mathbf{G}_i)$ and labor skills $(\mathbf{L}_i)$, that intermediate inputs are themselves produced by many distinct intermediate inputs, and that many outputs are used directly (and/or sequentially) or indirectly as inputs into their own production. In the particular case of $G_{11} \rightarrow \mathbf{Q}_1$, all the outputs also appear as inputs (either directly or indirectly) in their own production – that is, all of $\mathbf{Q}_1$ are produced means of production. This implies that both inputs and outputs are tied to technically specified differentiated uses, production is a circular flow, all intermediate inputs are produced inputs, and the elementary production schemas (2.3) for each output are all linked together on the input side. Consequently, the production of intermediate inputs is a differentiated, indecomposable, and hence emergent system of production that cannot be segmented, aggregated, disaggregated, reduced, or increased.[11]

A second feature is that an increase in any surplus good or service is technically dependent on intermediate inputs. Thus the production of any surplus good or service in $\mathbf{Q}_2$ requires the direct and/or indirect utilization of all intermediate inputs. As a result, the production of $\mathbf{Q}_1$ and the employment of L_{11} are dependent on the decisions to produce surplus goods and services for consumption, investment, and government use. Finally, the third feature of the structure of production is that the production of any Q_i must directly involve at least one g_{ij}, where $i \neq j$, which means that all of G_{11} is at least indirectly engaged in its production, making all intermediate inputs, $\mathbf{Q}_1$, Sraffian basic goods.[12] In short, in order to produce any Q_i, the entire sub-system of basic goods, G_{11}, is needed (Bortis 1997; Lee 1998; 2014; Roncaglia 2005; Trigg 2006; Miller and Blair 2009).

Circular production, non-produced inputs, and scarcity

Although resources and labor are not intermediate produced goods and services *per se*, neither are they non-produced inputs with naturally given indestructible productive capabilities and talents that exist prior to production and externally to the economy production schema as are 'original' factor inputs.[13] Being producible within the schema and the circuit of production more generally, goods and services used as intermediate produced means of production are not original factors, and a similar argument can be used for resources and labor as well. That is, while 'neutral stuff' in the form of attributes of nature exists, they are not resources with 'naturally' given capabilities that can be used for production until they have been shaped by technology and culture and placed under human control and direction. To be an input in a technologically specialized production process requires prior technological development in terms of converting nature into resources that have capabilities to work with other goods, services, and labor skills to produce an output that meets existing technological and/or cultural needs. Hence, nature-based resources are socially created inputs with technologically created capabilities. This implies that their 'fertility' is not knowable in physical terms. Thus they are produced, reproduced, augmented, eliminated, or even cyclically produced and eliminated by the structure of production in conjunction with changes in the social joint-stock of technical knowledge and technology (as represented in fixed investment goods) and therefore are not naturally fixed or finite in amount or quantity because they are not natural. In short, "resources *are* not, they *become*; they are not static but expand and contract in response to human wants and human actions" (Zimmermann 1951, 15, original italics). Consequently, resources are an expression of the human appraisal of nature and hence cannot be viewed as a non-produced input externally injected into the structure of production. Rather, resources are socially constructed, socially produced means of production and therefore function like goods and services used as intermediate produced means of production.

Similarly, labor is a socially produced input in that it is created or becomes through the social joint-stock of knowledge. That is, humans are acting persons that have capabilities to learn particular skills. A particular state of technical knowledge will produce and reproduce those skills or specific forms of labor while changes in it will render some skills obsolete (hence not reproducible) and create new skills. In addition, any particular labor skill or even the overall amount of labor can vary as a result of changes in technical knowledge. Therefore, like nature-based resources, labor is socially constructed; hence similar to, but not the same as, a resource or a good or service used as an intermediate input. Hence, while labor is not produced within the system of production like a ton of steel, it is socially created in conjunction with technical knowledge and then enters the system of production as 'input.'

With resources, labor, goods, and services being used as intermediate inputs co-created and co-existing internally within the circular circuit of production, there does not exist original factors of production with naturally given indestructible capabilities and given unalterable endowments. Consequently, none of the inputs in G or L can be scarce factor inputs, as defined in mainstream economics, which implies that none of the outputs (Q) can be characterized as relatively scarce products. Therefore, production is not an activity to overcome scarcity, exchange does not arise from scarcity, and prices are not scarcity indexes. In short, under circular production, scarcity has no theoretical meaning, and hence the price mechanism is not an organizing principle of economic activity in heterodox economics.[14] This does not mean that shortages of produced goods do not exist, but rather that shortages are not the basis of exchange, prices are not shortages indexes, and production is not solely organized to deal with shortages. Moreover, the absence of scarcity and the production of resources do not mean that nature (qua resources) is not fixed or exhaustible in some sense. Rather, its quantity available for production is variable since changes in technology, knowledge, social mores, legislation, business investment and production decisions, and government expenditure decisions can augment the quantity of a resource for production or can make a resource nature again. This does not imply that there are no environmental issues associated with production of resources, goods, and services; and it also does not imply that natural processes that contribute to the production of resources, goods, and services do not exist. But they are not relevant to the theoretical issue of scarcity as an organizing concept for economic inquiry being addressed. Finally, with the absence of scarcity, the 'fixity' of nature is not a constraint on production and a limit to the social provisioning process, which in turn implies that the concepts of production possibility frontier, opportunity cost, and the trade-off in the production of goods and services have no meaning in heterodox economics. The absence of original factors of production and scarcity means that with circular production, the restraints on the social provisioning process are not given quantities of scarce factor inputs located in production, but are located in the decisions (agency) and values that affect the production of the surplus (Q_2) and its distribution (Veblen 1908; Zimmermann 1951; Levine 1977; 1978; Eichner 1979; Matthaei 1984; De Gregori 1985, 1987; Tool 2001; McCormick 2002; Bradley 2007; Lee 2014).

Fixed investment goods, resource reserves, and the surplus

Behind the usage of intermediate inputs and the employment of differentiated labor skills for each product stands an array of differentiated fixed investment goods, some of which are currently being produced while others are not.

$$\mathbf{K}_{Si} = \left(k_{i1}, \ \ldots, k_{ik} \right) \tag{2.6}$$

where $\mathbf{K}_{Si}$ is a $1 \times k$ row vector of the stock of k_k fixed investment goods used in the production of Q_i; $k_{i1}, \ldots, k_{ir}$ are currently produced fixed investment goods; and $k_{ir+1}, \ldots, k_{ik}$ are fixed investment goods not currently produced.

The fixed investment goods are used in production, but they are not used up like intermediate inputs. Rather, they are separate from the intermediate and labor inputs (hence the colon in Schema 2.8 below) because they are repeatedly used in the repeated production of the output.[15] In addition there is also an array of differentiated resource reserves:

$$\mathbf{RR}_{Si} = (rr_{i1}, \ldots, rr_{ir}) \tag{2.7}$$

where $\mathbf{RR}_{Si}$ is a $1 \times r$ row vector of rr_r resource reserves used in the production of Q_i, and its element rr_{ij} is the amount of the j-th resource reserve available for the production of Q_i.

While resources used in production come from resource reserves, the resource reserves themselves are separate and are available for repeated acts of production, although the quantities of the reserves change as production takes place and the social joint-stock of knowledge changes.

Thus, the combined array of fixed investment goods ($\mathbf{K}_{Si}$), resource reserves ($\mathbf{RR}_{Si}$), intermediate inputs ($\mathbf{G}_i$), and differentiated labor skills ($\mathbf{L}_i$) used for the production of Q_i represents the complete technology of the elementary production schema:

$$[\mathbf{K}_{Si}, \mathbf{RR}_{Si} : \mathbf{G}_i \oplus \mathbf{L}_i] \rightarrow Q_i \tag{2.8}$$

The technology of the schema embodies a specific set of learned, socially created knowledge that makes it an emergent whole. In particular, the fixed investment goods, intermediate inputs, and the differentiated labor inputs are the physical manifestations of the uniquely specific social joint-stock of knowledge qua technology used in the production of Q_i. Being linked in an emergent technological arrangement for the production of Q_i, the elementary production schema cannot be separated into parts with each identified with a certain portion of the output;[16] its fixed investment goods and resource reserves cannot be viewed as separate 'dated output' to be hypothetically sold in the form of joint products (a point further discussed in the next chapter); and the schema itself cannot be treated as a joint output with Q_i. Finally, from Schema 2.8, the production schema of the economy as a whole can be represented as:

$$[\mathbf{K}_S, \mathbf{RR}_S : \mathbf{G} \oplus \mathbf{L}] \rightarrow \mathbf{Q} \tag{2.9}$$

or

$$\begin{bmatrix} K_{S1} & RR_{S1} : G_{11} \\ K_{S2} & RR_{S2} : G_{21} \end{bmatrix} \oplus \begin{bmatrix} L_{11} \\ L_{21} \end{bmatrix} \rightarrow \begin{bmatrix} Q_1 \\ Q_2 \end{bmatrix} \tag{2.9a}$$

where K_{S1} is a non-negative $n \times k$ matrix of the basic goods sector stock of fixed investment goods used in the production of Q_1; K_{S2} is a non-negative $(m - n) \times k$ matrix of the surplus sector stock of fixed investment goods used in the production of Q_2; RR_{S1} is a non-negative $n \times k$ matrix of the basic goods sector amount of resource reserves available for the production of Q_1; and RR_{S2} is a non-negative $(m - n) \times k$ matrix of the surplus goods sector amount of resource reserves available for the production of Q_2.

The social surplus of the economy consists of the excess of total goods produced over what is used up in production:

$$\left(eQ_d\right)^T - \left(eG^*\right)^T = Q - G^* = S^* \tag{2.10}$$

where e is a $1 \times m$ row vector of ones or a sum vector; Q_d is a positive $m \times m$ diagonal matrix of the total social product; $\left(eQ_d\right)^T = Q$ is a positive $m \times 1$ column vector of the total social product; G^* is an augmented G matrix with $n + 1$ to m columns consisting of zeros; $\left(eG^*\right)^T = G^*$ is a semi-positive $m \times 1$ column vector of intermediate inputs; and S^* is a semi-positive $m \times 1$ column vector of the goods and services that constitute the social surplus.

The social surplus includes 'extra' intermediate inputs and final goods that go into inventory. However, for a going concern economy, an inventory of goods and resources already exists. Since enterprises aim to maintain inventories at a particular level (which can change), total output for any good or resource is more or less equivalent to its sales, even if some of the goods and resources sold are recorded as produced in the previous accounting period and are replaced by goods and resources produced in the current accounting period. Because inventories constitute less than plus or minus one percent of total economic activity, they will for the moment be ignored.[17] Thus, it is assumed that all of Q_1 is used up in production or

$$\left(eQ_{d1}\right)^T - \left(eG\right)^T = 0 \tag{2.11}$$

This means that the surplus of the economy is equal to final goods and services, is technically defined (and, as will be argued later, is created by a particular social class), and consists of Sraffian non-basic goods and services:[18]

$$S = Q_2 \tag{2.12}$$

As a productive economy, it has the possibility through the circular circuit of production to continually replace all the output, Q_1 and Q_2, produced in the previous circuit. Moreover, if the social surplus is just sufficient to maintain without changing the society in which the economy is embedded, then the economy is viable and in a self-replacing state or stationary state qua simple reproduction. In a sense, as with Schumpeter's (1969) circular flow of economic life, the economy cannot change because it does not have the internal capabilities to do so. But, if the economy is sufficiently productive, it can, in a continuous manner, be in a viable and also in a non-self-replacing, non-replicating state – that is, the economy can be a going concern that changes.

The surplus is differentiated by its 'final' destination or their social accounts – government goods $(\mathbf{Q}_{2G})$ for the state, consumption goods $(\mathbf{Q}_{2C})$ for the household, and fixed investment goods $(\mathbf{Q}_{2I})$ for the business enterprise:

$$\mathbf{S} = \mathbf{Q}_2 = \mathbf{Q}_{2G} + \mathbf{Q}_{2C} + \mathbf{Q}_{2I} \tag{2.13}$$

where $\mathbf{Q}_{2G}$, $\mathbf{Q}_{2C}$, and $\mathbf{Q}_{2I}$ are semi-positive $(m - n) \times 1$ column vectors of surplus goods and services.

Since the different destinations are engaged with broadly different economic and social activities, the array and composition of the three vectors differ.[19] In particular, $\mathbf{Q}_{2I}$ not only differs in its array of goods from $\mathbf{Q}_{2G}$ and $\mathbf{Q}_{2C}$, it is also a differentiated array of goods and services due to the different technologies used to produce $\mathbf{Q}_{2G}$ and $\mathbf{Q}_{2C}$, which themselves are an array of differentiated goods and services. Moreover, as noted above, fixed investment goods affect both positively and negatively the amount of resource reserves available for the production of the social product. Finally, $\mathbf{Q}_{2I}$ is connected, as a flow of basic goods sector fixed investment goods K_{F1}, to the stock of basic sector fixed investment goods K_{S1} and, as a flow of surplus sector fixed investment goods K_{F2}, to the stock of surplus sector fixed investment goods K_{S2}. As a result, the stock of fixed investment goods gets augmented with the inflow of new fixed investment goods (and declines when old fixed investment goods are removed):

$$\mathbf{Q}_{2I}^T \rightarrow K_{F1\text{-}2} \rightarrow K_{S1\text{-}2}, RR_{S1\text{-}2} \tag{2.14a}$$

Thus, the economy is productively linked together by the circular flow of the production of intermediate inputs, by a second circular flow via the surplus from the production of fixed investment goods to their final destination as stocks and their subsequent use directly and/or indirectly in their own production as well as in the production of all intermediate inputs and final goods and services, which makes them a 'quasi-basic goods' in the Sraffian sense, and by a third quasi-circular flow from the production of fixed investment goods to their impact on the amount of resource reserves available for production (RR_{S1-2}).

The array of differentiated goods in $\mathbf{Q}_{2G}$ indicates the range of social activities supported by the state and its composition indicates their relative social importance. Therefore, the state's contribution to social provisioning is affected by the cultural values, beliefs, and norms and by agency qua decisions that compel the production of $\mathbf{Q}_{2G}$. But to make its contribution in terms of government services (GS), the state must draw upon government fixed investment goods and resource reserves (which it also produces as public assets and not as commodities) and employ differently skilled workers, managers, and politicians and combined them with $\mathbf{Q}_{2G}$ and government payments (GP):

$$\mathbf{K}_{S4}, \mathbf{RR}_{S4} : \mathbf{Q}_{2G}^{T} \oplus \mathbf{L}_{41} \oplus GP \rightarrow GS, \mathbf{K}_{F4} \rightarrow \mathbf{K}_{S4}, \mathbf{RR}_{F4} \rightarrow \mathbf{RR}_{S4} \qquad (2.14b)$$

where $\mathbf{K}_{S4}$ is a row vector of the stock of k government fixed investment goods used in providing of government services (obtained through past government purchases); $\mathbf{RR}_{S4}$ is a row vector of r government resource reserves available for providing government services; $\mathbf{Q}_{2G}^{T}$ is a $1 \times (m - n)$ row vector of surplus goods and services used in providing government services; $\mathbf{L}_{41}$ is a $m + 2$ row vector of z labor skills used in providing government services; GP is the amount of government payments in state money terms, such as unemployment or social welfare payments, to dependent individuals and households that do not have current employment hence wage income or other forms of income, and interest payments to bank and non-bank enterprises and households that hold government bonds; $\mathbf{K}_{F4}$ is a row vector of the flow of k government fixed investment goods into $\mathbf{K}_{S4}$; and $\mathbf{RR}_{F4}$ is a row vector of the flow of r government resource reserves into $\mathbf{RR}_{S4}$.

Thus, the state's production schema has as outcomes, government services (such as health care), a flow of government fixed goods (such as a hospital) that becomes part of its stock of hospitals, and a flow of resource reserves (such as discovering oil on government land) that also becomes part of its stock of resource reserves (such as oil). The government services support and enhance the economic activity in the basic and surplus goods (and banking) sectors as well as the business enterprises themselves; and it also supports households and contributes to the education and training of its members for participation in the economy.

Finally, the array of differentiated goods and services in $\mathbf{Q}_{2C}$ indicates the range of social activities undertaken by households, while its composition indicates their relative social importance:

$$\mathbf{Q}_{2C}^{T} \rightarrow HSA \qquad (2.14c)$$

where $\mathbf{Q}_{2C}^{T}$ is a $1 \times (m - n)$ row vector of surplus goods and services that contribute to household social activities (HSA).

In addition to maintaining the household as a going concern, HSA contribute to the skills that its members need to obtain employment in the economy and with it access to the social provisioning process.

There are three further implications arising from $\mathbf{Q}_2$ being produced by the economic system as a whole. The first is that since consumption and investment are based on current production, the former is not constrained by the latter and the latter is not based on 'savings.' That is, the economic system as a whole has the capability of producing varying amounts of $\mathbf{Q}_{2C}$ *independently* of $\mathbf{Q}_{2I}$ if below full utilization of capacity; and *cooperatively* with Q_{2I} if additional capacity is needed. Because workers consume currently produced Q_{2C}, this implies that there is no 'saved' wage fund that inversely links 'real wages' to employment or that links higher 'real wages' for some workers to lower 'real wages' for others. Secondly, since Q_{2I} is also currently produced, private investment is not dependent on 'savings' of any sort and increasing Q_{2G} does not 'crowd out' the production of Q_{2C} and Q_{2I}. This means that the production of Q_{2G} does not inhibit the growth of the economy, but instead contributes to it. Lastly, as Q_2 is produced for the purpose of maintaining an ongoing range of particular government services and household social activities, the overall array and composition of the social surplus is the physical component of the structure of the social provisioning process. But it also represents social relationships and decisions that produce it. This clearly makes the surplus socially (not naturally) constructed, hence a *social* surplus; the social determination of the volume and composition of the surplus also means the social determination of all means of production – resources, goods, services, and labor. Thus, all the actual economic activities that constitute the social provisioning process are manifestations of societal relations and decisions (Veblen 1908; Lower 1987; Ranson 1987; Kurz and Salvadori 1995; Lager 2006).

Social provisioning as a going plant

What emerges from above is that the structure of the social provisioning process in terms of resources, goods, services, and labor consists, in part, of the economy production schema representing the production of the social surplus (Schema 2.9a), and of the allocation qua contribution of the surplus to social provisioning through enabling state services and household social activities to occur and maintaining government and private sector productive capabilities (Schemas 2.14a–c). This can be schematically represented in terms of a stock-flow (in which the stocks and flows are identified and the flows of inputs into outputs and of outputs to their stocks delineated), social accounting (in which the flow of the surplus is connected to the three social accounts of the state, household, and enterprise) schema of the productive structure of the social provisioning process (see Table 2.1).[20]

As a whole, the social provisioning process acquires the structure of a going plant with unused capacity and fixed investment goods and resource reserves and the capability of producing additional capacity through producing fixed investment goods and resource reserves. So, as long as household social activities are ongoing and supported by government services, the economy circular production schema ensures the continuous reproduction of the intermediate inputs and fixed investment goods and production of resource reserves, thus maintaining the circular circuit of production. More specifically, the level of economic activity for the economy is completely determined by the decisions to produce consumption, investment, and government goods and services, that is, by effective demand. With the input requirements produced and reproducible simultaneously with the

Table 2.1 Stock-flow social accounting (SFSA) schema of the productive structure of the
social provisioning process

Basic goods sector	$K_{S1}, RR_{S1}: G_{11} \oplus L_{11} \rightarrow Q_1$
Surplus goods sector	$K_{S2}, RR_{S2}: G_{21} \oplus L_{21} \rightarrow Q_2 = Q_{2G} + Q_{2C} + Q_{2I}$
State	$K_{S4}, RR_{S4}: Q_{2G}^T \oplus L_{41} \oplus GP \rightarrow GS, K_{F4} \rightarrow K_{S4}, RR_{F4} \rightarrow RR_{S4}$
Household	$Q_{2c}^T \rightarrow HSA$
Enterprise	$Q_{2I}^T \rightarrow K_{F1-2} \rightarrow K_{S1-2}, RR_{S1-2}$

goods and services necessary for the household social activities and government
services to take place, the circuit of production (hence, the social provisioning
process) is potentially sustainable, and thus has an expected future; this is what
makes the economy a going plant. What this implies for the state and the household is that they are not external to the economy; rather, they are part of it on
par with the business enterprise. That is, since the economy as a going \plant is
an emergent entity, it is not possible to extract either the state or the household
from the economy and still have it as a going concern. In particular, the state
does not intervene into the economy; rather, it engages within the economy just
like the business enterprise and the household. Finally, although the economy
is a going plant, it is not necessarily a self-replacing, replicating one. That is to
say, the decisions that determine the production of the surplus generally alter
the absolute and relative quantities and composition of the goods, services, and
resources produced. Therefore, the production of goods, services, and resources
do not exactly replace what is used up in production; and nor do they necessarily
ensure the reproduction or replication of all of the individuals, households, and
groups that comprise the ruling, working, and dependent classes. The social provisioning process is a going plant, but one that constantly changes and access to
it also constantly changes.

Representing the relationship between the social surplus and income

The social provisioning process takes place through linkages between the money
incomes of workers, managers, and other members of society, profits of enterprises, and government spending on the social surplus – that is, consumption,
investment, and government goods and services. They exist because the social
surplus needs to be accessed qua distributed in a manner that maintains the economy as a going concern and particularly a capitalist going concern. Consequently,
class and agency-linked incomes are associated with agent-created goods and
services. Managers and owners of enterprises use their business income, that is
profits, to purchase fixed investment goods produced by other enterprises, while
workers use their wage incomes to purchase consumption goods and the state uses
its state money to purchase government goods both of which are also produced by
capitalists. The linkages are articulated through a social accounting matrix (Miller

and Blair 2009) or in terms of equations (the latter will be used in this book), often delineated in the form 'workers spend what they get and capitalists get what they spend.'

Classes, state, and state money

The particular forms that the linkages take involve exchange, markets, and state money, but they are based on a set of social relationships specific to capitalism. That is, under capitalism there exists a set of property rights that vest the ownership of the produced means of production, resource reserves, and output in a group of acting persons, either business people or the corporate enterprise;[21] and an associated set of legal rights that validate and 'empower' a hierarchical organizational structure which enables the board of directors and senior management of business enterprises to unilaterally direct their activities. These two groups of acting persons – business people/corporate enterprise and members of boards of directors/senior management – constitute the *capitalist class*. In addition, the state, as opposed to the political elite, owns its activities and 'property' while the elite, which also consists of acting persons, has the legal authority to direct its activities. Thus the combination of the capitalist class and the political elite constitutes the *ruling class* that owns the means of production, resource reserves, and output, and directs the economic and political activities of enterprises and the state. In contrast, there is a second class of acting persons who engage in the production of the output but do not own it or the means of production by which it is produced and who engage in activities that provide government services; neither can, in any substantive sense, direct, determine, or control (without workplace struggle) the 'working' activities in which they are engaged. These private and public sector employees constitute the *working class*. Finally, there is a third class of acting persons who are not engaged in social provisioning activities, such as children, retirees, and others, who constitute the *dependent class*.[22] Thus a twofold social relationship, denoted as *capital*, between the ruling class and the working and dependent classes exists: the former owns the 'going plant' – that is, the productive and administrative capabilities – and its output (which forms the foundation of social provisioning) and has the social power to direct it and to determine the conditions of access, while the latter have neither.[23]

As noted above, production is interdependent and diverse social activities exist; thus no elementary production schema of a single good or service can reproduce itself in isolation or ensure social provisioning. This implies that workers and managers, even if they own and hence have direct access to the total social product (**Q**), are not able to survive based on their own economic activities. In other words, it takes the entire economy as a whole to provide for social provisioning and thus to ensure the survival and reproduction qua continuation of households, business enterprises, and the state. This combined with the dominance of the ruling class means that the social provisioning process involves market exchange, which has three implications.

First, all goods, services, and resources (**Q**) are produced for exchange (hence are commodities in a Marxian sense), but since they are brought for their usefulness, they cease for the most part to be commodities after exchange is carried out – that is, they are not offered for further exchange. This is clearly the case for the intermediate inputs qua outputs, fixed investment goods, and resource reserves in that they are utilized directly for and in production. In addition, government and consumer goods and services are generally not brought to be offered for exchange.[24] Finally, in the case of fixed investment goods, they cannot be depicted as joint-products that are 'produced' as commodities to be hypothetically exchanged.[25] A second implication is that exchange is carried out in markets and involves prices, which means that individualistic, episodic, accidental exchanges for particular, personal needs have no analytical meaning or usefulness for explaining the social provisioning process, and that the only analytical-theoretical starting point is a system of systematic, coordinated, and unending multiple exchanges involving state money (which is not a commodity) as opposed to direct exchanges of commodities – that is, barter exchanges. The final implication is that prices are state money prices, which means that exchange, whether money for goods, services, or labor or *vice versa*, arises from the need of needy persons to gain access to a state-money monetized social provisioning process (rather than motivated by efforts to alleviate consumption constraints arising from relative scarcity, division of labor, and arbitrary allocation of scarce resources). Consequently, prices are correlated with state money incomes and the social rules governing the continually changing provisioning process, rather than with a 'substance' intrinsic or transferred to the commodities being exchanged or with exchange ratios required for the replicated reproduction of the economy – that is, 'prices of production.'[26]

State money (generally fiat money) is created when the government desires to purchase goods and services from business enterprises, hires employees to carry out its activities relevant to the social provisioning process, and at the same time requires such money in the payment of taxes, fines, and fees.[27] Following the Chartalist argument, the state creates its own money income for spending by crediting the bank accounts of enterprises and employees with state money that are located in bank corporate enterprises that constitute the banking sector; there it gets transformed into government financial assets (government bonds) and banking sector liabilities (demand deposits) and assets (bank loans). So while taxes co-exist with expenditures, they are not relevant with regard to expenditure decisions by the government and do not involve 'transferring' income from one group of households to another. Rather, the point of taxes is to create demand for the state's fiat money – in short, taxes are the 'cost' of having state money.[28] Complementing and reinforcing the Chartalist tax argument is that the demand for state money also arises through state and capitalist class power coupled with access to the social provisioning process. In this case, the government acquires the goods and services and hires the employees it needs by paying for them with fiat money that is backed by state power of simply acquiring them without any or little compensation. Accepting state money for its goods and services, the capitalist class in turn demands that all market exchanges for its goods, services, and resources are carried out in state money and the working class is paid with state money. By requiring all payments be made with state money, the capitalist class makes their own, and the working class' access to the social provisioning process depends on having it. So, it uses its class power over workers to impose on them the need to acquire state money as their only way to gain access to the social provisioning process, which means that members of the working class have to sell their labor for state money to be able to purchase goods and services necessary for their survival.[29] As a result, every exchange, every transaction that involves state money prices is a public manifestation of the dominant-subordinate social relationship between the ruling and the working-dependent classes (Levine 1978; Ingham 1996; Mosler 1997–98; Wray 1998; 2003; Bell 2001).

Government expenditures, state money, and the financial sector

Given the symbiotic relationship of the state through its ruling elite and the capitalist class over state money, the social relationship between the ruling class and the working and dependent classes is that the former owns-possesses the productive and administrative capabilities underpinning social provisioning, has the social power to direct the provisioning process, and controls the access to state money that is necessary for access to social provisioning, while the latter have none of the above. This tripartite social relationship defines what is meant by *capitalism* as a social, political, and economic system embedding the provisioning process; in doing so, it determines the particular structural form of the linkages between the money incomes of workers, managers, and other members of society, profits of enterprises, and state 'money income' and the expenditures on the social surplus. In particular, since all outputs are commodities that are exchanged in markets, they have prices in terms of state money. Hence, letting $\mathbf{p} = (p_1, \ldots, p_m)$ be a column vector of state money prices of all m resources, goods, and services produced in the economy, $\mathbf{p}_1 = (p_1, \ldots, p_n)$ be a column vector of prices of intermediate inputs, and $\mathbf{p}_2 = (p_{n+1}, \ldots, p_m)$ be a column vector of prices of all surplus goods and services, then the total value of the total social product is $\mathbf{Q}^T\mathbf{p}$, $\mathbf{Q}_1^T\mathbf{p}_1$ is the total value of the intermediate inputs, $\mathbf{Q}_{2I}^T\mathbf{p}_2$ is the total value of investment goods, $\mathbf{Q}_{2G}^T\mathbf{p}_2$ is the total value of government goods and services purchased, $\mathbf{Q}_{2C}^T\mathbf{p}_2$ is the total value of consumption goods and services, and the total value of the social surplus is:

$$\mathbf{Q}_2^T\mathbf{p}_2 = \mathbf{Q}_{2G}^T\mathbf{p}_2 + \mathbf{Q}_{2C}^T\mathbf{p}_2 + \mathbf{Q}_{2I}^T\mathbf{p}_2 \tag{2.15}$$

Consequently, to gain access to social provisioning, it is necessary that all household incomes, enterprise revenues, and government expenditures must be denominated in state money.

In terms of state money, government expenditures are equal to its purchases of final goods and services, to the wages and salaries of government employees and politicians, to government payments that are politically qua administratively determined income payments to the dependent class (GP_d), and to government interest payments to business enterprises (GP_{ib}), banks (GP_{iB}), and households (GP_{ih}) for holding state financial assets, that is, government bonds:

$$GOV_E = \mathbf{Q}_{2G}^T \mathbf{p}_2 + \mathbf{L}_{41}\mathbf{w} + GP_d + GP_{ib} + GP_{iB} + GP_{ih} = \mathbf{Q}_{2G}^T\mathbf{p}_2 + \mathbf{L}_{41}\mathbf{w} + GP_4 \quad (2.16)$$

where GOV_E is total government expenditures; $\mathbf{Q}_{2G}^T\mathbf{p}_2$ is government expenditures on goods and services; $\mathbf{w} = (w_1, \ldots, w_z)$ is a $z \times 1$ column vector of state money wage rates; $\mathbf{L}_{41}\mathbf{w}$ is the government's wage bill; and $GP_4 = GP_d + GP_{ib} + GP_{iB} + GP_{ih}$.

Because government expenditures are credited to accounts in the banking system, enterprises and households must use state money for provisioning and reproduction purposes; all enterprises must accept state money and utilize the banking system for making payments and receiving revenues. In addition, since the government does not actually produce $\mathbf{Q}_{2G}$ or the consumption goods and services purchased by government employees, politicians, and the dependent class, government expenditures are directly and indirectly spent on outputs owned by business enterprises and show up as a component of enterprise profits and hence in the total profits for the economy – so the more the state spends, the more profits (given tax rates) the capitalist class receives. Because profits are also generated by expenditures on fixed investment goods, total profits are equal to investment and government expenditures after taxes. This means government-generated profits are converted into financial assets through the purchase of government bonds by non-bank and bank corporate enterprises, and by households via the distribution of dividends out of profits.[30]

The symbiotic relationship of the state and the capitalist class regarding state money creates banking activities and hence the banking sector that is distinct from the basic and surplus goods sectors, and that could be managed by the state and/or capitalists.[31] Therefore, the banking sector is included in this book, but nothing of theoretical importance turns on whether banking activities are managed by the state or by capitalists. So with a stock of fixed investment goods ($\mathbf{K}_{S3}$), of resource reserves ($\mathbf{RR}_{S3}$), of financial assets-government bonds (FA_{SGB3}) and bank loans (FA_{SBL3}), and of financial liabilities-deposit accounts of business enterprises and households (LB_{S3}), the banking sector utilizes intermediate inputs and labor and income from the government bonds and loans minus the costs of demand deposits to produce qua create bank loans that are purchased by enterprises and households at the current bank interest rate;[32] so its elementary production schema is:

$$\mathbf{K}_{S3}, \mathbf{RR}_{S3}, FA_{S3}, LB_{S3}: \mathbf{G}_{31} \oplus \mathbf{L}_{31} \to Q_{3L} \quad (2.17)$$

where $\mathbf{K}_{S3}$ is a row vector of k_k fixed investment goods and $\mathbf{RR}_{S3}$ is a row vector of rr_r resource reserves used in the production of bank loans; $FA_{S3} = FA_{SGB3} + FA_{SBL3}$ is the total stock of financial assets of the banking sector and is a scalar;[33] $\mathbf{G}_{31}$ is the $m + 1$ row vector of n intermediate inputs used in the production of bank loans; L_{31} is the $m + 1$ row vector of z labor skills used in the production of bank loans; and Q_{3L} is a scalar and the amount of bank loans made to enterprises and households.

Since enterprises require bank loans for working capital on a continuous basis and, at times, for long-term investment projects, they have a stock of financial liabilities. Similarly, households take out bank loans to purchase various goods and services needed for household social activities and so have a stock of financial liabilities. Finally, the state carries out government expenditures that are not compensated by taxes and so has a stock of financial liabilities, called the national debt, that is represented by the outstanding government bonds owned by non-bank and bank enterprises and by households.[34] Combine this with Equation 2.16 and Schema 2.17, the schema of the productive structure of the social provisioning process (Table 2.1) is broadened to include a schematic representation of the financial structure of the economy and the stock-flow social accounting (SFSA) relationships of financial assets and liabilities.

Table 2.2 SFSA schema of the productive and financial structure of the social provisioning process

Basic goods sector	$K_{S1}, RR_{S1}, \mathbf{FA}_{S1}, \mathbf{LB}_{S1}: G_{11} \oplus L_{11} \rightarrow$	$\mathbf{Q}_1$
Surplus goods sector	$K_{S2}, RR_{S2}, \mathbf{FA}_{S2}, \mathbf{LB}_{S2}: G_{21} \oplus L_{21} \rightarrow$	$\mathbf{Q}_2 = \mathbf{Q}_{2G} + \mathbf{Q}_{2C} + \mathbf{Q}_{2I}$
Banking sector	$\mathbf{K}_{S3}, \mathbf{RR}_{S3}, FA_{S3}, LB_{S3}: \mathbf{G}_{31} \oplus \mathbf{L}_{31} \rightarrow$	$Q_{3L} \rightarrow FA_{S3} \rightarrow LB_{1,2,5}$
State	$\mathbf{K}_{S4}, \mathbf{RR}_{S4}, \qquad LB_{S4}: \mathbf{Q}_{2G}^T \oplus L_{41} \oplus GP_4 \rightarrow GS, K_{F4} \rightarrow K_{S4}, RR_{F4} \rightarrow RR_{S4}$	
Household	$FA_{S5}, LB_{S5}: \mathbf{Q}_{2C}^T \rightarrow HSA$	
Enterprise	$\mathbf{Q}_{2I}^T \rightarrow K_{F1-3} \rightarrow K_{S1-3}, RR_{1-3}$	
Financial structural balances	National debt $\qquad LB_{S4} = FA_{SGB1-3,5}$ Bank loans $\qquad FA_{SBL3} = LB_{1,2,5}$ Bank demand deposits $LB_{S3} = FA_{SDD1,2,5}$	

Notes: $\mathbf{FA}_{S1}$ and $\mathbf{LB}_{S1}$ are $n \times 1$ column vectors of the stock of financial assets-government bonds (FA_{SGB1}) and demand deposits (FA_{SDD1}), and liabilities-bank loans (LB_{S1}), associated with the production of intermediate inputs, $\mathbf{Q}_1$; $\mathbf{FA}_{S2}$ and $\mathbf{LB}_{S2}$ are $(m - n) \times 1$ column vectors of the stock of financial assets-government bonds (FA_{SGB2}) and demand deposits (FA_{SDD2}), and liabilities-bank loans (LB_{S2}), associated with the production of the social surplus, $\mathbf{Q}_2$; FA_{S3} and LB_{S3} are scalars and the stock of financial assets-government bonds (FA_{SGB3}) and bank loans (FA_{SBL3}), and liabilities-demand deposits (LB_{S3}), associated with the production of bank loans, Q_{3L}; LB_{S4} is a scalar and is the stock of financial liabilities (national debt) associated with providing government services (GS); and FA_{S5} and LB_{S5} are scalars and are the stock of financial assets-government bonds (FA_{SGB5}) and demand deposits (FA_{SDD5}), and liabilities-bank loans (LB_{S5}), associated with household activities.

The above schema shows that the national debt consists of the government bonds that are held by bank and non-bank enterprises and by households; thus an increase in the national debt arising from government expenditures exceeding taxes increases the private sector's and households' holdings of government bonds and hence their profits and incomes. Enterprises and households also take out bank loans (liabilities) that simultaneously create financial assets for the banking sector; but since bank loans are deposited in banks (thus creating financial assets), they also create banking sector liabilities. Therefore an increase in bank loans increases banking sector financial assets and liabilities at the same time. In short, government decisions to spend (given tax rates) and enterprise and household decisions to take out bank loans create, drive, and change the economy's financial structure. This outcome is not dissimilar from decisions concerning the production of the surplus driving the productive structure of the economy.

Profits, incomes, and the social surplus

To simplify the analysis, gross profits are defined as the difference between intermediate and labor input costs and revenues; thus, it includes depreciation (which is an 'income' stream to the enterprise) and interest income for the banking and non-banking enterprises.[35] So, drawing on Equations and Schemas 2.15, 2.16, 2.17, and Table 2.2, gross profits in a state money economy are:

$$\Pi = \mathbf{Q}^{\mathrm{T}}\mathbf{p} - e[\mathbf{Gp}_1 + \mathbf{Lw}] + \mathrm{TR}_3 - i_{\mathrm{D}}\mathrm{LB}_{\mathrm{S3}} - [\mathbf{G}_{31}\mathbf{p}_1 + \mathbf{L}_{31}\mathbf{w}] \qquad (2.18a)$$
$$\Pi = \Pi_{1\text{-}2} + \Pi_3 \qquad (2.18b)$$

where Π is a scalar and the total gross profits of the economy; $\mathbf{Q}^{\mathrm{T}}\mathbf{p}$ is the total value of the total social product; $\mathbf{Gp}_1$ is the value of the intermediate inputs by product used in the production of the social product; $\mathbf{Lw}$ is the wage bill by product incurred in the production of the social product; TR_3 is the total interest income of the banking sector and is equal to interest income from government bonds $(i_{\mathrm{G}}\mathrm{FA}_{\mathrm{SGB3}})$ plus interest income from bank loans $(i_{\mathrm{Bp}}\mathrm{FA}_{\mathrm{SBL3}})$; i_{G} is the rate of interest on government bonds; i_{Bp} is the rate of interest on past bank loans; $i_{\mathrm{D}}\mathrm{LB}_{\mathrm{S3}}$ is the interest costs of demand deposits to the banking sector; i_{D} is the rate of interest on demand deposits set by the banking sector; $\mathbf{G}_{31}\mathbf{p}_1$ is the value of the intermediate inputs by product used in the production of the bank loans; $\mathbf{L}_{31}\mathbf{w}$ is the wage bill by product incurred in the production of the bank loans; $\Pi_{1\text{-}2}$ is the total gross profits of the non-banking sector (Π_1 profits of the basic goods sector and Π_2 profits of the surplus goods sector); and Π_3 is the total gross profits of the banking sector.

Because demand deposits and interest payments on bank loans are a cost and an income to the banking and non-banking sectors, gross profits of the economy reduces to net profits (Π'), depreciation (D_{E}), interest on government bonds (that is, government interest payments to banks and non-banks enterprises, see Equation 2.16), and household interest income (HII), which is the difference between the interest income made on loans to the household sector ($i_{Bp}FAH_{SBL3}$) minus the interest payments made on household demand deposits ($i_D LBH_{S3}$):

$$\Pi = \Pi' + i_G FA_{SGB1\text{-}3} + D_E + HII = \Pi' + GP_E + D_E + HII \tag{2.19}$$

where $GP_E = GP_{iB} + GP_{ib}$ is government interest payments to enterprises; and $HII = i_{Bp}FAH_{SBL3} - i_D LBH_{S3}$.

Therefore again, we find that government debt makes a positive contribution to the gross profits of banking and non-banking enterprises.

Profit and income taxes (as well as other payments to the state) are necessary to maintain the demand for state money; thus with regard to profits, there is a profit tax rate, τ_p. In addition, the capitalist class allocates a percentage of its profits to dividends, and the rest is retained to purchase fixed investment goods, reduce liabilities, and acquire new government bonds. So gross profits after taxes are distributed between dividends and retained earnings:

$$\Pi(1 - \tau_p) = \Pi_R(1 - \tau_p) + \Pi_D(1 - \tau_p) \tag{2.20a}$$
$$\Pi^* = \Pi_R^* + \Pi_D^* \tag{2.20b}$$

where $\Pi(1-\tau_p) = \Pi^*$ is gross profits after taxes; $\Pi_R(1-\tau_p) = \Pi_R^*$ is retained earnings after taxes used to purchase fixed investment goods and government bonds, and to make payments to retire their bank loans; and $\Pi_D(1-\tau_p) = \Pi_D^*$ is dividends to be distributed to ruling class households.

From the above, the link between retained profits after taxes and fixed investment goods, assets, and liabilities is:

$$\Pi_R^* = Q_{2I}^T p_2 + FA_{BE} + LB_{BE} \tag{2.21}$$

where FA_{BE} is the amount of government bonds purchased by bank and non-bank enterprises; LB_{BE} is the amount of liabilities ($LB_{S1,2}$) paid off by non-bank enterprises.

In addition, dividends are distributed to ruling class households that use them to purchase government bonds (FA_{5RC}):

$$\Pi_D^* = FA_{5RC} \tag{2.22}$$

Thus, total profits after taxes resolve themselves into the purchase of investment goods and supporting production ($Q_{2I}^T p_2 + LB_{BE}$) and the purchase of government bonds ($FA_{BE} + FA_{5RC}$). This implies that decisions to demand investment goods, make government expenditures, and push workers into debt are the primary factors that determine profits (Erdos and Molnar 1990).

Finally, turning to households and their incomes, working class and dependent class households have bank loans and demand deposits, but do not own government bonds. Thus they spend their entire post-tax income (which consists of wages, government payments, and interest payments on demand deposits) on consumption goods and services and paying off bank loans (LB_{HWDC}) while maintaining their demand deposits. On the other hand, ruling class households spend only their post-tax salary and interest income on consumption goods and services, paying off bank loans (LB_{HRC}) and maintaining their demand deposits and utilize their post-tax dividend income to purchase government bonds. Thus, drawing from Equations and Schemas 2.16, 2.17, and 2.22, the link between total income and consumption goods and services is:

$$
\begin{aligned}
&L^{*}w(1-\tau_{i})+GP_{d}(1-\tau_{i})+i_{D}FA_{SDD5}(1-\tau_{i})+GP_{ih}+\Pi_{D}(1-\tau_{p})(1-\tau_{i}) \\
&= Q_{2C}^{T}p_{2}+FA_{5RC}+LB_{5}
\end{aligned}
\tag{2.23}
$$

where L^{*} is a $1 \times z$ row vector of all the labor skills; $L^{*}w$ is the total wage bill of the economy; τ_{i} is an income tax rate; $i_{D}FA_{SDD5}$ is interest income from demand deposits; FA_{5RC} is the amount of government bonds purchased by ruling class households; and LB_{5} is the amount of banking sector liabilities paid off by the households ($LB_{HRC}+LB_{HWDC}$).

The linkages between income-profit-government spending and the surplus delineated in Equations and Schemas 2.15, 2.16, 2.20–2.23 implies that incomes and profits before taxes equals the value of the social surplus; that the current government deficit is equal to the value of government bonds purchased by enterprises and the ruling elite; and that taxes represent the government's procurement of 'free' labor and goods and services for the benefit of society as a whole as interpreted by the ruling class.

Social provisioning as a going economy

Combining the equations and schemas of the productive and financial structure of the social provisioning process (2.15, 2.16, 2.17, and Table 2.2) and the above income-surplus linkages (2.19–2.23), we get Table 2.3 which shows the descriptively consistent stock-flow social accounting model of the monetary structure of the social provisioning process that produces social activities.

The model clearly distinguishes between stocks and flows and accounts for the social destinations of the various flows. For example, the model shows the flows of intermediate inputs into the surplus goods sector, and the flows of the various surplus goods and services into their social accounts of households, enterprises, and the state. At the same time, it mirrors these flows of goods and services with the flows of wage, profit, and state incomes required by households, enterprises,

Table 2.3 SFSA model of the monetary structure of the social provisioning process

Basic goods sector	K_{S1}, RR_{S1}, FA_{S1}, LB_{S1}: $G_{11}p_1 + L_{11}w + \Pi_1 = Q_{d1}p_1$
Surplus goods sector	K_{S2}, RR_{S2}, FA_{S2}, LB_{S2}: $G_{21}p_1 + L_{21}w + \Pi_2 = Q_{d2}p_2 \rightarrow Q_2p_2 = Q_{2G}^T p_2 + Q_2^T p_2 + Q_{2c}^T p_2 + Q_{21}^T p_2$
Banking sector	K_{S3}, RR_{S3}, FA_{S3}, LB_{S3}: $G_{31}p_1 + L_{31}w + \Pi_3 = TR_3 \rightarrow Q_{3L}(1+i_B) \rightarrow FA_{S3} \rightarrow LB_{S1-3,5}$
State	K_{S4}, LB_{S4}: $Q_{2G}p_2 + L_{41}w + GP_d + GP_{ih} + GP_E \rightarrow GS$, $K_{F4} \rightarrow K_{S4}$, $RR_{F4} \rightarrow RR_{S4}$
Household	FA_{S5}, LB_{S5}: $(L^*w)(1-\tau_i) + GP_d(1-\tau_p) + i_DFA_{SDD5}(1-\tau_i) + GP_{ih}(1-\tau_i) + \Pi_D(1-\tau_p)(1-\tau_i)$ $= Q_{2c}^T p_2 + FA_{5RC} + LB_5 \rightarrow HSA, FA_{S5}, LB_{S5}$
Enterprise	$\Pi(1-\tau_p) = Q_{21}^T p_2 + FA_{BE} + LB_{BE} \rightarrow K_{S1-3} \rightarrow RR_{1-3}, FA_{S1-3}, LB_{S1-3}$
Financial structural balances	National debt $\quad LB_{S4} = FA_{SGB1-3,5}$ Bank loans $\quad FA_{SBL3} = LB_{S1,2,5}$ Bank demand deposit $\quad LB_{S3} = FA_{SDD1,2,5}$
Current financial balances	Government deficit $\quad GOV_E - Taxes = FA_{BE} + FA_{5RC}$ Total profits after taxes $\Pi^* = Q_{21}^T p_2 + LB_{BE} + FA_{BE} + FA_{5RC}$

Notes: Π_1 is a $n \times 1$ column vector of profits for each intermediate input; Π_2 is a $(m-n) \times 1$ column vector of profits for each surplus product; Π_3 is the total gross profits of the banking sector; and i_B is the rate of interest on current bank loans.

and the state to purchase them. In this manner, the monetized social provisioning process is stock-flow social accounting consistent and hence acquires the structure of a going concern. With the provisioning process as a going plant, the flow of state money ties together market transactions and non-market activities that ensure the continuation of household social activities and government services through time. The model further identifies the core decisions that drive the provisioning process: the decisions that determine the social surplus, prices, profits, employment, wages, and interest rates. Because the ruling class (as opposed to the capitalist class by itself) through its acting persons has the productive and administrative capabilities and the legal rights to these decisions, it can direct the provisioning process in their own current and changing future interests. Therefore, the social provisioning process is a socially sustainable process in which each state money transaction is a manifestation and reproduction of the capitalist relationships and hence both sustains and promises a future for the ruling elite and their dependents – in short, the social provisioning process is a going concern. Given the going plant with ruling class agency, such a going concern economy is qualitatively different from Schumpeter's well-known circular flow of economic life and a commodity-based money, self-replacing, viable economy in that the latter two exist only as conceptual qua imaginary models of the economy whereas the former is grounded in the real world. The differences are found in the origins of profits, in the properties of prices, profit mark-ups, and wage rates, and in the causal direction of economic activity (Kregel 1975; Levine 1978; Bortis 1997; 2003; Lee 1998).

Agency, acting persons, organizations, and institutions

As it stands, the model of the monetary structure of the social provisioning process lacks both agency in terms of acting persons, and organizations and institutions through which they act. Acting persons do not act as isolated individuals outside or independent of social organizations and institutions. Rather, they are emergently embedded with them – that is, as the acting person makes decisions and acts, so do their organizations and institutions. Hence, without agency, organizations, and institutions, the core decision variables, such as the social surplus, bank loans, employment, interest rates, and prices, which drive economic activity and underpin the provisioning process lack determinacy. Moreover, acting persons and their organizations are enmeshed in social relationships with others, resulting in decisions that embody and hence reflect them. In short, acting persons are located in social organizations and institutions that make them emergent entities. This, in turn, means that acting enterprises, households, market governance organizations, and trade unions are not uniform but different, and the state is the site of different acting sub-organizations; and that all 'market' outcomes are causally determined – that is, they are the result of decisions made by acting persons and, hence, they can be ethically and socially judged. Markets do not 'do' things; rather, acting persons do things. Consequently, acting organizations and institutions are irreducible to any of their constituent parts and so constitute causal mechanisms that drive the provisioning process; they are irrevocably situated in an emergent web of social relationships that affect the decisions they make. These points about acting persons qua acting organizations and institutions mean that the (socially isolated) individual is not the primary unit of theoretical analysis, and, hence, is not the center of economic analysis. Instead, the emphasis will be placed on collective forms of decision-making in which individual acting persons have to engage and accommodate. After a discussion of the acting person, the rest of the section briefly describes the five acting organizations and institutions – the business enterprise, state, market governance organizations, trade unions, and households – that make the core decisions which affect and shape the social provisioning process.[36]

The acting person

It is a truism that economic agents are endowed with agency. However, often the nature of the economic agent is left unarticulated, a void that is often implicitly filled with a socially isolated individual making socially isolated, self-centered decisions. In contrast, heterodox economics endows the acting person with flesh and blood and social agency. Social agency is

> a temporally embedded process of social engagement informed by the past (in its habitual aspect), but also oriented toward future (as a capacity to imagine alternative possibilities) and toward the present (as a capacity to contextualized past habits and future projects within the contingencies of the moment).
> (Emirbayer and Mische 1998, 963)

Consequently, the acting person is situated within the flow of time and hence has an ongoing, repeated pattern of culturally particular, ethically informed differentiated set of social relationships that temporally overlap. Moreover, in a transmutable world where certain ends are not known, trust, fairness, and interpersonal comparisons along with social relationships affect every decision made by the acting person. Finally, in a world in which certainty or its opposite complete ignorance about the future does not exist, the acting person can act through creating purposes that lead to definable goals and make decisions and take actions to achieve those goals (all of which are constructed out of social meanings and values). Under these circumstances, the decisions and actions taken are not rational or irrational; nor are they compulsive, caprice, or random. Rather, acting persons set goals, make decisions, and take actions because they believe that they can, to a reasonable degree, influence if not make their future. Taken together, all decisions regarding the core variables that affect the social provisioning process are taken in the flow of time, are social, and are non-optimal acts taken to achieve particular goals qua provisioning outcomes that in turn have an impact on government services and household social activities. Thus, the acting person is not a neutered individual, undifferentiated, isolated agent, or a representative agent for any of the five acting organizations and institutions discussed below; neither is the acting person passive, simply reactive, and unwilling to make decisions and intentionally act to change the structures of the provisioning process and the acting person itself or herself. Rather, the acting person is the opposite of this and hence has the remarkable property of linking past actions and outcomes to various possible future outcomes (that is, the acting person constructs a narrative of its/her own activities and possible future outcomes) so as to take actions to affect current events and thereby making the social provisioning process non-self-regulating (Emirbayer and Mische 1998; Levine 1998; O'Boyle 2010; 2011; Davis 2011).

The business enterprise

As a going concern, the business enterprise consists of a going plant (productive capabilities), a going business (managerial capabilities), working rules, and routines. Its going plant includes technology, represented by fixed investment goods, intermediate inputs, labor skills, and the organization of the production and laboring processes, while the going business includes the legal and managerial organization of the business enterprise and its decision-making capabilities. What connects the going plant to the going business and molds them into a going concern are working rules, routines, and institutions, such as accounting rules, data collection procedures, occupational schedules and wage structures, and procedures for pricing, investment (including research and innovation), production-employment, wage-salary, and dividend decisions.

The theoretical significance of the business enterprise as a going concern is threefold. Firstly, it is the organizational means through which the capitalist economy is a going concern. Secondly, it is the organizational mechanism by which the capitalist class and their private sector employees gain ongoing access to the state-monetized social provisioning process, the former through a continuous flow of dividends and salary income and the latter by a continuous flow of wage and salary income. Thirdly, the going concern becomes a 'commodity' whose value is greater than its tangible assets to be bought and sold. How the acting business enterprise fulfills these theoretical roles depends upon its structures and causal mechanisms. The enterprise comprises of five structures: legal structure, organizational structure, decision-making structure, production-cost structure, and production-employment structure. The first will be briefly dealt with here, while the latter four will be dealt with in the following chapter.[37]

The legal structure of the business enterprise comprises of its legal organization that defines who owns it and who controls it. The enterprise is legally organized on a non-corporate or corporate basis. The former consists of sole proprietorships and partnerships. In either case, the acting enterprise is co-existent with the individual proprietor and the partners, and continues as long as they remain active in the enterprise. So any decisions and ensuring activities undertaken by the proprietor or partner in the name of the enterprise constitutes an acting enterprise. The non-corporate enterprise has two particular legal properties not found with corporate enterprises: (1) if the proprietor or any of the partners dies or leaves, the enterprise ceases operation and is dissolved, and (2) the proprietor and partners are subject to unlimited personal liability for all the obligations of the business, including liabilities flowing from wrongful acts of another partner. In contrast, the *corporate business enterprise* has a legal identity as an individual that is separate from those who own it; hence, it is, in a legal sense, an acting enterprise with an indefinite lifespan. Thus, it can own property, including the means of production and its output; employ workers, managers, and board of directors; and sue and be sued for breach of contract. However, it is the chief executive officer (CEO), its senior management, and, to a lesser extent, the board of directors of the corporation whose decisions and actions transform a legal acting enterprise into a truly acting enterprise. Finally, a corporate enterprise may have limited or unlimited status – the former means that the shareholders have limited liability whereas for the latter this protection is not available. Limited corporate enterprises are the most numerous and they can be divided into private and public enterprises.[38]

An acting enterprise means it has the power and capabilities to make core decisions – decisions that generally include aspects of justice, trust, and fairness. Core decisions include determining wage rates, salaries, profit mark-ups, and the division of profits between dividends and retained earnings; setting prices and private sector interest rates and demanding investment goods and bank loans; deciding on the production of output, the employment of personnel, and the choices of products to produce and where to market them; and deciding on which competitive and political strategies to pursue (for example, whether or not to cooperate with competitors over setting prices or influencing the political debate on minimum wage rates or tax rates on profits). Because such powers and capabilities are vested in the acting enterprise as an acting person, its legal ownership structure has no real impact on how it makes its core decisions. Rather, such power and capabilities stem, in large part, from the authority and dominance over day-to-day operations, the disposition of enterprise's resources, and (with the contributions and support of the board of directors) the planning and long-term decisions of the enterprise. That is, the CEO, senior management, and their employed subordinates devote their full time to doing the business of the enterprise, assessing its problems and prospects, and making and implementing plans for its improvement. By virtue of this concentrated effort and presence, they have special command over the technical details essential to an intelligent consideration of the problems the enterprise faces. They also make many immediate decisions that require experience, knowledge, and on-the-spot presence. While most of the specific decisions involved in day-to-day operations are made by middle managers, those at the top call the tune, set the parameters within which choices are made, and make the important decisions. These are built-in structures of activities that enable the CEO, senior management, and the board of directors to act collectively as an acting person, which generates the acting enterprise[39] (Berle and Means 1933; Eichner 1976; Herman 1981).

The size of the enterprise does make a difference. In small business enterprises that produce a single or a few closely related product lines and sell them at a few well-established locations, the owners generally work alongside their relatively few employees and personally make all the decisions. However, in large business enterprises, a bureaucratic structure is necessary for the management to manage and direct its different activities. While the particular bureaucratic structure in place in a business enterprise varies, it can generally be classified as a functional managerial structure with a centralized administrative structure and a divisional managerial structure with a decentralized administrative structure. In the former, the enterprise has few but closely related product lines in which their scale of production is quite large, so its activities are grouped and managed according to function, and all the decisions by the management are made in the central office. For the latter case, the enterprise has a quite diverse array of product lines that are in different markets and industries and geographically spread out; hence, the activities for each product line is categorized as a division, which is headed by a member of senior management who deals with the day-to-day activities. This enables the central office to concentrate on the enterprise overall and its long-term growth and development. The importance of the bureaucratic structure is that it enables the CEO, senior management, and the board of directors of large, diverse business enterprises to work effectively together so as to generate an acting enterprise.

The state

As implied above, the state is an organization that consists of fixed investment goods and resource reserves which it owns, has administrative and production capabilities, and has a workforce of both workers and the political elite who all together generate a wide range of government services. In addition, this is made possible by the state's unique capabilities of directly commanding the materials and labor to produce the services it desires and to issue state money to do the same. The entity within the state that makes the creation of government services happen is the political elite – that is, through the political elite there is an acting state. Since the political elite and the capitalist class constitute the ruling class, they are equals. The acting state is thus not subordinate to the capitalist class; nor does it stand apart from it. The role of the acting state is to ensure that the provisioning process is not disrupted and that it remains under the control of the ruling class. To deal with the former, the state makes decisions regarding the interest rates on government bonds and tax rates on incomes and profits, the purchases of goods and services from the private sector, the payments to the dependent class, and the employment of workers and the political elite and pays them wages and salaries. The aim of each of the decisions is to manage and direct the social provisioning process. To ensure the latter, the acting state mediates conflicts (such as market competition) within the ruling class, contains the demands of the working and dependent classes and their respective households for better working and living conditions, and protect business enterprises and their property from workplace demands. In short, the decisions of the acting state are all about ensuring that the economy remains a going concern under the control of the ruling class.

The household

The going household is conceived as a group of people located in a common residence who share market provisioning resources (such as wages, salaries, dividends, government payments, and interest income) and responsibilities to bring forth an array of social activities that maintains their existence into an indefinite, uncertain future (Todorova 2009, 8). The social activities include food provisioning, sheltering, caring, child-rearing, bonding with household members, and entertaining people outside the household, all of which occur outside the market and utilize time not spent on working.[40] And the social relations arising from social activity involve the active pursuit and maintenance of cooperative non-monetary, non-market relations with other identifiable persons in the household, and that, in such relations, the joint activity of mutual word-of-mouth interpersonal communication and mutual transfer of certain types of non-market services occurs. The aims of the household social activities are threefold: the first is to maintain the social relationships within the household so as to keep it a cohesive whole. The second is to reproduce and develop the capabilities of the members of the household so that they can continue to provide it with the necessary resources. And the third is to maintain harmonious relationships with various other households. Together, the three aims endow the going household with agency and, hence, transform it into an acting household. Therefore, the acting household is the basis of the spending decisions and hence makes various decisions about purchasing consumption goods and services produced by enterprises and utilizing government services for means of developing and sustaining social relationships; these decisions are related to its decisions regarding bank loans and their repayment, wages and salaries, and the providing of labor for employment by enterprises and the state. It is through these decisions that the acting going household engages with and penetrates into the social provisioning process; this has the result of linking together the reproduction of capitalist social relationships with the reproduction of the household.

The choice of goods and services purchased by the acting household is, as noted above, conditioned by the society in which it is located, by the social upbringing of the heads of the household, and by the current social demands made upon the household. Therefore, the actual choices of a single household are both socially conditioned and limited, but across households the choices are quite different. For example, because the goods and services have both an instrumental (use-value) dimension and a social dimension (which includes both ceremonial and routine conspicuous consumption), their demand can be stratified by income (as well as by class, culture, and other variables). In addition, the manner in which acting households are arranged and organized, the relationship among its members, and its demographics qua 'life cycle,' all have an impact on the kind of social activities it pursues and hence on its demand for goods and services. Thus over the life cycle of a particular household, its demand for goods and services will change significantly so that accumulated knowledge about past purchasing and consumption patterns are insufficient with regard to the future – hence, the structure of consumption for an individual household changes slowly; but, moreover, the lifestyle also changes. In short, because households are different via their social activities and the activities themselves are stratified by income and class, there exist differentiated goods and services to match the different classes that demand them. It is the purchase of these market goods and services with wages and salaries, interest incomes on demand deposits and government bonds, social welfare payments, and/or bank loans which links acting households to the market (Yanagisako 1979; Charusheela and Danby 2006; Todorova 2009).[41]

Market governance organizations

Market governance refers to the social, economic, and political processes that regulate horizontal market transactions and employment relationships among business enterprises in specific markets and industries, and with respect to organized workers, such as trade unions. The processes take on a variety of forms, denoted as market governance organizations and institutions, each involving the acting enterprises and some involving the acting state as well as acting trade unions. Concentrating first on the competitive relationship between enterprises in output markets, the purpose of the organization is to regulate market transactions through regulating the competitive relationships between enterprises. Its organizational structure and the 'collective' actions taken to regulate market transactions have a variety of forms, depending on the competition laws and the social network underpinning the relationships among the competing enterprises, such as informal or formal bilateral and multilateral cooperative relationships concerning technology or opening new markets. The most common organizational forms are associational such as a trade association, price leadership, and government regulation. In all cases, acting enterprises make decisions about prices (or interest rates), profit mark-ups, production and sales, and a host of ancillary decisions designed to reinforce those decisions. Trade associations are, for the most part, voluntary informal or formal organizations formed by acting enterprises to protect and advance interests common to all member enterprises. They are organized to carry out a range of beneficial activities for its members, such as representing them before governmental bodies, providing trading and commercial services, providing a common front for wage bargaining with trade unions (to be discussed below), and, most importantly, regulating market activities – for example, fixing market prices, determining output quotas or market shares, establishing and maintaining resale prices, and other forms of restrictive trade practices. Because the acting enterprises engage collectively through the trade association, this converts the latter into an acting trade association that is distinct from the acting enterprise.

Price leadership is a different market governance institution, which is only concerned with establishing and changing market prices. In particular, under price leadership a single enterprise regularly initiates price changes by changing its own price because all the other enterprises in the market follow and adopt those price changes. While it is possible for an acting enterprise to unilaterally determine the market price, in many cases this is made possible through associational activities in other areas that make the competing enterprises more 'cooperative' when dealing with market prices. Government regulation is also a market governance organization that combines the acting enterprise and/or the acting trade association with the acting state to regulate market prices and other competitive activities. This could take the form of regulatory agencies such as the Interstate Commerce Commission, the Federal Reserve Board, or a national marketing board for a particular product, where the agency, representing the acting state in a working relationship with acting enterprises and/or associations, is the acting market governance organization. Or it could be a combination of the acting state establishing a legal framework that enables the acting trade association, price leader, and/or business enterprises to control market competition and set 'acceptable' prices, such as enacting legislation to protect resale price maintenance or eliminating competing products. In all three general types of acting market governance organizations and institutions, it is the acting enterprise, the acting trade association, and the acting state that make the decisions affecting market prices, market interest rates, and profit mark-ups. In other words, none of these variables are determined independently of an acting market governance organization (Chapter 6 deals with trade associations and price leadership in detail with particular regard to 'regulated competition' and the market price).

When confronted by an organized workforce regarding workplace demands across many enterprises – either at the local, regional, or national level – and producing goods and services in the same set of markets, enterprises often establish an employers' association, either as an independent organization or as a component of an existing trade association. Like a trade association, an employers' association is a collective of acting enterprises with an internal organization that enables it to act as an acting association. This capability means that it can provide various services to its members, such as statistical data on the state of the 'labor market,' workplace conditions, and recent wage settlements; information on personnel practices; and administered insurance and other employee benefit plans. The primary concern of employers' associations is, however, to oppose organized labor in any form so as to retain the dominance of the business enterprise over the individual worker.[42] This takes the form of various collective activities, such as promoting open shops, blacklisting union workers, issuing 'yellow-dog' contracts, importing workers to break strikes, approaching the acting state to suppress unions and/or strike activities, opposing child-labor laws and workplace safety regulations, engaging in lockouts, and appealing to merchants not to support strikers. In addition, when forced to, the acting employers' association negotiates with trade unions over wages, salaries, working conditions, and the length of the working day and/or week. What is important is that the determination of wage rates and salaries or the length of the working day is determined between two acting 'collective' organizations, one representing acting business enterprises and the second representing workers; between them they regulate the 'labor market' (Bonnett 1956; Armstrong 1984; Derber 1984; Gladstone 1984; Windmuller 1984).

Trade unions

While individual workers are acting persons, an individual acting worker does not exist. An individual worker or employee does not have the capability to alter the actions of an acting enterprise. This can only be achieved through workers organizing as a collective – that is, as a union of workers. Such a union – that is, a trade (or industrial) union – has an informal or formal administrative structure through which acting individuals can direct to achieve collective outcomes. In particular, the acting trade union makes decisions to confront the individual acting enterprise or acting employers' associations over issues such as wage rates, salaries, length of the working day, retirement and health benefits, working conditions on the job, and closed shops. In doing so, the acting trade union is asserting that its individual acting members should have some degree of control over their working lives that are beyond the control and manipulation of the acting enterprise and the business class.[43]

Agency, acting persons, and core decisions

To summarize, the core decisions that affect and shape the social provisioning process are made by five acting organizations and institutions. The core decisions emanating from acting business enterprises set prices and private sector interest rates; demand investment goods and bank loans; determine the production of consumption goods, employment, profit mark-ups, dividends, and retained earnings; affect if not determine wage rates and salaries; and influence taxes on profits. Decisions emanating from the state set state interest rates on government bonds and tax rates on incomes and profits, demand government goods and services, determine government payments, employment, and wages and salaries, and influence private sector interest rates, while decisions emanating from acting households allocate their income to purchase the various consumption goods and services produced by enterprises, demand bank loans, and influence wages and salaries. Finally, the core decisions emanating from acting market governance organizations affect, if not determine, market prices, private sector market interest rates, wages and salaries, and profit mark-ups; the core decisions emanating from acting trade unions influence if not determine working conditions, and hence employment, wages, and salaries. These core decisions made by the five forms of acting agency are delineated in Table 2.4.

Modeling the economy as a whole

Combining the model of the monetary structure of the social provisioning process (Table 2.3) with acting organizations and institutions (Table 2.4) creates the economic model of the social provisioning process that produces social activities (see Table 2.5). This model analytically links agency qua acting organizations with core decisions qua economic variables embedded in the economic structures, thus linking agency with structures. Decisions about any economic variable, given

Table 2.4 Agency and core decisions

Core decision variables	Acting organizations and institutions				
	Business enterprise	*State*	*Household*	*Market governance organization*	*Class-based organization: Trade union*
Social surplus	Demand: Q_{2I} Determine: Q_{2C}	Demand: Q_{2G}	Choose among: Q_{2C}		
Bank loans	Demand: $LB_{1,2}$ Determine: Q_{3L}		Demand: LB_5		
Employment	Determine: L_{11}, L_{21}, L_{31}	Determine: L_{41}	Influence: $L_{11}, L_{21}, L_{31}, L_{41}$		Determine/Influence: $L_{11}, L_{21}, L_{31}, L_{41}$
Prices	Set: p			Set/Affect: p	
Wages/Salaries	Determine/ Affect: w	Determine: w	Influence: w	Determine/ Influence: w	Determine/ Influence: w
Profit mark-ups (r)	Determine: r			Determine/ Affect: r	
Dividends/ Retained earnings	Determine: Π_R, Π_D				
Interest rates	Set: i_B, i_D	Set: i_G Influence: i_B		Set/Influence: i_B, i_D	
Government payments		Determine: GP_4			Influence: GP_d
Taxes	Influence: τ_p	Determine: τ_r, τ_p			

Table 2.5 Economic model of the social provisioning process

		Structures
Basic goods sector	K_{S1}, RR_{S1}, FA_{S1}, LB_{S1}:	$G_{11}p_1 + L_{11}w + \Pi_1 = Q_{d1}p_1$
Surplus goods sector	K_{S2}, RR_{S2}, FA_{S2}, LB_{S2}:	$G_{21}p_1 + L_{21}w + \Pi_2 = Q_{d2}p_2 \to Q_2^T p_2 = Q_{2G}^T p_2 + Q_{21}^T p_2 + Q_{21}^T p_2$
Banking sector	K_{S3}, RR_{S3}, FA_{S3}, LB_{S3}:	$G_{31}p_1 + L_{31}w + \Pi_3 = TR_3 \to Q_{3L}(1+i_B) \to FA_{S3} \to LB_{S1-3,5}$
State	K_{S4}, RR_{S4}, $\qquad LB_{S4}$:	$Q_{2G}^T p_2 + L_{41}w + GP + GP_d + GP_{ih} \to GS$, $K_{F4} \to K_{S4}$, $RR_{F4} \to RR_{S4}$
Household	FA_{S5}, LB_{S5}:	$(L^*w)(1-\tau_i) + GP_d(1-\tau_i) + \tau_D FA_{SDD5}(1-\tau_i) + GP_{ih}(1-\tau_i) + \Pi_D(1-\tau_p)(1-\tau_i)$
		$= Q_{2c}^T p_2 + FA_{5RC} + LB_5 \to HSA, FA_{S5}, LB_{S5}$
Enterprise		$\Pi(1-\tau_p) = Q_{21}^T p_2 + FA_{BE} + LB_{BE} \to K_{S1-3} \to RR_{1-3}, FA_{S1-3}, LB_{S1-3}$
Financial structural balances	National debt	$LB_{S4} = FA_{SGB1-3,5}$
	Bank loans	$FA_{SBL3} = LB_{S1,2,5}$
	Bank demand deposit	$LB_{S3} = FA_{SDD1,2,5}$
Current financial balances	Government deficit	$GOV_E - Taxes = FA_{BE} + FA_{5RC}$
	Total profits after taxes	$\Pi^* = Q_{21}^T p_2 + LB_{BE} + FA_{BE} + FA_{5RC}$

	Agency
Acting organizations	*Core decision variables*
Business enterprise	Q_{21}, Q_{2C}, Q_{3L}, $LB_{1,2}$, L_{11}, L_{21}, L_{31}, p, w, r, Π_R, Π_D, i_B, i_D, τ_p
State	Q_{2G}, L_{41}, w, i_G, i_B, GP_4, T_i, T_p
Household	Q_{2C}, LB_5, w, L_{11}, L_{21}, L_{31}, L_{41}
Market governance organization	p, w, r, i_B, i_D
Trade union	L_{11}, L_{21}, L_{31}, L_{41}, w, GP_d

structures, push the provisioning process in a particular direction and doing so generates transfactual outcomes. But those same decisions may also transform the structures (and the economic variables and acting organizations as well) slowly most of the time but rather quickly at other times. This suggests that both structures and acting organizations are historically contingent – that is, they vary as capitalism changes. Moreover, given the social nature of the acting person, the acting organization is not separable from society. As social activities, economic activities are interlinked with various societal institutions (such as the legal system, the household, and the state); with cultural values (such as individualism and egalitarianism) that are evaluative criteria for establishing which social activities are worthwhile and desirable; with norms and beliefs (such as attitudes regarding the ownership of the means of production and the work ethic) that explain or justify particular social activities; with technology; and with the ecological system (such as land and law materials) that provide the material basis for conducting social and economic activities (Polanyi 1968; Hayden 1982; 1986; 2006; 2011; Stanfield 1995, Ch. 5; Natarajan, Elsner, and Fullwiler 2009).

The penultimate step to descriptively model the economy as a whole is to connect the social fabric to acting organizations. The social fabric, as noted above, consists of cultural values, norms and beliefs, societal institutions, the social joint-stock of knowledge, and the ecological system. These components of the social fabric influence the actions of the acting organizations and institutions. In turn, the acting organizations and institutions act on the social provisioning process and social activities, and the latter have an impact on the provisioning process. Thus, in Table 2.6 the model of the economy as a whole consists of the economic model of the social provisioning process (acting organizations and the provisioning mechanism) being bracketed at one end by the social fabric and at the other end by government services and household social activities. Hence, not only is the model of the economy socially encased, so is, quite clearly, the economic model of the social provisioning process. Therefore, all social provisioning qua economic activities and decisions are socially embedded, socially impregnated. Consequently, it is not possible to conceive of the economy as separate from society and operating under its own coordination mechanism, to conceive of the state (or the household) as external to the economy, and to assert that the state intervenes as an external force in the economy.

Since agency and structures change, capitalism and its social provisioning process change as well. In particular, the structures and agency that constitute capitalism can be relatively stable for a period of time, followed by a much shorter period of time in which they change more quickly, therefore giving rise to an ongoing stage-crisis-stage-crisis conceptual history of capitalism. Hence, the last step to descriptively model the economy as a whole is to historically contextualize it (McDonough 2010; 2011). Each historical stage of capitalism is distinguished by its ideology, by capital-capital harmony or competitive relationships between business enterprises, by its class-based capital-labor differences or nature of workplace control, and by the state's role in the economy. These features establish the concrete historical form of the model of the economy as a whole and, hence, of the

Table 2.6 Historically grounded model of the economy as a whole

Economy as a whole	Ideology → Social fabric	Acting organizations and institutions					Provisioning mechanism	Ideology → Social activities	
Delivering / **Receiving**	Cultural Values, Norms, Institutions, Social Joint-Stock of Knowledge, Ecological System	Business Enterprise	State	Household	Market Governance Organization	Trade Union	Social Provisioning Process	Government Services	Household Social Activities
Cultural Values, Norms, Institutions, Social Joint-Stock of Knowledge, Ecological System									
Business Enterprise	Influence								
State	Influence								
Household	Influence								
Market Governance Organization	Influence								
Trade Union	Influence								
Social Provisioning Process		Agency	Agency	Agency	Agency	Agency		Structural Impact	
Government Services		Demand/ Influence	Demand/ Influence	Demand/ Influence	Demand/ Influence	Demand/ Influence	Influence/ Impact		Structural Impact
Household Social Activities		Influence	Influence	Demand/ Influence			Influence/ Impact		

Historical stage of capitalist development — Capital-capital harmony, capital-labor differences, state's role

social provisioning process. In particular, for a given stage of capitalism, ideology informs both the social fabric and social activities; while the capital-capital harmony specifically informs market governance, the capital-labor differences specifically inform trade unions, the state's role specifically informs the state, and all three generally inform all acting organizations and institutions and the provisioning mechanism as well. With this last step, the historically grounded, descriptively consistent model of the economy as a whole can be represented (see Table 2.6) as a series of linked components: history linked to the model of the economy, social fabric linked to the economic model of the social provisioning process, agency linked to structures, and social provisioning linked to social activities.

While the historically grounded model of the economy as a whole provides the overarching framework in which heterodox microeconomic theory is situated, the remainder of the book is devoted to explicitly linking together the structures, acting organizations and institutions, and core decision variables. It starts first with, in Chapter 3, the business enterprise and its structures of organization, decision-making, and production and costs. In Chapter 4, core decisions concerning pricing and investment cumulating in a theory of the business enterprise are explained. The next step is to introduce the concepts of industry and markets and then develop a theory of demand for the social product (Chapter 5). This is followed by an examination of market competition and the theory of market governance (Chapter 6). The final step in this process is the development of the model of the going economy through the integration of an agency-based price and output-employment models with the economic model of the provisioning process (Chapter 7).

Notes

1 From this perspective, the notion of an isolated, asocial individual with asocial or arbitrarily given preferences (or natural needs) has no sense, no meaning. Hence, it is a fruitless, meaningless exercise to speculate about the choices an isolated individual would make in the context of the social provisioning process.

2 This 'paradigm' is distinct from the exchange paradigm that lies at the foundation of mainstream economics (Pasinetti 1986a; 2007, 18–20; Bortis 1997; 2003; Chiodi and Ditta 2008).

3 The economy 'embeddedness' controversy that has gone on for over sixty years essentially misses the point, starting with Polanyi (1944). That is, the economy is always socially embedded. On the other hand, there is a sustained ideological argument associated with both classical political economy and mainstream theory that place the economy outside of the 'social' so as to support the emergence of capitalism and/or maintain its continual existence. It is this fictitious, incoherent argument that has generated the controversy. In particular, if the argument delineating self-adjusting markets is incoherent and self-adjusting markets are in themselves fictions, then the notion of 'interference with the market mechanism' has no meaning, no sense. Therefore, Polanyi's double movement is without foundation (Dale 2010, Chs. 2, 5).

4 Produced means of production is often equated to capital goods. However, the term 'capital' in this book will only be used to refer to a specific social relationship between capitalists and workers. Therefore, the terms human capital, social capital, cultural capital, and capital as resources, goods, services, financial assets, and produced means of production will not be used in the book.

5 This implies that heterodox models that have heterogeneous outputs (and inputs) but homogeneous labor lacks a degree of meaning. This is especially the case when it is assumed that the model rests on the division of labor.

6 This point implies that both the usefulness of goods, services, and resources and the language used to identify and describe them are determined independently of the acting person.

7 The going concern conception of the business enterprise originated with Veblen and Commons is virtually identical to the conception of the business enterprise used by Post Keynesian and Marxist economists – see Dean (2013) for further discussion.

8 The significance of agency of the acting person is that the capitalist economy cannot be theoretically depicted, as for example Levine (1978) does, as a holistic, organic organism that is 'genetically' or 'logically' programmed, without the aid of conscious agency, to self-reproduce, self-expand, or self-organize. Sraffians also reject the role of agency and depict the economy solely in terms of structures, organizations, and institutions (Bortis 1997; 2003).

9 The issue of joint production of two goods or services emerging from the same production schema or process is not dealt with in this book.

10 The modern form of input-output tables was developed by Wassily Leontief in the 1930s. After 1945, governments around the world undertook the empirical construction of such tables. Hence after seventy years of work, there are hundreds of such tables in existence, depicting the world, national, and regional economies. In the United States, the Bureau of Economic Analysis produces input-output tables (see www.bea.gov). For further discussion of the history and methodology of Leontief, Sraffa, and input-output tables, see Clark (1984), Carter and Petri (1989), Kurz and Salvadori (1995; 2000; 2006), Foley (1998), Kohli (2001), and Miller and Blair (2009).

11 This implies that the removal of any one elementary production schema from G_{11} means that no production can occur, while an *ad hoc* introduction of a production schema is not possible.

12 As a result, it is not possible to reduce, through a series of $n - 1$ integrative steps, the intermediate inputs entirely to non-g_j inputs, such as a vector of labor skills and/or quality of resources. This point can be stated as follows: $Q_1^{-1}G_{11} = A_{11}$ where A_{11} is a non-negative, indecomposable matrix of production coefficients, where its element $a_{ij} = g_{ij}/Q_i$. Thus, $A_{11}^{n-1} > 0$, where n is the number of intermediate inputs and $A_{11}^m > 0$ as long as m is finite – that is, Sraffa's commodity residual exists. And, conversely, it is not possible to start with non-g_j inputs and to proceed in a 'forward' direct or in a 'roundabout' way to Q_i. Thus, the linear circuit of production and its linear structure of production with its one-way street to consumption goods are not compatible with the circular circuit of production in heterodox microeconomics. Moreover, it is not possible (or desirable) to abstract from intermediate inputs and circular production in favor of labor and some form of a labor value principle when explaining or theorizing about the social provisioning process (Pasinetti 1986b; 2007; Bortis 1997; 2003; Lee 2014).

13 Another way of stating this is that the quantity and/or reproduction of an original factor input are not dependent on any direct or indirect economic decisions (Lee 2014).

14 While scarcity is an organizing principle in mainstream economics, it is also a theoretically incoherent concept (see, Levine 1977, 180–186). The problem with scarcity is that it is an asocial or pre-social concept being used to organize explanations of what are inescapably social activities.

15 The issue of the physical and value depreciation of fixed investment goods and their relationship to production and costs will be dealt with in the following chapter. For the present chapter, it will be assumed that G_i and L_i include the intermediate goods, services and labor required to ensure that each element of K_{Si} maintains at constant efficiency. This, however, does not exclude the introduction of depreciation in value terms, as is done in Equation 2.19.

16 This means that none of the components of the production schema have intrinsic productive potency, which means that no single 'input' is in itself productive in the mainstream sense of having a marginal product.

17 Evidence can be found in the input-output accounts for the United States and United Kingdom (see, for example, Millard 1995; Kuhbach and Planting 2001; Stewart, Stone, and Streitwieser 2007).

18 This basic-non-basic model of the economy has a long history (see Chenery and Clark 1959, Ch. 6), which has been widely noted by heterodox economists but not really theoretically explored or used to articulate the surplus approach (see, for example, Pasinetti 1986b; for exceptions, see Robinson and Eatwell 1973; Bortis 2003).

19 Indicative evidence can be found in the input-output accounts for the United States and the United Kingdom (see Lee 1998, 221).

20 Stock-flow consistency in modeling the economy as a whole has a long history and has been extensively used by Post Keynesian economists; but it has been mostly concerned with financial stocks and flows (Godley and Lavoie 2007). However, it can also be applied to tracking via a schema the flows of surplus goods and services whether it is to the stock of fixed investment goods or to household social activities or government services. Social accounting modeling is based on the social accounting matrix (SAM) that is associated with input-output modeling (Miller and Blair 2009). It involves structurally relating the social surplus to various social institutions and organizations that need and purchase them. While it is often stated that SAM emerged in the 1960s, it has been around in an implicit form much longer – at least since the Kaleckian phrase: 'workers spend what they get and capitalists get what they spend.' In fact, it can be found in Marx's simple reproduction circuit of commodity where the value of luxury goods equals surplus value and the value of wage goods equals variable capital. In addition, it can be found in various commodity-based models which assume that each unit of labor has the same real wage (that is, the same bundle of wage goods) whose value equals the worker's wage income. But the most detailed development of this 'social accounting' approach is found in the economic writings of Father Maurice Potron (1872–1942) where he had *m* different categories of workers which include non-working consumers (unemployed workers, capitalists, and rentiers) each with their own bundle of consumption commodities; the value of each bundle is equal to the income of each category. Finally, Potron implicitly had the value of 'excess production' or investment goods and inventory stock equal to profits minus the 'income-dividends' given to the non-working consumers so that the investment goods are distributed among the *n* enterprises in the economy. Thus Potron linked the production of the surplus goods and services to various income categories associated with the *m + n* consumers and enterprises categories (Abraham-Frois and Lendjel 2006; Bidard, Erreygers, and Parys 2009; Bidard and Erreygers 2010). Hence social accounting modeling is an inherent component of modeling the economy as a whole.

21 In the United States, the corporate enterprise is legally considered an individual with constitutional rights: see the Supreme Court cases of Santa Clara County vs. Southern Pacific Railroad (1886) and Citizens United vs. Federal Election Commission (2010).

22 There is a possible additional class that gets income in terms of dividends, private sector interest payments, and government interest payments without engaging in any social activities that affect the provisioning process. Such a class, *rentier class*, is the dependent class of the extremely wealthy. However, the existence of individuals qua households that are not engaged in the social provisioning activities for which they get an income is problematical, and in any case is so small, so either can be ignored or subsumed into the ruling class, which amounts, theoretically, to the same thing.

23 This suggests that *capital accumulation* consists of increasing the number of workers and dependents that depend on the capitalist class for access to the social provisioning process, rather than massing more fixed investment goods and financial assets.

24 In the case of households, this means that their activities involving goods and services cannot be portrayed as production for exchange.

25 This point is further developed in Chapter 3 in the context of the business enterprise as a going concern, with the implication that the Sraffian depiction of fixed investment goods as joint-products is not a fruitful endeavor and should be left to one side (Sraffa 1960; Levrini 1988; Lager 2006).

26 If state money is not required for access to social provisioning, then there would be no prices, and social provisioning would be carried out by means other than exchange. In particular, production would not be separated from the consumer by the market of commodities, but rather they would be directly related – see, for example, Morris (1995, 36–43).

27 While historical accounts and 'logic' have the imposition of taxes being prior to government expenditures, in a going concern economy they are happening at the same time (Wray 1998). Moreover, this process of creating money means that it is not a scarce 'factor,' and hence compliments the non-scarce goods, services, and resources that make up the real monetary transactions of the economy.

28 A second role of taxes is to drain reserves out of the system, thereby affecting the expenditure decisions of enterprises and households.

29 This does not mean that workers' wage-money income is linked to a specific set of goods and services – that is, to a particular real wage.

30 Beginning with Kalecki ([1954] 1990, 242–243), this point is frequently argued in Post Keynesian literature (see, for example, Erdos and Molnar 1980; 1983; 1990 and Molnar 1981).

31 The starting point of the banking sector is the state and state money. Thus it is different from the monetary circuit theory approach. The latter starts with a stateless economy with no state money where the banking sector issues bank money. It then runs, unsurprisingly, into a variety of theoretical problems, such as the origins and existence of profits (see, for example, Graziani 2003; Rochon and Rossi 2003; Ponsot and Rossi 2009). However, these problems do not exist when the banking sector starts with or derived from the state and state money. It is also different from the Sraffian approach that posits a banking sector that is distinct from the sectors of production to account for the existence of the 'money' rate of interest which is also distinct from the rate of profit. In particular, the Sraffians connect a banking sector to a circular production model in order to establish that the 'money' rate of interest rules the rate of profit and ultimately affects prices of production and distribution (Panico 1985; 1988; Ciccarone 1998).

32 In a Chartalist monetary system where the state has a national debt and runs a current account deficit, banking system reserve requirements have no analytical relevance. Hence, they are not included in Schema 2.17.

33 It is assumed that the government backs all demand deposits at par, thus making demand deposits equivalent to state money.

34 It is assumed that the state does not own financial assets emanating from the private sector.

35 Depreciation is considered part of the cost of a product line and will be discussed as such in the following chapter. But for this chapter, it is considered a component of profits. While interest income is considered part of gross profits, interest payments on bank loans can be either included as part of the costs of a product line or charged against profits. The latter position is taken in this chapter.

36 There are also secondary acting organizations whose decisions affect the provisioning process, such as non-profit and foreign organizations. But they will not be dealt with in the book.

37 Editor's note: The production-employment structure has not been written.

38 The shares of private corporate enterprises are held by individuals and are not sold to the general public, whereas the shares of public corporate enterprises are sold to the public.

39 From the acting enterprise perspective, the separation of ownership, control, and management is of little importance for understanding the social provisioning process. That is, since the CEO, senior management, and the board of directors work together, ownership, control, and management are fused together into the acting person.

40 This means that household social activities do not involve the production of commodities or the use of paid labor. This implies that there is no household production function and the household is not a shadow market for unpaid labor, childcare, or sex. So, it is not possible to conceive of its activities as similar to the production of goods and services, or investment in plant, equipment, and human capabilities. However, in the context of proprietorships and partnerships, household activities do get mixed up with business activities; but analytically they are distinct (Charusheela and Danby 2006).

41 This implies that households (or individual workers) cannot be represented by a predetermined array of goods and services, such as a given real wage or subsistence wage. If households are to have at least some say over the purchase of goods and services, then there needs to be the opportunity to at least select among them on offer; this also implies that existence of markets (although not necessarily capitalist markets) (Levine 1998).

42 This attitude is somewhat damped when it is realized that through cooperation with trade unions, it is possible to curb and regulate the destructive price competition occurring in the output markets and control the entry of competitors (especially foreign competitors) into these markets (see Chapter 6 for further discussion).

43 Editor's note: This section is incomplete. Readers may refer to Lee (2009b) for a theoretical discussion of "job control and the key decisions and their variables that workers [through organizing themselves into trade unions] must take control of . . . in order to bring about the demise of capitalism and the flowering of socialism" (73). This discussion is based on the heterodox micro-macro integrated model of capitalism that is derived from the equations and schemas delineated in the present chapter.

3 The business enterprise

Structures

Organizational structure of the business enterprise

The acting business enterprise as a going concern is represented in a very elementary or fundamental schema. In it, the enterprise has a complement of plant and equipment and produces one product at a budgeted flow rate of output for a production period. Prior to production the business enterprise secures working capital to procure the necessary direct and overhead inputs. And then production takes place, the output sold, and the revenue collected. If earned profits are greater than working capital, the business enterprise grows and expands over production periods. What this 'reproduction' implies is that the business enterprise must have an accurate understanding of its costs (including wage costs) so that the prices it sets cover costs and generate a profit or a positive cash flow. A second implication is that the acting enterprise makes decisions about profit mark-ups and prices that are strongly connected to decisions about expenditures on fixed investment goods and on research and development of new products (this will be dealt with in Chapter 4), and somewhat connected to decisions about mergers and acquisitions, financial investments, and dividends policy. The final implication of the schema is that the enterprise makes decisions about output, employment, and wage rates.

The next section deals with decision-making by the acting enterprise, including the issue of motivation, the decision-making structure, and the role of accounting rules and procedures in providing the production, costs, sales, and cash flow (profits) information needed to make the aforementioned decisions. The following section covers the structure of production and costs for the enterprise's product line. That is, the going enterprise produces more than a single product line; however, virtually all heterodox (and mainstream) analyses that deal with prices, investment, production, and employment at the level of the enterprise and the market do so in terms of a single product and its price. Hence, it is necessary to enter the enterprise through the product line (and its structure of production and costs) and its price; in this process, substantive theories of production and costs (equivalent to and a substitute for that found in mainstream microeconomics) are developed.

Decision-making structure and the acting enterprise

Motivation

The theoretical significance of the going enterprise is that it is the organizational mechanism by which the capitalist class gains, with minimal working class interference, ongoing access to the state-monetized social provisioning process through the continuous flow of profit-derived dividends and salary income. Thus the motivation of the business leaders of a going enterprise is to maintain and augment this cash flow, which translates into the basic qualitative goals of survival qua reproduction and continuation of the business enterprise in a trade union-free environment.[1] This requires a positive business income – that is, profits – that is a clear quasi-concrete goal; but seeking profits is not an end in itself. Rather, profits are needed to maintain the going enterprise and for the capitalist class to have access via salaries and dividends to the social provisioning process. Consequently, business leaders are not seeking to maximize profits in the short-term but to generate a long-term flow of business income needed to meet their goals and access to social provisioning – in this sense, profits are not an immediate end goal of business leaders, but rather a long-term intermediate objective.[2] Therefore, the going enterprise adopts a variety of sub-goals that generally fall into categories that coincide with the principal decisions made by the enterprise: in particular, *production* which includes decisions about employment, and wages and salaries; *marketing* the output which includes both pricing and non-pricing decisions; *investment* which includes decisions about investment in plant, equipment, and technology and in research leading to product development; and *financial decisions* which include decisions about dividends, retained earnings, mergers and acquisitions, and financing real and monetary activities. Within each category there are clear sub-goals that concretely specify objectives connected with various business strategies with different temporal dimensions to attain them, such as increasing market share or sales (revenue), increasing the growth of profits or the profit margin through raising the profit mark-up or reducing costs, developing new products, entering new product markets, investing in fixed investment goods, branching out into financial markets, engaging in collective price-determination, and seeking government support or attaining political power.[3] Because of their longevity and importance to the continuation of the acting going enterprise, the basic goals and their associated sub-goals constitute institutional structures in which strategic decisions via the relevant causal mechanism are made. As long as the basic goals and sub-goals are socially legitimate, the decisions to attain them are legitimate as well (unless proscribed by law); for example, whatever the magnitude of prices, profit mark-ups, profits, wages, and salaries are, they are deemed fair and warranted (whether historically or currently) (O'Brien 1972; Eichner 1976; Wale 1989a; 1990; Napier 1990; Boyns and Edwards 1995; Taras 1997; Lee 1998; Downward 1999).

Decision-making structure

A business enterprise's decision-making structure consists of quasi-authoritarian, formalized hierarchical structures that establish the basic line of authority and primary responsibilities, underpinned by organized activities within the structure responsible for supporting and/or making particular decisions, and by working rules and routines or institutional patterns of activity. It can be either a centralized or decentralized structure. Under a *centralized decision-making structure* there is a central office that coordinates the various departments and directs them towards a common goal. It consists of the chief executive officer, his/her assistants, and the heads of departments. In turn, the department heads manage the departments, each of which consists of a single activity. Thus the administration of the enterprise is centered in the central office with control being dispersed along functional lines. The virtue of this structure is that the middle management specialists run the day-to-day activities of the enterprise, thus letting top management coordinate the activities of the various departments and become involved in long-term planning. Yet, it has a basic weakness – that is, very few individuals are entrusted with a great number of complex decisions. Moreover, the heads of the departments are often too busy with the running of their department to devote much time to the affairs of the enterprise as a whole. Their training proves to be a still more serious defect. Because the members of the central office spend most of their business careers within a single functional activity, they have little experience or interest in understanding the needs and problems of other departments or of the enterprise as a whole. As long as the enterprise stays in an industry (or industry group) whose markets, sources of intermediate inputs, and production processes remained relatively unchanged, few entrepreneurial decisions are needed; hence such a weakness is not critical. But when the enterprise's technology, markets, and sources of intermediate inputs become highly diverse as a result of the diversification and growth (especially into different industry groups), the defects of the structure become obvious. In a *decentralized decision-making structure*, the autonomous divisions continue to integrate production and distribution by coordinating flows from suppliers to consumers in different, clearly defined markets. The divisions, headed by middle management, administer their functional activities through departments that, in turn, are concerned with the day-to-day activities of the enterprise. The central office, consisting of top management and assisted by large financial and administrative staffs, supervises the multi-functional divisions. The general office monitors the divisions to make sure that their flows are tuned to fluctuations in demand, and that they have comparable policies in personnel, research, purchasing, and other functional activities. They also evaluate the financial and market performance of the divisions. Most important of all, they concentrate on planning and allocating resources (Channon 1973; Chandler 1977; 1990).

Within the formal structures, there exist organized activities in the form of departments, committees, and working groups whose responsibilities are to assist decision-making with regard to prices, investment, research and product development, production-employment, wage-salary, and dividends. Their membership consists of acting persons qua employees with expertise relevant to the decisions being made. To make reasonable decisions, they are dependent on various working rules and routines to ensure this. That is, the business enterprise consists of a loose coupling of rules (formal ways in which things should be done) and routines (informal practices actually in use) that generate overall institutional patterns of activity that provide both workers and managers ways of coping in a complex and uncertain world, and which enable individual managers to make sense of their own actions and the actions of others. Consequently, rules and routines are structures vis-à-vis the individual; they are relatively stable over time, although they do change. To continue to function on a day-to-day basis, managers need to know what working rules and routines to follow and when. Moreover, rules and routines help manage and contain the degree of intra-enterprise conflict so as not to be excessively disruptive. In this way, rules and routines help give form and social coherence to enterprise activities and provide the mechanism through which new employees learn how the enterprise works. Thus, the loose coupling of rules and routines provide stability to the enterprise while simultaneously enabling it to deal with changing circumstances (Burns and Scapens 2000; Lukka 2007).

Management accounting procedures

Among the plethora of working rules and routines that structure the activities of the enterprise, the one that is most significant with regard to production, pricing, recording business income, and allocating resources and income flows inside the enterprise are the accounting rules and procedures or management accounting procedures. As a relatively enduring structure, they are working rules that are particularly significant to the business enterprise, as they provide an important way of representing economic facts to management, directors, and owners of the enterprise as well as to external bodies.[4] For example, enterprise performance is reported and described, both internally and externally, according to accounting rules, conventions, and language. In addition, they define the rights of individual groups (shareholders, lenders, managers, and workers), provide a basis for prescribing actions such as how to carry out sales and bank reconciliations, carry forward knowledge of the procedures for budgeting and fixed investment goods expenditure, and contribute to the enterprise's decisions regarding research and development. Finally, cost accounting practices are used to construct product costs that are then used for pricing, for cost reductions, for decisions about producing or not producing various products, and for evaluating production processes and investment projects, which include make-or-buy decisions. Consequently, management accounting procedures provide the basis for decision-making and for the formation of expectations and beliefs. The extent to which accounting practices give social coherence and meaning to organizational behavior within the enterprise allows managers and other groups within the enterprise to give meaning to their day-to-day activities (Means 1939; Scapens 1994; Burns and Scapens 2000; Granlund 2001; Brierley, Cowton, and Drury 2006a; Lukka 2007).

The business enterprise adopts and develops cost and financial or, more generally, managerial accounting practices that are necessary for it to be a going concern. So long as the enterprise remains a going concern, its accounting practices remain relatively enduring, although changing in minor ways in light of changes in technology, inputs used in production, and the information needs of management. If an enterprise is not a going concern, it is a terminal venture in that it has a specific starting and ending date. Consequently, accounting for expenditures as deductions or one-time expenses against revenue and business income is straightforward. Moreover, the question of the value of the fixed investment goods and depreciation never arises. That is, the fixed investment goods are valued at the beginning of the venture and then revalued at the terminal date. Their initial value is their historical costs, while their liquidation value at the terminal date is added to the profit account for distribution (Litherland 1951). An enterprise as a strictly terminal venture is largely incommensurate with a going concern economy; rather, it is compatible with an exchange economy where repeatable and ongoing economic activities and provisioning 'processes' are absent.

For the going enterprise, the accounting practices must ensure an accurate delineation of costs that must be recovered if the enterprise is to be a going concern. More specifically, because a going enterprise engages in continuous sequential acts of production, its income (or profits) is calculated periodically, which is denoted as the *accounting period* and is generally taken to be a calendar year, and in a manner that permits distributing part of profits as dividends without impairing the enterprise's productive capabilities. This means that it is necessary to treat all material inputs (which are producible and reproducible) and labor inputs that contribute to the production of the output as reoccurring costs as opposed to one-time expenses against total revenue to arrive at profits.[5] In this manner, the expenses of resources, goods, services, labor skills, and depreciation of fixed investment goods used directly and/or indirectly in production are costs that are recouped so that the enterprise can repeat production. This means that all human performances are conceived as and treated no differently than that of material inputs and fixed investment goods. In addition, fixed investment goods are not viewed as commodities to be sold on the market for revenue purposes; rather, the going enterprise views them as essential non-commodities for maintaining the going plant whose historical value is considered a recoverable cost to be charged against revenue before determining business income.

The accounting practices essential to a going concern deal with (1) the tracing of the direct and overhead material, services, resources, and labor skills inputs relevant to the production of a unit of output, (2) the categorization of costs into direct (variable) and overhead (fixed) costs, (3) the determination of the cost of producing a unit of output which can be used for product costing, (4) depreciation, and (5) the determination of profits associated with a particular product and the business income for the enterprise as a whole. Evidence from archives of business enterprises show that, prior to the eighteenth century, merchants utilized accounting systems to keep records of purchases and sales; after that, industrial enterprises drew on these systems to keep records of purchases and sales, and to document the internal movement of inputs in the production process. In particular, sophisticated cost accounting systems for tracking direct inputs and direct costs in the production of a specific good have been in use since the 1700s. At almost the same time, enterprises developed accounting procedures that differentiated between direct and overhead inputs and costs, began identifying and measuring/quantifying them, and devised procedures to allocate the overhead costs among the various goods produced.[6] Thus, by 1900, comprehensive accounting systems of various degrees of sophistication were in general use and remain so to the present day. With developed cost accounting systems in hand, enterprises are able to engage in the costing of a good – that is, to arrive at its unit (or average) direct or direct plus overhead cost.[7] Costing systems utilized historical-estimated costs (or, sometimes in the twentieth century, predetermined standard costs) and employed various methods (based on, for example, output, direct costs, direct labor costs, labor hours, material costs, machine hours, or activity-based cost drivers) for the allocation of overheads.[8] However, changes in technology, the production of new goods and services, the need for new and better product line cost information, and competitive pressures have pushed enterprises to alter their cost accounting and costing systems, although not significantly, but their function of collecting cost information and use for estimating product line costs remains unchanged – as long as enterprises remain going concerns, cost accounting and costing systems will remain relatively stable and hence relatively enduring structures[9] (Garner 1954; Chatfield 1974; Jones 1985; Drury and Tayles 1994; Boyns and Edwards 1995; Alnestig and Segerstedt 1996; Boyns, Edwards, and Nikitin 1997; Fleischman and Parker 1997; Lee 1998, Appendix A; Lamminmaki and Drury 2001; Al-Omiri and Drury 2007; Fleischman 2009; Fujimura 2012).

Business enterprises have always made financial decisions, such as setting prices, whether to produce a good, close down a product line, or undertake an investment project; tying costing systems to the financial decisions (which occurred as early as the 1700s) helped immensely in making the decisions. This long historical emergence was, in part, due to an interlinked problem qua controversy grounded in the nature of a going concern. In particular, profits are defined as the difference between revenue and costs for a particular period of time, such as the accounting period, but whether that definition is consistent with the nature of the going concern depends on how expenditures on fixed investment goods are accounted for. From the 1700s into the early 1900s, expenditures on fixed investment goods were paid for and expensed out of revenues or profits and not included as a cost component – that is, depreciation – of a product. Being treated as a current expense and hence not added to the capital account, the capitalized value of the enterprise did not change. More significantly, it also meant that the enterprise's cost structure did not include all the costs to be a going concern – that is, it did not include the cost of the fixed investment goods needed for ongoing and future production. So when the fixed investment goods wore out or became technologically obsolete, and thus needed to be replaced, a 'cost-recovery' fund for their replacement purchase did not exist.

Enterprises dealt with the problem through adopting replacement accounting in which replacement (which could include repairs) investment was charged directly against revenues before profits were determined; having repairs to the fixed investment goods (which is a form of investment) charged directly against revenues before profits were determined; or establishing a depreciation fund of money based on assigned depreciation rates (based on reducing balance, straight line, or some other basis) to different categories of fixed investment goods based on their historical costs, which involved a charge against revenue before profits were determined or directly against profits.[10] However, the demand by shareholders of the enterprise for immediate dividends (which is part of their monetary access to the social provisioning process) irrespective of the negative impact on its capabilities of providing an ongoing stream of dividends and hence an ongoing access to the provisioning process resulted in a change in the way expenditures on fixed investment goods were dealt with.[11] Instead of being expenses charged against revenue, they are initially expenditures out of profits that become a cost of production.[12] To include depreciation as a cost of production, it is first necessary to value the fixed investment goods, which is generally done at historical cost or at replacement cost (so both in terms of state money). Then a method of depreciation, such as straight-line or accelerated, is deployed to determine the amount of depreciation to be allowed as a cost of production. Once depreciation is a cost of production, the accounting working rules of the enterprise ensure that, in principle, all inputs are traceable, all costs are identified and allocated, and the determination of business income or profits can be done without affecting the going plant of the enterprise[13] (Edwards 1980; 1986; 1989; Napier 1990; Wale 1990; Tyson 1992; Drury and Tayles 1994; Alnestig and Segerstedt 1996; Boyns and Edwards 1997; Fleischman and Parker 1997)

Structure of production and costs

The business enterprise produces an array of outputs – that is, goods and services – which are organized around a set of core product lines. A product line may consist of a single main product with numerous derivative but secondary products and/or by-products; a conceptually distinct product that is a differentiated array of products; or a generic 'capabilities' product line that can produce an array of products based on the specifications provided by the buyer, such as in the case of fixed investment goods or based on the nature of the product itself, such as books. In all cases, the structure of production of a single product in a product line is hard to isolate because fixed investment goods and labor skills are used to produce more than one product; and the costing of the product is difficult because of the problem of allocating various common shop costs among the different products. To overcome these problems, the enterprise is conceived as a multi-division, multi-product line producer. The *product line* is defined in terms of its core or main product – that is, a product line consists of a single homogeneous product; each division has a single product line. As a going concern, when producing any of its multi-product lines, the business enterprise engages in sequential acts of production through historical time; as a result, it incurs sequential costs of production also through time. These acts of production and the costs incurred in producing a product line are determined by the underlying relatively enduring structures of production and costs. The structure of production consists of plant segments-plant, shop technique of production, and the enterprise technique of production; correspondingly, the cost structure of the product line consists of direct costs, divisional or shop expenses, and general enterprise expenses (the latter two jointly called non-direct or overhead costs). The basic framework of analysis of the structure of production and costs is a two dimensional comparative analysis in which production and costs are examined relative to different flow rates of output (or degrees of capacity utilization) at a given unit of historical time. Hence, it concentrates on the 'virtual' movement of inputs and costs and the flow rate of output. The starting point is, thus, the conception of production from which emerges the structures of production and costs as they relate to plant segments, plants, and direct costs; followed by delineating the structures of production and costs regarding the shop and enterprise techniques of production and overhead costs, and concluding with the structures of production and average total costs for the product line.

Production, technology, plants, and direct costs

The delineation of how goods and services are actually produced constitutes, broadly speaking, the theory of production. Within it, it is possible to deal with the organization of production in the economy as a whole (as delineated in Chapter 2), in industrial districts, or within supply chains; the investment in fixed investment goods as it relates to the specifications of how production of a good is organized at the level of the plant or even the enterprise; and the production of different levels of output given existing plant and workforce. It is this latter area that is relevant to delineating a theory of production and costs of the business enterprise. The *plant*, as the basic aggregate unit of production, is an establishment that houses or encompasses the activities immediately involved in the production of the product line. It has a *practical capacity*, that is, the flow rate of output generally attainable for a specific time period, given operating rules (such as only operating sixteen hours a day and five days a week) and taking into account set-up times and maintenance; its degree of capacity utilization is the flow rate of output relative to practical capacity. Given the plant, production can be further delineated in that more than one plant may be used to produce the product line and/or that each plant may consist of a number of plant segments, each of which is also capable of producing the product line. Whether the plant is an emergent technological establishment, divided into separate plant segments, or a hybrid of the two depends on the technology and the organization of production that constitutes the plant.[14]

Production

The direct production of a good or service is organized in terms of tasks and elementary production processes that are arranged in a straight-line or job-shop pattern to produce a given amount or batch of output in a given period of time.[15] The tasks are carried out by skilled labor in conjunction with tools and material inputs and their differentiation arises from the combination of technology and the organization of production; thus, the division of labor is more accurately the division of tasks that are carried out by the same or different worker. Because the tasks of an elementary process cannot be sub-divided, they must be performed in a prescribed order using specific tools (fixed investment goods) and material inputs (some perhaps drawn from the resource reserves owned by the enterprise) and take a specific amount of time. Moreover, material and labor inputs qua tasks are fixed, which means substitution between tools that are specific for the task, labor skills needed to do the task, and material inputs required for the task is not possible.[16] As a result, the networks of elementary processes that constitute the *production process* that is 'housed' in the plant and produces the 'final' output are also sequentially or relationally arranged, take time (denoted as a *production period*), are indecomposable, and exhibit a fixed relationship between inputs and the given amount of output.[17] To change the amount of output per batch, a reorganization of the production process is needed. The reorganization involves different technology, tools, and tasks, a different prescribed order of the elementary processes, and a possible change in the production period. On the other hand, it is also possible to alter the production process while the output per batch does not change. In either case, production processes producing the same output can be organized differently, using different tools and labor skills. The expansion of output can also occur through utilizing more than one production process at a time, or it can occur by using a production process in sequences of production – the former takes place in a single production period and the latter takes place through a sequence of production periods. Both cases are based on the existence of a complement of fixed investment goods and an array of labor skills that are able to be continually used or not as long as they are maintained. So, in short, production consists of one or more plants that have one or more production processes, a complement of fixed investment goods, relevant resource reserves, and a pool of differentiated labor skills that can readily be utilized (as delineated in Chapter 2; in particular, Schema 2.8); the scale of production is the number of production processes-plants that can be simultaneously utilized in a single production period.[18] Even though the production of a product line may consist of many production processes and include many elementary processes, tasks, and tools, the enterprise's cost accounting procedures are capable of tracking the array of intermediate and labor inputs and their amount used directly in its production (Abruzzi 1965; Georgescu-Roegen 1970; 1971; 1986; Scazzieri 1983; 1993; Morroni 1992; Mir-Artigues and Gonzalez-Calvert 2007).

Plant segment, plant, and the structure of production

For the segmented plant (SP), the primary unit of production is the *plant segment* (PS) which consists of a production process that is represented as an input-output schema of direct intermediate inputs of resources, goods, services, labor skills, and an array of fixed investment goods and resource reserves needed to produce a given amount of output, g, of a product line in a specific period of time.[19] The period of time used in the specification of the PS is the *production period* and it denotes the amount of calendar time needed to produce g, starting with the first input and ending with the output (Morroni 1992, 73; Mir-Artigues and Gonzalez-Calvert 2007, 19, 26). Therefore, given the fixed investment goods and the resource reserves and their operating specifications, the unit of output, and the production period, the schema of the plant segment is delineated as follows:

$$\text{Plant segment (PS): } g \leftarrow \mathbf{a} \oplus \mathbf{l} : \mathbf{k}, \mathbf{rr} \qquad (3.1)$$

where g is the flow rate (or amount) of output per production period; $\mathbf{a} = (a_1, \ldots, a_h)$, a $1 \times h$ row vector of direct intermediate input technical coefficients and its element a_h is a direct intermediate input technical coefficient and is the amount of the h-th input needed to produce g amount of output; $\mathbf{l} = (l_1, \ldots, l_z)$, a $1 \times z$ row vector of direct labor input technical coefficients and its element l_z is a direct labor input technical coefficient and is the amount of the z-th labor input needed to produce g amount of output; $\mathbf{k} = (k_1, \ldots, k_k)$, a $1 \times k$ row vector of fixed investment goods associated with PS; $\mathbf{rr} = (rr_1, \ldots, rr_r)$, a $1 \times r$ row vector of resource reserves associated with PS; $\oplus$ means "combined with" as specified by the underlying production process; and ":" means "given."

Each PS is a recipe of fixed ingredients for producing a single batch or amount of output per production period. Hence, each technical coefficient is the absolute amount of the inputs needed to produce g amount of output and is fixed relative to the other inputs; therefore, it is impossible for any one PS to produce more than g per production period. Consequently, to increase the flow rate of output of a product line in a production period, the enterprise must bring on-line additional plant segments complete with their specific complement of fixed investment goods. It implies that the plant consists of more than a single plant segment to produce the product. This characterization of production and the flow rate of output means that the PS is not particular to any production period, but exists for all production periods, thus making it a component of the structure of production; that the PS is unaffected by the passage of time or by repeated usage through time even though it must exist in time. As a result, this relatively enduring structural property permits the PS to be used over and over again under the guise of sequential production. In this manner, the fixed technical coefficients are flow coefficients and g is a flow of output denominated in terms of a single production period.[20]

Consider the case for the segmented plant when the plant segments of a plant are not identical, meaning that each PS consists of different amounts of the same inputs or of different inputs.[21] If m plant segments are being used, where $1 < m <$ maximum number of plant segments in the plant, then we have

$$\text{Segmented plant (SP): } q_m = \sum_{j=1}^{m} g_j : \mathbf{k}_{sp}, \mathbf{rr}_{sp} \qquad (3.2)$$

where q_m is the plant's aggregate flow rate of output for m plant segments; $\mathbf{k}_{sp} = (k_{1m}, \ldots, k_{km})$ is a $1 \times k$ row vector of fixed investment goods associated with the segmented plant and its element k_{km} is the quantity of the k-th fixed investment goods associated with the m plant segments that constitute the segmented plant; and $\mathbf{rr}_{sp} = (rr_1, \ldots, rr_{rm})$ is a $1 \times r$ row vector of resource reserves associated with the segmented plant and its element rr_{rm} is the quantity of the r-th resource reserves associated with the m plant segments that constitute the segment plant.

The average amount of direct intermediate and labor power inputs used to produce a unit of output at a given flow rate of output is derived by dividing Equation 3.2 by q_m:

Average plant segment (APS): $\mathbf{a}^* \oplus \mathbf{l}^* : \mathbf{k}_{sp}, \mathbf{rr}_{sp}; k_{mu}$ (3.3)

where $\mathbf{a}^* = \mathbf{a}/q_m$ is a $1 \times h$ row vector of intermediate input production coefficients; $\mathbf{l}^* = \mathbf{l}/q_m$ is a $1 \times z$ row vector of labor input production coefficients; $k_{mu} = q_m/\tilde{q}$ is the degree of capacity utilization; and $\tilde{q}$ is the plant's practical maximum flow rate of output when all PSs are utilized.

The average plant segment (APS) and its production coefficients (which are input-output ratios) represent the plant's structure of production at different flow rates of output or degrees of capacity utilization. If the plant segments are different, then production coefficients will vary, as will the APS, as capacity utilization increases. However, if the plant segments of the plant are all identical, the outcome of an increase in the flow rate of output or k_{mu} is the degree of capacity utilization

$$q_m = \sum_{j=1}^{m} g_j \leftarrow \sum_{j=1}^{m} \mathbf{a}_j \oplus \mathbf{l}_j : \mathbf{k}_{sp}, \mathbf{rr}_{sp}$$

or

$$q_m \leftarrow q_m[\mathbf{a} \oplus \mathbf{l}] = \mathbf{a}q_m \oplus \mathbf{l}q_m : \mathbf{k}_{sp}, \mathbf{rr}_{sp} \qquad (3.4)$$

since $q_m = m \times g$. From Schemas 3.3 and 3.4, the average plant segment (APS) of the segmented plant is:

APS: $\mathbf{a}^* \oplus \mathbf{l}^* : \mathbf{k}_{sp}, \mathbf{rr}_{sp}; k_{mu}$ (3.5)

since $\mathbf{a}^* = \mathbf{a}(q_m/q_m) = \mathbf{a}$; and $\mathbf{l}^* = \mathbf{l}(q_m/q_m) = \mathbf{l}$.

So, when plant segments are identical, the intermediate and labor production coefficients do not vary with the flow rate of output, thus making them equal to their respective technical coefficients of the individual plant segments. Consequently, the plant's structure of production, as represented by the APS, does not vary with capacity utilization.

The technologically emergent plant is a single plant with a single production process; hence it is delineated as follows:

Emergent plant: $q \leftarrow \mathbf{a} \oplus \mathbf{l} : \mathbf{k}_{ep}, \mathbf{rr}_{ep}$ (3.6)

Average emergent plant (AEP): $\mathbf{a}^* \oplus \mathbf{l}^* : \mathbf{k}_{ep}, \mathbf{rr}_{ep}; k_{mu}$ (3.6.1)

where q is the plant's flow rate of (or amount of) output per production period; and $\mathbf{k}_{ep} = (k_1, \ldots, k_k)$ is a $1 \times k$ row vector of fixed investment goods associated with the emergent plant; and $\mathbf{rr}_{ep} = (rr_1, \ldots, rr_r)$ is a $1 \times r$ row vector of resource reserves associated with the emergent plant.

The emergent plant is either on-line or not; that is, it is either operating at a full capacity or not operating at all. Finally, there is the hybrid plant which can take many technological-organizational forms, but its production process can best be represented as amounts of labor skills that are given for all degrees of capacity utilization, with the intermediate inputs fixed per unit of output, and as an array of fixed investment goods that can operate at varying degrees of capacity utilization:

Hybrid plant: $q \leftarrow \mathbf{a}q \oplus \mathbf{l} : \mathbf{k}_{hp}, \mathbf{rr}_{hp}$ (3.7)

Average hybrid plant (AHP): $\mathbf{a}^* \oplus \mathbf{l}^* : \mathbf{k}_{hp}, \mathbf{rr}_{hp}; k_{mu}$ (3.7.1)

where $\mathbf{a}^* = \mathbf{a}q/q$ is a vector of intermediate input production coefficients; $\mathbf{l}^* = \mathbf{l}/q$ is a vector of labor production coefficients; $\mathbf{rr}_{hp} = (rr_1, \ldots, rr_r)$ is a $1 \times k$ row vector of fixed investment goods associated with the hybrid plant; and $\mathbf{k}_{hp} = (k_1, \ldots, k_k)$ is a $1 \times r$ row vector of resource reserves associated with the hybrid plant.

So, when k_{mu} increases to the practical full capacity utilization of all fixed investment goods, the intermediate production coefficient remains constant while the labor production coefficient declines, which means the hybrid plant's structure of production also varies.

To summarize, the basic aggregate unit of production is the plant. Whether it is a segmented, emergent, or hybrid plant, production is a recipe of fixed ingredients that results in fixed technical coefficients. Hence, the intermediate and labor power inputs are not individually productive; instead, to be productive all inputs must be used together along with the associated fixed investment goods and resource reserves. When the capacity utilization of the plant increases, the resulting production coefficients may increase, decrease, or remain constant, even though the underlying technical coefficients are fixed and production processes given; their changes are a result of the technology qua production processes embodied in the plant, not the outcome of some law of production. So how a plant's structure of production, as represented by APS, AEP, and AHP, varies with changes in k_{mu} can only be determined by empirical investigations, not by assumption (Dean 1976; Eichner 1976; Lee 1986).

Plant segment, plant, and the structure of average direct costs

With the introduction of intermediate input prices and wage rates, the plant segment becomes the plant segment direct costs of production of the product line (PSDCP):

$$PSDCP = \mathbf{ap} + \mathbf{lw} \tag{3.8}$$

where $\mathbf{p}$ is a $h \times 1$ column vector of direct intermediate input prices; and $\mathbf{w}$ is a $z \times 1$ column vector of wage rates.

From this, and drawing on Equations 3.2 and 3.3, we have

Segmented plant average direct costs (SPADC) =

$$\frac{1}{q_m} \sum_{j=1}^{m} PSDCP_j = \mathbf{a}^*\mathbf{p} + \mathbf{l}^*\mathbf{w}; \, k_{mu} \tag{3.9}$$

where $\mathbf{a}^*\mathbf{p}$ is the plant average direct intermediate costs (PADMC) and its element

$a_i^* p_i = \sum_{j=1}^{m} \dfrac{a_{ij} p_i}{q_m}$ is the PADMC of the i-th input; and $\mathbf{l}^*\mathbf{w}$ is the plant average direct labor costs (PADLC) and its element $l_i^* w_i = \sum_{j=1}^{m} \dfrac{l_{ij} w_i}{q_m}$ is the PADLC of the i-th input.

If the plant segments differ and assuming that the lowest PSDCP is used first, then SPADC will vary as k_{mu} varies since the production coefficients (a_i^*, l_i^*) vary and will increase as k_{mu} increases. In contrast, if all plant segments are identical, then SPADC will not vary as k_{mu} increases since each production coefficient (a_i^*, l_i^*) will not vary. Thus the plant's structure of costs, represented by SPADC, PADMC, and PADLC, will vary and increase or not as k_{mu} varies, depending on its underlying structure of production. In the case of the emergent plant, when it is in operation and, therefore, producing at practical capacity utilization, its direct costs of production (EPDCP) and its plant average direct costs (EPADC) are:

$$EPDCP = EPADC = \mathbf{ap} + \mathbf{lw}; \, k_{mu.} \tag{3.10}$$

Finally, for the hybrid plant, its direct costs of production (HPDCP) and its plant average direct costs (HPADC) are:

$$HPDCP = \mathbf{ap}q + \mathbf{lw}; \, k_{mu.} \tag{3.11}$$
$$HPADC = \mathbf{a}^*\mathbf{p} + \mathbf{l}^*\mathbf{w}; \, k_{mu} \tag{3.11.1}$$

where $\mathbf{a}^*\mathbf{p} = \mathbf{ap}q/q$ is the plant average direct intermediate costs; and $\mathbf{l}^*\mathbf{w} = \mathbf{lw}/q$ is the plant average direct labor costs.

So as k_{mu} increases PADMC is constant since the intermediate production coefficients are constant, while PADLC declines as k_{mu} increases because the labor production coefficients decline; thus, as k_{mu} increases up to full capacity utilization, PADC declines because of its underlying structure of production. To summarize, the plant's structure of average direct costs, as represented by SPADC, HPADC, PADMC, and PADLC, can vary in any direction with changes in k_{mu} depending on its underlying structure of production (Lee 1986).

Multi-plant production and enterprise average direct costs of production

Business enterprises may employ up to n plants to produce a product line. Thus the number of plants actually used in production depends on the total flow rate of output as well as the flow rate of output of each plant. Consequently, the shape of the enterprise's average direct costs (EADC) curve depends on which plants are being utilized and the degree of utilization of each plant. Focusing on the k-th plant and assuming its full capacity utilization, we have:

$$\text{Segmented plant: } \tilde{q}_k \leftarrow \tilde{\mathbf{a}}_k \oplus \tilde{\mathbf{l}}_k : \mathbf{k}_{spk}, \mathbf{rr}_{spk}; \tilde{k}_{mu} \tag{3.12.1}$$

$$\text{Emergent plant: } \tilde{q}_k \leftarrow \tilde{\mathbf{a}}_k \oplus \tilde{\mathbf{l}}_k : \mathbf{k}_{epk}, \mathbf{rr}_{epk}; \tilde{k}_{mu} \tag{3.12.2}$$

$$\text{Hybrid plant: } \tilde{q}_k \leftarrow \tilde{\mathbf{a}}_k \oplus \tilde{\mathbf{l}}_k : \mathbf{k}_{hpk}, \mathbf{rr}_{hpk}; \tilde{k}_{mu} \tag{3.12.3}$$

where $\tilde{q}_k$ represents the maximum flow rate of output of the k-th plant; $\tilde{\mathbf{a}}_k$ is a vector of the amounts of intermediate inputs needed to produce the maximum flow rate of output of the k-th plant; $\tilde{\mathbf{l}}_k$ is a vector of the amount of the labor inputs needed to produce the maximum flow rate of output of the k-th plant; $\mathbf{k}_{spk}$, $\mathbf{k}_{epk}$, and $\mathbf{k}_{hpk}$ are the arrays of fixed investment goods for the segmented plant, emergent plant, and hybrid plant, respectively; $\mathbf{rr}_{spk}$, $\mathbf{rr}_{epk}$, and $\mathbf{rr}_{hpk}$ are the arrays of resource reserves available for the segmented plant, emergent plant, and hybrid plant, respectively; and $\tilde{k}_{mu}$ is full capacity utilization of the k-th plant.

Thus the enterprise's average direct inputs structure of production (EADSP) for the product line is:

$$\text{EADSP: } \frac{1}{q_e} \sum_{k=1}^{n} \tilde{\mathbf{a}}_k \oplus \tilde{\mathbf{l}}_k = \tilde{\mathbf{a}}_k^* \oplus \tilde{\mathbf{l}}_k^* : \mathbf{k}_d, \mathbf{rr}_d; k_{mue} \tag{3.13}$$

where $q_e = \sum_{k=1}^{n} \tilde{q}_k$ is the enterprise's flow rate of output for k plants with each plant producing at full capacity; $\tilde{\mathbf{a}}_k^* = \frac{1}{q_e} \sum_{k=1}^{n} \tilde{\mathbf{a}}_k$ is the vector of intermediate production coefficients at q_e;

$\tilde{\mathbf{i}}_k^* = \dfrac{1}{q_e}\displaystyle\sum_{k=1}^{n} \tilde{\mathbf{i}}_k$ is the vector labor input production coefficient at q_e;

$\mathbf{k}_d = \displaystyle\sum_{k=1}^{n} \mathbf{k}_{spk}, \sum_{k=1}^{n} \mathbf{k}_{epk}, \text{ or } \sum_{k=1}^{n} \mathbf{k}_{hpk}$ is the array of fixed investment goods across all plants that are 'directly' used in the production of the product line;

$\mathbf{rr}_d = \displaystyle\sum_{k=1}^{n} \mathbf{rr}_{spk}, \sum_{k=1}^{n} \mathbf{rr}_{epk}, \text{ or } \sum_{k=1}^{n} \mathbf{rr}_{hpk}$ is the array of resource reserves across

all plants that are 'directly' used in the production of the product line; and $k_{mue} = q_e / \tilde{q}_e$ is the degree of capacity utilization of the product line where $\tilde{q}_e$ is the enterprise's maximum flow rate of output when all plants are used and producing at full capacity.

If the plants are identical, then the production coefficients ($\tilde{\mathbf{a}}_k^*, \tilde{\mathbf{i}}_k^*$) are constant as k_{mue} increases, but if the plants are not identical then the production coefficients vary as k_{mue} increases.

Adding intermediate input prices and wage rates to EADSP results in the enterprise average direct costs (EADC) of production for the product line:

$$\text{EADC} = \tilde{\mathbf{a}}_k^* \mathbf{p} + \tilde{\mathbf{i}}_k^* \mathbf{w} : \mathbf{k}_d, \mathbf{rr}_d; k_{mue} \qquad (3.14)$$

where $\tilde{\mathbf{a}}_k^* \mathbf{p}$ is the enterprise average direct intermediate costs (EADMC); and

$\tilde{\mathbf{i}}_k^* \mathbf{w}$ is the enterprise average direct labor costs (EADLC).

As noted above, if the plants are identical, then the production coefficients are constant as k_{mue} increases, resulting in constant EADC, EADMC, and EADLC.[22] However, if the plants are not identical, then they will change as k_{mue} changes. That is, if technology and the organization of production change over time, then each plant may be different in terms of intermediate and labor inputs used and the flow rate of output. Consequently, it is not possible to determine the order in which the various plants are used to produce the output without first comparing their average direct costs (Gold 1981). Assuming that the business enterprise tries to produce any flow rate of output as cheaply as possible, it will use plants with lower PADC at full capacity utilization first and plants with higher PADC later:

$$\text{PADC}_1 < \ldots < \text{PADC}_k < \ldots < \text{PADC}_n \qquad (3.15)$$

where PADC_k is the plant average direct costs of the k-th plant at full capacity utilization; and PADC_n is the highest cost and last plant used by the business enterprise.

Consequently, as capacity utilization increases and more plants are brought on-line, EADC will increase due to the use of more costly plants:

if $PADC_k < PADC_{k+1}$,
then $EADC_{k+1} > EADC_k$, and $EADC_{k+1} - EADC_k > 0$ (3.16)

where $PADC_{k+1}$ is plant average 'incremental' costs.

If variations of k_{mue} take place within the k-th segmented plant, the production coefficients ($\tilde{\mathbf{a}}_k^*, \tilde{\mathbf{l}}_k^*$) will increase, even if the plant segments are all identical so that the plant coefficients ($\mathbf{a}^*, \mathbf{l}^*$) are constant as plant capacity utilization increases, which implies that enterprise average direct costs increase, even though average direct costs within the plant are constant. That is, the least costly plant segments are used first and the most costly later:

$$PSDCP_1 < \ldots < PSDCP_j < \ldots < PSDCP_m \qquad (3.17)$$

where $PSDCP_j$ is the direct costs of the j-th plant segment.

Therefore, if $PSDCP_j < PSDCP_{j+1}$ and $PADC_{k-1} < PADC_k$, then $PSDCP_{j+1} > EADC_{km}$ and $EADC_{km} < EADC_{km+1}$. So if segmented plants have different costs irrespective of whether the plant segments within a plant have the same costs or not, enterprise average direct costs will increase as k_{mue} increases. On the other hand, if the EADC is based on hybrid plants, then it will exhibit spiked costs even if overall costs are constant (Blinder et al. 1998, 103). That is, if $HPADC_k = HPADC_{k+1}$ at full capacity utilization so that $EADC_k = EADC_{k+1}$, for $k = 1, \ldots, n$, then if $HPADC_{k+1}$ is partially utilized ($q < \tilde{q}_{k+1}$), $EADC_{k+1q} > EADC_{k+1}$, but tends to equality as q approaches $\tilde{q}$, implying declining plant average incremental costs. Spiked costs can also occur if the EADC is increasing and k_{mue} increases, but they will not be as pronounced.[23]

The outcomes of the above analysis of enterprise average direct costs are that (1) under single plant production both EADC and its incremental costs can be constant, increase, or decrease as k_{mue} increases; (2) under multi-plant production EADC can be constant or increase as k_{mue} increases while its incremental costs can be increasing, decreasing, or constant; and (3) average direct intermediate input and labor costs can increase, decrease, or remain constant as k_{mue} increases. These varied outcomes are due to the possibility that plants (and plant segments) have the same or different technology and organization of production that generates a structure of production whose production coefficients vary or remain constant as k_{mue} varies. In particular, over time technical and organizational innovations occur that become embedded in the production processes that make up the plant and produces a lower PADC. The lower costs may arise, for example, from large-scale production through the use of specialized equipment, better organization of production flows, and use of different kinds of skilled or unskilled labor. But the

point is that technical and organizational knowledge and capital-labor relationships continually change and supersede the existing knowledge and conventional
ways of working. Hence the difference between the technological make-up and
work organization of plants is not just time, but a wholly new unforeseen body of
technical and organizational knowledge and capital-labor relationships that makes
for greater cost reductions per unit of output; thus, it is possible to view a plant
as a particular time-specific embodiment or 'vintage' of technical and organizational knowledge and capital-labor relationships.[24] Since the older vintage plants
have higher PADC, an increasing EADC is a result of technological progress;[25]
in contrast, if technological progress and social change is absent, then EADC is
constant so that vintage plants are the same as new plants. Thus, it is the existence
of technological, organizational, and social change which creates vintage plants
that makes the EADC increase as k_{mue} increases, not the existence of inefficient
technology and backward manning practices; an assumption of constant EADC is
an assumption of technological stagnation or at least the absence of technological
progress[26] (Salter 1966; Eichner 1976; Gold 1981; Lee 1986).

Shop technique of production and shop expenses

As noted above, the costs a business enterprise incurs in the production of a product line are divided into direct costs and overhead costs. The former are specified in terms of a production period, while the latter are specified in terms of an
accounting period that is generally a calendar year and often consists of a number
of production periods. Overhead costs, in turn, are divided into two categories:
shop expenses and *enterprise expenses* (which are dealt with below). Shop and
enterprise expenses can be further divided into indirect costs and depreciation.
Indirect costs consist of the labor and intermediate input expenses required to
supervise and manage the production of a product line; hence, they must be able
to accommodate many different flow rates of output in a single production period
and a succession of flow rates of output over a number of production periods. That
is, for a business enterprise to engage in sequential acts of production over time as
well as to be able to vary how much it produces in any production period, it must
continually incur labor and intermediate input expenses that permit this. Shop
expenses are those non-direct costs associated with the production of a particular
product line in a plant and across plants and generally include the salaries of fore-
men, support staff, and supervisors; the intermediate inputs needed to maintain
the support staff and the technical efficiency of the plant(s) used directly in production; and the depreciation allowance associated with the plant(s).

Shop technique of production

Each plant involved in the production of a product line utilizes an array of labor
and intermediate inputs in conjunction with an array of fixed investment goods
(k_{se}) and resource reserves (rr_{se}) to oversee production for the accounting period
that constitutes the plant's managerial technique of production (PMTP). Although
the technical coefficients that make up the PMTP are not rigid, they are specified

at the same time the technology of the plant is determined. Assuming the number of production periods in the accounting period to be f, the PMTP for the k-th plant is the following:

$$\text{PMTP}_k = \mathbf{a}_{sek} \oplus \mathbf{l}_{sek} : \mathbf{k}_{sek}, \mathbf{rr}_{sek} \tag{3.18}$$

where $\mathbf{a}_{sek}$ is a $1 \times b$ row vector of managerial intermediate input technical coefficients for the k-th plant in absolute amount for the accounting period; $\mathbf{l}_{sek}$ is a $1 \times c$ row vector of managerial labor input technical coefficients for the k-th plant in absolute amount for the accounting period; $\mathbf{k}_{sek}$ is the array of fixed investment goods associated with the k-th PMTP; and $\mathbf{rr}_{sek}$ is the array of resource reserves associated with the k-th PMTP.

The technical coefficients are made up of flows of inputs over successive production periods that constitute the accounting period, and their amount for any f-th production period is given and sufficient to manage any degree of capacity utilization of the plant. This implies that incremental variations in the amount of any coefficients have no impact on the degree of capacity utilization. While the flow of the managerial inputs need not be absolutely uniform over the production periods, their variations cannot be too great, and in the end they have to add up to the absolute amounts needed for the accounting period. To simplify the analysis, it is assumed that the managerial inputs are uniformly distributed over the f production periods; therefore, the PMTP_k for the f-th production period is represented as:

$$\text{PMTP}_{kf} = \frac{1}{f} [\mathbf{a}_{sek} \oplus \mathbf{l}_{sek}] = \mathbf{a}_{sekf} \oplus \mathbf{l}_{sekf} \tag{3.19}$$

Since PMTP_{kf} can accommodate any variation in its flow rate of output, the average PMTP_{kf} is

$$\text{APMTP}_{kf} = \frac{1}{q} [\mathbf{a}_{sekf} \oplus \mathbf{l}_{sefk}] = \mathbf{a}^*_{sekf} \oplus \mathbf{l}^*_{sekf} ; k_{mu} \tag{3.20}$$

where $\mathbf{a}^*_{sekf}$ is a $1 \times b$ row vector of plant managerial intermediate production coefficients for the f-th production period and q flow rate of output; and its element $a^*_{serkf} = a_{serk} / f \cdot q$ is the r-th plant managerial intermediate input production coefficient for the f-th production period and q flow rate of output; $\mathbf{l}^*_{sekf}$ is a $1 \times c$ row vector of plant managerial labor input coefficient for the f-th production period and q flow rate of output; and its element $l^*_{seskf} = l_{sesk} / f \cdot q$ is the s-th plant managerial labor input production coefficient for the f-th production period and q flow rate of output.

Thus, as k_{mu} increases, APMTP_{kf} varies and the plant managerial production coefficients for the f-th production period decline, reaching their lowest value when the plant is at full capacity utilization.

If the enterprise uses more than one plant in the production of a product line, it has more than a single PMTP. As a group they are the shop technique of production (STP) and represent the enterprise's 'technical organization' of its managerial supervision of the production of the product line:

$$\text{STP} = \sum_{k=1}^{n} \text{PMTP}_k = \sum_{k=1}^{n} \mathbf{a}_{sek} \oplus \mathbf{l}_{sek} = \mathbf{a}_{se} \oplus \mathbf{l}_{se} : \mathbf{k}_{se}, \mathbf{rr}_{se} \qquad (3.21)$$

$$\text{STP} = \sum_{r=1, s=1}^{b, c} a_{ser} \oplus l_{ses} = \mathbf{a}_{se} \oplus \mathbf{l}_{se} : \mathbf{k}_{se}, \mathbf{rr}_{se} \qquad (3.21.1)$$

where $a_{ser} = \sum_{k=1}^{n} a_{serk}$ is the r-th shop intermediate input technical coefficient for the accounting period; $l_{ses} = \sum_{k=1}^{n} l_{sesk}$ is the s-th shop labor technical coefficient for the accounting period; $\mathbf{a}_{se}$ is a $1 \times b$ row vector of managerial intermediate input technical coefficients in absolute amounts for the accounting period; $\mathbf{l}_{se}$ is a $1 \times c$ row vector of managerial labor input technical coefficients in absolute amounts for the accounting period; $\mathbf{k}_{se}$ is the array of fixed investment goods associated with STP; and $\mathbf{rr}_{se}$ is the array of resource reserves associated with STP.

Because STP is based on PMTP, its technical coefficients are made up of flows of inputs over successive production periods that constitute the accounting period, and their amount for any f-th production period is given and sufficient to manage any degree of capacity utilization for the product line, k_{mue}. Since managerial inputs are assumed to be evenly distributed over the production periods that constitute the accounting period, the shop technique of production for the f-th production period is:

$$\text{STP}_f = \frac{1}{f}\text{STP} = \frac{1}{f}[\mathbf{a}_{se} \oplus \mathbf{l}_{se}] = \mathbf{a}_{sef} \oplus \mathbf{l}_{sef} : \mathbf{k}_{se}, \mathbf{rr}_{se} \qquad (3.22)$$

Finally, for any production period, the STP can accommodate variations in the flow rate of output in terms of bringing a plant (or plant segment) on-line or closing a plant (or plant segment) down. Therefore, the average shop technique of production (ASTP) for the f-th production period is

$$\text{ASTP}_f = \frac{1}{q_e}\text{STP} = \mathbf{a}_{sef}^* \oplus \mathbf{l}_{sef}^* : \mathbf{k}_{se}, \mathbf{rr}_{se} ; k_{mue} \qquad (3.23)$$

where $\mathbf{a}_{sef}^*$ is a $1 \times b$ row vector of shop intermediate input production coefficient for the f-th production period when the enterprise's flow rate of output is q_e; and its element $a_{serf}^* = a_{serf}/q_e$ is the r-th shop intermediate input production coefficient for the f-th production period when the enterprise's flow rate of output is q_e; and $\mathbf{l}_{sef}^*$ is a $1 \times c$ row vector of shop labor input production coefficient for the f-th production period when the flow rate of output is q_e; and its element $l^*_{sesf} = l_{sesf}/q_e$ is the s-th shop labor input production coefficient for the f-th production period when the flow rate of output is q_e.

Thus, as k_{mue} increases, $ASTP_f$ varies and the average shop production coefficients decline, reaching their lowest value when k_{mue} reaches full capacity utilization.

Indirect costs: costs of the shop technique of production

With the introduction of intermediate input prices and salaries, the STP_f becomes indirect costs or the cost of the shop technique of production (CSTP):

$$CSTP_f = \mathbf{a}_{sef}\mathbf{p}_{se} + \mathbf{l}_{sef}\mathbf{w}_{se} : \mathbf{k}_{se}, \mathbf{rr}_{se} \tag{3.24}$$

where $CSTP_f$ is the cost of shop technique of production for the f-th production period; $\mathbf{p}_{se}$ is a $b \times 1$ column vector of managerial intermediate input prices; and $\mathbf{w}_{se}$ is a $c \times 1$ column vector of managerial labor salaries.

The $CSTP_f$ shows that indirect costs are cost flows over the production periods that constitute the accounting period, but they are also invariant with respect to different flow rates of output within the f-th production period. Therefore, the average $CSTP_f$ and the average intermediate and labor input costs will vary inversely with the flow rate of output or degree of capacity utilization:

$$ACSTP_f = \frac{CSTP_f}{q_e} = \mathbf{a}^*_{sef}\mathbf{p}_{se} + \mathbf{l}^*_{sef}\mathbf{w}_{se} ; k_{mue} \tag{3.25}$$

$$\frac{\Delta ACTP_f}{\Delta q_e} < 0 \tag{3.25.1}$$

$$\frac{\Delta SAMC_f}{\Delta q_e} < 0 \tag{3.25.2}$$

$$\frac{\Delta SALC_f}{\Delta q_e} < 0 \tag{3.25.3}$$

where $SAMC_f = \mathbf{a}^*_{sef}\mathbf{p}_{se}$ is the shop average intermediate costs for the f-th production period; $SALC_f = \mathbf{l}^*_{sef}\mathbf{w}_{se}$ is the shop average labor power costs for the f-th production period.

Costs of the shop technique of production are contractual expenditures; thus, although fixed with regard to variations in the flow rate of output within a production period, they are not deferrable over production periods but have to be paid-out on a regular, sequential basis.

Depreciation

As noted above, depreciation of fixed investment goods is a cost denominated in state money that is incurred in the production of a product line. To determine it, the fixed investment goods involved in its production have to be identified. From Equations 3.1, 3.2, 3.6, 3.7, 3.13, 3.16, and 3.21, the array of fixed investment goods associated with the production of the product line is:

$$\mathbf{k}_{dse} = \mathbf{k}_{d} + \mathbf{k}_{se} \tag{3.26}$$

With the fixed investment goods associated with the production of the product line identified, their individual values are determined based on their historical costs. Then using straight-line or declining charges methods, the depreciation allowance of each fixed investment good for the accounting period is determined, from whence they are aggregated into a single value amount for the accounting period, D_{se}. Distributing D_{se} equally across all production periods, depreciation allowance for the f-th production period is $D_{sef} = D_{se}/f$. Since D_{sef} is invariant with respect to variations in the flow rate of output, average depreciation costs and hence the shop depreciation production coefficient varies inversely with as the degree of capacity utilization:

$$d^{*}_{sef} = \frac{D_{sef}}{q_{e}} \tag{3.27}$$

$$\frac{\Delta d^{*}_{sef}}{\Delta q_{e}} < 0 \tag{3.27.1}$$

where d^{*}_{sef} is the shop depreciation production coefficient for the f-th production period when the flow rate of output is q_{e}.

Shop expenses

Shop expenses (SE) for the f-th production period is obtained by adding together D_{sef} and $CSTP_{f}$:

$$SE_{f} = \mathbf{a}_{sef}\, \mathbf{p}_{se} + \mathbf{l}_{sef}\, \mathbf{w}_{se} + D_{sef} \tag{3.28}$$

Since $CSTP_{f}$ and D_{sef} are cost flows, SE_{f} is also a cost flow; thus it cannot be seen as 'fixed' even though it is invariant with respect to different flow rates of output. Average shop expenses (ASE) for the f-th production period is

$$ASE_{f} = \frac{SE_{f}}{q_{e}} = \mathbf{a}^{*}_{sef}\, \mathbf{p}_{se} + \mathbf{l}^{*}_{sef}\, \mathbf{w}^{*}_{se} + d^{*}_{sef} : \mathbf{k}_{se}, \mathbf{rr}_{se}; k_{mue} \tag{3.29}$$

and as the degree of capacity utilization increases, ASE_f declines (Equations 3.25.1 and 3.27.1). That is:

$$\frac{\Delta ASE_f}{\Delta q_e} < 0 \tag{3.29.1}$$

Enterprise technique of production and enterprise expenses

Because the going enterprise is generally a multi-product producer, it incurs expenses that are common to all of its product lines, that are necessary if it is to stay in existence as a going concern, and hence that are identified as enterprise expenses (EE). In general, these costs are associated with those activities that the enterprise must engage in in order to coordinate the production flows of its various product lines, to sell its various product lines, and to develop and implement enterprise-wide investment and diversification plans. EE include the salaries of management, stationary, selling and other office expenses, and the depreciation of the central office fixed investment goods. This array of labor and intermediate inputs in conjunction with an array of fixed investment goods ($\mathbf{k}_{ee} = k_{ee1}, \ldots, k_{eek}$) and resource reserves ($\mathbf{rr}_{ee} = r_{ee1}, \ldots, r_{eek}$) are used to manage the enterprise as a whole for the accounting period which includes the various degrees of capacity utilization for any one product line and all product lines; it can be thought of as the *enterprise technique of production* (ETP):

$$ETP = \mathbf{a}_{ee} \oplus \mathbf{l}_{ee} : \mathbf{k}_{ee}, \mathbf{rr}_{ee} \tag{3.30}$$

where $\mathbf{a}_{ee}$ is a $1 \times o$ row vector of enterprise intermediate input technical coefficient for the accounting period; and its element a_o is the o-th enterprise intermediate input technical coefficient for the accounting period; $\mathbf{l}_{ee}$ is a $1 \times y$ row vector of enterprise labor technical coefficient for the accounting period; and its element l_y is the y-th enterprise labor technical coefficient for the accounting period.

The technical coefficients are made up of flows of inputs over the accounting period that are not synchronized with the production periods of the various production lines, which would not be possible in any case since they are not necessarily the same. Therefore, it is not possible, as with the STP, to allocate the flow of the inputs to any and all product lines; rather, the allocation is done in terms of state money.

With the introduction of intermediate input prices and yearly salaries, the ETP becomes indirect costs or the cost of the enterprise technique of production (CETP):

$$CETP = \mathbf{a}_{ee}\mathbf{p}_{ee} + \mathbf{l}_{ee}\mathbf{s}_{ee} \tag{3.31}$$

where $\mathbf{p}_{ee}$ is a $o \times 1$ column vector of enterprise intermediate input prices; $\mathbf{a}_{ee}\mathbf{p}_{ee}$ is the enterprise intermediate costs for the accounting period; $\mathbf{s}_{ee}$ is a $y \times 1$ column vector of enterprise yearly salaries; and $\mathbf{l}_{ee}\mathbf{s}_{ee}$ is the labor costs for the accounting period.

Given the CETP for the accounting period, it is allocated to each of the enterprise's j product lines. Once a given percentage of CETP, αCETP, is allocated to the j-th product line for the accounting period, it is then allocated equally over all the production periods. Therefore, the CETP for the enterprise's j-th product line and the f-th production period is:

$$\text{CETP}_{jf} = \alpha_j \frac{1}{f}\left(\mathbf{a}_{ee}\mathbf{P}_{ee} + \mathbf{l}_{ee}\mathbf{s}_{ee}\right) = \mathbf{a}_{eeif}\mathbf{P}_{ee} + \mathbf{l}_{eeif}\mathbf{s}_{ee} \tag{3.32}$$

where $\mathbf{a}_{eeif}\mathbf{P}_{ee}$ is the enterprise intermediate costs for the j-th product line and f-th production period; $\mathbf{l}_{eeif}\mathbf{s}_{ee}$ is the enterprise labor costs for the j-th product line and f-th production period; and α_j is the percentage of CETP allocated to the j-th product line.

Like with the CSTP_f, the CETP_{jf} shows that indirect costs are cost flows over the production periods that constitute the accounting period, but they are also invariant with respect to different flow rates of output in the f-th production period. Therefore, the average CETP_{jf} and the average intermediate and labor input costs will vary inversely with the flow rate of output or degree of capacity utilization:

$$\text{ACETP}_{jf} = \frac{\text{CETP}_{jf}}{q_{je}} = \mathbf{a}^*_{eeif}\mathbf{P}_{ee} + \mathbf{l}^*_{eeif}\mathbf{s}_{ee} \tag{3.33}$$

$$\frac{\Delta\text{ACETP}_{jf}}{\Delta q_{je}} < 0 \tag{3.33.1}$$

$$\frac{\Delta\text{EAMC}_{jf}}{\Delta q_{je}} < 0 \tag{3.33.2}$$

$$\frac{\Delta\text{EALC}_{jf}}{\Delta q_{je}} < 0 \tag{3.33.3}$$

where $\text{EAMC}_{jf} = \mathbf{a}^*_{eeif}\mathbf{P}_{ee}$ is the enterprise average intermediate costs for the j-th product line and f-th production period; and $\text{EALC}_{jf} = \mathbf{l}^*_{eeif}\mathbf{s}_{ee}$ is the enterprise average labor costs for the j-th product line and f-th production period.

Costs of the enterprise technique of production are also contractual expenditures; thus, although fixed with regard to variations in the flow rate of output within a production period, they are not deferrable over production periods, but have to be paid-out on a regular, sequential basis.

Since the array of fixed investment goods $(\mathbf{k}_{ee})$ associated with the ETP are known, the depreciation allowance for enterprise expenses, D_{ee}, for the accounting period is determined in the same manner described above in reference to shop expenses. It is then allocated to the various product lines so that the enterprise depreciation allowance of the j-th product line for the accounting period is $D_{eej} = \alpha_j D_{ee}$; for the j-th product for the f-th production period, it is $D_{eejf} = \frac{1}{f}\alpha_j D_{ee}$. Finally, although D_{eejf} is invariant with respect to variations in the flow rate of output, the enterprise depreciation production coefficient for the j-th product line and f-th production period varies as the flow rate of output varies:

$$d^*_{eejf} = \frac{D_{eejf}}{q_{je}} \tag{3.34}$$

$$\frac{\Delta d^*_{eejf}}{\Delta q_{je}} < 0 \tag{3.34.1}$$

where d^*_{eejf} is the enterprise depreciation production coefficient of the j-th product for the f-th production period when the flow rate of output is q_{je}.

Finally, the enterprise expenses for the accounting period consist of the cost of the enterprise technique of production and depreciation; thus the enterprise expenses (EE) for the j-th product line in the f-th production period are:

$$EE_{jf} = CETP_{jf} + D_{eejf} = \mathbf{a}_{eejf}\mathbf{p}_{ee} + \mathbf{l}_{eejf}\mathbf{s}_{ee} + D_{eejf} \tag{3.35}$$

Since each of its components is a cost flow, the EE_{jf} is also a cost flow. Thus it cannot be seen as 'fixed' even though it is invariant with respect to different flow rates of output. Average enterprise expenses for the j-th product line and f-th production period is:

$$AEE_{jf} = \frac{EE_{jf}}{q_e} = ACETP_{jf} + d^*_{eejf} = \mathbf{a}^*_{eejf}\mathbf{p}_{ee} + \mathbf{l}^*_{eejf}\mathbf{s}_{ee} + d^*_{eejf} : \mathbf{k}_{ee}, \mathbf{rr}_{ee}; k_{mue} \tag{3.36}$$

and as the degree of capacity utilization increases and AEE_{jf} declines (Equations 3.33.1 and 3.34.1). That is,

$$\frac{\Delta AEE_{jf}}{\Delta q_e} < 0 \tag{3.36.1}$$

Structure of production and costs of a product line

The average structure of production (ASP) for the business enterprise's j-th product line in terms of the f-th production period and for a flow rate of output of q_{je} (derived from equations 3.13, 3.23, 3.30, and 3.33) is:

$$ASP_{jf} = \tilde{\mathbf{a}}^*_{kjf} \oplus \mathbf{a}^*_{sejf} \oplus \mathbf{a}^*_{eejf} \oplus \tilde{\mathbf{l}}^*_{kjf} \oplus \mathbf{l}^*_{sejf} \oplus \mathbf{l}^*_{eejf} : \mathbf{k}_z, \mathbf{rr}_z; k_{mue} \tag{3.37}$$

where $\mathbf{k}_z = \mathbf{k}_d + \mathbf{k}_{se} + \mathbf{k}_{ee}$ and $\mathbf{rr}_z = \mathbf{rr}_{se} + \mathbf{rr}_{ee}$.

Equation 3.37 clearly shows that the enterprise's ASP consists of an array of material and service inputs and labor inputs whose production coefficients are jointly determined by technology and the flow rate of output. So while the structure itself remains stable in face of variations of the flow rate of output, the production coefficients can vary: (1) a^*_{sejf}, a^*_{eejf}, l^*_{sejf}, and l^*_{eejf} all decline as the flow rate of output (q_{je}) increases; and (2) $\tilde{a}^*_{kjf}$ and $\tilde{l}^*_{kjf}$ can vary in any direction as output increases. Therefore, the product's structure of production and, hence, its ASP changes when the underlying technology and social/labor relationships change, resulting in changes in the material and labor inputs. This generally occurs when new plants (or plant segments) are brought on-line and as vintage plants (plant segments) are dropped, as well as when managerial and enterprise techniques of production are altered, but it can also occur after a failed (or successful) strike. When considering the structure of costs for a single product, we are essentially considering the enterprise's average total costs of production (EATC) for the j-th product line, the f-th production period, and the flow rate of output of q_{je} (derived from equations 3.14, 3.29, and 3.36):

$$\text{EATC}_{jf} = \text{EADC}_{jf} + \text{ASE}_{jf} + \text{AEE}_{jf}$$
$$= \tilde{a}^*_{kjf}\mathbf{p} + a^*_{sejf}\mathbf{p}_{se} + a^*_{eejf}\mathbf{p}_{ee} + \tilde{l}^*_{kjf}\mathbf{w} + l^*_{sejf}\mathbf{w}_{se} + l^*_{eejf}\mathbf{s}_{ee} + d^*_{sejf} + d^*_{eejf}; k_{mue}$$

(3.38)

where EADC_{jf} is the enterprise average direct costs for the j-th product line, f-th production period when the flow rate of output is q_{jef}; ASE_{jf} is the average shop expenses for the j-th product line, f-th production period when the flow rate of output is q_{jef}; and AEE_{jf} is the average enterprise expenses for the j-th product line, f-th production period when the flow rate of output is q_{jef}.

Restricting the structural analysis to a single production period, the relationship between EATC_{jf} and the flow rate of output can be shown in the following manner:

$$\frac{\Delta \text{EATC}_{jf}}{\Delta q_{jef}} > 0, \text{ if PADC}_{jk+1} > \text{EATC}_{jf}$$
$$= 0, \text{ if PADC}_{jk+1} = \text{EATC}_{jf}$$
$$< 0, \text{ if PADC}_{jk+1} < \text{EATC}_{jf}$$

(3.39)

Thus we find that the specific forms of the relationship depend on a tug-of-war between the rising incremental costs and the falling ASE_{jf} and AEE_{jf}. Since there is no necessary reason for the relative dominance of one side over the other, a positive, negative, or U-shaped EATC_{jf} are possible. The empirical evidence does suggest, however, that EATC_{jkf} is declining as the flow rate of output increases. Still, it should be noted that whatever the shape of the average total cost curve is, the shape is solely due to technological and organizational change and changes in capital-labor relationships and, hence, is solely an empirical issue.

The heterodox theory of production and costs

The beginning point of the heterodox theory of production and costs is not the business enterprise *per se*, but a circular circuit, circular production, surplus producing economy. For such an economy, production and the surplus are delineated in terms of a Leontief-Sraffa input-output model complete with industry- or market-level production coefficients. However, what is lacking is a connection between the business enterprise that actually does the production and the industry-level coefficients. The heterodox theory of production and costs of an enterprise's product line delineated in this chapter fills this gap by developing the theoretical 'micro' foundations of the industry production coefficients that consist of a product-based input-output structure, an explanation of the movements of production coefficients, and finally an explanation of average and incremental cost curves. Given this, how does the heterodox theory of production and costs stand relative to neoclassical theory? Because it is based on the going business enterprise with its relatively enduring (but not unchanging) accounting rules and unceasing sequential acts of production, the theory cannot be located in the short- or long-period. Rather, the relevant time periods for theoretical purposes are the production period and the accounting period, both of which are calendar or real time periods and not solely analytical time periods defined in terms of fixed and variable inputs. The going enterprise is also predicated on reproducible, differentiated intermediate inputs, and differentiated labor power. This implies the rejection of inputs being characterized as relatively scarce factors of production and of the 'linear' reduction of intermediate inputs to an objective or subjective quantity of homogeneous labor power or effort. Finally, the role of a going enterprise's accounting rules in determining what constitutes the reoccurring costs of a product line makes costs a socially constructed concept as opposed to an unambiguous, unmediated objective concept. These three points fundamentally differentiate the heterodox theory of production and costs from its neoclassical counterpart: the former is in the theoretical universe of historical time, reproducible inputs, non-reductionism, and social joint-stock of knowledge, whereas the latter is in a universe of analytical time, relative scarcity, reductionism, and socially unmediated knowledge.

Heterodox theory also differs from neoclassical theory on the particulars. That is, the heterodox characterization of production as a recipe embedded in a plant is incompatible with intensive rent qua the productivity of individual inputs qua marginal products, fixed-variable input distinction, and the full utilization of a fixed input requirement for the existence of marginal products; without marginal products (and relative scarcity), the law of diminishing returns does not exist. Consequently, such theoretical concepts such as cost minimization, marginal cost curves and their upward slope, the marginal rate of technical substitution, and constant output factor input demand curves are irrelevant. Since vintage plants differ by knowledge and capital-labor relationships that are historically contingent, factor substitution via changes in relative factor input prices and returns to scale have no substantive meaning. Finally, the inclusion of depreciation solely as a money cost and the rejection of the rate of interest or normal profits as a cost make the meaning of heterodox and neoclassical average total costs quite different. Therefore, the choice between neoclassical and heterodox production and cost theory is based on the empirical validity and theoretical superiority of the latter.

Although fundamentally different at the theoretical level, heterodox and neoclassical production and cost theory are similarly organized. Both theories start with a structure of production in which inputs are connected to outputs (although the actual production processes are left unarticulated in the neoclassical theory); from the structures, the movement of production coefficients (average products) and 'incremental' plants (marginal products) are delineated. In short, both theories see production as a technological, organizational, and (at least for heterodox economists) social activity central to understanding the business enterprise. The transformation of production into costs is carried out in a similar manner, which gives rise to similar looking cost curves. However, since their theoretical content is, for both theories, located in the theory of production, the curves' superficial resemblance obscures their profound theoretical differences. This tight connection between production and cost theory means for both theories that it is illegitimate to discuss the costs of the business enterprise independent of its structure of production. This point can be further extended for heterodox economics in that it is illegitimate to aggregate structures of production and costs across product lines. That is, the heterodox theory of production and costs is predicated on an input-output relationship of a well-defined product line. So long as the production of the goods and services needed for social provisioning require distinct and differentiated reproducible inputs, labor inputs, fixed investment goods, and resource reserves, it is not possible to aggregate the different product lines and their corresponding structures of production into a single homogeneous input-output (such as in a corn model or a labor-based production model). Therefore the input-output relationship is the foundation of both the going capitalist economy and the going business enterprise. From this, it can be inferred that production and cost theory provides, in part, the foundation from which all heterodox theory emanates.

Notes

1 If the enterprise is tied to a specific resource at a specific geographical location, such as a colliery in Northumberland (UK), the motivation of the owners and managers may be to make its profitable finite life-span as long as possible so as to secure long-term dividends and salary incomes, and therefore long-term access to the social provisioning process. This would involve spreading out production evenly, rather than exploiting the resource quickly so as to shorten the life-span of the enterprise (Wale 1989b).

2 As noted in Chapter 1, in a historical, transformative world, terms such as maximization (and minimization) have no meaning in terms of objective or goal to achieve through time. It is also argued in Chapter 2 that the acting person makes decisions to attain such goals that cannot be defined as either rational or irrational. Finally, as will be argued later in this chapter and in subsequent chapters, there is no functional law-like relationship between price and sales or between price and production-costs on which to base an optimizing relationship. That is, for the enterprise to act, it must

know what is to be attained prior to acting. To say profit maximization or cost minimization, without concretely identifying what it is, is for the acting enterprise to establish no goals upon which to act. Hence, non-rational acting enterprises do not maximize profits or minimize costs, but have profit attainment and cost reduction goals that they actively pursue.

3 Some objectives have a three-year horizon, whereas others have only a one-year horizon. Moreover, some objectives and their attainment are reviewed every year, while others are reviewed in a shorter or longer time period. In some cases, although periodically reviewed, the same objective is retained for six to ten years (O'Brien 1972). In addition, overlapping time periods also exist in production as well as in the determination of cost. Consequently, it is not possible to argue in terms of short-period or the classical-Marxian long-period, or any other kind of analytical, ahistorical time period. The only permissible analytical time period for theorizing is historical time: the business enterprise, prices, output, and the rest of the economy must be analytically examined in historical time.

4 As relatively enduring structures, management accounting procedures (now in most cases embedded in software packages) remain relatively unchanged for decades at a time, or, in the case of DuPont Powder Company, for nearly one hundred years (1804–1902). Moreover, when change is introduced, it can take nearly a decade to make it happen, which means that changes are not made very often. Finally, even when a change is introduced, it may have a very small impact on the overall management accounting procedures used by the enterprise. So, overall accounting rules and procedures are relatively enduring structures (Anderson 1995; Granlund and Malmi 2002; Fujimura 2012; Quinn 2014).

5 That is, costs are defined in terms of the going enterprise, so that what constitutes costs are reoccurring expenses derived from the use of reproducible intermediate inputs, labor skills, and fixed investment goods. Such costs are objective and irreducible to a homogeneous unit such as labor or subjective disutility. Moreover, non-produced items that are not utilized on a reoccurring basis are not costs but expenses that are charged against revenue. Therefore, scarce factor inputs are not costs in the context of the going enterprise – that is, the category of costs of the going enterprise is conceptually distinct from the category of costs in neoclassical theory in that the former is not based on relative scarcity.

6 'Direct' inputs/costs refer to inputs/costs that are directly associated with the production of a good, while 'overhead' inputs/costs refer to inputs/costs that are not directly associated with the production of a good. Direct and overhead inputs/costs are not the same as 'variable' and 'fixed' inputs/costs (as in neoclassical theory); accountants and business enterprises generally did not use those latter concepts until the latter part of the twentieth century, when the accounting profession began acquiring them from economics. While not identical, they are in practice pretty much the same, and for theoretical purposes with regard to pricing and the determination of profits, the differences are not important. Thus, for this book, direct and overhead inputs/costs will be used.

7 The costing of unit direct costs (or what is called 'direct' or 'marginal' costing) is done only under special circumstances: when the accounting procedures employed do not permit more detailed costing to take place, or when management is not interested in a better understanding of its costs. But in general, enterprises undertake total (absorption) costing, which includes both direct and overhead costs.

8 There are two types of costing procedures: historical-estimated and standard costing. In the former, costs are determined by methods that range from a perfunctory guess to a very careful computation based upon past experience; in either case, past costs are used as the basis to determine the costs of a good that will be produced in the future. In the latter, costs are determined in advance of production by a process of scientific fact-finding that utilizes both past experience and controlled experiments. However,

in spite of the differences, both historical-estimated and standard costing arrive at the costs of producing a good that will be used in setting the price in the same way. Hence, in this chapter reference will only be made to costing.

9 In recent decades various studies have noted the relative stability in management accounting practices used by enterprises. They show that enterprises slowly make marginal changes while retaining basic practices, even when faced with a changing environment. Other studies on the adoption of new cost accounting methods, such as activity-based costing, indicates that there is often resistance inside enterprises to significant changes in the status quo. The reasons range from perceived lack of benefits coming from the new methods relative to the costs of implementation to the realization that the new methods will change power positions within the enterprise and/or result in redundancies. Moreover, it is sometimes found that the new methods, when introduced alongside existing methods, perform no better than the existing method in calculating, say, accurate product costs. In short, enterprises retain the same management accounting practices for decades at a time (Staubus 1990; Emore and Ness 1991; Bright et al. 1992; Anderson 1995; Malmi 1997; Innes, Mitchell, and Sinclair 2000; Granlund 2001; Major and Hopper 2005).

10 Allocations to the depreciation fund often varied directly with profitable years (Stone 1973–74; Edwards 1980).

11 There was another controversy that involved whether 'interest' on the paid in 'capitalized value' of the enterprise was a cost or not. In some partnerships, interest charges were included as costs in order "to ensure that individuals were properly remunerated for differential capital contributions rather than to produce a more accurate costing of business operations" (Edwards 1989, 312; also see Stone 1973–74; Hudson 1977). While this case seems to be the basis of mainstream arguments that includes normal profits as costs, generally interest charges are not considered costs.

12 This means that fixed investment goods are not seen as commodities to be sold to raise revenue, but as a cost of production to be recovered.

13 The old method of expensing the purchases of fixed investment goods meant that the capitalized value of the enterprise did not alter. Consequently, the concept of the rate of profit under this system had no precise meaning, making it useless as a theoretical concept. Although the introduction of depreciation partially redresses this issue, the use of historical cost makes the rate of profit a backward looking concept, hence not well-suited for making strategic decisions.

14 For evidence of the three types of plants, see Lee (1986).

15 There is a difference between the production process delineated in terms of a batch or amount of output and the production of product lines that remain stable for long periods of time relative to those that change seasonally, annually, or with every change in fashion. These latter product lines are considered 'custom or batch' products, while the former are mass produced-bulk products. For further discussion of custom-batch products, see Scranton (1991); for mass produced-bulk products, see Chandler (1977; 1990) and Hounshell (1984).

16 Being task complements implies that fixed investment goods, differentiated labor skills, and material inputs combine together to complete the task and ultimately produce the final good. However, they do so at different conceptual levels: one as a material throughput, a second as a reoccurring technical process, and a third as repeating labor skills. As a result, what does not happen is that fixed investment goods and labor become physically incorporated into the 'output' in completing the task and, thereby, are at the same time quantitatively reduced in some manner. If this were possible, then the fixed investment goods, labor, and the material inputs would be homogeneous in essence and hence quantitatively comparable (Mir-Artigues and Gonzalez-Calvert 2007, 8).

17 While each elementary process generates an 'output,' it may or may not be 'marketable.' It is assumed that the final output of the sequences of elementary processes is the only marketable output from the perspective of the business enterprise.

18 The scale of production is independent of the amount of output. That is, if the production process is changed in order to have a larger batch of output, then the number of the production process needed to produce a particular amount or level of output could be less. So 'large scale production' does not necessarily imply a large amount of output.

19 The production process uniquely determines the elements in the vector, but the vector does not uniquely identify a production process (Scazzieri 1993, 84).

20 This characterization of the PS qua production process sweeps away the property of single (or multiple) input-output variation – that is, the marginal products for intermediate and labor inputs do not exist. Since an increased flow rate of output requires additional plant segments, it is impossible to argue that an increase in the flow rate of output can occur by simply increasing one, some, or all the direct intermediate and labor inputs, and/or fixed investment goods (Morroni 1992, 28–31). Consequently, not only are marginal products, the law of variable proportions, and 'convexity' inapplicable to this analysis, but the traditional distinction between fixed and variable inputs is also undermined.

21 It is possible that technically different plant segments can produce different flow rates of output, but this will be ignored.

22 This assumes that input prices do not change with changes in the usage of the inputs. But if p_i is based on the quantities of the i-th intermediate input bought and used in the production of the good, then as k_{mue} increases, p_i declines and hence EADC declines even though the production coefficients do not change.

23 It is possible that the segmented and hybrid plants have different relative costs at different degrees of capacity utilization. Thus, it is possible that all plants are in use but at different k_{mue}. While it complicates the theory of costs of the business enterprise, it does not fundamentally alter it (Westfield 1955).

24 This differentiation between plants is not compatible with the neoclassical economies of scale that is based on proportional increases in the inputs and the absence of technological change and new knowledge (Gold 1981).

25 This statement may have exceptions if changes in wage rates, profit mark-ups, technology, and social conditions of work generate an array of input prices and wage rates that results in $PADC_{k+1} < PADC_k$. This reordering of vintage plants is analogous to the reswitching of techniques of production in the capital controversies.

26 The concept of vintage plants bears a strong resemblance to the different fertility of plots of land in Ricardo's theory of extensive rent, and the increase in EADC as k_{mue} increases is akin to the Ricardian expansion of the production of corn to less and less fertile land.

4   The business enterprise

Agency and causal mechanisms

In this chapter, we will first deal with the causal process through which the business enterprise sets prices (that is, costing and pricing), and the properties of going concern prices; the outcome is a substantive theory of pricing, which is equivalent to and substitute for the mainstream marginalist analysis of pricing.[1] The remainder of the chapter deals with investment decisions and decisions regarding wage rates, employment, and output; it concludes with the delineation of the 'formal' theory of the going, acting business enterprise that is based upon the substantive theories of production, costs, pricing, investment, and employment, output, and wage rates.[2]

Costing and pricing

For the going enterprise to engage in economic activity, such as setting prices, making investment decisions, and hiring workers, involves decision-making by an acting person or a collective of acting persons. This decision-making activity is a causal mechanism. In the case of setting or changing the price of a product line, this causal mechanism involves acting pricing administrators that determine prices and administer them to the market. Pricing consists of institutionalized patterns of behavior (that is, micro-structures) known as accounting, costing, and pricing procedures and acting administrators that make decisions in this structural context with regard to costs, profit mark-ups, and prices. And the prices that emerge from the pricing process have specific properties. To set or change the price of a product line, the acting pricing administrators of a business enterprise – such as its owner and a committee of business administrators or managers drawn from different departments and levels of management – engage in a two-set process: first involving *costing* the product and then *pricing* it.

Costing involves the use of the enterprise's management accounting procedures to determine the product's EADC, ASE, AEE, and EATC at a budgeted flow rate of output. However, what costs are included in costing the product varies across enterprises depending on the type of procedures used. In particular, enterprises could use historical data from the past year or past few years; or it could use a form of standard costing in which the quantity and quality of the inputs used in the production of a product line are subject to careful scrutiny. Either approach works well for direct costs, but overhead costs, especially in enterprises with multi-product lines pose more of a problem. In such enterprises, the various components of overhead costs are often commonly used. For much of the nineteenth and twentieth centuries, costing systems used a volume-based driver such as direct labor hours for overhead cost allocation across the product lines. This worked well enough as long as the number of product lines was not too great. However, in recent decades some enterprises have increased their product lines significantly; as a result, a product's consumption of the common overhead resources may not be strictly related to units produced. Moreover, in recent decades the portion of overhead costs in many products' total costs has also increased significantly, in part because of the decline in direct labor costs. This has made the conventional costing procedures for some product lines less and less appropriate for providing accurate cost information to the pricing administrators.

Activity-based costing (ABC), which emerged in the 1980s, is a method of assigning indirect or overhead costs according to the factors that cause the costs. Conventional costing procedures are familiar, easy, and inexpensive to implement, but the information obtained may not be very accurate, whereas the ABC procedure solves this problem but is expensive and time-consuming to implement. Given the strengths and weaknesses of the two costing systems, pricing administrators utilize as appropriate both of them with varying degrees of the scope and sophistication, although ABC is still used by a minority of enterprises (Stratton, Lawson, and Hatch 2009). Once the product's costs to be used for costing have been identified, it is necessary to determine their average values; this requires the use of the tool called the budgeted flow rate of output. That is, since EADC, ASE, AEE, and EATC vary with different flow rates of output, it is necessary for pricing to select a particular budgeted flow rate of output if product costs for pricing are to be determined before production takes place and the actual costs of production are known. The budgeted rate selected could be practical capacity, normal capacity, or current year's budgeted capacity, with the latter being in recent decades most widely used.[3]

Utilizing costing procedures that are derived from the management accounting procedures used by the enterprise, the pricing administrators determine the product's budgeted costs. With the budgeted costs administratively determined, the pricing administrators select a profit mark-up to be applied to costs to set the price.[4] This pricing procedure means that the price of the good is set before the good is produced and exchange takes place. The pricing administrators then take their administratively determined price and administer it to the market – that is, the administered price is determined outside the market and then imposed upon it.[5] However, whatever method is used, the costs used as the basis for setting the price are based on a pre-determined flow rate of output, rather than the actual flow rate of output.

Since prices are determined through costing procedures and the profit mark-up, pricing procedures can be distinguished by the emphasis they place on costing relative to the mark-up. In other words, one group of the pricing procedures is predicated on different costing procedures, taking the mark-up simply as given (or customary), whereas a second group is defined according to the profit mark-up processes, taking their relevant cost base as given whatever the costing procedure is. Thus, it is necessary to differentiate between the two pricing procedures and identify them as *costing-oriented pricing* and the *mark-up-oriented pricing* respectively[6] (Gu and Lee 2012; Lee 2013b).

Costing-oriented pricing

Costing-oriented pricing is predicated primarily on various costing procedures. The basic foundation, which has been in existence since the early 1700s, is the calculation of budgeted enterprise average direct costs ($EADC_B$); but the determination of average overhead costs (AOHC) is another matter. There are three general types of costing-oriented pricing: direct cost pricing, total cost pricing, and ABC cost pricing. Direct cost pricing consists of marking up $EADC_B$ to set the price, with the mark-up being sufficient to cover overhead costs and produce profits:

$$\text{Direct cost pricing: } p = EADC_B (1 + k) \tag{4.1}$$

where p is the price of a product or a single product line; $EADC_B$ is the enterprise average direct costs at the budgeted flow rate of output; and k is the mark-up for overhead costs and profits.

Total cost pricing has two forms: one is to mark up $EADC_B$ to cover overhead costs, which gives $EATC_B$, and then apply a profit mark-up to $EATC_B$ to set a price; the other applies the profit mark-up directly to $EATC_B$ to set the price:

$$\text{Total cost pricing: } p = EADC_B (1 + z)(1 + r) \text{ or}$$
$$p = EATC_B (1 + r) \tag{4.2}$$

where z is the mark-up for overhead costs based on budgeted output; and
        r is the mark-up for profits

Finally, ABC cost pricing is formulated in the following manner:

$$\text{ABC cost pricing: } p = EADC_B \left(1 + \sum_{i=1}^{n} x_i\right)(1 + r) \tag{4.3}$$

where x_i is the mark-up to cover an allocated part of i-th overhead cost according to the product's consumption of the activity that causes the overhead cost.

It should be noted that the difference between total cost pricing and ABC cost pricing lies in the specific method by which to determine the mark-up for the overhead costs. With more than one product line which a business enterprise produces, total cost pricing allocates the total amount of the overhead costs to each product based on each product's budgeted volume which may be irrelevant to the causes of the overhead costs, whereas ABC cost pricing utilizes each product's relative consumption of each overhead cost to allocate the total amount of the overhead costs among its products.

Mark-up-oriented pricing

Mark-up-oriented pricing procedures are differentiated according to a variety of profit mark-up processes after presupposing a cost base such as $EADC_B$ or $EATC_B$, and regardless of what its costing procedure is. The best-known mark-up-oriented pricing procedures are fair rate of return pricing and target rate of return pricing. In addition, there is also a refined pricing procedure, which is divided into three sub-groups: product based mark-up pricing, competitor motivated mark-up pricing, and class induced mark-up pricing.

Firstly, fair rate of return pricing is a pricing procedure in which the mark-up is predetermined by convention or a fair rate of profit, based on the industry norms – that is, customs and practices established within an industry and with which enterprises comply. These customs and practices are known by the industry, and the industry will expect that all business and trading conform to these customs and practices. In the context of pricing, these customs and practices are manifested as 'acceptable' and 'expected' mark-ups.

Secondly, target rate of return pricing is a pricing procedure in which the mark-up is determined exclusively by organizational conditions. Suppose that a business enterprise installs plant equipment to produce a product and aims to generate a desired flow of funds from that investment for whatever goals or objectives it wants to achieve. A possible target rate of return pricing consists of marking up $EATC_B$ by a certain percentage to generate a volume of profits at budgeted output that will produce a specific rate of return with respect to the value of the enterprise's capital assets connected with the production of the product. That is, given the value of the capital assets (VCA) associated with the production of the product, the enterprise wants to obtain a specific target rate of return (TRR) on those assets. Therefore, the profits required to meet the target rate of return is TRR × VCA = target profits, π_t. To incorporate the target profit figure into the price, π_t is first divided by budgeted output (q_B) to get the targeted costing margin, and then divided by $EATC_B$ to get the targeted profit mark-up (θ):

$$\text{Target rate of return pricing:} \quad p = EATC_B\left(1 + \frac{\pi_t}{q_B \times EATC_B}\right) \quad (4.4)$$

$$= EATC_B(1 + \theta)$$

Given the targeted profit mark-up, if the business enterprise produces at budgeted output, enough profits will be generated to attain the desired target rate of return on the capital assets. Because actual output can differ from budgeted output, the enterprise will not always achieve its target rate of return or desired profits, some-times being above it and other times being below it over the business cycle.[7]

Thirdly, product based mark-up pricing is a pricing procedure in which the mark-up is adjusted to reflect characteristics or life cycles of products. Product charac-teristics have much to do with complementarity and supplementarity between the enterprise's products; thus, enterprises sometimes use a joint mark-up rate for a group of complementary products. Product life cycles are mostly determined by technological changes and market growth; hence, the mark-up rates of unfash-ionable products are occasionally curtailed. This procedure is closely related to specific pricing practices or tactics such as price bundling and skimming pricing.

Fourthly, competitor motivated mark-up pricing is a pricing procedure in which the mark-up is set mainly to be responsive to the strategies of competitors in the same industry. Depending on the price leader-follower relations, business enter-prises position themselves in setting mark-up rates and thus prices. Practically, there are four possible tactics: leader pricing, parity pricing, low-price supplier, and opportunistic pricing. In the majority of industries, large business enterprises set the rules of the game, leaving smaller ones with limited price discretion and no other option than to follow the leader's (or leaders') pricing initiatives, since the price leader tends to maintain its superiority in technology.

Lastly, class induced mark-up pricing is a pricing procedure in which the mark-up differs primarily according to its primary target class. Frequently, business enterprises aim to create markets for their products and set desirable mark-up rates by manipulating the purchasing habits of their consumers – for example, developing conspicuous consumption by the upper class – by means of pricing practices such as perceived-value pricing, price signaling, and image pricing. They sometimes try to increase their total profits by providing discounts for the lower class – that is, expanding their customer group – in the case of reference pricing and second-market discounting (Rothschild 1947; Eichner 1976; Lee 1998; Downward 1999; Hall, Walsh, and Yates 2000; Forman and Lancioni 2002; Indounas 2009; Rao and Kartono 2009).

Going concern prices

The administered prices set by enterprises have properties that are quite different from prices determined in the market. The first is that the administered price is not based on or related to actual costs, and immediate or current market forces do not affect the profit mark-up. That is, irrespective of the pricing procedures used by enterprises, the shape of the product's average direct cost curve or its average total cost curve is immaterial for pricing purposes. This is because the costs used for pricing are determined prior to production and are based on budgeted output. Con-sequently, the price is based on budgeted costs, while actual costs vary inversely around it as actual output varies around budgeted output.

The second property is that administered prices are stable within the pricing period in that they remain unchanged for extended periods of time, many trans-actions, and for short-term or momentary variations in sales.[8] This 'intrinsic' stability is based on the pricing procedures used by the enterprise where costs are based on budgeted rather than actual costs, and the profit mark-up is given for the pricing period and relatively stable over a number of pricing periods. Consequently, administered prices are neither exchange-specific nor responsive to immediate variations in sales.[9] This implies that markets that have stable, budgeted, cost-based prices are not organized like auction markets or oriental bazaars, where the retailer engages in individual price negotiation for each transaction. Rather, an enterprise that desires to enter these unorganized markets must first announce a price for its product and then enter into direct buyer-seller interaction to obtain sales. Since buyer-seller interactions take place both simultaneously and through time, business enterprises find that stable prices are cost-efficient in terms of selling costs, reduce the threat of price wars, and facilitate the establishment of goodwill relationships with customers.[10]

Following from the stability property, the third property of administered prices is that they are not related to any specific quantity of sales and, hence, are not set to achieve a specific volume of sales. In studies of price determination, business enterprises state that variations of their prices within practical limits, given the prices of their competitors, produce virtually no change in their sales, and that variations in the market price, especially downward, produce little, if any, changes in market sales in the short-term. Moreover, when the price change is significant enough to result in a significant change in sales, the decline in profits has been enough to persuade enterprises not to try the experiment again. Consequently, there is a disjuncture between price and actual output.

The fourth property is that administered prices can change over time – that is, over a sequence of pricing periods. The empirical evidence shows that enterprises maintain pricing periods of three months to a year in which their administered prices remained unchanged; and then, at the end of the period, they decide on whether to alter them. The factors that are most important to enterprises in this regard are changes in labor and material costs, changes in the mark-up for profit, and changes in budgeted output. Factors prompting the enterprises to alter their profit mark-ups include short-term and long-term competitive pressures, the stage that the product has reached in its life cycle, and the need for profits. Moreover, since budgeted output is administratively determined, it is possible for the enterprise to alter it cyclically over the business cycle, resulting in the $EATC_B$ increasing in the downturn and decreasing in the upturn. If profit mark-ups remain constant, then the enterprise would be setting counter-cyclical prices. Consequently, administered prices can change from one pricing period to the next in any direction, irrespective of the state of the business cycle. Prior to 1980, evidence shows that within short periods of time (such as two-year intervals), changes in costs dominated price changes, whereas over longer periods of time changes in the mark-up played a more important role. However, since 1980, it appears that when costs decline, assuming no change in budgeted output, enterprises increase their profit mark-ups, with the result that prices are quite stable across a number of pricing periods (Lee 1998; Blinder et al. 1998; Álvarez et al. 2006; Fabiani et al. 2007).

The stability of administered prices within the pricing period (due to the intrinsic nature of administered pricing procedures) and across a number of pricing periods (due to the extrinsic nature of enterprises' capabilities to simultaneously adjust in opposite directions of budgeted costs and profit mark-ups) is a pervasive feature of capitalist economies and a fundamental property of administered prices as they relate to the going nature of the business enterprise. So, the fifth and final property of administered prices is their role in the reproduction of the business enterprise – that is, prices enable the enterprise to engage in sequential acts of production over time and thereby reproduce itself and grow. This property can be illustrated using a very simple model. First, assume that the enterprise has its complement of plant and equipment, and that it produces a single product line at budgeted output for the pricing period. Now for production to occur, the enterprise must have enough working capital on hand to procure the necessary amount of direct and overhead material and labor inputs. Once obtained, production occurs, the output sold, and the revenue collected. If the amount of total revenue received at the end of the pricing period equals the initial expenditure of working capital for the inputs, the enterprise can repeat the process for each succeeding production period, thus 'reproducing' the enterprise on an ongoing basis as long as the original sum of money advanced is returned – see Table 4.1. Thus, the enterprise can only engage in sequential acts of production at the budgeted output if total costs equal total revenue, or, more specifically, the enterprise sets its price equal to its budgeted average total costs: $p = EATC_B$.[11] The model can be extended beyond the simple reproduction of the enterprise by postulating that total revenue is greater than total costs at the budgeted flow rate of output. That is, if $TR_B > TC_B$, then $p = EATC_B (1 + r)$ which will produce a profit at budgeted output that can be used to expand the enterprise's scale of production.

One implication of the model is that for an enterprise to grow and expand over pricing periods, it must mark up its costs when determining its price, where the mark-up becomes, as noted above, a strategic variable for reproduction and growth. A second implication is that if price declines are not tied to declines in budgeted costs, the targeted or desired mark-up is not attained and hence the going nature of the enterprise is threatened. In particular, if a price decline fell below $EATC_B$, the enterprise would cease to be a going concern.

Table 4.1 Simple reproduction of the business enterprise

Production period 1:	$M_{WC} \rightarrow TC_B \rightarrow P_B \rightarrow TR_B$
Production period 2:	$M_{WC} \rightarrow TC_B \rightarrow P_B \rightarrow TR_B$
. . .	
Production period n:	$M_{WC} \rightarrow TC_B \rightarrow P_B \rightarrow TR_B$

Notes: M_{wc} is the cash advanced in the form of working capital; TC_B is total costs at budgeted output; P_B is production at budgeted output; and TR_B is the total revenue at budgeted output.

Together, the five properties transform the administered price into a going concern price. A going concern price is one that embodies the enterprise's multi-temporal, open-ended strategies, collectively known as the enterprise's pricing policy that will allow it to continue it as a going concern. But if price instability emerges via competition with other enterprises resulting in price declines without commensurate cost declines, the enterprise will be pushed towards bankruptcy. Consequently, going enterprises within a market are driven to establish market institutions that would eliminate the problem of destructive price competition and establish a stable market price and an orderly market (Wood 1975; Eichner 1976; Harcourt and Kenyon 1976; Çapoğlu 1991; Sawyer 1995; Downward and Reynolds 1996; Lee 1998; Downward 1999).

Pricing and the profit mark-up

The final aspect of the pricing mechanism that needs to be dealt with concerns the profit mark-up used for setting the administered price. To set prices, the pricing administrators use a profit mark-up. The determination of this mark-up and its selection in pricing constitutes what can be thought of as a profit mark-up causal mechanism. Its role in pricing makes it a sub-causal mechanism with regard to pricing. On the other hand, its relationship to investment and the flow of profits or retained earnings makes it a complete causal mechanism by itself. Although profit mark-up is central to heterodox microeconomics (and to macroeconomics), there exists no empirically grounded explanation of its determination and its use in pricing. Consider the following facts:

1 Profit mark-ups do not change quickly – mostly they change over a series of accounting periods (excluding price wars).
2 Changes in profit mark-ups are not due to fluctuations in market sales/demand.
3 Changes in profit mark-ups can be due to changes in competitive pressures.
4 The determination of the profit mark-up is based on competition and custom.
5 In some cases, profit mark-ups used for a product are borrowed from another product.
6 Changes in the profit mark-up are sometimes considered at the same time costs have changed and changes in the price are being considered.

If we are to delineate a profit mark-up causal mechanism, we would first need to delineate its structures – demand structures and institutional patterns of behavior such as accounting, uses of profits regarding the enterprise as a going concern, and uses of profits for social purposes. The next thing is to identify the administrators that determine the profit mark-up and delineate how they make their decisions. The final step is to put it all together to delineate the causal mechanism. One point to note is that the profit mark-up and its determination is dependent on decisions about the use of profits and this use of profits is largely dependent on investment decisions and dividend decisions.

Market governance and market prices

Because the going enterprise exists in markets with other competing enterprises, competitive conditions may generate market prices that seriously affect the going enterprise's ability to reproduce and expand. That is, since they have capabilities of setting their own prices and engage in other competitive activities, going enterprises have the ability to inflict unacceptable consequences upon competitors. In particular, they have the ability to eliminate positive net cash flows, insofar as the cash flows are derived from, or depend upon, activities in the markets in which they participate. Competition between enterprises in the production and the sale of goods involves the use of these capabilities in the attempt to make a profitable volume of sales in the face of the offers of other enterprises selling identical or closely similar products. Aspects of competition include advertising, service, product development, and price. The combination of capabilities to affect market transactions and competition creates the all too real possibility of price wars and destructive competition. So, given the immediate impact a price war has on the enterprise's profit mark-ups and hence cash flow, enterprises are driven to establish market governance organizations that attempt to eliminate the problem of destructive price competition and establish a stable market price: going enterprises are always in search of orderly markets through collective, cooperative action.

Organizations that engage in market governance and regulate competition include trade associations, cartels, open price associations, price leadership, and government regulatory commissions; in addition, governments enact legislation that also regulates competition.[12] Their primary role is to set a market price that will be a going concern price for at least most of the enterprises in the market. In virtually all instances, the market governance organizations use the same costing and pricing procedures as do business enterprises to set the market price, but with the caveat that some, most, or all of them will have to adjust their profit mark-ups in order to set the same price.[13] Hence, the pricing equation for a market is not significantly different from an enterprise pricing equation (Lee 1998). We will discuss pricing and prices in the context of competition and market power in Chapter 5 and of market governance in Chapter 6.

Investment

As discussed in the previous section, the price-setting mechanism within the going enterprise is closely linked to other sub-mechanisms (such as, profit mark-up determination mechanism and cost accounting procedures) and structures (such as, the structure of costs embodying production technology/capacity of the going enterprise, and the organizational structure of the business enterprise). It is also noted earlier that pricing is tied up with investment and financing (or the use of profits/retained earnings). In this section, we deal with enterprise investment decisions.

Long-range planning

Long-range planning is a structural activity assisting decision-making. By structural activity it is meant a reoccurring or institutional pattern of activity within the business enterprise. Long-range planning is a type of planning for periods in excess of one year, which encompasses all functional areas of the business, and is effected within the existing and long-term future framework of economic, social, and technological factors. When initially established, most entrepreneurs do not engage in long-range planning *per se*, but as their enterprise grows, various factors push them towards establishing a specific group of employees who engage in long-range planning. The following are the internal conditions to an enterprise necessitating the development of long-range planning.

Trend to industrial decentralization. A formal structure is required to coordinate and relate decentralized corporate planning efforts among many relatively autonomous and functionally integrated divisions. Underlying this change is the increased scope and magnitude of enterprise operations and the greater complexity and diversity of the product mix. The existence of a decentralization policy, coupled with growth and diversification, stimulates the need for the establishment and centralization of long-range planning functions. Approaching stagnation in profit divisions and the change from a homogeneous one-industry enterprise to a diversified decentralized administrative structure enterprise further motivates the desire to develop a far-future planning effort.

Enterprise growth and complexity. In the case of a highly divisionalized enterprise, there is a tendency for each division to optimize its own operations and plans as it understands them without full knowledge of the corporate activity directed toward the same goal. When the enterprise is small, this coordination is relatively simple and effective; as the enterprise grows, it is more and more time-consuming for the top management to perform this function unaided; a gradual evaluation to more formalized handling of this responsibility is to be expected. Thus, the long-range planning effort effected by a staff agency evolves along with the growth and complexity of the enterprise.

Internal dissatisfaction with decentralized units and enterprise profit margins. Over-concentration of sales in one general product line or a need for growth and diversification at an accelerated rate to overcome the depressing effect of the declining sales of one product motivates the need for long-range planning.

In addition, there exist other internal conditions that require the development of long-range planning, such as growing obsolescence of equipment, aging of key executive personnel and ultimate retirement of founders, and prudent allocation of resources for strategically selected enterprise sponsored research and development programs.

The business enterprise also faces external factors, such as competitive elements, production techniques, and trade union influences, that push the enterprise towards long-range planning. Let us briefly elaborate on each factor.

Competitive elements. Competitive elements motivating the need for long-range planning include such factors as the expansion of markets and increasing competition, particularly since World War II. Increasing research and development costs incurred in order to keep pace with the dynamic move of technological change, coupled with the rise of research and innovation in all fields of functional works, require a revision of existing planning policies and procedures of the competitive business enterprise. In order to remain competitive, the enterprise is required to increase its research commitments in 'frontier products.' Financial outlays involved for the research and development programs thus become so huge that long-range planning becomes necessary. So research and development expenditures involved are compatible to the probabilities of the pay-off. The decline in funding for traditional products, coupled with an increasing product obsolescence and an increased demand fostered by an expansion of markets, makes a longer view mandatory for business units. As technology develops and products become more complex, the period required for product development lead time increases; product substitutes are offered with increasing frequency both from domestic and foreign competitors. Higher capital costs are incurred and profit margins are reduced accordingly. Collateral with these changes, the business unit increases in size and complexity and the number and rapidity of major changes affecting business increases. Business becomes more competitive depending upon (1) diversification by other enterprises; (2) saturation of markets and excess capacity; (3) competitors' innovations, improvements, and new strategies; (4) foreign production; and (5) increasing size and term of capital commitments.

Production techniques. Increasing mechanization and automation, stimulated by technological influences in manufacturing methods and processes, requires long-range planning by management groups before committing the large capital outlay required to support these programs.

Trade union influence. Trade union contracts combined with growing fringe benefits, provisions for guaranteed annual wages, and contributions for supplemental unemployment benefits necessitate long-range planning for labor costs.

Another factor explaining the attention to long-range planning is that financial analysts in search of growing companies react favorably to situations where management has attempted to forecast the specific shape and scope of potential growth, and then take positive action in anticipation of future demands. The fact that some of the leading corporations in the United States, in particular, developed a philosophy of long-range planning no doubt forced competitors to do likewise in order to compete adequately.

As a result of the need for planning for dealing with the unknown, enterprises generally construct a set of long-range plans – such as, a best long-range plan, an alternative long-range plan, and a growth and contractions long-range plan – and engage in continuous long-range planning.

The enterprise undertakes two kinds of long-range planning. The first kind consists of activities that operate in the present but also has a significant impact on the enterprise's future. The most significant of these is *price setting*, especially with respect to the determination of the profit mark-up. The procedures used to set the price, especially the cost aspect of the price, are originally determined by the central office and then are 'mechanically' used by the lower level managers when setting and changing the price. Likewise, the profit mark-up is determined by the central office and then routinely used by the lower management in price setting. It should also be noted that lower management handles price changes even if it involves changes in the profit mark-up if it falls within agreed upon competitive conditions, such as meeting the prices of competitors.

The second kind of long-range planning deals mainly with activities that concern the enterprise's future. Consequently, it is a function of the central office, although the actual planning is generally undertaken by a sub-committee that includes individuals from the areas of marketing, engineering, economics, management, statistics, finance, and production. The purpose of the sub-committee is to determine which line of activity the firm should allocate its profits in order to maintain itself as a growing concern. Some of the activities include investment in existing commodity lines, creation of new commodity lines, diversification, and forward and backward integration via enterprise mergers and acquisitions. The business enterprise is also concerned with major changes of profit mark-up on existing and new products when such changes have significant impact on the enterprise's future.

Investment decisions

Financing investment decisions from profits or retained earnings puts pressure on knowing costs accurately. That is to say, since enterprises fund investment projects internally, they need to manage costs and hence put an emphasis on accurate cost accounting; careful cost records are to be maintained of capital construction (Fleischman and Parker 1997).

In the nineteenth century, some enterprises financed new/expanding investment by calling on partners to supply more capital or going to the financial markets. Profits, on the other hand, were simply paid out in dividends, while at the same time repairs and replacement investment were paid directly out of revenue. However, this inhibits the enterprise as a going concern in that it does not have direct access/control over its earnings/profits for expansionary purposes (Edwards 1980; 1986).

New investment expenditures in the nineteenth century, if paid for from revenue generally, were not capitalized for the enterprises. This means that value of capital assets used in production had no meaning and, hence, the rate of profit had no meaning. Enterprises that financed new investment expenditures from revenue/earnings meant that profits were under-reported. But it also meant that the enterprise did not incur debts that could hurt them (Edwards and Baber 1979).

Whether the fund for depreciation is established through deductions for revenue (or profits) or it is established via depreciation as a component of costs, enterprises can use it to replace or expand fixed investment goods. That is, the depreciation is viewed generally as a fund to be used for purchasing fixed investment goods irrespective of whether it is replacement or expansion. Generally, the depreciation fund combined with reserves or retained earnings and increases in share capital are used to finance gross/net investment. In some cases, the obsolete/replaced fixed capital equipment is sold and the funds obtained from it are considered part of the funds used to purchase the new fixed investment goods (Napier 1990).

Costing estimates are made of all investment expenditures (and this has been done from at least the 1800s onwards) and it is part of the investment decision-making process. And after the investment decision is made, it is then possible to compare the costing estimate with the actual cost of the investment project. While this post-project comparison is not always done, it has been done from at least since the early 1840s (Fleischman and Parker 1997). In terms of investment decisions, enterprises do not make decisions based on the objective difference between the normal profit rate and the actual profit rate. Rather, other factors are involved, including agency and expectations. The former is used to remove agency (Bortis 1997; 2003).[14]

Notes

1 A theory of pricing is not a theory of prices as it is generally understood. The latter is relevant only when it is thought that prices coordinate and regulate economic activity such as through the mainstream scarcity-based price mechanism or through the classical-Sraffian reproduction-based price mechanism. This point is further discussed in Chapter 7.

2 Editor's note: The section on investment is incomplete, and the sections on financing, wage rates, employment, and output have not been written.

3 Practical capacity of a product line is the amount of output generally attainable from its array of fixed investment goods or 'plant'; normal capacity is the 'average' capacity of the plant utilized during the previous three to five years or over the business cycle; and budgeted capacity is the amount of practical capacity expected to be used in the coming accounting period or year. From the 1700s to sometime after 1970, enterprises used the term normal capacity instead of budgeted capacity. Normal capacity was based on past data and thus considered to be relatively stable. Budgeted capacity, in contrast, suggests that it is responsive to management decision-making and thus could be changed from one pricing period to the next (Hertenstein, Polutnik, and McNair 2006; Brierley, Cowton, and Drury 2006b). While practical capacity appears to be determined independently of expectations and uncertainty, it, like normal capacity, is based on the belief (or the expectations) that the past is a good guide for the future. Thus expectations and uncertainty are directly embedded in the costs derived from the costing procedures. In short, their commonality and importance is that they fix the level of output on which costs are determined. This clearly suggests a disjunctive between price, actual costs, and output

4 The profit mark-up used in pricing is derived from its own causal mechanism that is delineated in the following section.

5 Not all administratively determined prices are based on costing procedures. In the case of destructive price wars, especially associated with rapid technical change and innovation, administrators frequently set and re-set prices without regard to costs. There are, of course, prices that are not administered, such as those found in auction markets and commodity exchanges.

6 For an historical survey of costing and pricing studies and of Post Keynesian approaches to pricing, see Lee (1983; 1984; 1985; 1994; 1998); and also Coutts and Norman (2013).

7 Target rate of return pricing is often tied to the Post Keynesian arguments by Ball (1964), Wood (1975), Harcourt and Kenyon (1976), and Eichner (1976) that investment decisions determine the target mark-up and hence prices – see Lee (1998, 175–184).

8 There exists extensive historical evidence of price stability, which is found in the archival records of business enterprises that date back to the 1760s (Fleischman and Parker 1997).

9 In case of price wars, administered prices become more exchange-specific, like prices in auction markets where retail prices are individually negotiated. However, it must be noted that price wars generally affect only a small part of the transactions and volume of sales in any particular market and the reduction in price is not very large.

10 In many instances, competing enterprises establish market governance organizations, such as trade associations, and press for changes in the legal system that would support their desire for market price stability. This will be discussed in Chapter 6.

11 Since $TC_B = TR_B$ and TR_B = price × budgeted output, then price equals $EATC_B$.

12 Whether the degree of market concentration is high or low or the barriers to entry are significant or not, they have little impact on market governance *per se*; rather, they only affect the organizational form that market governance takes.

13 The evidence on trade associations, cartels, price leadership, and government regulations controlling market competition and regulating prices is so extensive that it is plausible to argue that regulated competition has always existed under capitalism – see Lee (1998, 208, n. 15) for a number of references. For references with an international flavor, see Schaede (2000), Viton (2004), and Connor (2008). This issue will be dealt with in Chapter 6.

14 Editor's note: This section on investment is incomplete. What appears here is long-range planning as a basis of the investment decision-making process, which is inextricably connected to cost-accounting, pricing, and financing. For this issue, I would refer readers to Eichner (1976; 1987a; 1987b), Lee (2011c), Dzarasov (2015), and Jo (2015; 2017), which are in line with what Fred Lee would have developed in this section. It should also be noted that Lee also planned to articulate the link between investment and other causal mechanisms within the enterprise, such as wage, employment, and production decision-making process. These causal mechanisms qua decision-making processes will constitute a heterodox theory of the business enterprise (see a list of readings in Appendix I, Section IV, in this volume).

5   Markets and demand for the social product

Market, industry, and the social provisioning process

All capitalist economies produce a differentiated array of goods and services and they are for the most part exchanged in markets. Because the economy is also a social system of production, market exchange and competitive activities within the market are also social activities. This conceptualization of the market as a social institution does not fit well with mainstream economics, which sees the market as an asocial, natural, timeless entity.

In this chapter, the market and industry is viewed as a social structure qua institution and whose existence is predicated on continuous and sequential transactions of a specific product. The market is also the site of socially structured competition, which means that variations in the social structures result in different kinds of competition within and across markets. It follows that the market must be carefully crafted and competition suitably regulated so that it can be a safe home for going enterprises. With this concept of the market and industry, we shall also deal with the structure of market demand.

Market as an institution for social provisioning

As a structure, the market consists of a set of property rights, a social and physical infrastructure that facilitates transactions, legal rules and informal practices that facilitate transactions, and legal rules and practices that specify how enterprises are organized and engage with each other in the market. The rules define who can transact with whom and guarantee that the conditions surrounding the transactions are met. The rules must be established as related to shipping, billing, insurance, and exchange of money. These conditions are important, not just within societies, but become even more important across societies. Clearly, states are essential to the creation and enforcement of the rules of exchange.

Laws specify how enterprises cooperate, compete, or merge. These laws, generally called anti-trust, competition, or anti-cartel laws, are contested as well. All advanced industrial societies have some form of these laws. This contested context occurs over their evolution from proposal, to passage, to enforcement, and to judicial interpretation. In addition, there are also views within enterprises about what constitutes legal and illegal behavior of enterprises vis-à-vis one another. This leads to the issue of competition and market control. Enterprises in markets are interested in controlling their internal organization and their environment so as to be able to ensure their reproduction and growth. In order to do so, enterprises must have a set of understandings of how their world works, which structures their perception of their world and allows them to interpret their world and act. This kind of local knowledge means that enterprises with two different conceptions of control will analyze the same situation in different ways. One can also conceive of a conception of control as a political compromise that management across enterprises uses to stabilize their relations with one another. The purpose of action in a given market is to create and maintain the stable world within and across organizations in the market. This requires a conception of control that implies a cultural view of the world specific to the market and a set of enforcement mechanisms whereby that view is held in place. The state must ratify, help create, or, at the very least, not oppose the conception of the control of markets. The specific form of control will reflect agreement on the principles of internal organization, the tactics for competition and cooperation, and the hierarchy or status ordering of enterprises in the existing market.

Market: defined and delineated

Products within an industry can be distinguished according to their technical (specific use-value) and income dimensions and hence can be considered as well-defined 'islands.' Thus the market is defined conventionally as an abstract concept which collectively denotes all the exchanges of a specific product – that is, an 'island' product – between buyers and sellers irrespective of the quantity involved, value of the exchange, or the time and places the exchanges take place. If this is the case, the market exists simultaneously with the product in abstract and disappears when the product is no longer exchanged. The market is, however, not defined in terms of a specific/actual product or its quantity involved in the exchange, its price, and the time and place of the exchange. But for the sequence of transactions in the market to take place, the enterprises that engage in the transactions must be able to reproduce themselves. Thus the market exists when enterprises are able to derive revenue from the sequential transactions in the market (more on this below).

The strengths and properties of this definition are fourfold. First, because of the income dimension, not all the products within the market need to be technically identical and carry identical price tags; rather, as long as the product fulfills the specific social needs in question and its price is consistent with the particular income class in question, its price and technical specifications can differ from those of the competing products which inhabit the same market. But such differentiation of price and technical specifications has little economic importance since they are the same in the eyes of the market.

Second, because the framework sustains both the ideas of sequential acts of production and enterprise interdependency, products are continually being produced and sold in the markets; conversely, the continual need for products ensures that there is an unbroken demand for the products to be produced for the market. Moreover, because of the flow dimensional nature of the framework, it is easy to envision buyers and sellers coming to the market in an irregular but continuous manner, thus never leaving the market 'empty' of a transaction. In this context, the idea that the market can be cleared has no theoretical basis; rather, the market must be seen as a *non-clearing* market.

Third, closely aligned with the idea of a non-clearing market is that exchanges cannot clear markets. That is, because the framework sustains the idea of non-clearing market, it must reject the notion that exchanges clear the market. Rather, the purpose of exchange must be to ensure that buyers and sellers are always in the market – that is, the continuance of sequential acts of production and exchange.

Lastly, the notion of product differentiation can now be clearly understood and its importance ascertained – a product can be 'differentiated' within a market, but such an endeavor has little economic importance. On the other hand, product differentiation could refer to the creation of a new product/market with a specific social use-value but the same general social use-value and, in this respect, its importance for economics cannot be underestimated. It is in this role that product differentiation becomes somewhat indistinguishable from technical change.

Product types and characteristics of markets

The technical dimension of investment products is derived from the technical specifications of the product to be produced, the existence and technical specifications of the intermediate products to be used in production, the expected flow rate of output to be produced by the investment product, and the organizational structure of the buying enterprise. The technical determinism of the first two attributes is obvious – the investment product's specific use-value must be appropriate for the kinds of product to be produced and for the type of intermediate products to be used since, if the former attribute is not fulfilled, the investment product will not be bought and, if the latter attribute is not fulfilled, the investment product cannot be used efficiently. The expected flow rate of output provides an additional technical characteristic in that investment products are constructed for a minimum and/or maximum flow rate of output and to be most efficient at a particular flow rate of output. Hence the specific use-value of an investment product is closely tied to a narrow range of flow rates of output. Closely aligned to this attribute is the organizational structure of the business enterprise. Since the existing organizational structure of an enterprise is based, in part, on the flow rate of output of each product line individually and collectively, investment products that require amendments or changes to the structure which are more appropriate to or more easily undertaken by enterprises with different flow rates of output will not be bought. Rather, the technical specifications of the investment product to be produced, although affected by the flow rate of output, must be compatible with the existing organizational structure.

The impact of the income dimension on investment products comes about in two complementary ways. First, an enterprise's income restricts it to a particular price class of investment products; second, for a particular species of investment product, the various subspecies products are directed at particular enterprise income levels. The first attribute is easily seen in terms of a small enterprise with its correspondingly small income being prevented from buying investment products with large price tags, while large enterprises with their correspondingly large income being able to buy those same products. The second attribute is easily seen in terms of an enterprise producing a great many subspecies investment products, each of which is designed for a particular enterprise income class. To summarize, investment products can be identified as those output-products that are used to produce a product and can be delineated by its technical characteristics and the enterprise income class in which it resides.

The technical and income dimensions of consumption products are similar to those of investment products. Like investment products, the use of consumption products as 'inputs' and the products they use as inputs determine the technical specifications of consumption products, and, hence, specific use-value. That is, consumption products are used to fulfill biological and social needs of the individual and, therefore, must be specified in terms of these needs. For example, the need for housing, clothing, food, medicine, intellectual stimulation, recreation, and the like determines the general use-value for various species of consumption products and, at the same time, prevents all other products from having the same general use-value. In turn, each species of consumption good can be decomposed into subspecies with the results that the specific use-values of the inclusive products become more pronounced. Eventually, the point is reached where the subspecies contains a single product with a specific use-value, which is designed to meet a particular social need. In this manner, the 'use' to which a consumption product is put determines its specific use-value and, thus, is one attribute of its technical dimension. The other attribute of the technical dimension is that a consumption product cannot require a product (as an input) that the economy does not produce. Thus the manner in which a species of need is fulfilled depends upon the kinds of intermediate products produced by the economy.

The income dimension of consumption products is similar to that of investment products. Like enterprises, individuals and families have an income constraint, which restrains them to particular price classes; conversely, a particular species of consumption products will have various subspecies products that are designed for particular consumer income levels. The first attribute is easily seen in terms of low income individuals and families being restricted to low priced consumption products while high income individuals and families have a broader range of products to select from. The second attribute is seen in terms of an enterprise producing a great many subspecies of consumption products with each designed for a particular consumer income class. To summarize, consumption products can be identified as those output-products that are used for consumption and can be delineated by its technical characteristics and the consumer income class in which it resides.

The implications of the above discussions are twofold. First, investment and consumption products are distinct and thus inhabit well-defined markets. However, because of the income dimension, not all the products within the market need to be technically identical and carry an identical price tag; rather, as long as the product fulfills the particular social need in question and its price is consistent with the particular income class in question, its price and technical specifications can differ from those of the competing products which inhabit the same market. But such price differentiation and technical specifications have little economic importance since in the eyes of the market they are the same. This argument undermines the view that product differentiation within a market is an important economic phenomenon to investigate. Rather, the argument suggests that product innovation, creation of new needs, and cheapening of products are the relevant economic phenomena to investigate. Secondly, by tying the output-products to either the production of products or the maintenance and reproduction of the individual and families, their essential contribution to sustaining the economy's ability to engage in continuous sequential acts of production is clearly brought out.

Market and industry

In Chapter 2, the economic activity of the economy was classified in terms of product groups and by the use to which products were put, either as intermediate products or as final demand. However, product groups are not adequate categories for the analysis of microeconomic activity. In particular, the competitive, social, industrial environment of the business enterprise is either more general or more specific than the product groups. Therefore, it is necessary to recast the product group into categories that are appropriate for economic analysis of the activity of the business enterprise. Using the framework of standard industrial classification of economic activity as a basis, the product group will provisionally be recast in terms of industries and markets. This will simply serve as an introduction to markets and industries.

The economic activity of the whole economy can be classified into 2-digit North American Industrial Classification System (NAICS) sectors, such as those in Table 5.1. Each sector contains a number of 3-digit sub-sectors. For example, the NAICS sector 31–33 Manufacturing contains twenty-one sub-sectors – see Table 5.2. In turn, the sub-sector 327 Nonmetallic Mineral Product Manufacturing consists of five industry groups – see Table 5.3. Each industry group contains a 6-digit United States industry. In the case of the industry group 3272, it contains four US industries – see Table 5.4. Finally, each 6-digit industry includes a large number of similar products, each of which constitutes a market – see Table 5.5.

An industry is defined as consisting of business enterprises, which operate 'similar' kinds of production processes (which implies the possession of substantially similar technical resources), produce 'similar' kinds of products (that is, an industry produces products with the same general social use-value), and distributes

Table 5.1 2017 NAICS United States structure

Sector	Name	Subsectors (3-digit)	Industry groups (4-digit)	NAICS industries (5-digit)	6-digit industries		
					U.S detail	Same as 5-digit	Total
11	Agriculture, Forestry, Fishing and Hunting	5	19	42	32	32	64
21	Mining, Quarrying and Oil and Gas Extraction	3	5	11	24	4	28
22	Utilities	1	3	6	10	4	14
23	Construction	3	10	28	4	27	31
31–33	Manufacturing	21	86	180	265	95	360
42	Wholesale Trade	3	19	71	0	71	71
44–45	Retail Trade	12	27	57	17	49	66
48–49	Transportation and Warehousing	11	29	42	25	32	57
51	Information	6	11	25	12	19	31
52	Finance and Insurance	5	11	31	15	26	41
53	Real Estate and Rental and Leasing	3	8	17	11	13	24
54	Professional, Scientific, and Technical Services	1	9	35	20	29	49
55	Management of Companies and Enterprises	1	1	1	3	0	3
56	Administrative and Support and Waste Management and Remediation Services	2	11	29	25	19	44
61	Educational Services	1	7	12	7	10	17
62	Health Care and Social Assistance	4	18	30	16	23	39
71	Arts, Entertainment, and Recreation	3	9	23	3	22	25
72	Accommodation and Food Services	2	6	10	8	7	15
81	Other Services (except Public Administration)	4	14	30	30	19	49
92	Public Administration	8	8	29	0	29	29
	Total	**99**	**311**	**709**	**527**	**530**	**1057**

Source: 2017 NAICS, United States Census Bureau (www.census.gov/eos/www/naics/).

Table 5.2 NAICS sub-sectors of the sector 31–33 Manufacturing

NAICS number	Sub-sector
311	Food Manufacturing
312	Beverage and Tobacco Product Manufacturing
313	Textile Mills
314	Textile Product Mills
. . .	. . .
327	Nonmetallic Mineral Product Manufacturing
. . .	. . .
339	Miscellaneous Manufacturing

Source: 2017 NAICS, United States Census Bureau (www.census.gov/eos/www/naics/).

Table 5.3 NAICS industry groups of the subsector 327 Nonmetalic Mineral Product Manufacturing

NAICS number	Industry group
3271	Clay Product and Refractory Manufacturing
3272	Glass and Glass Product Manufacturing
3273	Cement and Concrete Product Manufacturing
3274	Lime and Gypsum Product Manufacturing
3279	Other Nonmetallic Mineral Product Manufacturing

Source: 2017 NAICS, United States Census Bureau (www.census.gov/eos/www/naics/).

Table 5.4 NAICS industries of the industry group 3272 Glass and Glass Product Manufacturing

NAICS number	Industry
327211	Flat Glass Manufacturing
327212	Other Pressed and Blown Glass and Glassware Manufacturing
327213	Glass Container Manufacturing
327215	Glass Product Manufacturing Made of Purchase Glass

Source: 2017 NAICS, United States Census Bureau (www.census.gov/eos/www/naics/).

Table 5.5 NAICS products of Industry 327211

Antique Glass	Blown Glass	Glass Cast
Colored Glass	Sheet Glass Drawn	Figured Glass
Glass Flat	Float Glass	Flat Glass
Glass Plate	Glass Rolled	Tinted Glass
Glass Window	Glass Wire	

Source: 2017 NAICS, United States Census Bureau (www.census.gov/eos/www/naics/).

them in the same general manner. The significance of this definition of industry is that it delineates the boundaries of the immediate competitive environment of the enterprises producing the similar products. It achieves this in part because it limits the time period in which enterprises can alter their methods of production to be in a position to produce the similar products. However, if the time period is lengthened so that enterprises in neighboring industries could put in place the methods of production and distribution necessary for the production and selling the similar products, then the competitive environment of the business enterprise enlarges. Thus, depending on the time horizon, the competitive environment of the business enterprise can be as narrow as the industry or cover many industries. More concretely, the definition of industry is most congruent with the NAICS 6-digit industry and, as the time horizon increases, the competitive environment of the enterprise expands from similar NAICS 6-digit industries within the same NAICS 5-digit product group and then to similar NAICS 5-digit product groups. There are other significant aspects of this definition of industry: (1) the relationship between products with the same general social use-value can be delineated, and (2) the interdependency between enterprises can now be shown to cross industry lines, not because of input flows, but because of 'profit competition.'

Demand for the social product

The heterodox approach identifies at least four types of demand (corresponding to acting persons and organizations delineated in Chapter 2): demand for consumption goods, for investment goods, for intermediate inputs, and for non-market goods such as government goods and services. There is also a demand for labor power, but heterodox economists consider it quite differently from the demand for goods and services. The factors that influence the demand for the four categories of demand are quite distinct and therefore will be considered separately. In particular, we shall consider consumption demand. The other types of demand will be considered later.[1]

Acting household and consumption demand

As discussed in the previous section, markets for consumption goods are distinguished by their specific use-value and by their income class. We also know that consumers directly purchase a wide range of goods that fall into a variety of markets. Thus what we are interested in is the process by which the consumer decides on the goods to purchase and the quantity of the purchase. We shall deal with this consumption decision-making process in the following.[2]

In our approach, it will be assumed that purchasing decisions are made by the household as a social organization rather than by an asocial person. Consequently, the choice of goods purchased by the household is conditioned by the society in which it is located, by the social upbringing of the heads of the household, and by the current social demands made upon the household. Therefore, the actual choices of the household are both socially conditioned and limited. The socially conditioned choices also have another impact besides choice – that is, they also determine the appropriate quantities for consumption by specifying recipe-like consumption or socially acceptable limits (more on this below). But this does not mean that the purchase of consumption goods and services necessarily only takes place within the household. Individual members of the household do circulate among other non-household members and within an array of non-household functional physical environments. But their purchases are made within the context of household spending decisions. So the household is the basis of spending decisions while the actual purchases and consumption of the goods and services can take place outside the household.

Within the household, the consumption activity is viewed principally as a process of social relations. That is, social relations in consumption activity involve the active pursuit and maintenance of cooperative non-monetary relations or personal encounters with other identifiable persons face to face. In such social relations the joint activity of mutual word-of-mouth interpersonal communication and mutual transfer of certain types of non-market services occurs; physical market goods are used as a means of facilitating such functional social relationships.

In an advanced society, the basic material needs of the individual/household are easily satisfied, at least for the great majority of persons living in those societies. Hence, the choice among consumption goods reflects idiosyncratic preferences rather than just objective needs. Thus individuals consume goods that have both a *use-value (instrumental) dimension* and a *social (ceremonial) dimension*.[3] Idiosyncratic preferences, however, are not innate or inherited. They are the result of a social conditioning or learning process that begins with the acquisition of language and continues throughout the individual's lifetime. First parents and relatives, then friends and acquaintances will instruct the neophyte consumer as to what items are the proper ones to use under varying circumstances. When two adults join together to form a household, they become the more immediate influence on each other's behavior, with any conflicting views necessarily having to be reconciled through some interpersonal or proto-political process. The norms developed through continuous interaction with other human beings are then modified, though only in part by other social mechanisms such as the formal educational system and the mass media. Of course, the choice among different consumption goods never depends solely on a person's prior social conditioning or on current social mores. There is usually some room for individual discretion. Nonetheless, once both the objective and social constraints on the choice among consumption goods have been taken into account, the room for individual discretion may be quite limited. The scope for deliberate, conscious choice is even further narrowed by the need to reduce as much as possible the burden that the multiplicity of available consumption goods places on the household's decision-making capability.[4]

The material needs (preferences) of the household are lexicographically ordered based on the separability and hierarchy of their needs.[5] The material needs of household members are discrete, variegated, and socially conditioned. This means that each household, viewed as a social organization, requires a large number of different items that are not substitutable for one another. What is not possible is that the household has unlimited desire for any particular good or for goods in general: households have satiable needs.[6] The food that must be consumed in order to provide the minimum daily intake of calories will not provide protection against the vagaries of the climate. And among the different types of food consumed, meat does not provide the same nutrients as fruits and vegetables. Likewise, the different means of sheltering do not offer the same protection as a dwelling. In other words, the material needs of households are qualitatively distinct, or separable. It is for this reason that, in specifying the material needs of a household, one must speak in terms of a consumption basket.

The different goods represented by this consumption bundle can be grouped together into discrete categories, with the items that are included within any one category more nearly alike in the need they serve than the items excluded. Fourteen major categories of household consumption can be delineated: housing, fuel and power, food and non-alcoholic drinks, alcoholic drinks, tobacco, clothing and footwear, household goods, household services, personal goods and services, motoring, fares and other travel costs, leisure goods, leisure services, and miscellaneous. Within each major category, various subcategories can be further delineated on the basis of the same rule – namely that the items included are more nearly alike in the need they serve than the items excluded.

An individual household must be able to make a large number of decisions on a continuous basis. Even if one ignores all the other aspects of daily living and focuses only on the question of how any income is to be spent, the number of choices is quite large. This is not to suggest that human beings, organized into households or other types of social groups, are incapable of making a 'rational' choice. The point rather is that it is not easy for them to do so. Even if all the necessary information is at hand – something that cannot always be counted on – it requires time and mental effort to weigh the options and make a choice that everyone within the group will find tolerable. The larger the number of decisions that must be made is, the greater the strain on the group's decision-making capability. The difficulty is compounded with a large number of persons in the household. It is for this reason that, faced with the task of having to make a large number of decisions on a continuous basis, the representative or typical household can be expected to adopt a *two-part behavioral rule*, at least insofar as the purchase of consumption goods is concerned.[7]

The first pat of the rule is that the household will continue to maintain whatever pattern of consumption that it has already established, especially in the case of food, clothing, and other non-durable goods. Only in response to some new information – information that indicates a change either in the household's own circumstances or in the availability of consumption goods – will the household consider altering that pattern. In this way the household is able to minimize the number of conscious, deliberate decisions it needs to make. The second part of the rule is that when new circumstances require that the household consider a possible change in its pattern of consumption, it will transform whatever multiple options it has into a series of discrete, preferably dichotomous, choices. The household can then use whatever power of discrimination it has to rule out a succession of alternatives until only one good – the item that best meets its need – remains to be chosen. In this way, the household is able to follow a relatively simple algorithm, one that does not place too great a strain on its ability to make decisions.

The household is able to transform its multiple options into a series of discrete choices through the three-step sequential decision-making process that it usually follows in selecting any particular basket of goods for purchase at the store. The first step in the process is for the household to determine the maximum amount of income it wishes to spend under each major category of consumption – usually as part of the exercise it goes through in drawing up a household budget. The minimal number of consumption goods that need to be purchased is determined by the adult members of the household at the time they establish a separate household. At the very least they must decide how much to spend on food, clothing, and shelter while still leaving themselves enough income to cover any incidental expenses. Indeed, it is only if there is enough income to meet those minimal needs that a separate household will be established. Thus an initial budget can be assumed to have been determined at the time a separate household is formed, with that budget then revised with every significant change in either the composition of the household or its real income. As long as the budget previously worked out remains in effect, the household needs to make no further decisions as to how its income should be apportioned among the major types of consumption goods. All it has to do is to limit its purchases within any one category to the amount allowed for in the budget.

The second step in the sequential process by which the household decides which items to purchase is for the household to draw up a shopping list prior to visiting the store. Once established, a household will try to keep a certain stock, or inventory, of the goods it needs, replacing those items through periodic visits to the store only as they are used up. In this way, the household can compile a separate shopping list for each of the major types of consumption goods it needs simply by noting what items have been consumed since the last visit to the store that sells those items, with the frequency of any visit to the store depending on how quickly those types of goods are normally used up. Thus the shopping list for food and other household items is likely to be compiled daily or weekly, the shopping list for clothes seasonally, and other shopping lists as items need to be replaced. The compiling of a shopping list is, however, likely to be the occasion for taking into account any new information and, on the basis of that information, for revising the list of items normally purchased. Adding a new item to the shopping list may mean that the household is not able to stay within its budget. In that case the household will find itself back at the first step in the sequential decision-making process – having to decide whether to revise its budget. More typically, however, the household simply purchases the new item instead of some other good, one that, with the inclusion of the new item, need not be purchased as frequently or indeed even at all. It may be that the good dropped from the regular shopping list is a more expensive one. In that case, the household will find a way to reduce the cost of satisfying the present set of needs allowed for within the budget.

The third step in the sequential process is for some member of the household actually to visit the store and then based on the shopping list previously compiled, select specific items. This third step in the process provides one last opportunity for the household's buying plans to be revised. While visiting the store, the member of the household with the responsibility for doing the shopping can take cognizance of any significant change in prices or in the items available for sale. A change in price may cause a revision in buying plans for either of two reasons. If there should be a decline in the price of some good – one that is normally kept in stock by the household but is not on the current shopping list because it does not yet need to be replaced – the person doing the shopping may decide to take advantage of the bargain and add the item to the basket of goods being purchased. Alternatively, if the good was already on the shopping list, there will be money left over either to spend on other items or to be added to the household's unspent cash balances, thereby augmenting its discretionary funds or savings. Conversely, if the price of some good on the list has increased, the person doing the shopping will need to reconsider the tentative choices represented by the shopping list. The person can decide that the higher price is only a temporary deviation from the price that normally prevails and, in anticipation of the price subsequently falling, may simply avoid making a purchase at the present time. To this extent, the person will necessarily be speculating as to what is the normal price of the good. However, the person may instead decide that the higher price is permanent rather than temporary, in which case he or she will need to make some allowance for the loss of real income involved. This can range from going all the way back to the first step in the sequential decision-making and deciding whether to revise the household budget to merely cutting back on the purchase of some other goods so as to stay within the present budgetary limits.[8]

Purchases by the household consist of two kinds – one that is routine or continuous and the second that is non-routine. As a result, the household income is divided into two categories – that which is claimed for the routine purchases and that which is claimed for discretionary (non-routine). To obtain these latter goods, the household must accumulate sufficient funds in the form of liquid assets and/or after the necessary financing has been arranged. While most of the latter items are durable goods of one sort or another, such as a home, a car, or various household furnishings and appliances, they may also include outlays on non-durable goods and services that go beyond the amounts normally budgeted for, such as university tuition or special holidays.

Purchases are primarily affected by money income while price variation has no independent role. Each household can be assumed to have an order of priority in which it selects any one of the items in its consumption basket as its income increases. This order of priority reflects both the household's objective material needs and the types of social conditioning to which the members of the household have been subject. It will therefore depend on: (1) the current stage in the life cycle of the household, as proxied by the number of persons constituting the household and their respective ages; (2) the household's social class, as proxied by the educational background and occupation of its adult members; and (3) the larger culture to which the household belongs, as proxied by nationality, language, religion, and other ethnic characteristics. These three sets of factors suffice to define the household's socioeconomic profile, with the distinguishing features of that profile serving as the parameters of the household's consumption behavior.

Because of the lexicographically ordered material needs, each household with a similar socioeconomic profile can be expected to add a particular item to its normal inventory of consumption goods and thus to its regular shopping list, once its income in real terms reaches a certain threshold limit – that is, once all the items with a higher priority are already being purchased on a regular basis.[9] However, there is no reason to believe that, for all households with the same socioeconomic profile, the threshold level of income at which a particular item of consumption will be added to the shopping list is the same. On the contrary, it seems more reasonable to assume that the threshold level will vary.

This way of conceptualizing the household's decision process, the choice is never whether to purchase more of the same good, but rather whether to purchase some additional item for the first time or whether to purchase some variant of an item already on the household's regular shopping list. It also means that for a given product and price, increasing money incomes could have a positive or negative impact on the demand for the product. If the increase in income for households means that more households can enter the market for the good (due to its income class characteristic) then the demand for the product increases; but if, at the same time, households already buying the goods start to buy a different good because of their increase in income, then the demand for the product could decline. Whether the demand for the product increases or decreases as income increases depends on how that increase in income is distributed and what households get the increase in income. This result means that a good's price and its sales are not connected – that is, there is no law of demand as in neoclassical economics.[10]

This very important result is reinforced by the lack of *substitutability* between goods. That is, lexicographically ordered material needs means that when determining the degree of substitutability between any two consumption goods, it is not enough just to identify the items in broad terms, such as food or clothing. At that level, replacing one consumption good with another is simply not feasible. For substitution to be a real possibility, the various items of consumption need to be specified in sufficient detail. In addition, substitution is only feasible between closely aligned goods on the lexicographic continuum – only the items listed immediately before or after one another are likely to be close substitutes. The greater number of other goods separating any two items, the less likely it is that one good can be used in place of the other to satisfy the same need. Thus, for example, only chicken not a necktie can be considered a substitute for beef – and even then, if the recipe for making stew calls for beef, using chicken may not, as a particular matter, be an option. Indeed, the material requirements or needs of the household may be governed by recipes, not to mention habits. The consequence of this is that, in general, the reduction of a good's price will generally not induce the household to increase its demand for it by substituting it in place of another good.

The lack of substitutability and the importance of money income in determining the household's demand for a particular good means that there is no relationship between a good's price and its sales. Rather, it is variations in money income that is the determinant of market demand and sales. Because money income is linked to effective demand (that is, private investment and government expenditures) and the distribution of income, it is effective demand that drives market sales, not prices.

Structure of market demand and the market price

If we reject the law of demand or the neoclassical price mechanism, how can we analyze the relationship between market price and market sales? We will deal with this issue in this section with regard to the structure of market demand.

Differential prices and fluidity of market shares

Generally more than one enterprise produces the same product – that is, more than one enterprise inhabits the same market. Thus we are immediately faced with the task of explaining how the market is divided up among the enterprises and the effect of a non-uniform market price on the fluidity of market shares. In a market with a uniform market price, the market sales are distributed among the enterprises in the market according to their goodwill. That is, for the sake of convenience of acquisition, the maintenance of easy access to supplies, the maintenance of a regular clientele that permits smooth (predictable) production runs for the selling enterprise over the accounting period, and the convenience of accounting, buyers and sellers strive to establish mutually rewarding social relationships that go under the title of goodwill. But the buyer-seller relationship is not impervious to the price the seller charges. Because of the nature of enterprises which inhabit industrial markets in which the product bought becomes part of the costs of another product sold, the buyer enterprise would institute routine searches to make sure that the price it pays for the product is, over time, no more than its competitors. This is necessary since different behavior would increase its costs relative to its competitors and, therefore, place it at a competitive disadvantage. Thus, a buying enterprise would not continually prefer a higher-priced product over a lower-priced product from the same market – the higher-priced product means that the product is placed in a different (higher) 'income bracket' due to the price. As a result the selling enterprise will experience a rapid and permanent reduction in its flow rate of production/sales and hence its market share as its buying enterprises transfer their orders and goodwill to the other lower price enterprises in the market.

This transference will come about in two ways: first, the higher price will result in an immediate decline in the selling enterprise's sales as its buying enterprises immediately transfer their orders to the lower price enterprises. The size of the transference will depend on the size of the price differential. In addition, the size of the transference for any initial price difference will increase with time if the initial difference is held for a period of time since other buying enterprises begin to realize that the price difference is permanent and thus transfer their orders and goodwill so as to reduce their costs.

The above discussion can be delineated in the following manner. Let us consider an enterprise in a market of the j-th good that is also inhabited by other enterprises. Let us also assume that the time period under consideration is a production period and that the enterprise has many possible buyers at this time. And finally let us assume that some or all competitors are also in the market at the same time. If all the enterprises in the market charge the 'same' price, then the enterprise's market share or the share of the market's flow rate of output in the f-th production period is q_{jkf} (see Figure 5.1). However, if the enterprise's price is greater than the 'market price' charged by its competitors, then some of its buyers will transfer their orders and goodwill immediately to the other competitors in the market. Consequently, the enterprise's flow rate of output/sales reduces to q_{jk-1f} or q_{jk-2f} depending on the price differential. Of course, if it reduces its price below the market price, then it will be flooded with orders/sales to the extent that it is operating at full capacity. The line that traces out this relationship can be called a sales-price line.

Now let us extend the above analysis over a single accounting period. Assuming for simplicity's sake that the market flow rate of output is the same for each production period throughout the accounting period, then the enterprise's flow rate of output would diminish over the accounting period as its buyers switch their orders and goodwill to the lower price enterprises (assuming $p_{ej} > p_{mj}$). Of course, if $p_{ej} < p_{mj}$ over the accounting period, then it will be operating at full capacity with a possible backlog of sales as shown in Figure 5.2.

Finally, assuming at the end of the accounting period (which is also assumed to be the pricing period) the enterprise matches the lower market price or the higher market price will match the lower enterprise price. In both cases the market will

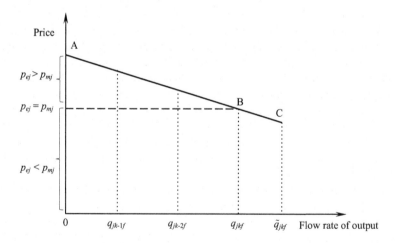

Figure 5.1 A sales-price line over a single production period

Notes: p_{ej} is the enterprise's price of the j-th good; p_{mj} is the market price of the j-th good; q_{jkf} is the enterprise's market share (or share of flow rate of output) in the f-th production period; $\tilde{q}_{jkf}$ is the enterprise's maximum flow rate of output for producing the j-th good; and ABC is the sale-price line.

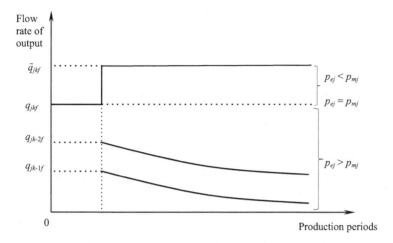

Figure 5.2 A sales-price line over an accounting period (with multiple production periods)

now be divided up solely along the lines of goodwill. But because the goodwill of the previous accounting period has been rearranged because of the price differential, the realignment of prices will not restore the pre-existing market shares. In the former case (assuming the market flow rate of output remains unchanged), the enterprise has a lower flow rate of output (hence higher costs and lower profits) than its competitors who have lower costs and higher profits and who have increased their flow rate of output at its expenses. (The reverse case occurs when the enterprise's price is below the market price.) Hence, to prevent the erosion of sales at a production period, accounting period, or over multiple accounting periods, enterprises will strive to maintain the same market price. Moreover, because of the nature of goodwill, enterprises know that once goodwill is lost it is difficult to regain. Thus, they will not, in general, adopt a price policy that promotes or accepts short- or long-term price differentials since such a policy would reduce their flow rate of output to the point of driving them out of the market. In short, market shares, whether in the production period, accounting period, or over many accounting periods, are extremely fluid with respect to price differentials.

Relationship between the market price and market sales

The above discussion implies that enterprises in a market would not pursue a price policy that would result in differentiated prices in the market. The discussion also implies that, for a given production period, a negatively sloped sales-price curve could be constructed but that it has no place in the enterprise's price policy. Now we want to consider a more aggregate relationship between the market price and market sales. Let us assume that the time period under consideration is a production period, a single price reigns in the market, technical change is absent from the economy as a whole, and the level of aggregate investment is given. The question being asked is whether a fall in the market price will generate an increase in market sales. Given the assumptions above, the answer is generally no. First of all, a decrease in the market price is in fact a reduction in the 'market' profit mark-up. That is, the market price is set by a target rate of return pricing procedure, which for the moment we shall assume to be that of the market's price leader. Since NEATC (enterprise average total costs at the normal flow rate of output) is given, price variation can only come at the expense of the target profit mark-up. Consequently, the market price can only vary within a limited range, depending on the response of market sales, since the profits arising from the profit mark-up must maintain the existing level of aggregate investment.

Second, a reduction in the market price of an intermediate, investment, or state product will not result in an increase of market sales for two reasons: (1) with given technology, enterprises already buying the intermediate input cannot buy more of it (we are ignoring speculation) and enterprises who may want to buy it cannot buy it – if the enterprises did in fact buy the input, it would remain unused because they would not have the technology to utilize it, and (2) the demand for investment and state goods are generally based on factors other than the price, such as needs for cost reductions and expansion of output; therefore, a price reduction in itself would not increase sales since the sales of the buying enterprises are unaffected by the price change. However, a decline in the market price could stimulate sales of an investment product if it dropped the product to the next lower income class. But such a possibility is remote since the necessary price reduction would place the market price outside its limited range and since enterprises will not rearrange their long-term investment plans based on a price alteration in a single production period.

Third, the demand for a consumption product, given its use-value, depends on the income class in which it is placed – that is, on its price. However, such a price reduction, while possible, would probably place the price outside its limitative range. Thus, we can conclude that a price change for a consumption product will not result in an increase in market sales. So we can conclude that there is no functional-structural relationship between the market price and market sales, given the above assumptions.

Going enterprise, sequential production, and the market price

We are now in the position to describe the price-sales relationship between enterprises in the market in a given accounting period. Let us consider Figure 5.3.

The question that we want to answer now is whether this hybrid relationship is sustainable over the accounting period and in face of fluctuations in the market flow rate of output. Assuming given technology for the enterprise and the economy as a whole and given market prices in all other markets in the economy, then fluctuations in the market flow rate of output over the accounting period will have the following impact upon the enterprise and the market price.

A decline in the market flow rate of output, resulting in a decline in the enterprise's flow rate of output from one production period to the next, will not induce

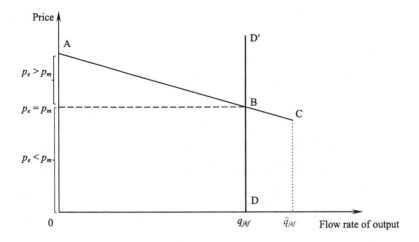

Figure 5.3 The price-sales relationship between enterprises

Notes: p_e is the enterprise price; p_m is the market price; ABC is the enterprise's sales-price line if the enterprise alone varies the selling price; ABD is the enterprise's market sales-price relationship in that if the enterprise raises its price ($p_e > p_m$), then sales will decline, and if it lowers its price, then all enterprises in the market will match the price ($p_e = p_m$, but both p_e and p_m decline); D′ D is the market sales-market price 'relationship' for the single enterprise in that throughout its length, $p_e = p_m$, although the absolute value of p_e and p_m can vary.

enterprises to reduce their price by cutting their profit mark-up because the net result would be a reduction of net profits for each enterprise and therefore a greater possibility of bankruptcy. That is, since a reduction in price by any one enterprise would be matched by all other enterprises in the market, thus maintaining relative market shares at any flow rate of output, and since a reduction in market price would result in no increase in the market flow rate of output, any reduction in the market price would only result in a fall in net profits to all enterprises. Continuing, since actual average total costs (generally) increases as the flow rate of output falls, a reduction in the market price increases the possibility that enterprises would be unable to cover them. Therefore, enterprises would not maintain such pricing policies. On the contrary, they would try to promote market wide price maintenance schemes to prevent such occurrences as weak selling.

An increase in market sales also would not induce enterprises to increase their price by increasing their profit mark-up because the net result would be a reduction in their ability to survive and grow. The reasons are twofold. First, within the market, an arbitrary increase in the profit mark-up probably would not command the adherence of all enterprises, even if sanctioned by the trade association or initiated by the price leader. Consequently, the enterprises that do increase their price would not only lose goodwill and market share in the production period, but also continually lose them over the accounting period. Second, if the arbitrary increase in the profit mark-up is accepted by all enterprises within the market, then not only would the enterprises lose goodwill, thus making it easier for enterprises in general to enter the market, but also the increased profit mark-up would increase the ability of enterprises outside the market (but within the industry) to enter easily and quickly, possibly by the next accounting period. Since the entry of new enterprises would disrupt the market price and reduce the market shares of the existing enterprises, the existing enterprises would not adopt such a price policy.

Thus we can conclude that the above hybrid relationship represented by D' D in Figure 5.3 captures in part the forces that support a stable market price policy in face of variations in the market flow rate of output over the accounting period. That is, the hybrid relationship shifts over the accounting period as the market flow rate of output varies, but its form remains the same. Yet, because the relationship does not explicitly show why 'depressed' market prices are detrimental to the enterprise over the accounting period and over many accounting periods, the relationship between sequential production and the market price is not completely delineated.

To start off this discussion, let us first construct a very simple model in which we assume that the enterprise exists and has its complement of the plant and equipment, that it produces one product at a standard flow rate of output for each production period during the accounting period, and that overhead expenses are evenly dispersed over the accounting period. Now for production to occur, the enterprise must have enough working capital on hand to procure the necessary amount of direct and overhead inputs. Once obtained, production occurs, the output sold, and the revenue collected. If the amount of total revenue received at the end of the production period equals the initial expenditure of working capital for the inputs, the enterprise can repeat the process for each production period throughout the accounting period, thus 'reproducing' the entire enterprise. If conditions do not change, this process can continue on over many accounting periods (thus reproducing the enterprise over many accounting periods) as long as the original sum of money advanced is returned – see Table 4.1.

Thus in this simple model, the enterprise can only engage in sequential acts of production at the normal flow rate of output if total costs equal total revenue, or, more specifically, the enterprise sets its price equal to average total costs at the normal flow rate of output (p = NEATC). Moreover, by setting p = NEATC, the enterprise can not only partially 'reproduce' the enterprise in each production period, but also completely reproduce itself over accounting periods.

The model can be extended beyond the simple reproduction of the enterprise by postulating that total revenue is greater than total costs at the normal flow rate of output. That is, by marking up average total costs at the normal flow rate of output, the enterprise can set a price that would cover costs and produce a profit at the normal flow rate of output which could be used to expand its scale of production. Assuming that p = NEATC $(1+r)$, that budgeted capacity utilization occurs at all times, that profits in any accounting period are divided between expanding working capital and increasing capacity, and that the new capacity comes on line in the subsequent accounting period, the model in Table 4.1 can be amended as the expanded reproduction of the business enterprise in Table 5.6.

The expanded reproduction model demonstrates that for an enterprise to grow and expand over accounting periods, it must not only mark up its costs when

Table 5.6 Expanded reproduction of the business enterprise

Accounting period 1

Production period 1:
$$q^1_{jn1} : M^1_{wc1} \to TC^1_{n1} \to P^1_{n1} \to TR^1_{n1} = q^1_{jn1}[NEATC_1(1+r)] = TC_{n1} + B^1_{11} + B^1_{12}$$

$$\cdots$$

Production period f:
$$q^1_{jnf} : M^1_{wcf} \to TC^1_{nf} \to P^1_{nf} \to TR^1_{nf} = q^1_{jnf}[NEATC_2(1+r)]$$
$$= TC^1_{nf} + B^1_{f1} + B^1_{f2}$$

Accounting period 2

Production period 1:
$$q^2_{jn1} : B^1_{11} + \ldots + B^1_{f1} = M^2_{wc1} \to TC^2_{n1} \to P^2_{n1} \to TR^2_{n1} = q^2_{jn1}[NEATC_2(1+r)]$$
$$= TC^2_{n1} + B^2_{11} + B^2_{12}$$

$$\cdots$$

Production period f:
$$q^2_{jnf} : M^2_{wcf} \to TC^2_{nf} \to P^2_{nf} \to TR^2_{nf} = q^2_{jnf}[NEATC_2(1+r)]$$
$$= TC^2_{nf} + B^2_{f1} + B^2_{f2}$$

$$\cdots$$

Notes: q^t_{jnf} is the normal flow rate of output (j-th good) for the f-th production period in the t-th accounting period; $p_t = NEATC_t(1+r)$ is the price of j-th good in the t-th accounting period; B^t_{f1} is the portion of profits of the f-th production period in the t-th accounting period set aside for use as working capital in the next accounting period – that is, $M^t_{wcf} = \sum_{t=1}^{t} B^{t-1}_{f1}$; and B^t_{f2} is the portion of profits of the f-th production period in the t-th accounting period set aside for expanding capacity in the next accounting period.

determining the price, but the price must remain stable throughout the accounting period if the profit objective is to be met (more on this below).

Finally, the above model can be extended to include variations in the flow rate of output and in the disbursement of profits for the procurement of the plant and equipment needed to expand capacity. To do so, however, requires the explicit use of funds from the banking sector. The model can also be extended to the case of a multi-product enterprise. But these extensions will not be undertaken here.

The implication of the above models is that the price and price stability are crucial to the reproduction and expansion of the enterprise over time. That is, models in Tables 4.1 and 5.6, where the flow rate of output does not vary and always occurs at normal capacity utilization and where overhead expenses do not vary from production period to production period, price stability is necessary if the enterprise is to reproduce and expand. If the price ever falls below the 'target return price' then the enterprise in Table 4.1 cannot continue to engage in sequential production and the enterprise in Table 5.6 cannot fulfill its investment plans or, in the extreme, continue to engage in sequential production. Moreover, the models suggest that an unstable price would seriously constrain the enterprise's ability to reproduce and expand, even if access to bank credit is possible, since increasing interest payments can push the enterprise towards bankruptcy simultaneously as the price falls. Consequently, enterprises within a market are driven to establish market institutions that would eliminate the problem of destructive price competition and establish a stable market price. Such organizations include trade associations, cartels, open price associations, and price leadership.

The administered price used in the above models is a stable and *common* price, since it is conceptually the same for the f production periods. The models also clearly show the market specific property of the price. That is, the target return price set by the enterprise, 'in theory,' would permit the enterprise to reenter the market in a continuous sequential manner; hence, the price 'embodies' the conditions that will maintain the market through time, at least from the perspective of the enterprise. Contrary to this is the exchange-specific price that, because of the manner of its determination, does not 'embody' the conditions that would permit the enterprise to reenter the market in a continuous sequential manner. Hence, the exchange-specific price does not, in principle, maintain the market through time.

Competition, market power, and the going market price

Market power and price instability

All enterprises have some sort of market power and this creates problems. Market power is the ability to inflict unacceptable consequences upon competitors, suppliers, and/or customers. Enterprises with market power have the ability to eliminate the positive net cash flows of competitors, suppliers, and/or customers insofar as that cash flow derives from, or depends upon, activities in the markets in which the holder of market power trades. The basis of market power are the following: nature of market, demand, and inter-dependency; controlling inputs/outputs of competitors; raising input prices of competitors; lowering output prices/cost advantages; financial strength – banks and funds generated in other unaffected markets; and relative market concentration.

Since all enterprises in the market have some degree of market power, the problem of establishing a common uniform market price emerges through the interaction between enterprises because of their different characteristics. One such difference between enterprises can be located in their cost structure with respect to sequential production. To show this, let us first consider a *descriptive market cost curve*. To construct such a curve, the number of enterprises in the market is given and fixed, and each enterprise is producing at normal (or standard) capacity utilization. Given these assumptions, the enterprises can be ranked by their NEATC. A descriptive market cost curve (DMCC) that shows this ranking is drawn in Figure 5.4.

Assuming that the market price is fixed, that each enterprise has decreasing enterprise average total costs (EATC), and that relative market shares remain

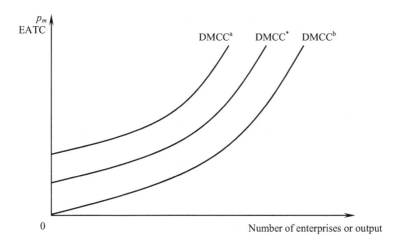

Figure 5.4 Descriptive market cost curve

Notes: p_m is the market price; EATC is the enterprise average total costs; DMCC* is the descriptive market cost curve when each enterprise in the market is producing at the normal flow rate of output; DMCCᵃ is the descriptive market cost curve for the *i*-th enterprise when its actual flow rate of output is less than its normal capacity utilization ratio; and DMCCᵇ is the descriptive market cost curve for the *i*-th enterprise when its actual flow rate of output is above its normal capacity utilization ratio.

constant in face of fluctuations in market output, the descriptive market cost curve (DMCCᵃ) lies above the DMCC* if the actual flow rate of output of the *i*-th enterprise is less than its normal capacity utilization. Conversely, the descriptive market cost curve (DMCCᵇ) lies below DMCC* when actual enterprise flow rate of output is above its normal capacity utilization ratio. Given this analysis of the DMCC, let us now investigate it within the context of sequential production.

Figure 5.5 clearly shows the movement of the DMCC over six production periods and the movement of EATC of the high, medium, and low cost enterprises over the same time period. It also lets us make the following significant points. First, if the flow rate of output for each enterprise in the fifth production period is considered 'normal' and p_{m3} the market price, then each enterprise in the market has a positive profit mark-up and is making a profit in the fifth production period. Secondly, when the market level of output falls below that of the fifth production period, the DMCC shifts upward and the profit margin of the high and medium cost enterprises disappears or becomes negative while the profit margin for the lowest cost enterprise is less than its costing margin. Thirdly, given the market price, a decline in the market (hence enterprise) flow rate of output would reduce the profit margin for each enterprise. If the depressed market flow rate of output continues for a number of sequential production periods, the high cost enterprises may run out of liquid funds needed to sustain sequential production. Consequently, instead of passively going bankrupt, they will break rank and set

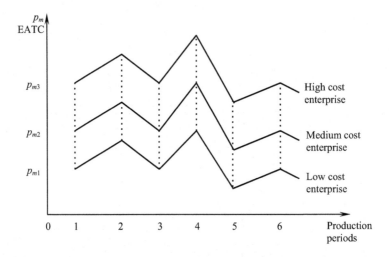

Figure 5.5 Descriptive market cost curve over multiple production periods

Notes: High (medium or low) cost enterprise means high (medium or low) EATC; DMCC of each enterprise shows the movement of EATC over production periods.

a price that is lower than its competitors' prices in an effort to increase sales and to produce a positive profit margin. If all enterprises in the market immediately match the lower price, the net result will be a lower costing margin (hence profit margin) at any flow rate of output. This can be seen in Figure 5.5: if the market price falls to p_{m2} or p_{m1} all the enterprises in the market will be worse off, especially the high and medium cost enterprises. The above conclusion indicates that any price reduction will be fruitless and implicitly undermines the enterprise's ability to engage in sequential production. Therefore, the question to be asked is 'why do enterprises initiate such acts of self-destruction?' The answer is found in the nature of sequential production. If an enterprise can set a price lower than its competitors' prices without them knowing it, then its sales will increase relative to the other enterprises as the floaters and less strongly attached buyers change their buying patterns. The price differential will last only as long as its existence is kept from the other enterprises. Thus, because price information is not generally instantly available to all enterprises in the market, individual enterprises can engage in one-upmanship economic behavior that can generate immediate profits but ultimately results in a completely demoralized market and individual self-destruction. This argument can be illustrated in Figure 5.6.

As Figure 5.6 indicates, the price policy of one-upmanship leads to extremely low market prices and to the self-destruction of the initiating enterprise. To eliminate it, the enterprises in the market need to control future prices.

A second difference between enterprises can be found in market sales growth rate expectations. To illustrate this, assume that over many production periods

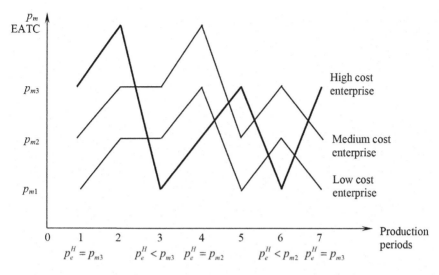

Figure 5.6 One-upmanship price setting of the business enterprise

Notes: p_e^H is the price charged by the high cost enterprise; $p_e^H = p_{m2}$ when $p_e^H < p_{m3}$; and $p_e^H = p_{m1}$ when $p_e^H < p_{m2}$.

and accounting periods that have experienced fluctuations in market output, the market has grown at a certain rate each year. This can be illustrated by Figure 5.7.

Figure 5.7 can be put into a more recognizable mathematical form. Assuming that the steady market growth rate is g^*, then the market flow rate of output for any point in time would be:

$$q_{mt}^* = q_{m0} e^{g_t^*} \qquad (5.1)$$

where t denotes an accounting period from 0 (initial period) to t (current period); q_{m0} is the initial market flow rate of output; q_{mt}^* is the 'steady' market flow rate of output; and e is the natural exponential function.

Assuming that the actual market growth rate for any production period is g^a and that it varies over production periods, then the actual market flow rate of market in any production period would be:

$$q_{mt}^a = q_{m(t-1)}(1 + g_{t-1}^a) = q_{m0} A(1 + g_{t-1}^a), \text{ where } A = \left(1 + g_1^a\right)\left(1 + g_2^a\right)...\left(1 + g_{t-2}^a\right) \qquad (5.2)$$

Mapping Equations 5.1 and 5.2 together, we get Figure 5.8.

The above analysis can also be shown at the level of the enterprise in the market. Assuming that the market growth rate can accommodate individual enterprise's

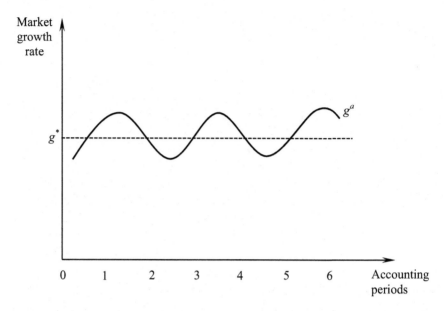

Figure 5.7 Market growth rate and instability

Notes: g^* is the steady growth rate and is derived from the actual movements of the market's growth rate; hence, it is dependent primarily on the factors which determine the market's actual growth rate over time; g^a is the actual movement of the market's growth rate over the business cycle or fluctuations in market output.

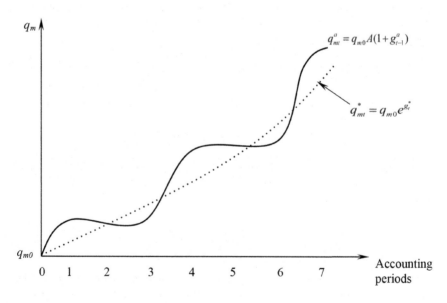

Figure 5.8 Market flow rate of output over accounting periods

growth rates, the steady and actual growth rates of the *i*-th enterprise in the market can be denoted as:

The steady growth rate: $q_{it}^* = q_{i0}e^{g_{it}^*}$ $\qquad\qquad$ (5.3a)

The actual growth rate: $q_{it}^a = q_{i0}A\left(1 + g_{it-1}^a\right)$ $\qquad\qquad$ (5.3b)

Now assuming input prices given, the movement of the *i*-th enterprise's NEATC and EATC[11] can be denoted as:

$$\text{NEATC}_{it} = \text{NEATC}_{i0}A(1 - c_{it-1}) \qquad\qquad (5.4)$$

$$\text{EATC}_{it}^a = \text{EATC}_{i0}^a(1 + z_{it})A(1 - c_{it-1}) \qquad\qquad (5.5)$$

where NEATC_{it} is the NEATC for the *i*-th enterprise in the *t*-th accounting period; NEATC_{i0} is the NEATC in the initial accounting period; c_{it-1} is the reduction in NEATC in the *t*-th accounting period due to the technically new plants introduced in the previous accounting period, $t-1$; EATC_{it}^a is the actual EATC of the *i*-th enterprise in the *t*-th production period; and z_{it} is the percentage change in EATC due solely to a change in the *i*-th enterprise's level of output in the *t*-th production period.

Mapping Equations 5.4 and 5.5 together, we get Figure 5.9.

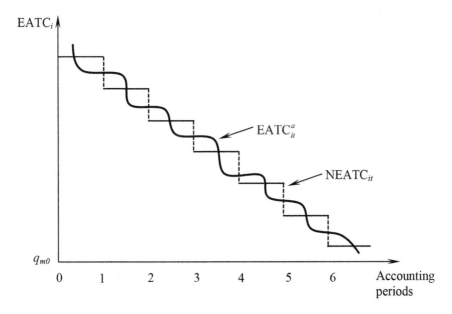

Figure 5.9 The movement of NEATC and EATC over time

Now assume that there occurs a radical and permanent change in the market's growth rate to a lower growth rate. Such a change at the level of the market is illustrated by Figures 5.10 and 5.11. The important point of Figures 5.10 and 5.11 is that when the actual growth of the market declines, so does the steady growth rate; moreover, a decline in the market steady growth rate means that the growth of market sales has declined in relative terms (although not in absolute terms). The implication of a lower market growth rate is that the enterprises in the market are experiencing a lower growth rate in output/sales. In turn this has a twofold impact on the enterprise's cost structure. First, because the enterprise's growth rate has decreased, its NEATC will not decrease as fast over time; secondly, because the enterprise's growth rate has decreased, the rate of decline of its actual EATC will also diminish.

Now we are in a position to discuss the impact of a change in the market growth rate on market price stability and enterprise profitability. Because enterprises initiate plans to increase capacity ahead of actual sales, a change in the market (hence enterprise) growth rate will initially exhibit itself as a slump in sales or no growth. Thus $EATC_{it}^a$ would most likely be higher than its counterpart $NEATC_{it}$. Therefore, given any market price, there will generally be some high cost enterprises that will try to shade it in order to increase its short-term sales and degree of

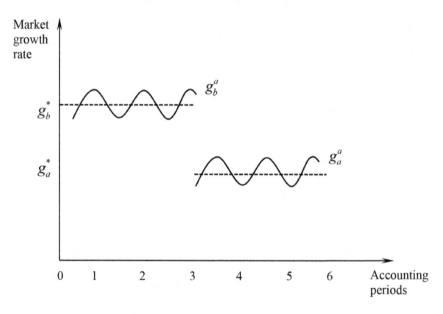

Figure 5.10 A change in the market's growth rate I

Notes: g_a^* is the steady market growth rate after the change; g_b^* is the steady market growth rate before the change; g_a^a is the actual market growth rate after the change; and g_b^a is the actual market growth rate before the change.

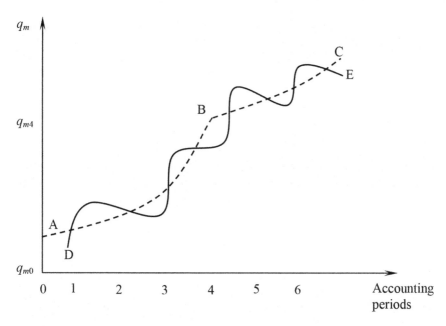

Figure 5.11 A change in the market's growth rate II

Notes: AB is $q_{mt}^{*} = q_{m0}e^{g_{bt}^{*}}$, $t = 1, ..., 4$.; BC is $q_{mt}^{*} = q_{m0}e^{g_{at}^{*}}$, $t = 4, ..., t$.; DE is $q_{mt}^{a} = q_{m0}A\left(1 + g_{at-1}\right)$.

capacity utilization. However, such an enterprise policy, as noted above, would only be successful if it remained hidden from its competitors; but that is generally unlikely except for the briefest of time. Consequently, destructive price competition generally will break out in this transition period, leading to price instability and lower enterprise profits. Underlying this, a 'superficial' response to the change in the market growth rate is the overall conflict of the enterprises' growth plans within the market. That is, some enterprises in the market might try to maintain their accustomed growth through eliminating the higher cost enterprises by a price war and occupying their economic space. Thus market price instability and low enterprise profits will exist for the period of time while the enterprises in the market 'work out' their mutually inconsistent growth plans.

There are other reasons and characteristics of enterprises that make it impossible for a group of individual enterprises to arrive at the same market price. Consequently, there emerges a set of market institutions and arrangements established by the enterprises themselves to do the trick. These institutions and arrangements go under the names of trade associations, price leadership, government regulation, and collusion. The next chapter will deal with this issue.

Price instability and the going enterprise

To maintain its existence in a capitalist economy, the enterprise must continually invest in plant, equipment, and product innovation in order to maintain its cost competitiveness and to grow. In making its investment decisions, it must, in a decentralized economy, look to the market for the necessary information, such as sales trends, stock movements, state of orders, or market share. Because each of the indicators are singularly dependent on the prices charged in each act of exchange, exchange specific prices cannot generate the information needed by enterprises for making investment decisions. On the one hand, buyers cannot make long-term buying plans, such as the buying of investment goods or consumption durables, based on the goods' relative prices since these relative prices could change in a haphazard, unpredictable manner. On the other hand, if the total sales of the enterprise are associated with many different prices, then it could not make long-term sales predictions based on sales trends, stock movements, state of orders, or market share. Consequently, the information needed by the enterprise to make investment decisions would simply not exist.

Although enterprises themselves would establish common prices (as opposed to exchange-specific prices), competitive pressures may prevent their wishes from being realized. So to eliminate these pressures, enterprises within the market would develop codes of behavior to prevent the occurrence of destructive price competition, hence exchange-specific prices, and market organizations to enforce the codes. For example, to eliminate secret price shading and therefore the possibility of price wars, a rule against price cutting would be propagated throughout the market and backed by market organizations such as open price associations, price notification schemes, cartels, trade associations, or price leadership. Specifically, to eliminate fluctuating exchange-specific prices, enterprises would establish codes of behavior and market institutions that would generate a single market price that would remain unchanged for many exchanges. That is, the market price must not only be 'uniform' over many exchanges at a given point in time (i.e., for a given production period) but also stable and uniform over time (over many production periods). In addition, the market price must also be conceptually the same over all the exchanges (i.e., a common price). Therefore, the market price must be established in the same manner as individual enterprises establish their prices and have the same kinds of properties. If a common market price were established, then sales trends, for example, would provide the information enterprises needed to make long-term investment decisions, since the price/quantities combinations would not be related to short-term market conditions, but instead would reflect permanent/evolving market conditions.

Notes

1 Editor's note: This section is incomplete; only consumption demand is dealt with here.
2 Editor's note: See Hamilton (1973; 1987) for an institutionalist approach to consumption and see Lavoie (1994; 2004) for a Post Keynesian approach to consumption.

3 It should be noted that the social dimension of making choices means the households may care about their relative position to other households in terms of consumption.

4 The choice of goods to buy also cannot be fully understood independently of the system of economic activity that provides it. In other words, enterprises can affect choice and mold social perception, as they are members of the society itself.

5 What this means is that while households purchase goods for consumption, the goods themselves may also be bought for other reasons. In addition, consumption goods differ significantly. This means that generality across consumption goods is not possible, due to a hierarchy of needs.

6 Goods that households choose to meet their material needs are socially defined, not individually defined.

7 In adopting this two-step rule, we are saying that the households are 'procedurally rational.'

8 Note that what is desired are the characteristics, experiences, services, etc. of the goods not the goods *per se* themselves. This permits substitutability is some ways.

9 By allowing for the additional possibility that the increment of income will not be spent on any item of consumption but will instead simply be used to increase the household's discretionary funds or savings, it is possible to encompass all the different purposes for which an increment in household income can be used.

10 It is normal within a capitalist economy for the demand for a good to increase/decrease as income increases. It is also normal that product development co-exists with changes in income. Since all consumption is socially conditioned, the appropriate distinction is between routine and discretionary goods. Thus, for example, conspicuous consumption is not extraordinary consumption but perhaps routine consumption designed to fulfill a particular social (ceremonial) function (say, desired by the rich). Of course, when value judgments are used for evaluating the capitalist economy, then routine goods for the rich can be effectively evaluated. Furthermore, the notion of income elasticity is problematical because income, price, and productive variation/development are interdependently linked with aggregate investment and the distribution of income. Thus, increases in income cannot be considered independently but must be related to all the other factors.

11 Note that NEATC is associated with the accounting period (that is, it is updated over accounting periods), while EATC is with the production period (that is, actual EATC changes over production periods).

6 Competition, the market price, and market governance

Heterodox approach to market competition and market governance

When it comes to the determination of market prices and the significance of market competition, heterodox economists have little to say beyond that price leaders determine the former while the latter varies. This is the general position of Post Keynesians, while the Marxists accept the former to some degree but argue that competition is much more severe than Post Keynesians (and the monopoly capital school) say it is. However, much of the discussion appears to rest on the implicit assumption of methodological individualism in that business enterprises operate as isolated individuals, that they engage qua compete with other enterprises as isolated individuals, and that all market outcomes are traceable to the actions of individual enterprises. In this chapter, I challenge this by arguing that competing enterprises in markets are embedded in an array of social networks, social relationships that manage how they competitively relate to each other to arrive various market outcomes, such as a market price. As a result, market competition does not 'manage' enterprises, but enterprises manage competition. This is most clearly seen in markets where competition and market outcomes are managed by private market governance organizations, such as trade associations, cartels, and price leadership.

A cartel or trade association, for example, is an organization made up of competing business enterprises whose objectives are to set agreed upon market prices, sales quotas, and/or market shares, to establish agreed upon ancillary restrictions relevant to market transactions such as the structure of quantity discounts, and to establish a private judicial system with fines to deal with infractions such as a member enterprise selling goods and services at below the cartel price. From a mainstream perspective, cartels have two problems. The first is that they violate methodological individualism in that it is not the individual agent making price, output, and sales decisions, but an emergent collective organization doing so. In this manner, the individual agent is analytically decentered. The second problem is its negative impact on the price mechanism and hence the optimal allocation of resources. The mainstream approach assumes that collective or cartel price fixing mimics the price fixing of a monopolist resulting in a market price higher than under competitive conditions and market sales lower than under competitive conditions. The 'failure' of the market to produce competitive optimal outcomes arises in part because of the assumed inverse relationship between market price and market sales – that is, the law of demand.

Heterodox economics also has the same problems with cartels. In spite of claiming to reject methodological individualism, most heterodox analysis of the determination of market prices assumes a lone, isolated price leader. Moreover, heterodox economists often depict competitive activities among business enterprises against all others in a war of all against all. This scenario is not weakened with the introduction of oligopolistic markets – here just a few enterprises compete with each other but still remain methodologically isolated. In short, as with mainstream economics, the isolated enterprise is the analytically central agent when theorizing about market prices. Heterodox economists also consider monopoly price fixing undesirable because it reduces the level of economic activity and hence employment, in much the same way as mainstream economics. Utilizing a simple Kaleckian model, for example, where national income is a function of the Kaleckian multiplier and effective demand (investment), an increase in the profit mark-up which increases prices, given level of demand in monetary terms, operates through the reduction of the wage share to reduce national income and employment.[1] On the other hand, if the degree of monopoly declines, hence the profit mark-up and prices decline, the wage share will increase and so will national income and employment. Thus, monopoly and higher prices lead not only to market failure but also to system failure, which can be avoided if the economy is more competitive.

From both mainstream and heterodox perspectives, monopoly or collective-cartel price fixing leads to market and system failure that can only be alleviated by introducing more competition. However, there are a number of problems with this conclusion. The first is that it is predicated on the twin suppositions that a law-like relationship between price and sales or price and the level of economic activity exists, and that more competition is better for economic outcomes than less. Certainly, within some strands of heterodox analysis, neither of the suppositions is accepted; so there is some basis to question the conclusion. Moreover, given the rejection of methodological individualism by heterodox economists, it is plausible to argue that collective forms of price fixing should be included in heterodox economics, thus decentering the extreme emphasis on the individual enterprise. Thus, the aim of this chapter is threefold: first is to dethrone the role of prices and competition as the regulators of economic activity; second is to introduce market governance and 'managed competition'; and third is to establish that collective price fixing, illuminated through the use of trade associations and cartels, is the basis for the general determination of market prices. This is to be carried out in four steps. The first section discusses the notion of competition and the degree of competition (or concentration) vis-à-vis the size of the business enterprise. The second sets out the basis for the need for managed competition, followed in the third section with the introduction and discussion of the concept of market governance. The fourth and fifth sections deal with specific market governance organizations – the trade association qua cartel and price leadership; a brief discussion on the public market governance mechanism and its impact on the market price follow.

Competition and market concentration

The most important form of potential instability in a market is price competition and the major objective of the enterprises in markets is to produce a form of control that will produce a stable market. Let us first discuss the notion of competition and what affects its degree of severity within a market.

Competition between enterprises in the production and sale of goods is the effort of such enterprises, acting independently of one another, each trying to make a profitable volume of sales in the face of the offers of other enterprises selling identical or closely similar products. Aspects of competition include: price, selling costs, advertising and service, and product development.

The factors that might affect the strength of market competition include the size of the business enterprise and market concentration. To investigate the relationship between the enterprise size and market concentration, we first need to define what is meant by size and then determine whether it is appropriate for our use in discussing market concentration. Enterprise size can be defined in a variety of ways in terms of, for example, total assets, value added, invested capital, sales, and employment. Because we are interested in market concentration and its relationship with the enterprises in the market with respect to the determination of the market price, the only relevant definition of enterprise size is sales. More specifically, because we are only interested (for the moment) in the enterprise's size with respect to a single market, its size can only be defined in terms of its specific market sales. Therefore, a multi-product enterprise might have a total sales of X but only a percentage of it is found in any one market; hence the enterprise's size for any particular market can be defined as $y = aX$, where y is the total sales in a particular market per accounting period, a is the percentage of total enterprise sales, and X is total enterprise sales per accounting period.

Now we are in the position to discuss market concentration. Like enterprise size, market concentration can be defined in terms of total assets, value added, invested capital, sales, and employment, but we are only concerned with it being defined in terms of sales. Moreover, market concentration can be measured in a variety of ways, each providing a specific kind of information. These measures can be sorted into 'absolute measures' and 'inequality measures.'

Three measures – the market concentration curve, the 4 (8)-enterprise concentration ratio, and the marginal concentration ratio – fall into the absolute measures of market concentration. Firstly, the concentration curve simply traces out in a cumulative manner the percentage of market sales with respect to the cumulative number of enterprises starting with the largest enterprise first. The curve is illustrated in Figure 6.1.

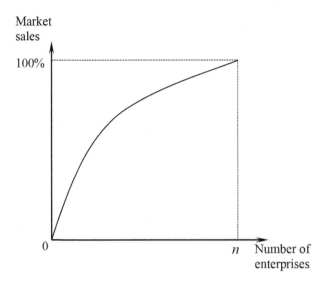

Figure 6.1 The market concentration curve

Secondly, the 4 (8)-enterprise concentration ratio is the points on the market concentration curve which denote the top four (eight) enterprises' share of total market sales. However, the 4 (8)-enterprise concentration ratio does not indicate the dispersion of the sizes of the enterprises involved; hence, important information concerning inter-enterprise relationships is lost. Therefore, an incremental concentration ratio is needed, which would not only summarize relative size differences between the enterprises, but also indicate how rapidly market concentration is increasing. This ratio – the marginal concentration ratio (MCR) – is obtained by $MCR_j = CR_{n+j} - CR_n$, where n is the number of highest ranked enterprises in the market, and j the last unit(s) of the enterprise. For example, $MCR_8 = CR_8 - CR_4$, that is, the marginal concentration ratio of enterprises ranked five through eight (in terms of market share), is the difference between the 8-enterprise concentration ratio (CR_8) and the 4-enterprise concentration ratio (CR_4) (see Miller 1967; 1971).

The above measures of concentration deal with only part of the enterprises in the market and have a difficulty in expressing the impact of the dispersion of enterprise sizes might have on our understanding of market concentration. Hence, a summary measure that accounts for firm size inequalities is needed.

The Gini coefficient is derived from the Lorenz curve, which shows as a continuous function the percentage of total sales accounted for by any given fraction of the total enterprise population, with the enterprises ranked in order of market

share. Lorenz curves can be characterized numerically by means of the Gini coefficient, which measures the departure between the Lorenz curve actually observed
and the curve that would appear if all enterprises had equal market shares (see
Figure 6.2). A Gini coefficient of zero ($G_0 = 0$) indicates perfect equality of enterprises shares; a coefficient of 1 indicates total inequality. The principal problem
with the Gini coefficient, however, is that it does not readily distinguish between
markets that have few enterprises of equal size and many enterprises of equal size.

Another inequality measure is the Herfindahl-Hirschman index, which is
defined as $H = \sum_{i=1}^{n} s_i^2$, where s_i is the market share of the i-th enterprise and n is
the number of enterprises in the market. When a market is occupied by only one
enterprise, the index attains its maximum value of 1. The value declines with the
increase in the number of enterprises n and increases with rising inequality among
any given number of enterprises. By squaring market shares, the index weighs
more heavily the values for large enterprises than for small enterprises.

Of all the measures of market concentration, the Herfindahl-Hirschman index
comes the closest to providing an understanding of the correlation between market forms and the number of enterprises and market concentration. A low H-value
would indicate that there are many enterprises in the market and that size differentials are not great compared to the market as a whole. Hence, jumping ahead
a bit, such a market could be characterized as an 'associate' market in that the
enterprises must cooperate, say through a trade association, to set a stable uniform
market price. On the other hand, a high H-value would indicate that there are
few enterprises in the market and that size differentials are great compared to the

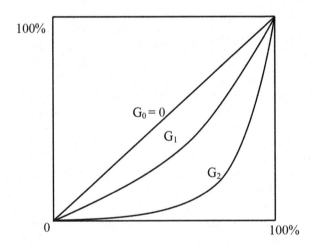

Figure 6.2 Gini coefficient

Notes: The vertical axis denotes the percent of market sales; the horizontal axis denotes the percent
of business enterprises cumulated from the smallest to the largest size business enterprises; and
$G_0 = 0 < G_1 < G_2 < 1$.

market as a whole. Hence, such a market could be characterized as a 'leadership' market in that a price leader could exist and it would set a stable market price. Finally, an in-between H-value would characterize a 'leadership or associative' market. However, the index does have one weakness: it is an aggregative measure of concentration and thus does not indicate what high or low market concentration means at the level of the enterprise. To explore this point, let us turn to the relationship between a multi-plant enterprise and enterprise size/concentration.

Business enterprises are, in general, multi-plant producers in the same market. The reasons for this are: (1) if major distribution areas are widely dispersed, a business enterprise might locate its plants close to them in order to save on transportation costs; (2) if major production areas based on the availability of specific raw materials are widely dispersed, a business enterprise might locate its plant in many of the areas so as to save on transportation costs; and (3) if the enterprise wants to be able to vary its flow rate of output for any particular production period, it must employ more than one plant. Consequently, it appears that the enterprise's size (market share) is not simply a technical/efficiency result, rather it appears to be based on its need to be a flexible going concern.

Let us consider the relationship between plant and market concentration. Empirical data show that the share of market sales belonging to the 4 (8) largest plants (irrespective of ownership) varies across markets and is generally less than the share of market sales belonging to the top 4 (8) enterprises. Since plant size is generally considered to be technically determined, the 4 (8) plant share of the market is also technically determined. Consequently, variations in this share between markets at a point in time or in the same market over time are due to technical change (assuming equal market size).

Now let us consider the relationship between enterprise size (or share of the market) and its largest plant size (or share of the market). Data indicate (and general reasoning support) the argument that enterprise size and plant size differ, with the former being larger than the latter. This divergence will always be the case if the enterprise is a multi-plant producer for the reasons given above. Therefore, we must conclude that the enterprise's size or share of the market (or the top four enterprises' share of the market) cannot be explained with reference to technology alone.

Since plant size cannot explain enterprise size and since multi-plant production is not necessarily correlated with a large enterprise size relative to the market (or large market share), a multi-plant enterprise may simply be a 'by-product' of its desire to grow with the market. If this were simply the case, however, then the statistics showing that a high degree of market concentration – typically measured by 4 (8)-enterprise concentration ratio – is significantly correlated with the existence of multi-plant production would not generally exist. Since they do, a reason is needed to explain it. The reason that will be advocated here is that enterprises become multi-plant producers in the course of pursuing a policy that would give them enough market power to 'control' the market price. Therefore, multi-plant production is not simply a product of cost reduction, of output augmentation, or of growing with the market; rather, it is an essential ingredient on an enterprise's plan to gain 'control' of the market price and maintain the control by erecting additional plants so as to grow sufficiently as the market grows. The conclusion that can be drawn from the above discussion is that an enterprise's size (market share) or its ability to grow is not determined by the technology embodied in its plant and equipment; rather, size and growth result from a specific plan adopted by the enterprise to maintain itself as a going concern. This argument can be supported by the structure of the business enterprise delineated in Chapter 3.

Management can take on different forms as the enterprise goes from a single product producer to a highly diversified producer. It should also be obvious that the form can change as newer technology and managerial techniques (methods of organization) become available; the form could also change in response to a growth in the enterprise's size. In particular, it must be recognized that the enterprise and shop technique of production for a specific product will change as technology and organizational methods change and as the maximum/normal flow rate of output increases. That is, when the enterprise decides to produce at a specific (normal) flow rate of output, it will employ a shop and enterprise technique of production appropriate to it and that is also appropriate to variations in the flow rate up to a maximum. However, as the enterprise increases its normal flow rate of output through the addition of more plants (and the retiring of obsolescent ones), the shop technique of production will continually alter, thus 'accommodating' the large flow rates of output. The net result will be that over accounting periods (assuming constant prices and a normal flow rate of output) average total costs and average shop and enterprise expenses will decrease. Thus there does not exist a managerial constraint on the size of the enterprise or with respect to any particular product. Hence, the size of the enterprise in any particular market is not solely determined by technology; rather, its market size and growth is determined by enterprise policy. Consequently, enterprise size and market concentration depends in part on the policies adopted by the enterprises within it.

Basis for managed market competition

The issue of managed market competition stems from the nature of the business enterprise as a going concern, as discussed in detail in Chapter 2. To be a going enterprise, its business leaders must maintain a positive cash flow. This is accomplished by adopting a range of business strategies, such as increasing market share (through intra-market competition via advertising or cost-led price reductions), increasing the profit mark-up through raising it or reducing costs, developing new products and creating new markets, entering new markets that promise significant growth in sales and profits, engaging in collective price-determination, and/or seeking government support. To achieve a positive cash flow, the going enterprise needs to set a price that both covers costs and generates profits. That is, as discussed in Chapter 4, assuming that the going enterprise is producing at budgeted capacity utilization, then it can only engage in sequential acts of production when its total costs equal total revenue, or, more specifically, only when the enterprise sets its price equals to average total costs at budgeted capacity utilization:

p = EATC$_\text{B}$. If total revenue is to be greater than total costs at budgeted capacity utilization, then the price must cover average total costs and produce a profit: p = EATC$_\text{B}$ $(1 + r)$. Through the use of cost-plus pricing procedures, the going enterprise can (assuming budgeted capacity utilization or greater) ensure that it remains as a going concern that both generates incomes for the business leaders and at the same time enables the enterprise to reproduce and expand itself.

The implication of the strategic price decision-making process within the going enterprise is that the price set by the going enterprise is crucial to its reproduction and expansion over time. So, if the enterprise's price falls below costs, EATC$_\text{B}$ $> p$, then it cannot long continue to engage in sequential acts of production and reproduction. Moreover, if its price is below EATC$_\text{B}$ $(1 + r)$ so that the 'target' profit mark-up is not achieved, then the enterprise will have a cash flow short-fall resulting in delaying or dropping investment and product development plans and a reduction of dividend payments. Thus, the going enterprise is driven, irrespective of competitive market conditions, to adopt and utilize various cost-plus pricing procedures to first ensure that the price covers costs at budgeted capacity utilization and secondly to apply a profit mark-up consistent with its cash flow or profit needs. Determined through administrative action within the enterprise prior to production (hence knowledge of actual costs) and market exchange, the enterprise administers its budgeted-cost prices to the market.

As we discussed in Chapter 5, a market is a social structure whose existence is predicated on continuous and sequential transactions of a specific product. Because products are continually produced and sold in the markets combined with the continual need for products, there is an unbroken demand for the products to be produced for the market. Consequently, the market cannot be cleared; rather it must be seen as a *non-clearing* and that exchanges cannot clear markets. The significance of a non-clearable market is that it cannot be defined in terms of structured relationships between prices and sales. In terms of the production of goods and services, the quantities produced qua supplied are, in a demand-driven economy, determined by state decisions to spend and enterprise decisions to invest and to produce consumption goods and services. That is, quantities 'supplied' are determined by effective demand and not by the 'supply price' of the goods and services produced. Moreover, each of the demand decisions is not a function of prices and, in fact, prices do not figure in the decision-making process. This is particularly clear regarding state demand for goods and services and enterprise demand for intermediate goods and services and for fixed investment goods. Moreover, household demand for consumption goods and services is a derivative outcome of being employed, hence having an income by which to buy them. What households can do is to choose between various consumption goods produced, but cannot actually determine what is produced. The most significant point is that there is no analytical argument in heterodox economics that establishes a demand curve-like relationship for households or for the market that is law-like. In addition, the empirical evidence on price stability reveals quite clearly that market sales vary independently of market prices. Without a structured relationship between market prices and sales, there is no mechanism inside the market to modify the negative impact of price reductions on the cash flow of the business enterprise. That is, since goods and services are homogeneous in a specific market, it is not possible for competing enterprises to have differential prices without having significant changes in their market shares. In particular, if an enterprise reduces its price in the market and the other enterprises do not match it, then its sales and market share increases; and since the enterprise's average total cost curve for the good declines, the decline in costs offsets the price reduction, and so the enterprise comes out ahead. On the other hand, the other enterprises in the market suffer a reduction in sales, which means higher average total costs and, given the price, a reduction in the profit margin, hence a reduction in its cash flow. Hence, enterprises will match all price declines, which means a reduction in their profit mark-ups and hence their cash flow; there is no mechanism within the market to correct this.

With no built-in mechanism linking prices to sales, a reduction of the market price does not generate an increase in market sales; and so profits are reduced. This situation is made much worse if there is a decline in overall market sales due to either a recession or secular changes in the market's growth rate of sales. As delineated in previous chapters, all going business enterprises have the capacity to set prices and carry out other competitive activities – that is, the business enterprise has the ability to inflict unacceptable consequences upon competitors. This means that if market sales decline, business enterprises may engage in price wars as a way to increase their sales; but this is only possible if others do not follow immediately. The going enterprise always has the capability to pursue this strategy, especially in markets in which competitive enterprises are not collectively organized. However, the outcome of price competition is inherent potential market instability, and with it a potential threat to the going enterprise. This threat is made even more real when business cycles and technological and secular economic changes are taken into account. This potential and real threat to price stability and the viability of the going enterprise is the basis for managing market competition. Since the 'market' (as a 'structure') cannot correct this problem, it is up to the acting enterprises in the market to do it. This brings us to market governance organizations. That is, given the immediate problem of destructive price competition and the need to establish a stable market price, going enterprises are always in search of orderly markets through collective, cooperative action. Such organizations that engage in market governance and regulate price (and other forms of) competition include trade associations, cartels, open price associations, price leadership, and government regulatory commissions; in addition, governments enact legislation that also regulates competition.[2]

Market governance: controlling instability through regulating markets

Market governance refers to the social, economic, and political processes that regulate horizontal market transactions among business enterprises in specific markets. The processes take on a variety of specific forms, denoted as market governance mechanisms, each of which involves purposeful actions by business enterprises, deals with relationships between business enterprises, and regulates actual market transactions. Hence, hierarchy in the form of a vertically integrated enterprise is not a market governance mechanism. Moreover, the market mechanism as conceived by mainstream economists is also not a market governance mechanism, in part because it reduces the importance of purposeful actions by enterprises. A market is a socially constructed institution or a social structure in that it represents and delineates recurrent and pattern interactions between acting persons/organizations vis-à-vis a specific product, which are maintained through various social, economic, political, and legal sanctions.[3] It is concretely reflected in the product's characteristics, demand, and production, and in the social network between the active economic agents engaging in market transactions. Within this structure economic agents are engaged in purposeful and causal actions, which reinforce the pattern interaction but can also slowly change it.[4] The social network represents the social and economic interaction of the agents in terms of codes of moral-economic behavior, trust, familiarity, and business customs. Thus, it constrains the set of actions the agents can choose as well as facilitates market transactions.[5] Consequently, the social network provides the foundation for all market governance mechanisms. The most basic form is the social network itself; more developed mechanisms are obligational and promotional networks, which include informal and formal bilateral and multilateral relationships and associational relationships including trade associations (Granovetter 1985; Campbell and Lindberg 1991; Lindberg, Campbell, and Hollingsworth1991; Larson 1992; Grabher 1993; Hakansson and Johanson 1993; Swedberg 1994; Fligstein 1996; Uzzi 1996; White 1997).

The important point is that any form of market governance requires acting enterprises and that market transactions are embedded in the same set of social relationships as are the enterprises. To ignore this is to make collective activity to regulate competition unintelligible except as an individualistic, profit maximizing or opportunistic exercise. In other words, 'trust' rather than 'opportunism' is the norm among the enterprises.[6]

There are studies of market governance mechanisms, but they generally have not taken into account the social network of the 'social' market and have not connected the mechanism directly to the relevant market transactions. In addition, the studies rely on conventional economic wisdom to analyze and explain the origins, effectiveness, and social impact of the market governance mechanism. The most stark examples of this are studies of American price-output fixing trade associations of the latter part of the nineteenth century, which refer to the existence of extensive social networks among the owners of the enterprises, their agents, and superintendents of their mills and factories. While the networks in these studies had a societal component, much of it was based on common commercial interests, such as keeping abreast of technological developments, collecting and disseminating trade statistics, concern with labor and impending labor laws, and dealing with tariffs on competing or raw material imports. These common interests led to close relationships, as exhibited in volumes of correspondence or attendance at dinner clubs, which constrained individual action and generated propensities for common responses to common economic problems, such as declining profits and prices (Robinson 1926; Cox 1950; Cooper 1953; Galambos 1966; Becker 1971; Fickle 1980).

However, the studies tend to overlook the fact that the social network acts as a market governance mechanism *per se* and, therefore, do not recognize that an associational arrangement to control prices, for example, is a more developed form of a social network. The second drawback is their reliance on conventional economic dogma to examine the trade association and its activities. Consequently, statements – such as, trade associations emerge because of high fixed costs combined with intense competition that creates price instability and drives down profits; trade associations raise prices, restrict output, and hence are a threat to the public; and trade associations are unstable and liable to fail because of the inherent propensity of members to cheat on prices – are made based on the dogma but with virtually no supporting evidence. That is, the studies rely largely on newspapers, trade papers, journals and other publications, government publications, manuscript collections of trade associations, and relevant individuals; so when marshaled together, the resulting story is concerned only with the association itself (and specific member enterprises) and hence does not shed light on actual market transactions. Without this detailed enterprise-transaction connection, the trade association is effectively severed from the market it is governing and, therefore, the above statements are left with no empirical grounding and only dogma to support them.

With the social network in place, it is possible for enterprises to go further and deal with price fixing, establishing output quotas or market share, and dealing with ancillary issues concerning market transactions. Such networks also provide the foundation for price leadership and government regulations. So the combination of inherent market instability, acting enterprises, and market social networks means that market governance organizations exist in all markets to manage competition. Hence, whether the degree of market concentration is high or low or the barriers to entry are significant or not, they have little impact on market governance *per se*; rather, they only affect the organizational form that market governance takes. Therefore, all markets are characterized by 'managed competition' constructed by going enterprises. So all markets are equally competitive; all enterprises take into account other enterprises when making pricing (and investment, research and development, and marketing) decisions.[7] And most significantly, the going enterprises create a form of market governance that regulates competition in their interests – that is, competition is pervasive but not pernicious or destructive.

Breakdowns of market governance occur, but they are exceptions, not the rule. And when they occur, efforts are immediately undertaken to reestablish some form of market governance. In fact, in many cases, the breakdown of one form of market governance was the result of the establishment of a different form of market governance. Moreover, there are cases where new entrants into a market are incorporated into the existing form of market governance as a way to reestablish market stability. Uncertainty in the market rises as the social network/

market governance weakens. Under such uncertainty, investment declines (Clark and Baglione 1998).

Private market governance mechanisms are not independent of the state. The state is always present in the mechanisms, insofar as it provides an institutional and legal framework that influences the selection of different governance mechanisms and thereby permanently shapes the economy. The state, as both an actor and a political-institutional structure, does this through the defining and enforcing of property rights.

Institutionalists appear to approach the whole issue of market governance from the dichotomy of 'free market' and government regulation. In this respect, government regulation is seen as a mechanism through which well-organized and public-spirited technical expertise is used to curb the excesses of predatory capitalism and to mitigate and perhaps solve a great variety of more particular and less encompassing problems. The institutional structure of government regulation involving an expert regulatory commission is that an enabling act is passed by the legislative, which sets forth in general terms what is to be regulated, to what purpose, and sets limits on the powers of the commission. Complementing the enabling act is a set of administrative procedures that set procedural standards to govern the operations of their commissions. The commission makes rules, which have the force of law, and it engages in judicial activity to deal with contested cases. The activities of the commission are predicated on the view that regulation is an ongoing activity if it is to be effective, and that to judge contested cases requires expertise. For a commission to be effective in curbing the predatory activities of capitalists, it has to encompass the entire geographical scope of the industry being regulated; be capable of fielding sufficient expertise; be reinforced by an independent, technically competent and energetic assemblage of public representatives to balance the vested interests in proceedings where the agency takes the role of the neutral decision-maker; and hence least technically effective regulation be defeated through the capture of the agency by the regulated interests (Sheehan 1988).

Regulation and deregulation are different forms of market governance. The former is based on the state and the latter is not so directly, and the enterprises involved have a significant say in what the governing mechanism should be. In the case where government regulation is taken away, then the 'implicit' rules of the market take over. In the new market environment, the enterprises develop private control of competition as a substitute for public control – for example, in the case of the US trucking industry in the 1970s and 1980s, increasing the degree of concentration was a way to stabilize freight rates in face of rate cuts and discriminatory rates demanded by big shippers (Kling 1988).

Institutionalists also argue that government regulation is neither more or less a potential object of influence peddling than the private market or public enterprise (Miller 1985). This view fits in quite well with the notion of market governance and the Post Keynesian view of the market. Given the concept of market governance that implies various degrees of private and public social control, then it becomes plausible within this context to ask the question as to the best form of market governance. Such a question may be answered from a socio-economic perspective and involves value judgments. It is, however, not possible to construct a general theory of regulation (and market governance) in the sense of a universal, descriptive, and explanatory body of thought. This is because regulation-market governance is historically contingent. Industries that constitute part of the community infrastructure are prime candidates for government regulation; but, in a broader sense, this same argument can be extended to all basic and non-basic goods markets and industries.

Inter-organizational linkages exist between enterprises. They can be at the level of management in terms of corporate control or at the level of markets. In either case, the business enterprise finds it necessary to regulate its market relationships with important organizational actors. The resulting social network becomes an important social structure that can be brought to bear in the continual process of maintaining a stable economic and social environment. Such networks are important for establishing cartels and price leadership, especially in the latter case, if one enterprise is most central to the network (Martinson and Campbell 1979).[8]

Since market governance is a social institution qua relationship (which includes market power)[9] it can be regulated. In this case, regulation is really specifying acceptable and unacceptable relationships and, therefore, specifying acceptable and unacceptable activities and outcomes. Since market power exists at all times by enterprises operating in the market, the issue is not the elimination of market power *per se*, but how it is used and for whose advantage. Institutionalists simply want to regulate this power so that certain segments of society get the advantage (Miller 1996).

Business enterprises shape markets. Hence, one factor relevant to shaping markets is the enterprise's own vision of its future and the power it has to make 'markets' conform to it. Thus, in a sense markets do not do anything if this view is to hold or make sense – that is, markets do not coordinate economic activity or force directions on enterprises. Rather, enterprises with varying degrees of power strive to achieve their goals by shaping and governing the market. In this regard, the profit maximizing neoclassical firm, which follows the pre-existing rule of the market, is irrelevant (see, Nix and Gabel 1996; Clark and Baglione 1998).

Given the above conception of markets, market governance, and the social network, the notion of market failure does not exist – nor does the invisible hand exist. That is, the market cannot fail unless it is conceived as a coordination mechanism in the neoclassical sense. The market itself does not coordinate economic activities. It is the acting persons and organizations through the market governance-regulation mechanisms that coordinate economics activities. It further implies that the transaction cost approach to the firm and to hierarchy (à la Ronald Coase and Oliver Williamson) can be dismissed, since it posits that markets exist 'naturally' and firms emerge in order to economize the use of scarce resources (Coase 1937; Williamson 1975). The market failure or transaction cost argument is incompatible with the heterodox approach to markets and should thus be rejected by heterodox economists.

Private market governance and the market price: trade associations

Trade associations are voluntary, non-profit making organizations formed by business enterprises to protect and advance interests common to all member enterprises. They can cover a whole industry, such as the British Iron and Steel Federation; a certain area of trade, such as the Food Machinery Association; or a particular product, such as the Fish Hook Makers Association. Of particular interest are those trade associations of competitors in a given market or, more generally, product group or industry, which band together to present a united front. Their primary purpose is to organize the conduct of the market (product group or industry), within the competitive system and on the basis of maintaining the essential independence of the enterprises involved, so as to make the market more orderly. In particular, they promote market stability in terms of production and prices by preventing the build-up of unsold inventory or unused capacity, radically changing market shares, and destructive price competition, to spread trade information that would make for intelligent or reasonable competition, to eliminate unfair business practices, and to reduce costs both on the technical and commercial side. To achieve these goals, trade associations take on various forms depending on the problems involved and the state of law. There are trade associations that simply set prices while others only allocate output among its members. Then there are trade associations, called 'cartels,' which fix prices and allocate output among the member enterprises. Finally, there are trade associations called 'open price associations,' which deal with the dissemination of past price information.

Legal form

A trade association generally has a constitution or memorandum and articles of the association which set out (1) its objective or purpose, area of coverage, membership, and organizational structure; (2) procedures on elections, meetings, making decisions and policies, and enforcing agreed upon policies, finance, activities, and relationship to other trade associations; and (3) its duration and conditions for dissolution.

Legally, a trade association may be a company, an unincorporated body, or a trade union. If a trade association is incorporated it almost always adopts the legal form of limitation by guarantee.[10] In this case, each member enterprise guarantees to contribute a certain sum in the event of winding-up, but there is no share capital and no profit-making is allowed. The advantages to a trade association that flow from registration as a company arise from the legal personality it acquires. Though associations are not trading concerns, they may need to make contracts of a commercial character, such as to own property, to make contracts, and to sue and be sued in their own name. It also makes possible the amendment of the objects of the association without the completely unanimous support otherwise required. The only disadvantage of company status, to an association that is eligible, appears to be that certain documents must be available for public inspection.

Thus the memorandum, articles of the association, and annual returns giving the list of directors and the year's accounts must be sent to the Registrar of Companies (UK), for example, and these are available to the public. In addition, these documents must give the address of the officers of the association. The major constraint on becoming a company is that the trade association cannot have, as a major activity, the restraint of trade.

Section 16 of the British Trade Union Act Amendment Act of 1876 defines a 'trade union' as:

> any combination, whether temporary or permanent, for regulating the relations between workmen and masters, or between workmen and workmen, or between masters and masters, or for imposing restrictive conditions on the conduct of any trade or business, whether such combination would or would not, if the principal Act had not been passed, have been deemed to have been an unlawful combination by reason of some one or more of its purposes being in restraint of trade.

Thus, if the major purpose and activity of a trade association is the restraint of trade, then it is a trade union.[11] As a result, according to Section 5 of the Trade Union Act of 1871, a trade union may not register under the Companies Acts, the Friendly Societies Acts, or the Industrial Provident Societies Acts. However, they may register themselves as trade unions or become certified as a trade union with the Registrar of Friendly Societies.[12] When the trade association is registered as a trade union, it has the following organizational advantages: being able to sue and to be sued in its own name, to hold property through trustees with full continuity, and to make contracts in its own name. On the other hand, the trade association is obliged to lodge with the Registrar a copy of the rules and of any amendments and to send annual returns of accounts to the Registrar; these are available for public inspection. Certification is a simpler matter. It merely involves satisfying the Registrar about the objects of the trade association. It does not entail either the privileges or the obligations of registration, and its purpose is merely to assure the trade association and, if necessary, the courts, that it is, in fact, a trade union.

Being a registered or certified as a trade union means that the trade association is immune from liability in tort.[13] This immunity means that any association which injures others by its restrictive activities cannot be sued for conspiracy, defamation, or any similar matter, and none of its harmful actions, if *intra vires*, can be questioned in a court of law. The protection of the Act extends only to the trade association itself and not to members or officials; but the wording suggests that it even covers torts about to be committed, and that it prevents, therefore, injunctions to restrain trade associations from committing these acts.[14] Initially, being a trade union also meant that, under the Trade Union Act of 1871, the courts would not directly enforce agreements between members about conditions on which they transact business or agreements to pay subscriptions or penalties.[15] However, by 1920 the situation had changed so that the Courts would not enforce unreasonable restraints on trade while enforcing the reasonable ones.

The majority of trade associations are neither companies nor registered or certified trade unions. There are many informal trade associations that have no corporate legal existence. This means that property must be held for the trade association by a trust or by individual members. In most circumstances, the council of the association would find themselves fully liable for all actions that they have authorized, including any contractual ones. The trade association cannot sue or be sued in its own name. Finally, in theory, every member enterprise must consent to the trade association's actions and to changes in its rules. But these disadvantages do not appear important to member enterprises since trade associations do not often own much property or enter into many contracts. Trade associations would rather do without the right to sue or be sued and indemnify the individuals who are held responsible instead, and members are willing enough to consent to any acts on which a majority of the association decides.

Constitution and purpose

For those trade associations that are incorporated, their constitutions are set out in their memorandum and articles of the association; those trade associations, which are registered or certified as trade unions, have a full constitution in their rules; and informal trade associations will have less formal and shorter documents. Central to all constitutions are statements that establish the objective of the trade association, determine membership and relevant geographical area, organization and management, method of reaching association decisions, and finance. Essential to all forms of trade associations is the statement of purpose or types of activities it will be engaged in. If the trade association is incorporated, its memorandum and articles of the association will state its purpose, such as for the Tyre Manufacturers' Conference Ltd.:

> To safeguard and promote the interests of those engaged or concerned in the United Kingdom or elsewhere in the British Commonwealth and Empire in the manufacture, sale, distribution or use of tires, to facilitate co-operation, co-ordination and common action on all or any matters affecting the Industry and ancillary trades and branches.

On the one hand, the memorandum must clearly state that the trade association eschews any activity in restraint of trade, and in fact the memorandum will often include some such phrase as "not to act as or carry on the business of a trade union." On the other hand, those trade associations that are registered or certified as trade unions explicitly state in their purpose that they are engaged in restrictive trade practices. For example, one object in the Rules of the Notts Lace and Net Dressers Association was

> to prevent unfair competition, and price-cutting, and unfair attempts to get work for themselves from the customers of other members.

And another example is the Rule of the National Association of Crankshaft and Cylinder Grinders, which was to

> prevent the operation of unscrupulous traders who prejudice good workman-ship, reduce prices below an economic level, violate trade agreements, and adopt trading methods inimical to the trade.

Finally, there are the trade associations that are not incorporated, registered, or certified in any way, and their statement of purpose may include restrictive prac-tices or prohibit them. For example, the Society of British Soap Makers states that:

> The society shall not promote, encourage or sanction any steps tending to pre-vent or restrict competition between one member of the society and another, or as between members of the society and non-members, and whether by way of price-fixing, allocation of markets or otherwise.

On the other hand, the British Silk Throwsters Association states its object that:

> To fix and regulate the minimum selling prices of all classes of thrown silk yarns and the conditions of sale so as to eliminate price-cutting. . . . The fix-ing of such prices shall take place on Monday and Wednesday in each week.

Similarly, the object of the Cold Rolled Brass and Copper Association is "to fix the prices and terms on which the manufactures of the Members shall be quoted for and (or) sold."

Organization and management

Membership of a trade association is generally open to any geographically rel-evant enterprise engaged in the line(s) of business covered by the association, which agrees to comply with the provisions of the constitution, bylaws, and other rules of the organization, and to pay the required subscriptions and fees. For example:

> The [Manufactured Copper] Association consists of Manufacturers in the United Kingdom engaged in the production of Non-Ferrous goods who have undertaken to abide by the provisions of those Heads of Agreement and of the Rules and Regulations of the Association for the time being in force. . . . The moneys necessary from time to time for the purpose of financing the operations and meeting the expenses of the Association shall be provided by a tonnage levy on the output of Association good.
>
> Membership shall be open to all Producers of Washed Sand and Gravel in Scotland who subscribe to this Constitution as amended from time to time, who have paid the deposit of £500 and who have been admitted to

membership at a General Meeting of the Association. . . . The expenses of the Association shall be met by a levy upon each member. Such levy shall be one penny per ton on members' actual outputs or such other sum as may be decided upon by the Association in General Meeting.

The organization of a trade association consists of an administrative structure, which deals with the day-to-day affairs, and a governing structure. The former can be very informal and has been done as a secondary activity by a member enterprise. That is, in some cases it is agreed that the necessary secretarial work for an association shall be carried out by each of the member enterprise or each member of the governing body, in turn. Or, alternatively, the administration of the association's affairs may be put permanently into the hands of one of its members. If the work involved is at all substantial, the association may make some payment to its members for the service. The administrative structure of many trade associations around 1900 was indeed like this, but by the 1950s this had changed. Instead of trying to do the administrative activities in-house, associations hired specialists to do the tasks. In some cases, trade associations have made arrangements with major chambers of commerce or federations to carry out the secretarial work.[16] The practice of these large organizations is to allocate members of their staff to take charge of association work. In other cases, trade associations band together to share accommodation and employ staff in common. Further, an association may have an enterprise of accountants to carry out the secretarial duties.[17] Finally, trade associations establish their own administration to carry out the secretarial duties.

In this last case, the constitution of the trade association usually establishes the administrative structure as well as its principal officials.[18] The head of the administrative side of the trade association generally goes under the name of director or secretary and is independent of the enterprises in the association. One of the major duties of the director is to supervise the day-to-day administration of the services that the trade association provides for its members. In addition, the director usually plays a part in the determination of wider policy. Associations find that they need to employ high-quality staff not only for their general advantage, but also in order to meet government departments and other bodies with officials of equivalent caliber. But the discretion allowed to these officials varies considerably from association to association. Some directors work with the minimum of references to governing bodies and have considerable influence on the determination of policy. Others seem expected to consult their chairman or even their executive on every point that departs at all from routine. There can exist below the director a variety of personnel, including heads of departments dealing with statistics, legal advice, and standards, architects, engineers, research workers, technical assistants, public relations officers, and general office staff, depending on the daily and long-term services desired by the member enterprises of the association.

The governing structure of the trade association is set out in the constitution. It generally consists of a council, executive committee, committees, and general meetings. The main governing body is the council that has the power to make all decisions necessary to the running of the association; on the other hand, the executive committee is derived from the council and is generally charged with overseeing the daily affairs of the trade association. To assist the council and the executive committee, various specialized committees are usually established. These committees deal with financial, technical, and standardization matters as well as with prices and members' complaints regarding violations of association rules and agreements. The members of the trade association exercise control over the policies of their organization by electing the governing bodies, not by meeting and making decisions themselves. This election occurs at the annual general meeting. The general meeting is also where general policy debate occurs and policy resolutions are passed.

General activities

Trade associations undertake a range of activities for their members which can be broken down into three areas: putting the views of their members before other bodies, providing common trading and commercial services for their members, and regulating market activities.

Representational activities

The representational activities include dealing with government departments, public corporations, and suppliers and customers. The recognition of the need for collective representation on the part of industry has been a principal motive for the formation of many trade associations, and, as stated in their constitutions, one of the chief objectives of trade associations is to make the views of their members known to the government of the day. Indeed, most trade associations specifically refer, in their constitutions, to the need of the industry in question to speak with one voice in negotiations with government departments; to promote helpful and resist unfavorable legislative and administrative developments; to cooperate with government departments; and to act as a channel of communication between government departments and member enterprises. Some of the topics that are discussed between trade associations and government departments include promotion of exports, import licensing, taxes, tariff negotiations, health and safety regulations, technical and research problems, and statistics. For those government departments that buy goods and services from the private sector, the topics that are discussed with trade associations include the conditions and terms of contracts, prices, tendering procedure and allocation of orders among suppliers, standards and specifications, and guarantees of workmanship and materials. Trade associations will also have contact with public corporations, such as the National Coal Board and Central Electricity Authority, who buy significant amounts from their members through, for instance, regular meetings at which many things including prices are discussed.

Trading and commercial services

Trade associations provide numerous trading and commercial services for their members. These activities fall into three areas. The first is promotional and publicity work in which the association channels information from their industries to their markets. The work includes organizing exhibitions and displays; producing press releases, pamphlets, directories, and buyers' guides; developing advertising campaigns; giving advice to members about advertising media; and providing technical information and advice on the applications and use of their members' products.

The second area involves collecting trade information and statistics and their dissemination to their members, together with the provision of services that facilitate members' trading activities. For example, a number of larger trade associations have overseas departments that handle export matters. A few have permanent representatives in their chief export markets, while others organize overseas visits by their members, or disseminate reports about trade conditions overseas. Among the services provided by these associations which have a considerable exporting interest are the circulation of statistics and market intelligence; fairly continuous contact with government departments on the preparation of briefs for trade negotiations, the lodging of objections to increases in overseas tariffs, and so on; and an information service for members' individual inquiries. Smaller trade associations that do not have special staff dealing with exports may simply circulate overseas information in their bulletins and deal with individual inquiries as they arise. Trade associations also provide trade statistics concerning the domestic market in the form of monthly statistical bulletins and statistical yearbooks;[19] collect and disseminate cost statistics of member enterprises and undertake industry cost studies; pass on inquiries from prospective customers to members; advise individual members on transport, on insurance, and on the existence of patents, trademarks and styles on the products of the industry; run status and credit bureaus; provide library services and legal advice; and support members' cases in the courts when they involve a point of principle deemed to be important to the industry as a whole.

The third area of activity related to trading and commercial services concerns the production efficiency of their members. For example, a trade association distributes a technical information bulletin that sets out the results of members' research and development in production techniques. Further, many UK trade associations are in contact with the British Standards Institute and have special departments concerned with standardization and simplification,[20] and behind those departments there are numerous technical committees concerned with different products and processes. In addition, many associations are closely linked with the research agencies of their industries. In some instances they are responsible for starting research groups that have become research associations jointly financed by industry and government. Finally, many associations prepare and publish estimating and costing manuals on modern methods of costing and endeavor to get members to adopt modern costing and accounting procedures; they are also concerned with the education and training of new workers.

Regulating market activities

The third area of general activities of the trade association concerns regulating market activities. The practices used by trade associations are many and varied and include price-fixing, quota systems, and resale price maintenance. Other restrictive trade practices, such as collective boycott, exclusive dealings, discriminatory rebates, restriction of association membership, restriction of supplies to customers, and aggregate rebate arrangements, are done as a way to support their price-fixing arrangements, quota systems, and resale price maintenance systems. Quite often trade associations use a number of the practices together as a way to control both prices and output and thus to regulate market activities. Consequently, most trade associations are cartels as opposed to simply price-fixing associations. Let us look closely at three major regulating market activities undertaken by trade associations.

Associational price-fixing involves the trade association fixing the market price that its members agree to follow. Generally, the trade association establishes a committee to deal with price determination, and the committee in turn employs various methods to fix prices.[21] Some of the costing methods used on which to base the price include determining a weighted average total costs of the three largest enterprises or taking the average total costs of the lowest-cost or of the largest member. Once the cost-base is determined, the committee proposes a particular profit mark-up and, thereby, determines the price. The proposed mark-up may be a customary one or one that takes into account a number of market factors and policies of the association. After setting the price, the committee may either have the power to impose it on the members of the association or need to have the council approve it. In either case, once the market price has been fixed by the association, its members are in many cases constitutionally bound to accept it.[22]

A quota system involves allocating market sales among the members of the trade association. That is, the trade association determines the amount of market sales by its members for a given base time period and then determines the percentage share of each member.[23] This percentage share or quota for each member enterprise is then monitored closely to see whether it is being exceeded or not. If it is being exceeded, then financial penalties will be imposed, perhaps in the form of a pool account that is then used to compensate members who did not reach their quota of sales. For example, under the Hard Fibre Cord and Twine Manufacturers' Association quota scheme, each enterprise was allocated a percentage, based on its pre-war sales, of the total available home trade in packing cord and twine; the participants were obliged to make payments into a pool or entitled to receive sums from it, according to whether their turnover exceeded their percentage quota or fell below it. From time to time the trade association will alter the quotas, usually basing the new quotas on a new base time period. Quota systems are generally seen as an insurance system against the conditions of cutthroat competition and grabbing of market share.

A resale price maintenance system refers to a system of marketing whereby the supplier of a product – in practice, generally one which is branded or otherwise identified – prescribes, as a condition of sale, the price at which (or above which) it may be offered for resale by the retail trader together; in some cases, with a similar stipulation as to prices to be charged by wholesalers and in other intermediate transactions in the chain of distribution. Trade associations often encourage or require as a basis of membership member enterprises to establish their own resale price maintenance system. In other cases, the trade association itself sets up a resale price maintenance system based on the prices its sets. Whether individual or associational-based, the success of the resale price maintenance system generally hinges on whether both wholesalers and retailers agree to it; we find that where successful, wholesalers and retailers are part of the manufacturers' trade association. In cases where there are violations, either fines will be imposed or the individual enterprise concerned or all the enterprises in the association will boycott it.

The significance of all these regulating market activities is that the trade association or cartel is much like a going enterprise in that it has administrative capabilities to administer prices and sales. That is to say, trade associations are centers of administrative competence and expertise. They can manage markets and competition effectively and competently, so much so that any acting business enterprise or acting state can. What is important here is twofold. The first is that the policies being administered are derived from collective actions that are grounded in any array of social relations – so the policies come from the trade association as opposed to a simple aggregation of decisions made by individual enterprises.[24] Thus, the trade association is the 'link' or 'network' that connects the individual enterprise to the market. Consequently, the enterprise does not enter the market on its own without any social protection, but rather enters the market through a 'social cocoon' that attempts to protect the enterprise (and the market) from destructive forces. Secondly, the outcomes of the policies regarding prices and output are embedded with 'social intentions,' such as to ensure that individual enterprises remain going concerns, that the 'social network' tying the enterprise together is maintained, and that market disorder and disruptions are avoided and the current array of enterprises in the market is not greatly upset. In short, by managing market competition, the trade association (or its specific form, cartel) is a positive force for promoting the stabilization of a potentially very unstable capitalist economy at the level of the market and even the industry.

Private market governance and the market price: price leadership

Price leadership describes the situation in which a single enterprise regularly initiates market price changes by changing its own price because all the other enterprises in the market follow and adopt those price changes. The former is the 'price leader' and the latter 'price followers.' Therefore, the questions that need to be answered are how an enterprise attains the position of price leadership and how it commands allegiance to its price. These two questions will be dealt with considering three situations: the first will be the archetype price leadership situation in which a dominant enterprise 'controls' the market price; the second will consider the situation in which price leadership has failed and enterprises have engaged in collusion to set the market price; and the third situation considered will deal with large enterprise price leadership as exercised through a trade association.

As indicated above, the notion of price leadership emerges when a dominant business enterprise in a market is able to dictate its price to the other enterprises in the market, and the following enterprises accept the dominant enterprise's price because they believe that it is the best thing to do. In stating this, a number of unanswered questions immediately comes to the fore: (1) how is a dominant enterprise identified (or quantified)?; (2) why would such an enterprise appear in a particular market?; (3) why is its price accepted by the remaining enterprises in the market?; (4) what impact does it have on the market price?; and (5) how stable is it in terms of being a price stabilizing market institution? In answering these questions, we will come to a better understanding of what dominant enterprise price leadership is.

The dominant enterprise defined and identified

The most obvious characteristic of a dominant enterprise, especially one formed via a horizontal merger, is that it is extremely large in comparison to the market and to the other enterprises in the market. To quantify this two-fold characteristic, we must first specify the manner by which the enterprise's size is measured. As delineated earlier in this chapter, enterprise's size can be measured in a variety of ways – for example, in terms of total assets, value added, employment, and sales. For the sake of our present discussion on the dominant enterprise's relationship to the other enterprises in a particular market with respect to the determination of the market price, it would be reasonable to utilize sales as the relevant measure of enterprise size. To deal with this we can define the enterprise's size for any particular market in which the dominant enterprise exists as $y_d = aX$, where y_d is the dominant enterprise's total sales in a particular market per accounting period, a is the percentage of total sales accorded to the market, and X is the dominant enterprise's total sales per accounting period.

Now we are in a position to quantify the statement that the dominant enterprise is large in comparison to the market. This is done by determining the dominant enterprise's share of market sales, $s_d = y_d/y_m$, where y_m is total market sales and s_d is the dominant enterprise's percentage of market sales or market share. To be a dominant enterprise with respect to the market $s_d > 50$ percent. Historically, dominant enterprises – normally, emerging as a result of a merger – have s_d much greater than 50 percent. Insofar as we are interested in a summary measure of quantifying the size of dominant enterprise vis-à-vis the other enterprises in the market, we can use the Herfindahl-Hirschman index, $H = \sum_{i=1}^{n} s_i^2$, where s_i is the market share of the i-th enterprise, n the number of enterprises in the market (see the first section of the chapter for a general discussion of the index). In the case that there exists the dominant enterprise, the index should be greater than 0.25. If n is less than, say, 5, $H > 0.4$; and if n is greater than 5, then $H > 0.3$. To summarize the above discussion, the dominant enterprise in a market can provisionally be identified if its market share is $s_d > 50\%$, and if $H > 0.3$ (if $n > 5$) or $H > 0.4$ (if $n < 5$). Given this two-fold characteristic, we can conclude that the dominant enterprise has in part the ability to simply dominate the remaining enterprises in the market.

The size of the dominant enterprise, as discussed above, does not by itself permit it to dominate the other enterprises in the market. Therefore, the size of the dominant enterprise must convey upon it a competitive advantage that the other enterprises in the market do not have. The most important and necessary advantage the dominant enterprise must have, if it is to impose its price upon the market, is a cost advantage. A second, but less important, advantage is a financial advantage.

If a dominant enterprise obtains a cost advantage from a horizontal merger, it is most likely to occur in the area of production. To illustrate this, let us assume that two enterprises are merging and each has three plants. The costs of the two enterprises are as follows:

Table 6.1 The cost structure of two enterprises before merger

Enterprise A

Plants	PCP	Plant output	Cumulative output	PADC	EADC	ASE	AFC	AEE	EATC
A1	300	200	200	1.50	1.50	2.00	3.50	2.00	5.50
A2	325	175	375	1.85	1.67	1.07	2.74	1.07	3.81
A3	275	125	500	2.20	1.80	0.80	2.60	0.80	3.40

Enterprise B

B1	300	200	200	1.50	1.50	2.00	3.50	2.00	5.50
B2	250	125	325	2.00	1.69	1.23	2.92	1.23	4.15
B3	300	100	425	3.00	2.00	0.94	2.94	0.94	3.88

Notes: PCP is the plant costs of production; PADC the average direct costs at the plant level; EADC the average direct costs at the enterprise level; ASE the average shop expenses; AFC the average factory costs, AFC = EADC + ASE; AEE the average enterprise expenses; and EATC the enterprise average total costs, EATC = EADC + ASE + AEE (on these costs see Chapter 3).

Assuming that the normal flow rate of output for enterprise A is 375, then its normal average factory costs (AFC) is \$2.74; likewise, if the normal flow rate of output for enterprise B is 325, then its AFC is \$2.92. Upon merger, the dominant enterprise has a total capacity of 925. Assuming that the normal flow rate of output of the dominant enterprise is 700 and maximum flow rate of output is 825 (that is, B3 is shut down after merger), the dominant enterprise's structure of costs is delineated as follows:

Table 6.2 The cost structure of the dominant enterprise after merger

Dominant enterprise

Plants	PCP	Plant output	Cumulative output	PADC	EADC	ASE	AFC	AEE	EATC
A1	300	200	200	1.50	1.50	2.00	3.50	3.50	7.00
B1	300	200	400	1.50	1.50	1.00	2.50	1.75	4.25
A2	325	175	575	1.85	1.61	0.70	2.31	1.22	3.53
B2	250	125	700	2.00	1.68	0.57	2.25	1.00	3.25
A3	275	125	825	2.20	1.76	0.48	2.24	0.85	3.05

At the normal flow rate of output, we find that the dominant enterprise's AFC is $2.25, which is less than the pre-merger AFC of enterprises A and B (that is, $2.74 and $2.92 respectively). This reduction in costs is due to the small reduction in EADC from concentrating production in the most efficient plants, and to the reduction in shop expenses following the re-organization of production and the scrapping of the inefficient plants (B3 in the above example). Turning to enterprise expenses, we can expect that when the integration of the two enterprises is complete, the total enterprise expenses will decrease (or remain nearly the same) with the elimination of duplicate activities (such as sales expenses). Assuming enterprise expenses to be $700 (as opposed to $800, assuming enterprises A and B have enterprise expenses of $400 each), the dominant enterprise's average total cost (EATC) schedule is shown in Table 6.2. And since the normal flow rate of output of the dominant enterprise is 700, NEATC$_d$ is $3.25.

Since NEATC$_d$ ($3.25) < NEATC$_A$ ($3.81) < NEATC$_B$ ($4.15), it can be concluded that the dominant enterprise has access to cost reductions via merger, which are not available to the other enterprises in the market. Therefore, it implies that, in most instances, the dominant enterprise will have lower average total costs at the normal flow rate of output than the remaining enterprises in the market. Given this cost advantage, the dominant enterprise is in a position to set a price that will be less than the prices that the smaller, more costly enterprises would desire. Therefore, as we shall see below, the smaller enterprises are 'forced' to accept the dominant enterprise's price.

Because of its size, the dominant enterprise's financial position is much stronger than that of its smaller competitors. That is, the dominant enterprise has easier access to borrowing short- and long-term working capital at lower rates of interest than its competitors. In addition, it has access to capital markets, whereas the smaller enterprises are generally frozen out of those markets. As a result, as will be shown below, the dominant enterprise is in a much stronger competitive position vis-à-vis its smaller competitors, especially with respect to setting predatory prices as a way to establish its price as *the* market price.

Thus the dominant enterprise of a market can be defined as one that is able to control to a degree the competitive environment in which all other enterprises in the market operate. This enterprise's actions will shape the market outcome, especially with respect to the market price, without the explicit (or even implicit) consent of the other enterprises in the market. The principal characteristics of such a dominant enterprise can be summarized as:

1   Market share > 50 percent;
2   H > 0.3 (if $n > 5$) or H > 0.4 (if $n < 5$);
3   NEATC$_d$ significantly lower than the NEATC of any of the other enterprises;
4   Access to the capital markets;
5   Easier access to short- and long-term borrowing; and
6   Significantly lower interest rates compared to its competitors.

Determining the market price

It is generally accepted that the dominant enterprise's price is accepted as the market price by the other enterprises in the market because of its cost and financial advantages. Still, the question as to why the smaller enterprises accept the dominant enterprise's price has not been completely answered. To provide a complete answer, let us undertake the following analysis.

Consider a two-enterprise case in which one of the enterprises is a dominant enterprise. Considering the two enterprises together, it would be unusual if both enterprises have the identical view about the most desirable market price. That is, in light of their differences in normal average total costs and their different financial requirements, the two enterprises would have different ideas as to what the market price should be. More specifically, because of the dominant enterprise's significantly lower $NEATC_d$, its ideal market price will most likely be lower than the smaller enterprise, even if its profit mark-up is greater than the smaller enterprise's ideal profit mark-up. Therefore, the dominant enterprise's price will rule in the market.

It is sometimes argued that the dominant enterprise can use its financial advantage to force following enterprises that have an ideal market price less than its own to adopt its market price. First of all, it must be clear that financial advantage can in part be seen as a cost advantage and has therefore been analyzed above. At stake here is the financial ability of the dominant enterprise to engage in predatory pricing to force the following enterprise(s) to adopt its ideal market price. In this case, the dominant enterprise sets a price which is below its ideal price and which is far below the ideal prices of the following enterprises – in extreme instances it could be below the normal average total costs of some (or all) of the following enterprises. Because the dominant enterprise has recourse to the banks and financial markets, the decline in its flow of profits due to the reduction in its profit mark-up will not affect its ability to grow and expand. That is, over the foreseeable accounting periods, the dominant enterprise will set a 'low' price that will reduce its profit flow; however, this reduction in profits will not affect its investment projects because it can borrow money from financial institutions or issue new stocks to make up the difference. Therefore, the dominant enterprise is not under pressure to raise its price for a considerable period of time. On the other hand, since the smaller enterprises will face economic hardship because they do not have access to external financial support, they will have to reduce their investment expenditures or cease them altogether. Therefore, after a period of time the enterprises will either have to accept the dominant enterprise's ideal price or be forced into a permanently crippled state (or out of the market altogether).

The dominant enterprise and the market price

Because the dominant enterprise's price is the market price, the market price will move over accounting periods in accordance with the movements in $NEATC_d$ and profit mark-up. Moreover, because the dominant enterprise uses normal cost (or target return) pricing procedures, the price will be stable within the accounting period.

Let us take a closer look at the market price upon the emergence of the dominant enterprise. Prior to its emergence, the market price fluctuated greatly following the business cycle. In the case of depression both costs and profit mark-ups declined, while during the boom, both increased. However, with the emergence of the dominant enterprise, price fluctuations over the business cycle (accounting periods) would primarily reflect variations in costs since the determinants of the profit mark-up are largely unaffected by the fluctuations in effective demand associated with the business cycle. Therefore, the dominant enterprise reduces price fluctuations over the business cycle.

Because the dominant enterprise usually comes into existence following a destructive price war, the market price is below the ideal price of all enterprises in the market, including the dominant enterprise. Thus we find the phenomena of the dominant enterprise being associated with a significant rise in the market price and defending the price rise as being reasonable. Once the ideal market price has been set, however, its value over time is closely connected to changes in $NEATC_d$ and the profit mark-up set by the dominant enterprise, and thus explainable in terms of the dominant enterprise's cost structure and plans for investment and growth.

Appearance and stability of the dominant enterprise

The emergence of the dominant enterprise is based on many factors, such as mergers, patents, innovation/invention, and product superiority. United Shoe Machinery Corp., for example, which owed part of its position of dominance to a merger, also relied on product superiority (loyalty) generated through its leasing policy and the trust as an organizational innovation. Mergers played a role in Pullman's acquisition of dominance, but they occurred simultaneously with invention and patent protection. At least one of the acquired enterprises approached Pullman because it was having difficulty competing without access to the Pullman patents. Kodak, Gillette, and Campbell also invented their products, but patents were required to prevent imitators. In addition, they were able to generate product loyalty as a result of the quality superiority of their products, advertising, and dealerships. Coca-Cola followed a similar pattern. Although it did not invent the soft drink, it was associated with the development of franchised bottlers, a marketing innovation. Its formula for Coke was protected by secrecy rather than patents. However, in spite of all these factors, a common thread runs through them, which is that they all help the dominant enterprise escape destructive competition and thus have more control over the market price.

As an industrial institution, the dominant enterprise is subject to change over time. That is, the factors that gave rise to its dominance can also contribute to its decline as well as to its continued dominance. To determine the conditions under which the dominant enterprise institution can change over time, let us consider two distinct situations: the first concerns costs and the second concerns competitive strategy.

The evolution of the dominant enterprise: costs

Let us consider the market and the enterprises within it in the context of sustained market growth over a period of time. Let us assume that, given input prices and wages, market growth gets translated into lower NEATC through the adoption of new plant and equipment by the enterprises in the market. For the dominant enterprise and the market price, this assumption implies the following: (1) $NEATC_d$ declines over time, (2) the market price will decline over time if the profit mark-up is held constant or does not rise as fast as costs fall, and (3) thus we conclude that there is an inverse relationship between the size of the dominant enterprise in the market and the market price. For the price following enterprise, the implications are as follows: (1) the price following enterprise's NEATC will decline over time, (2) its profit mark-up will increase, decrease, or remain constant as the decline of its NEATC is greater than, less than, or equal to that of the dominant enterprise, and (3) thus we cannot conclude that growth in size will ensure that the price following enterprise's profit mark-up will increase.

Putting the above results together, we can reach the following conclusions. First, assuming the profit mark-up of the dominant enterprise (r_d) is constant, then the market price will decline over time as the market grows and hence $NEATC_d$ declines, since $NEATC_d(1+r_d) = p$; and if $\Delta NEATC_f / \Delta NEATC_d < 1$, then the profit mark-up of the following enterprise (r_f) declines. Therefore, in this case the price following enterprises are being driven out of the market because their profit mark-up is being reduced. In extreme cases, $r_f < 0$ when the market price becomes less than $NEATC_f$. With the elimination of the smaller price following enterprises, the dominant enterprise strengthens its dominant position in the market. Second, assuming r_d constant and a declining market price, if the price following enterprise is more energetic in introducing new technology than the dominant enterprise, then its profit mark-up will increase over time. Therefore, its financial position with respect to the dominant enterprise will increase. More interestingly, if $NEATC_f < NEATC_d$ occurs because of its relatively aggressive stance towards technology, the smaller price following enterprise is in a position to become a price leader in the market. Lastly, the above two cases clearly indicate that, except for a fluke, market growth combined with technical change will lead to changes in the market structure, whether it be the relative growth of the dominant enterprise vis-à-vis its competitors or the relative decline of the dominant enterprise to the point that another enterprise will become the price leader. Thus we must conclude that (1) changing market structure is the state of affairs in growing markets faced with technical change, and (2) the dominant enterprise cannot maintain its market dominance (even though it has maintained its size dominance) if it does not keep up with the new technology. But it should be noted that up until the dominant enterprise is challenged as a price leader, the market price will remain stable throughout the accounting period.

Let us now consider the situation in which wage rates change while all other input prices and technology are held constant. The result will be a change in $NEATC_d$ and, therefore, the market price, assuming r_d is constant. Since the price following enterprise faces the same wage rate changes, its cost/competition position vis-à-vis the dominant enterprise will not change significantly. Let us now introduce two new wrinkles into this state of affairs. Firstly, assume that the dominant enterprise's labor force is unionized and the following enterprise's labor force is not. Since the union will press for and obtain larger increases in the wage rate than will occur in the non-unionized enterprises, the dominant enterprise's cost will increase faster than the costs of the following enterprises. Thus, the situation can emerge when the dominant enterprise loses its cost dominance in the market and, along with it, its price setting dominance. Secondly, assume that the wage costs associated with the new technology is very much lower than those associated with the vintage technology. Therefore, since the dominant enterprise employs more of the new technology than the following enterprises, changes in the wage rate will affect the following enterprises more severely. Consequently, as the wage rate increases r_f will generally decrease. Hence dominant enterprise's position in the market will be strengthened not only because $\Delta NEATC_f < \Delta NEATC_d$, but also because the following enterprises' profit mark-ups are declining and, hence, reducing their ability to obtain the funds needed to buy the new technology. Consequently, we can conclude that wage changes can lead to significant changes in the organization of the market, especially when tied to technology or to unions.

The last situation that will be considered is the growth of the following enterprises' market share in a growing market. Let us assume that the dominant enterprise is willing to grow but not at a rate which will maintain its market share. The result will be that the following enterprises will be growing at rates faster than the market with the results being $\Delta NEATC_f > \Delta NEATC_d$ and $\Delta r_f > 0$. As a result, the dominant enterprise will be losing its dominance in terms of size, costs, and pricing within the market. Consequently, a time will come when a new form of market organization will be needed to ensure a stable market price.

The evolution of the dominant enterprise: competitive strategy

The question being considered here is: what kind of competitive strategy must the dominant enterprise undertake if it expects to maintain its dominance in the particular market? It must be noted that a dominant enterprise can maintain its dominance in a market while simultaneously losing it in other markets. Moreover, the dominant enterprise could control a particular market, while its competitors create new substitute markets or simply new markets, with the net result being that the dominant enterprise stagnates while its competitors grow. While such situations are important when dealing with the growth of the enterprise, they are outside the confines of the present analysis. Rather, what we are specifically interested in are the kinds of competitive strategy the dominant enterprise must undertake if it expects to maintain its dominance.

With the *first mover strategy*, the dominant enterprise maintains its position in the market by being the first enterprise in the market to, say, introduce novel additions to the product being sold or novel ways of selling the product in the market. Consequently, the other enterprises are always trying to 'catch up' with the dominant enterprise and therefore are never in a position to surpass it. The second strategy, similar to the first mover strategy, involves the *creation of barriers to entry and growth*. One such barrier would be the control of patents that could be used to 'block entry' or 'inhibit growth' through burdensome licensing agreements. Another barrier could be the control of inputs, such as the ownership of the cheapest resource inputs. And the third strategy would be to *build capacity* ahead of the growth in market sales so as to always be in a position to capture the 'new sales' and thus prevent any of the other enterprises from getting them. Each of these strategies, while designed to maintain the dominance of the dominant enterprise, could in fact lead to its downfall because they violate the antitrust laws.[25]

Public market governance and the market price: government regulations

In this chapter, 'regulation' is defined as a process consisting of the intentional restriction of a subject's choice of activity by an entity not directly party to or involved in that activity. In stating this, there are a number of points that need to be made. Firstly, regulation is a process – that is, it is an ongoing, continuous activity. Therefore, if we are going to talk about regulation of a particular market, the enterprises in the market must continually come to the market to sell their goods and enterprises/individuals must continually come to the market and buy the goods. Hence we must not only view the regulated enterprises as going concerns, but the economy itself must be seen as evolving through time. Secondly, regulation is an intentional restriction of a subject's choice of activity. There are three aspects to this: (1) there are regulatory goals such as stabilizing the market, preventing destructive competition, the continuation of the enterprises involved, etc.; (2) these goals are achieved by constraining the activities of the enterprises in the market and/or the enterprises that would like to enter the market – in fact, if the regulatory commission deals with competing markets/enterprises, constraints might be placed on enterprises in both markets in order to achieve the desired goals; and (3) the restraining activities can change/evolve over time to meet new conditions while the goals remain constant. Thirdly, since regulation is a process through time, the goals of regulation at one point in time might be changed at a future point in time. As a result the constraining activities might also change to accommodate the new goals. Finally, the party directing the activity can be private (cartels, for example) or public, and the public party can be a government agency or commission. In this chapter we shall primarily be concerned with government commissions and 'agencies' (such as Parliament and the Courts' involvement in resale price maintenance).

There are a number of explanations for the origin of government regulation of industry, but we will be discussing only the 'private interest' explanations. Before discussing the private interest explanations, let us first briefly discuss the 'public interest' explanations. Public interest theories of regulation assume that regulation is established largely in response to public interest related objectives. Unless one assumes that the state or public mystically acts for itself in seeking the regulation, public interest theories require in effect that parties seeking regulation be agents for the public interest. These agents may satisfy their self-interest instrumentally through pursuit of public interest objectives, but the theory requires that at least some preferences for the public interest be genuine and terminal. The form which public interest takes in these theories are as follows:

1   *Balancing* concept in which the public interest results from the simultaneous satisfaction of selected aspects of several different particularistic interests. The balancing result gives satisfaction to interests that may to some extent be contending or competing.
2   *Compromising* concept in which particularistic interests are made to concede part of what they desire so that the overall result is in the public interest.
3   *Trade-off* concept in which particularistic interests affected by regulation are made to provide some costly service or other benefits judged to be in the public interest in exchange for certain private benefits to them.
4   An overriding *national* or *social goals* concept in which certain social, societal, or national objectives are held to be in the public interest and supersede private interests.
5   *Particularistic, paternalistic,* or *personal dictated* concept, unitary in character, in which the public interest is equated with the preferences of a particular person, group or organization, or system.

There are many different public interest theories of the origin of regulation, but they will not be discussed here. Rather, what needs to be noted is the general argument that lies behind them. The argument is based on two assumptions: one being that the economy (market) is very fragile and therefore can easily operate in a manner which is not in the public interest, and the other being that regulation is costless and does not make matters worse. With these assumptions, it is easy to argue that regulation is simply a response of government to public demands to correct the problems in the market, and that the government can in fact make conditions better. However, there are many problems with this argument – some related with the assumptions and others with the notion of responding to public interests. But the principal problem that we shall be concerned with is that, in many cases, industries and enterprises themselves ask to be regulated rather than have regulation imposed on them.

Private interest explanations of the origin of regulation are based on the assumption that enterprises in a market actively seek government regulation in order to achieve a goal or a range of goals particular to them. It is conventionally argued that the primary goal sought by the enterprises is the maximization of profits, and the method sought to achieve it is the use of government regulation to control entry, to affect competing goods and services, to fix prices, and to grant subsidies. The first three methods are desired because of the 'free rider' problem. That is, enterprises request regulation because there is no legal way to make all the enterprises in the market conform to a common goal such as setting the same market price. Rather, because of the lack of legal control, enterprises are able to engage in one-upmanship and thus plunge the market into chaos. Therefore, legal assistance is sought to prevent this and thus, at the same time, maximize (long- or short-term) profits.

The problem with the above explanations is that they attribute the origins of government regulation to 'greed' – that is, to the desire of enterprises to simply maximize profits. However, the notion of profit maximization cannot be sustained theoretically in a sequential production framework. Rather, the enterprise is interested in growing (expanding) and, therefore, will engage in activities that will promote it. Hence, it will request government regulation if it believes that is the only way to maintain itself as a going concern. Specifically, it can be argued that enterprises request government regulation in order to eliminate destructive price competition or the potential for it (by either fixing prices, controlling entry, or affecting competing commodities) so as to maintain themselves as going concerns.

Given the above discussion, it is obvious that the notion of 'regulatory capture' has little meaning in its most common sense, since the regulations (or regulatory commissions or agencies) are designed with the enterprises in mind in the first place. However, regulatory capture does have some meaning when it refers to the dominant role of the enterprises in the continuing regulation of the market. In this latter case, the enterprises ensure that the regulations (or commissions) fully reflect their views as the market conditions change over time.[26]

Market competition and the control of the social provisioning process

This chapter suggests that going business enterprises are embedded in a regulated competitive environment of their own making.[27] So competition is perceived as pervasive, but generally shorn of its destructive potential. In this context, competition affects the life span of a particular going enterprise, but not the going enterprise in general. That is, competition is something that individual enterprises are concerned about, but it does not create profits, only partially at best determines the magnitudes of the profit mark-up, and has an ambiguous impact on the level and direction of economic activity. What competition obscures are the class relationships that enable the capitalist class to make decisions which are carried out through the business enterprise that collectively ensures its reproduction, with the survival and reproduction of the working class an irritating incidental. Whether the enterprise is small or large, the number of enterprises in a market few or many, profit mark-ups big or little, or the concentration of economic activity is in a few or many enterprises, does not affect these class relationships. If for some reason capitalists' propensity to invest declined, resulting in a decline in profits, their access to consumption and the provisioning process would not be impaired. Moreover, the state would increase its expenditures (without increasing taxes), thereby increasing profits for the enterprises – the state is the profit-maker for capitalist of last resort.

Competition is now just, perhaps, an incidental irritant to capitalism since its most destructive properties regarding prices, price wars, and price stability is controlled through market governance organizations. What is of more significance is the going enterprise and its capabilities to change the structures of the economy that shapes the social provisioning process and affects profits and profit mark-ups. But in the hands of a going concern managed competition may be the legitimating social mechanism to concentrate the ownership of wealth and control over the social provisioning process into a smaller capitalist class and corresponding political elite. Speculative suggestion, of course, yet it does give importance to the study of competition that is far beyond the question of the profit mark-up.

Notes

1 This argument provides the basis for the claim that monopoly prices reduce workers' consumption, leading to under-consumption and depression.
2 The evidence on trade associations, cartels, price leadership, and government regulations controlling market competition and regulating prices is so extensive that it is plausible to argue that regulated competition has always existed under capitalism – see Lee (1998, 208, fn. 15) for a number of references and Lee (2012) for a critical examination of the connection between competition, profit mark-ups, and economic activity using a two-industry production model and a labor based mark-up pricing model. For references with an international flavor, see Schaede (2000), Connor (2008), and Viton (2004).
3 The preconditions for the existence of a market are not the concern in this chapter. However, it should be noted that there are three preconditions: (1) a clear definition of property rights; (2) general social rules that define relations of competition, cooperation, and market specific definitions of how enterprises should be organized; and (3) rules of exchange.
4 To be able to engage in causal actions suggests that the economic agent has power; in a social network, the agent's power is dependent on its network position vis-à-vis market transactions (Powell and Smith-Doerr 1994).
5 It should be noted that networks work because of mutual dependency and hence reliance; gains are to be made by pooling resources/relationships (Powell 1990).
6 Trust is part of social networks; hence, opportunism is not universally there. When opportunistic behavior occurs, it does not necessarily break up the social network.
7 Oligopoly exists when enterprises recognize the existence of other competing enterprises and thus realize that their strategic decisions regarding prices, for example, will elicit responses from their competitors. While oligopoly does suggest fewness (and corresponding large size and high barriers to entry), the exact number is indeterminate. In fact, through social networks and associational relationships, enterprises and their business leaders can recognize interdependency over a very large number of competitors that can be geographically dispersed and so adopt a motto that an injury to one is an injury to all.
8 The social network exists because of social discourse between the members. Since social discourse involves the sharing of experience, hope, aspirations, and resolutions

of conflicts, it is plausible to argue that social discourse is a contributing factor to managing competition (Kesting 1998).

9   A distinction between *power to set prices* in the market which comes with, for example, social networks, and *power to control access to the market* should be made. For the purpose here, I am concerned only with the former and not the latter.

10 For example, in 1955, there existed about 184 incorporated manufacturers' trade associations in the UK, with the earliest date of incorporation being 1892 for the Pianoforte Manufacturers Association Ltd.

11 In British Association of Glass Bottle Manufactures v. Nettlefold (1911) and Performing Right Society, Ltd. v. London Theatre of Varieties, Ltd. (1924), it was held that the mere fact that the memorandum of the association of a company empowers it to enter into arrangements for the regulation of output or prices, does not constitute a company as a trade union, provided that this is not one of its main objects.

12 In 1955 in the UK there were at least twenty-three trade associations registered as trade unions and twenty-nine trade associations which appeared in the Registrar of Friendly Societies as certified trade unions.

13 Section 4.1 of the British Trade Disputes Act of 1906 states that:

An action against a trade union, whether of workmen or masters, or against any members or officials thereof on behalf of themselves and all other members of the trade union in respect of any tortious act alleged to have been committed by or on behalf of the trade union, shall not be entertained by any court.

14 'Tort' is defined as a breach of legal duty with liability for damages.

15 The relevant sections of the Trades Union Act of 1871 read as follows:

3. The purposes of any trade union shall not, by reason merely that they are in restraint of trade, be unlawful so as to render void and voidable any agreement or trust.

4. Nothing in this Act shall enable any court to entertain any legal proceeding instituted with the object of directly enforcing or recovering damages for the breach of any of the following agreements, namely, (1) any agreement between members of a trade union as such concerning the conditions on which any members for the time being of such trade union shall or shall not sell their goods, transact business, employ, or be employed. . . . But nothing in this section shall be deemed to constitute any of the above-mentioned agreements unlawful.

16 These would include the Federation of British Industries, National Union of Manufacturers, London Chamber of Commerce, Manchester Chamber of Commerce, and the Birmingham Chamber of Commerce.

17 This approach is frequently used by associations whose main purpose is the fixing of common prices. Decisions about prices are rarely arbitrary: some formula related to costs is usually applied. Accountants are therefore necessary for purposes of computation, and, being neutral, they can collate production costs and other information in confidence.

18 For example:

The affairs of the Cold Rolled Brass and Copper Association shall be directed by the Members assembled in General Meeting and (subject to the control and directions of the Members in General Meeting) by the following officers of the Association namely the Chairman, Vice-Chairman, Director, Assistant Director, Secretaries, and Auditor.

19 Trade statistics are statistics relating to business activity, including statistics on one or more of such subjects as inventories, production, sales, shipments, and orders.

20 Standardization refers to the establishment of uniform product sizes or dimensions and, in the case of quality standards, of criteria of properties and performance as the

basis for grading, certification, and labelling; simplification refers to the reduction of the number or variety of product sizes, dimensions, types, models, patterns, and lines.

21 Many times the committee is constitutionally established – see, for example, the constitutions of the Non-Electrical Copper Association and the Cold Rolled Brass and Copper Association.

22 For example, the constitution of the H. C. Copper Association states: "No Member is at liberty to sell any goods, the prices of which are, for the time being, controlled by the Association on terms or at prices more favourable to the Buyer than those for the time being in force."

23 In some cases, as with the Hard Fibre Cord and Twine Manufacturers' Association, a separate company was set up to run the quota system.

24 This cannot be viewed as enterprises giving up freedom of decisions. This kind of notion of freedom is based on the methodological individualism that faces no social ties. But in a socially embedded context that is not the case of the acting enterprise. What is going on here is a particular *social decision process* in which decisions are collectively arrived at.

25 The dominant enterprise is a legal industrial institution and therefore is stable in that sense. That is, although the dominant enterprise is large compared to the market and provides the basis by which the market price is stabilized, it is not in *per se* violation of, for example, the various 'monopolies' statues in the UK.

26 Editor's note: This section is incomplete. Fred Lee left only a very rough draft on 'Laws and market control in a historical context,' which is intended to explain private enterprise's engagement in political activity to pass 'laws of regulation' that might give them a competitive advantage in the market.

27 Editor's note: The concluding section is from Lee (2012).

7 Microeconomics and the social provisioning process

Social provisioning and social surplus

Heterodox economics is about developing theoretical explanations of the actual (as opposed to a hypothetical or imagined) social provisioning process that is a continuous, non-accidental series of production-based, production-derived economic activities through historical time that provide 'needy' individuals and families the goods and services necessary to carry out their sequential reoccurring and changing social activities through time. Hence, as discussed in Chapter 2 (in particular see Table 2.6), economic activities are interlinked with various cultural values, norms and beliefs, societal institutions, technology, and the ecological system that provide the material basis for conducting social and economic activities. These components of the social fabric affect the acting organizations and institutions and, hence, the pattern and organization of economic activities delivering the goods and services that make government services and household social activities possible: they give this delivery mechanism or the social provisioning process its meaning and its value (Polanyi 1968; Hayden 1982; 1986; 2006; 2011; Natarajan, Elsner, and Fullwiler 2009). This means that the social provisioning process is embedded in a production-with-a-social surplus 'paradigm.' Consequently, the social surplus consists of the goods and services determined by the values and forces that create the social activities, which the provisioning process underwrites.

There are a number of variants of the social surplus approach, one being the Sraffian approach and another being the heterodox approach, which is developed in this chapter.[1] Like the Sraffian surplus approach, the heterodox surplus approach starts with some assumed givens that characterize an actual (rather than imagined) capitalist economy: technology, class, capitalist state, and a viable economy. However, unlike the former, the latter does not presume both the level and composition of the social product and a self-replacing-with-a-surplus economy. In their place agency is embedded in the social structure qua social relationships qua social institutions. By 'embedded' it is meant that agents, either individually or collectively, carry out particular roles assigned by the present social structures. The defining social structures of capitalism are the capitalist state (with its state money), the class structure, and the structure of production in the sense that individual workers' economic activities are directed by the state's and capitalists' production and employment decisions. The embedded agency regarding private sector pricing, investment, output, and employment decisions is the business enterprise qua capitalist class who make the decisions for the purpose of continuing as a going concern or enterprise through making positive monetary profits, while state expenditure decisions (which include employment and investment decisions) are made by the political elite with the view of primarily supporting the interests of the capitalist class (O'Connor 1973). In this context the social surplus is defined as the difference between the total social product and the total amount of intermediate inputs at a point in time; and the total social product is agency-determined by the business enterprise and political elite expenditure decisions, and economic activities are organized and directed toward the creation of the surplus. That is, in the heterodox surplus approach with the inclusion of agency (as well as structures), the social product is not given and the surplus is not a residual. The indispensability of agency to determine the social surplus makes it, contrary to Pasinetti's (2005) argument, a necessary core component of the heterodox surplus approach and its theory of value. In addition, because agents make socially structured decisions in a transmutable and uncertain world that generate objective, quantitative outcomes, the adjectives of 'subjective,' 'rational,' or 'optimal' are not appropriate or relevant to describe their decision-making activities and outcomes. Thus, agents in the heterodox social surplus approach (and heterodox economics in general) are distinctly different from the mainstream notion of agent that Sraffa rejected when adopting his objectivist methodology (Kurz and Salvadori 2005; Kurz 2006; Sinha 2010, 307–308).

This property suggests that the heterodox surplus approach generates its own theoretical accounts of prices, output, and employment, and its own theory of value. This chapter delineates the former and their associated theory of value, based upon heterodox microeconomic approaches to the structure, agency, and the social provisioning process developed in previous chapters. In the first two sections, corresponding to the productive, financial, and monetary structures of the heterodox model of the economy are delineated with respect to the social surplus and social provisioning in Chapter 2, the pricing model and an output-employment model are developed and their structural-theoretical properties are delineated. The third section brings together the productive, financial, and monetary structures of the provisioning process with the price and output employment models to create an emergent, concatenated heterodox model of the going economy and delineates its theoretical core. Drawing upon this, the chapter concludes with a heterodox theory of value. The outcome of the chapter is that unexpected but not unfamiliar or impossible arguments, claims, and conclusions emerge. To be receptive to the unexpected, the reader needs to be more like the Queen and less like Alice in *Through the Looking Glass*:

> "There's no use trying," she [Alice] said: "one *can't* believe impossible things." "I daresay you haven't had much practice," said the Queen. "When I was your age, I always did it for half-an-hour a day. Why, sometimes I've believed as many as six impossible things before breakfast."
>
> (Carroll 1902, 93)

Pricing model and theory of prices

The business enterprise is a specific social organization for coordinating and carrying out economic activities in a manner that mirrors the social relationships in capitalist society and, most importantly, reproduces the capitalist class. It consists of an organizational component, a production and cost component, a series of routines that transmit information (such as costs, sales, and prices) to enable workers and managers to coordinate and carry out their activities, and a management that has agency to make strategic decisions about prices, investment, production, and employment. The organization of the business enterprise is a social technique for the production of goods and services. Hierarchical in structure and authoritarian in terms of social control, the organization of the enterprise enables senior management to make decisions that, in turn, are carried out by lower management and workers. The enterprise has three tools by which to affect economic activity and hence the social provisioning process for its own interest: setting prices, undertaking fixed investment, and making production and employment decisions. When making decisions, the management of an enterprise is motivated by different goals, the most fundamental being the survival and continuation of the enterprise, followed by various strategic goals, such as growth of sales, developing new products, entering new geographical regions or markets, generating dividends for shareholders, and attaining political power. Given that the enterprise has an unknown but potentially very long life span, the time period to achieve each of the goals is likely to differ, and management cannot be sure that it can achieve them. Thus the goals are not ends in themselves, but are established so as to direct the activities of the enterprise in a transmutable and uncertain environment. As a result, profits are not an end goal for management, but rather an intermediate objective that facilitates the directing of its desired activities.

Management views price setting as a strategic decision designed to meet its goals (see Chapter 4). In particular, it utilizes cost-plus pricing procedures that first involve calculating the enterprise average total costs ($EATC_B$) of producing the product at budgeted output or normal capacity utilization[2] and then multiplying the $EATC_B$ by a profit mark-up to set the price.[3] The resulting price remains fixed for a period of time (and many transactions) and does not change when sales increase or decrease. Its two most important properties are its potential, depending on the state of demand (sales), to generate a cash flow for the enterprise that will cover its costs of producing the product(s) and to generate profits, and its strategic capabilities, such as penetrating markets and altering market shares. Once set, the price is then administered to the market as the enterprise's market price. However, the business enterprise sells its goods and services in markets that include products from other competing enterprises; thus there needs to be a market arrangement, such as trade associations and price leadership, by which the market price is set (see Chapter 6). Therefore, the price equation for the i-th market, as delineated below, is not significantly different from the enterprise pricing equation (Lee 1998; 2013b):

$$[\mathbf{m}_i\mathbf{p}_{1t} + \mathbf{h}_i\mathbf{w} + d_i][1 + z_i][1 + r_i] = p_{it+1} \tag{7.1}$$

where $\mathbf{m}_i = (m_{i1}, \ldots, m_{in})$ is a row vector of material pricing coefficients at normal capacity utilization; p_{1t} is a given column vector of input prices at time t; $\mathbf{h}_i = (h_{i1}, \ldots, h_{iz})$ is a row vector of labor pricing coefficients at normal capacity utilization; $\mathbf{w}$ is a column vector of state money wage rates; d_i is the depreciation pricing coefficient (in terms of state money); z_i is the overhead mark-up for the i-th good; r_i is the profit mark-up for the i-th good; and p_{it+1} is the actual market price for the i-th good at time $t+1$.

Since a market refers to all the transactions of a specific product, the economy consists of as many markets as there are products. Thus, there are m markets that can be classified as intermediate, government, fixed investment, and consumption goods markets. Common to all the markets is that the relationship between the market price and market sales is nonexistent; so a reduction in the market price by itself will generate little, if any, increase in market sales. Finally, the *price model of the economy* is:

$$[R_d][Z_d][M\mathbf{p}_{1t} + H\mathbf{w} + \mathbf{d}] = \mathbf{p}_{it+1} \tag{7.2}$$

or in a disaggregated form:

Basic goods sector prices: $[R_{d1}][Z_{d1}][M_{11}\mathbf{p}_{1t} + H_1\mathbf{w} + \mathbf{d}_1] = \mathbf{p}_{1t+1}$ (7.3)
Surplus goods sector prices: $[R_{d2}][Z_{d2}][M_{21}\mathbf{p}_{1t} + H_2\mathbf{w} + \mathbf{d}_2] = \mathbf{p}_{2t+1}$

where R_d is a $m \times m$ diagonal matrix of profit mark-ups and the i-th element is $(1 + r_i)$; Z_d is a $m \times m$ diagonal matrix of overhead mark-ups and the i-th element is $(1 + z_i)$; M is a $m \times n$ matrix of material pricing coefficients that are invariant with respect to short-term variations in output and the i-th row is $\mathbf{m}_i$; H is a $m \times z$ matrix of labor pricing coefficients that are invariant with respect to short-term variations in output and the i-th row is $\mathbf{h}_i$; $\mathbf{d}$ is a $m \times 1$ vector of depreciation pricing coefficients and the i-th element is d_i; $\mathbf{p}_1$ is a $n \times 1$ column vector of prices of intermediate inputs; and $\mathbf{p}_2$ is a $(m - n) \times 1$ column vector of prices of all surplus goods and services.

The *structural properties* of the price model and its prices are well known and can be briefly stated:

1 because M_{11} is based on G_{11} (intermediate inputs used in the production of basic goods), it may be decomposable to some degree, but has an irreducible sub-matrix that has a positive maximum eigenvalue less than one;
2 given 'reasonable' values for R_d, Z_d, $\mathbf{w}$, and the material, labor, and depreciation pricing coefficients (M, H, $\mathbf{d}$), prices are determined, and $\mathbf{p}$ is strictly positive, which means that the price model is internally, structurally coherent:[4]

$$\mathbf{p}_1 = [I - R_{d1}Z_{d1}M_{11}]^{-1}R_{d1}Z_{d1}[H_1\mathbf{w} + \mathbf{d}_1]$$

$$\mathbf{p}_2 = R_{d2}Z_{d2}M_{21}[I - R_{d1}Z_{d1}M_{11}]^{-1}R_{d1}Z_{d1}[H_1\mathbf{w} + \mathbf{d}_1] + R_{d2}Z_{d2}[H_2\mathbf{w} + \mathbf{d}_2]$$

(7.4)

3 the material and labor pricing coefficients cannot be reduced to a homogeneous quantity of labor;
4 with given values for **w** and **d**, different compositions of M, R_d, Z_d, and H produce different prices; and
5 as **d** and **w** are in terms of state money, so are prices.

The *theoretical properties* are, however, not so well known, but can also be briefly stated. First, with irreducible material and labor pricing coefficients, prices cannot be reduced to and hence conceived of as a comparable homogeneous substance such as a homogeneous quantity of labor power. Consequently, the relative comparability of prices is not governed by the relative amounts of a measurable common substance supposedly embodied in them.[5] And even if it is possible to do such a reduction process, prices would still not be reduced to an amount of the common substance such as quantity of labor power because of the existence of depreciation that is in terms of state money. Secondly, price models with structurally different pricing equations produce different prices, which imply that price models must structurally represent the range of pricing equations actually used in the economy if their prices are to be theoretically accurate and hence relevant for theoretical and applied research. Thirdly, because prices exist as long as both the profit mark-ups and the wage rates are positive, then it is the 'basic' price system that determines the 'basic' prices, p_1; while it is the price system as a whole that determines the 'non-basic' prices, p_2, that is, the prices of the goods and services that comprise the social surplus. However, since the price system reflects and is embedded in the social system of production, it is the latter that determines prices or, more accurately, provides the material and social basis for their existence. Lastly, the price model, prices, and wages are embedded in a monetary production economy denominated in the state monetary unit (and hence denominated by state money, not commodity money). Consequently, wage rates in terms of the monetary unit and the profit mark-up (which is denominated differently as a percentage on costs) are determined independently of each other and hence can independently vary. So in the absence of a commodity *numeraire*, the state-money prices of goods and services are free to vary in response to changes in the wage rate or the profit mark-up. Thus an increase in wage rates does not require a structural reduction in profit mark-ups and vice versa (Pivetti 1985; Nell 2003). In particular, an equal percentage increase in wage rates will not appreciably alter the price-wage rate ratio, p_i/w_{iz}, or affect at all the profit mark-up or the price-cost ratio, $(p_i - \text{EATC}_B)/\text{EATC}_B$, whereas an equal percentage increase in the profit mark-up will do so. This asymmetrical outcome occurs because money wages do not equal real wages, whereas due to its nature of being a percentage of costs, the profit mark-up appropriates in a sense real goods and services and thus is equivalent to the real wage but for capitalists. Hence, as will be argued in the penultimate section, that in the context of distribution, the profit mark-up has a more significant impact on the economy relative to the money wage rate.

The structural-theoretical properties do not completely determine the outcomes of the price model; there is also a role for *agency*. In particular, actual prices (p_i) are set, changed, and re-set through agency. Price changes occur only when enterprises decide to vary money wage rates or profit mark-ups or by altering the pricing coefficients (which is predicated on changing the underlying technology, an alteration in the capital-labor relationship within the enterprise, or changes in the laws and/or rules governing depreciation). Thus, prices in the economy reflect agency, the costing-pricing structures of the business enterprise, and the structures of the social system of production. Price setting as an act of agency within a set of structures raises an important theoretical issue of structurally determined prices relative to agency-structure determined prices or what is known as the issue of convergence of agency-set market prices to structural-solution short-period or long-period prices. As argued in Lee (1996; 1998, Ch. 11), agency can decide to change prices at various time periods, such as every six months or a year, with the result that it can take a long time for structural-solution prices to be reached. However, if agency, when setting the market prices, also changes the pricing coefficients, overhead/profit mark-ups, and/or wages rates, then structural-solution prices are never attained and actual prices are not 'imperfect production prices' (Lavoie 2011). This suggests that instead of carrying out economic analysis in terms of actual-price convergence to structural price solutions (or long-period/ short-period positions), which imply a closed system methodology, economic analysis should be in terms of open-systems and agency-structure interaction – that is, as a historical analytical story.[6] This is why the price model (Equations 7.2 and 7.3) has input prices at time t and output prices at time $t + 1$ and the two prices are not the same. In short, the heterodox theory of prices so far consists of the pricing equation, the price model, the structural, theoretical, and agency properties of the model, and the accompanying narrative, all of which explains how prices are set and changed relative to the state monetary unit. What remains to be articulated is the purpose of prices, which will be dealt with in the going economy section below.

Output-employment model and the social surplus

Agency – that is, decisions to produce the surplus – resides with the capitalist class and the political elite or the ruling class (Lee 2011). For the economy as a whole, the total demand for investment goods (Q_{2I}) is determined by business enterprises and based on a range of criteria most of which are more important than the rate of interest, the rate of profit, or the difference between them.[7] In addition, although the dependent, working, and ruling class households demand consumption goods (Q_{2C}), they do not directly order the production of the goods they consume. So, they partake in the social surplus, but not entirely of their own choosing. Drawing upon past and possibly new consumption patterns of various kinds of households differentiated by income qua class,[8] enterprises make production and employment decisions that result in the production of a differentiated array of consumption goods for the dependent class (Q_{2Cd}), the working class (Q_{2Cw}), and the ruling class (Q_{2Cr}), where $Q_{2C} = Q_{2Cw} + Q_{2Cd} + Q_{2Cr}$. Being produced ahead of payments,

households exercise limited agency by only choosing among the already produced goods for them. This implies a global 'real wage' for each class, but does
not imply a particular real wage for any individual household within the working,
dependent, or ruling class. Finally, the political elite also demands government
goods $(\mathbf{Q}_{2G})$ necessary to produce government services. Thus, the output of the
economy $(\mathbf{Q})$ is represented as:

$$\mathbf{Q} = (e\mathbf{G}^*)^{\mathrm{T}} + \mathbf{Q}_{2C}^* + \mathbf{Q}_{21}^* + \mathbf{Q}_{2G}^* = (e\mathbf{G}^*)^{\mathrm{T}} + \mathbf{S}^* \tag{7.5}$$

where $\mathbf{Q}_{2C}^*$, $\mathbf{Q}_{21}^*$, and $\mathbf{Q}_{2G}^*$ are $m \times 1$ column vectors with the first n row zeros
and the last $m - n$ rows semi-positive; and $\mathbf{S}^*$ is a $m \times 1$ column vector
with the first n row zeros and the last $m - n$ rows strictly positive.[9]

Letting $\mathbf{Q}_{d1}^{-1}\mathbf{G}_{11} = \mathbf{A}_{11}$ and $\mathbf{Q}_{d2}^{-1}\mathbf{G}_{21} = \mathbf{A}_{21}$, then $\mathbf{Q}_d^{-1}\mathbf{G}^* = \mathbf{A}^* = \begin{bmatrix} \mathbf{A}_{11} & 0 \\ \mathbf{A}_{21} & 0 \end{bmatrix}$ is a $m \times m$

augmented matrix of material production coefficients that vary with output; and

letting and $\mathbf{Q}_{d1}^{-1}\mathbf{L}_{11} = l_1$ and $\mathbf{Q}_{d2}^{-1}\mathbf{L}_{21} = l_2$, then $\mathbf{Q}_d^{-1}\mathbf{L} = l = \begin{bmatrix} l_1 \\ l_2 \end{bmatrix}$ is a $m \times z$ matrix

of labor production coefficients that vary with output, the *output-employment
model of the economy* is:

$$\begin{aligned} \mathbf{Q} &= \mathbf{A}^{*\mathrm{T}}\mathbf{Q} + \mathbf{S}^* \\ \mathbf{L}^* &= \mathbf{L} + \mathbf{L}_{41}^{\mathrm{T}} = l^{\mathrm{T}}\mathbf{Q} + \mathbf{L}_{41}^{\mathrm{T}} \end{aligned} \tag{7.6}$$

where $\mathbf{L}^*$ is a $z \times 1$ column vector of total labor skills employed in the economy;
$\mathbf{L}$ is a $z \times 1$ column vector of total labor skills employed in the private sector – that is, the basic goods sector $(\mathbf{L}_{11})$, the surplus goods sector $(\mathbf{L}_{21})$, and
the banking sector $(\mathbf{L}_{31})$; and $\mathbf{L}_{41}^{\mathrm{T}}$ represents the total labor skills employed
in providing government services.

Thus, given the ruling class agency qua decisions regarding the amount of
the social surplus to be produced, total social product, total labor employed
in the private sector, and their composition are structurally determined while
agency by the state determines total number of government employees and their
composition:

$$\begin{aligned} \mathbf{Q} &= [\mathbf{I} - \mathbf{A}^{*\mathrm{T}}]^{-1}\mathbf{S}^* \\ \mathbf{L}^* &= l^{\mathrm{T}}[\mathbf{I} - \mathbf{A}^{*\mathrm{T}}]^{-1}\mathbf{S}^* + \mathbf{L}_{41}^{\mathrm{T}} \end{aligned} \tag{7.7}$$

or in a disaggregated form:

Output-basic goods sector : $\mathbf{Q}_1 = [\mathbf{I} - \mathbf{A}_{11}^{\mathrm{T}}]^{-1}\mathbf{A}_{21}^{\mathrm{T}}\mathbf{S}$ $\tag{7.8}$

Output-surplus goods sector : $\mathbf{S} = \mathbf{Q}_2 = \mathbf{Q}_{2C} + \mathbf{Q}_{21} + \mathbf{Q}_{2G}$

Total employment : $\mathbf{L}^* = l_1^{\mathrm{T}}\left[\mathbf{I} - \mathbf{A}_{11}^{\mathrm{T}}\right]^{-1}\mathbf{S} + l_2^{\mathrm{T}}\mathbf{S} + \mathbf{L}_{41}^{\mathrm{T}}$

The *structural properties* of the output-employment model are also well established and hence can be briefly stated:

1   A_{11} is at least semi-positive, indecomposable, and has a maximum eigenvalue (λ_{m11}) less than one and greater than zero since A_{21} is semi-positive;

2   $[I - A_{11}^T]^{-1}$ is the Leontief inverse matrix, which is finite and strictly positive since $0 < \lambda_{m11} < 1$;

3   $[I - A_{11}^T]^{-1} A_{21}^T$ is a strictly positive $n \times (m - n)$ matrix and is the output-employment multiplier in that it is used both in the determination of Q_1 and L^*;

4   for any given values of S and L_{41}, total social product Q, total intermediate inputs Q_1, and total employment L^* are strictly positive;

5   for any change in S ($\Delta S = S_1 - S_0$) where all elements are zero except one which is either a plus or minus one will produce same direction changes in Q_1 and L^*; and

6   any change in any element of S is independent of any other element of S, which means ΔQ_{2C}, ΔQ_{2I}, and ΔQ_{2G} are independent of each other.

Its *theoretical properties* are, on the other hand, not so obvious. First, the actual economy, as represented in the output-employment model, is an emergent going plant that has the productive potential to produce the surplus – that is, it is the system of production of intermediate material and labor inputs as a whole that is productive.[10] Consequently, the production of any surplus good or service requires the direct and/or indirect utilization of all intermediate inputs and labor skills necessary for their production as well as for the production of the surplus goods and services. This implies that the total social product does not adequately represent the economy and the social surplus is not a residual. A better way to represent the economy is the output-employment model qua a going plant that is directed by the demands of the surplus and the total social product emerges as a necessary by-product. With the economy as a going plant, the physical real cost of producing the social surplus in any quantity and its composition is represented by the multiplier, $[I - A_{11}^T]^{-1} A_{21}^T$, and summarized by the maximum eigenvalue of A_{11} (λ_{m11}). That is, the lower λ_{m11} the greater is the amount of intermediate inputs that can be used to produce the social surplus. This suggests that λ_{m11} represents the productive fertility of the economy directly in terms of A_{11} and generally in terms of increasing the production potential of the surplus.[11] Moreover, the variation in the real costs of producing the surplus is captured by variations in λ_{m11}. An increase in the social surplus requires more intermediate material inputs and the possible use of vintage technology, which means that the material production coefficients may increase; the overall impact is that a sufficient number of the production coefficients in A_{11} will decline so that λ_{m11} remains relatively stable or declines; and the same can be said for A_{21}. As a result, the productive fertility of the system as a whole remains the same or increases.[12] Consequently, the system of production as a whole has the fundamental capacity to produce increasing quantities of the social surplus, somewhat akin to Baran and Sweezy's (1966) 'law' of the stable or rising surplus. This means that limitations on its production is not technological, but emanates from the decisions of the ruling class.[13]

A second theoretical property is that the economic activity for the economy as a whole is determined by the decisions to produce consumption, fixed investment, and government goods and services: the demand for the surplus generates current production. With the 'input' requirements produced (and reproduced) upon the demand for the surplus goods and services, the coordination of the production of the total social product is effectuated independently of prices. That is, the output-employment multiplier represents the technical coordination of economic activity while the surplus through the multiplier determines the level and composition of the total social product and private sector employment. Hence, although the notion of the 'anarchy of production' is a misleading description of production under capitalism, the 'anarchy' of the ruling class' demands for the social surplus is not.

The last theoretical property of the output-employment model arises from the productive independence of the goods and services that comprise the surplus, and the demand for the surplus generates its production. In particular, since consumption and fixed investment goods are created from the current production they call forth, the former is not constrained by the latter and the latter is not based on 'savings.' The economic system as a whole, represented by the output-employment model, has the capability of producing varying amounts of Q_{2C} independently of Q_{2I}, if below full utilization of capacity and co-operatively with Q_{2I}, if additional capacity is needed.[14] It also has the capability of producing varying amounts of class-linked consumption goods without affecting the production of other class-linked consumption goods, which means that the production of Q_{2Cw}, Q_{2Cd}, and Q_{2Cr} can vary independently of each other. Because workers as households consume currently produced Q_{2C}, this implies there is no 'saved' wage fund that inversely links 'real wages' to employment or that links higher 'real wages' for some to lower 'real wages' for others. Similarly, since Q_{2I} is also currently produced, private fixed investment is not dependent on 'savings' of any sort. Moreover, because the economic system as a whole also has the capability of producing varying amounts of Q_{2G} independently of Q_{2I} and Q_{2C}, increasing Q_{2G} does not 'crowd out' the production of Q_{2C} and Q_{2I}.

The structural-theoretical properties do not entirely determine the outcome of the output-employment model; *agency* also has a necessary role. It is clear that the agency-decisions of the capitalist class working through the business enterprise and the political elite working through the state determine the actual amount and composition of the total social product and employment. It is also obvious that the decisions are coordinated to some degree, but also uncoordinated to, perhaps, a greater degree, thus generating a misplaced perception of the anarchy of production. Moreover, given the productive output-employment multiplier, the social provisioning process is potentially sustainable and thus has an expected, but transmutable and uncertain, future – that is, the social provisioning process is not necessarily a self-replacing, replicating one. So while the actual-current decisions of the ruling class that determine the current production of the social surplus are continuous and hence result in continuous production (implying that market transactions do not clear markets but rather ensure continuous market transactions so that markets are non-clearable), they are at the same time generally altering the level and composition of the total social product. Therefore, the actual production of goods and services do not exactly replace what is used up in production, so the economy is not reproduced qua replicated; nor do they necessarily ensure the survival and reproduction of all of the individuals and groups that comprise the ruling, working, and dependent classes. All of this implies that because of agency with its uncertainty and expectations in a transmutable world, there are no long-period positions that are 'centers of attraction' for the actual output and employment resulting from the actual decisions made by the ruling elite. Consequently, the heterodox theory of output and employment consists of the output-employment model and multiplier; the structural, theoretical, and agency properties of the model and multiplier; and the accompanying narrative, all of which provides a plausible explanation of what determines the social surplus, total social product, and employment and how they change in response to decisions made by the ruling class.

The going economy and its theoretical core

In Chapter 2, we delineated the structure of the going economy. This can be combined to the price model and the output-employment model to form a model of the going economy as a whole. That is, linking together the SFSA (stock-flow social accounting) models of the productive, financial, and monetary structures of the social provisioning process (Tables 2.2 and 2.3) with the disaggregated price model of the economy (Equation 7.3), and the disaggregated output-employment model of the economy (Equation 7.8) creates an emergent concatenated heterodox model of the going economy as a whole.

In terms of its productive structure, the economy is a going plant with unused capacity and fixed investment goods and the capability of producing additional capacity through producing fixed investment goods. So as long as household social activities are ongoing and supported by government services, the structure of production ensures the continuous reproduction of the intermediate inputs and fixed investment goods. More specifically, the level of economic activity for the economy as a whole is completely determined by the decision to produce government, consumption, and investment goods and services – that is, by the decisions to produce the surplus. With the input requirements produced and reproducible simultaneously with the goods and services necessary for the household social activities and government services to take place, the social provisioning process is potentially sustainable, and thus has an expected future; this is what makes the economy a going plant. On the other hand, the financial structure (as delineated in Table 2.3) shows that the national debt consists of government bonds that are held by business enterprises and households; thus an increase in the national debt arising from government expenditures exceeding the interest payments by enterprises and households to the government increases private sector and households holding of government bonds and hence their incomes and profits. Enterprises and households also take out state bank loans, which simultaneously create financial assets for the state. Hence, government decisions to spend and enterprise and household decisions to take out state loans create, drive, and change the economy's financial structure, an outcome not dissimilar from decisions concerning the production of the surplus driving the productive structure of the economy noted above.

The monetary structure model shows the flows of intermediate inputs into the surplus goods sector, and the flows of the various surplus goods and services into their social accounts of households, enterprises, and the state. At the same time, it mirrors these flows of goods and services with the flow of wage, profit, and state incomes required to purchase them. In this manner, the monetized social provisioning process acquires the structure of a going concern. With the provisioning process as a going plant, the flow of state money ties together market transactions and non-market activities that ensure the continuation of consumer activities and government services through time. The model further identifies the core decisions that drive the provisioning process: the decisions that determine the social surplus and employment, prices, profits, wages, and interest rates. The impact of the former decisions is shown in the output-employment model, and the impact of pricing decisions is shown in the price model. Because the ruling class (as opposed to the capitalist class by itself) has the productive and administrative capabilities and the legal rights to these decisions, it can direct the provisioning process in their own current and changing future interests. Therefore, the social provisioning process is a socially sustainable process in which each state money transaction is a manifestation and reproduction of the capitalist relationships, and hence both sustains and promises a future for the ruling elite and their dependents – in short, we have a going economy.

This model of the going economy is unusual in that it consists of four concatenated models, each of which is an emergent model with their own potential locations of agency. Thus, it is not possible to reduce the model of the going economy to a single 'homogeneous' system where everything is determined simultaneously. Hence, the theoretical core of the going economy consists of different but linked components, each drawing on the four models in different ways: (1) the separation of price and output-employment decisions; (2) prices and the going business enterprise; (3) social surplus, the state, and wages and profits; and (4) the social surplus and social provisioning. Together the components delineate the heterodox narrative picture of how the social provisioning process works under capitalism – that is, the heterodox theory of value (more on this below).

Prices and output-employment decisions

The first component of the theoretical core is the separation of price and output-employment decisions, which implies that prices and outputs are not structurally related in terms of a deterministic functional relationship, as in the case of demand or supply curves; that prices and output-employment are not determined simultaneously; and that the output-employment multiplier has no impact on prices and hence is not the cause of price increases qua inflation. As a result, prices are relatively stable in face of output-employment variations; conversely, the changing of prices is not predicated on output-employment variations. Indicative of this separation is that the pricing coefficients matrices (M, H) are different from the production coefficients matrices (A, *l*), so that the structure of the pricing equations differs from their corresponding structure of production and cost equation. The absence of a dual between the two sets of matrices implies that prices are not profit maximizing prices, and that neither prices nor output and employment converge to Sraffian long-period positions, which explicitly depend on the existence of the dual. The non-simultaneous decisions of prices and output-employment, combined with non-profit maximizing prices and the absence of long-period positions, also result in the dismissal of the concepts of equilibrium and the tendency towards it, cost minimization, profit maximization, and implicitly market clearing. What this means methodologically is that the actual variables and magnitudes of prices and output-employment are theoretical variables, and the actual economy is the theoretical economy. What it means theoretically is that neither the distribution of the social product (so that production can take place again) nor the coordination of economic activity is possible via prices (and interest rates and profit rates).[15]

Prices and the going business enterprise

Since prices neither coordinate nor make economic activity happen, their theoretical role in a going economy has to be located elsewhere. In a capitalist going economy, it is necessary that enterprises generate sufficient revenue through the prices they set to cover their costs and generate profits. Thus, prices of goods and services are the primary mechanisms through which business enterprises obtain their revenue to continue as a going enterprise. So the second theoretical component of the going economy is that prices, as abstract indexes of credit qua debt obligations, are 'going enterprise' prices. In particular, as credit-debt indexes, prices are not grounded intrinsically in commodities and hence are not 'reproduction prices' – that is, prices that only permit the 'commodity' replication of the enterprises and the economy. They are more since the settling of debts enables enterprises to acquire new debts, but not necessarily debts that will replicate it on a constant or expanding basis. This has the obvious implication that even with a state banking system and the absence of private financial enterprises, Minsky's financial instability hypothesis is still relevant. Moreover, because they are credit-debt indexes, price increases (inflation) occur because price declines make it more difficult for enterprises to meet their debt obligations. Finally, going enterprise prices permit the location of agency to be in the business enterprise; it is this agency qua the business enterprise working through the output-employment multiplier that (along with state expenditures) drives, coordinates, and changes economic activity of the going economy.[16]

Social surplus, the state, and wages and profits

The third component of the theoretical core deals with the origins of the social surplus, the analytical categories of profits and wages, and the relationship between the social surplus and wages, profits, and state expenditures. Since the economy, as represented by the output-employment model, has the productive potential to produce the social surplus (and hence the total social product and employment), the origin of the social surplus under capitalism is found in the agency of the ruling class and the correlative existence of the working class, whose members are compelled to work for capitalists and the state to get state money so as to have access to the social provisioning process; unlike the ruling class, the working (and dependent) class has no fundamental-structural control over their access to social provisioning because they have no access to the means of production or the productive capabilities of the economy. Utilizing this class and state imposed dependency on state money, the ruling class' desire to acquire particular surplus goods and services results in their commanding state moneyless unemployed labor power to produce it, with the unintended by-product of also having to produce, as part of the surplus, consumption goods for the working and dependent classes.[17] In short, with the economy as a going plant, the origin of the social surplus (and hence the total social product) is found in agency-demanded class- and state-linked goods and services.

The most significant implication that flows from the agency-driven surplus is that it generates the analytical categories of wages, profits, and state expenditures and the corresponding surplus-acquiring, provisioning-accessing variables of wage rates, profit mark-ups, and state money.[18] That is, the decision by business enterprises to demand and purchase fixed investment goods requires them to also have an income variable, the profit mark-up, by which to acquire them. Similarly, the decision by the state to demand and purchase government goods and services requires it to also have an income variable, state money, by which to acquire them and the business enterprise to have a profit mark-up to capture the state expenditures as profits. Finally, the decision to produce consumption goods and services requires the existence of income variables, the wage rate (which includes salaries), and government payment for households to purchase them. Thus, the production of the social surplus requires the simultaneous 'production' of income variables (and prices) – wage rates, profit mark-ups, government payments, and state money – in order for the state, business enterprises, and households to gain access to the social provisioning process.[19] In fact, it is not just that the income variables are produced simultaneously with the production of the surplus, the production of the social surplus also generates the incomes by which they are purchased. Since government expenditures have the tripartite role of directly and/or indirectly purchasing goods and services, of becoming part of business enterprise profits, and of ending up as financial assets purchased by ruling class households (FA_{5RC}) and enterprises (FA_{BE}), the value of the surplus ($Q_2^T p_2$) plus the purchase of government bonds equals private sector wages $e(L^* w)$, net profits (Π'), depreciation (D_E), and the net government income qua expenditures (GOV_E) that is equal to the deficit:[20]

$$e(L^* w) + \Pi' + D_E + GOV_E = Q_2^T p_2 + FA_{BE} + FA_{5RC} \qquad (7.9)$$

Subtracting out the equivalent of government expenditures qua deficit from both sides, we have the value of the surplus equaling private sector wages, plus net profits and depreciation, plus a residual of state financial assets and liabilities (due to $\mathbf{p}_{1t} \neq \mathbf{p}_{1t+1}$). So if the ruling class decides to produce more social surplus goods and services, then the result will be an increase in private sector wages and profits, and at the same time 'produce' private financial assets in the form of government bonds purchased by the ruling class.[21] In short, being producible means that agency qua demand for the social surplus creates the income variables that give access to the social surplus, the provisioning process, and the incomes to purchase it: demand creates the surplus *and* income to purchase the surplus or 'demand creates its own supply.'

Two subsidiary implications follow from 'demand creates its own supply.' The first is that saving behavior has no theoretical role in explaining incomes, specifically profits; the second is that underconsumption and overproduction do not exist – rather only Keynesian unemployment exists. This well-known relationship of 'demand creates its own supply' is a result of an agency-structure relationship deeply embedded through the output-employment multiplier in the productive-monetary structure of the social provisioning process; it is an outcome that is independent of the competitive nature of the markets (Pasinetti 1997; 2001). But even more significantly, this relationship, in the context of a state money economy, creates state financial assets for the ruling class (and simultaneously state liabilities) that extend into the future. Hence, the ruling class not only directly determines the current social provisioning process, it can, through its accumulation of financial assets, also determine its future. Therefore, the state can never be a neutral arbitrator in a class-based economy; rather, it must always work in the interests of the ruling class – those who control the future also control the present.

A second implication is that the classical-Marxian distinction between productive and unproductive labor power is not relevant. That is, according to Table 2.3 and Equations from 7.1 to 7.6, it is evident that all the labor employed is necessary to produce, on an ongoing basis, the surplus goods and services for the state to carry out its government services and households to engage in their social activities. Moreover, the employment pattern of the labor power among the various economic and social activities does not intrinsically limit the production of the surplus, limit the creation of profits, and hence potentially generate a lower rate of accumulation. If there is a problem with the size, growth, and composition of the social surplus, its solution lies with the agency of the ruling class and not with the pattern of employment. The solution, however, is a ruling class solution, which may mean higher unemployment for the working class and worsening living standards for working and dependent class households.

Social surplus and social provisioning

The final theoretical component of the going economy is the social surplus itself and the implications for differential access to the social provisioning process. As noted above, the output-employment multiplier represents the physical real cost of producing the social surplus and that this real cost declines (or at least remains constant) as the amount of the surplus produced increases. So instead of a technological barrier to increasing the surplus, there is an agency barrier in terms of the decisions made by the ruling class. In particular, as long as the ruling class makes the decisions needed to sustain (but not necessarily replicate) the technological capabilities of the multiplier, the production of the social surplus remains unimpeded. Thus, much of the surplus is discretionary in that its quantities and composition between and within consumption, fixed investment, and government goods and services are not dictated by the multiplier but by the discretionary decisions of the ruling class.

This gives rise to two significant implications. Since the production of fixed investment goods is independent of the production of consumption goods, variations in the ratio of the value of fixed investment goods to the value of consumption goods have little economic relevance either to the issue of the distribution of income or to understanding economic growth. As noted above, the production of the surplus simultaneously creates the income variables that give access to it. However, the 'discretionary' decisions by the ruling class generate a differentiated composition of the surplus, and particularly of fixed investment and consumption goods. And this in turn generates a hierarchical array of profit mark-ups and household incomes. So the second implication is that the distribution of consumption goods between the working, dependent, and ruling classes is varied in that enterprises produce specific kinds of goods and services for each of the social classes, with each array of goods priced so that they equal the particular incomes of the three classes. Thus, capitalist production decisions create a structure of household incomes and within them a structure of wage rates and government payments. It also creates a structure of household incomes within the working and dependent classes and within the ruling class, but there is no necessity that all household incomes of the former provide at least a minimal subsistence access to social provisioning.[22] The same can be said for profit mark-ups, in that the production of differentiated fixed investment goods with different prices associated with different kinds of technology and enterprise organization creates the basis for differentiated profit mark-ups and differential business incomes.[23] Hence the distribution of household and business enterprise income is determined by the ruling class outside the market and prior to the determination of the various income variables and prices, and the income variables and prices simply 'adjust.' In short, production decisions by the ruling class concerning the surplus drives distribution; and this clearly makes the differential access to social provisioning a social-political issue.

Theory of value and heterodox microeconomics

The heterodox theory of value emerges from the model of the going economy and its theoretical core, which means that it is much more than simply a theory of prices. Its narrative is linked with a quantitative analysis (usually a model or a concatenated set of models) that succinctly explains why and how the particular goods and services that constitute the social provisioning process get produced and the households, business enterprises, and the state get access to them.

Consequently, the particulars of the explanation include the origins of the income variables (wage rates and profit mark-ups) that give access to the surplus and hence to the provisioning process; the determination of prices and their role in affecting economic activity; the determination of the social surplus, total social product, and employment; the 'real costs' of producing the social surplus; the distribution of the consumption goods between and within the three social classes; and the distribution of fixed investment goods and state financial assets among business enterprises and the ruling class (Dobb 1945, 1–33). The explanation also includes an examination of the state as the political unit in which the provisioning process is located and its role in affecting and directing economic activity.

The narrative of heterodox value theory starts with the observation that the material basis of the social provisioning process is determined by the ruling class – the capitalist class and the political elite of the dependent capitalist state – for the society as a whole. That is, since the composition and amount of the total social surplus is determined by the ruling class, they have the dominant influence qua control over the economy and society; since the capitalist class via the business enterprise administratively set going enterprise prices, profit mark-ups, and wages while the state sets wages, employs people, and makes government and interest payments, the ruling class determines through non-market decisions both the general access and the differential access to social provisioning. Underpinning the narrative of the heterodox value theory is the theoretical core that delineates the structures and agency and that gives it its form and character. In particular, the quantity of the surplus is not technically constrained, and the distribution of consumption goods among households is not technically determined by their productivity or the market value of what they produce. Rather, the creation and distribution of the surplus is effectuated through the social relationships that sustain the ruling class, while the trappings of market forces and the ideology of individualism are veils that obscure them. The heterodox theory of value through its model of the going economy pierces these veils and reveals what is hidden or obscured. It is evident that the heterodox theory of value is quite different from its neoclassical counterpart, which is restricted to a theory of prices and a narrative of market interaction of non-social individuals all located independently of the social realm. It also differs (but much less so) from the classical and Marxian theories of value because of its emphasis on both agency and structures, as opposed to just structures, in the determination of the social surplus, total social product, prices, and profit mark-ups. Thus, the heterodox theory of value derived from the model of the going economy as a whole is distinctive. But it is more than that – it is also an integrating force (or 'center of gravity') for all of heterodox economics. For the last quarter century and more, efforts have been made to create a heterodox synthesis (see Lee 2009a, Ch. 10). The arguments in this chapter and the resulting model of the going economy and the theory of value are part of these efforts. Whether dealing with the structure of production, classes, money, prices, or social provisioning, many of the ideas, arguments, and even conclusions are drawn from Marxian-radical, Post Keynesian-Sraffian, institutional, social, and feminist economics. There are also novel arguments whose introduction facilitates bringing them together, most notably being critical realism with its emphasis on structures, agency, and causal mechanisms that provide a common methodological foundation and situates economics in actual historical time, whether it be past or present. Finally, there are hybrid novel arguments that consist of using accepted ideas and arguments from different approaches in unexpected ways: the application of agency to the creation of the surplus, of circular production and non-basics to separate and unconstrained production of the different components of the surplus, and of the separation of price and quantity decisions and the non-duality between pricing and production coefficient matrices. Overall, the model of the going economy with its theoretical core and accompanying theory of value constitutes a comprehensive, coherent theoretical foundation for heterodox economics – one that does not privilege macro over micro, money over real, or structure over agency. Can it be further developed? Of course. But for the present, it is a good point of departure for further integrative work in heterodox economics.

Notes

1 For a critical comparison of the Sraffian and heterodox social surplus approaches, see Lee and Jo (2011). See also Roncaglia (1989), Davis (1992), Aspromourgos (2004), and O'Hara (2008).

2 When budgeted capacity utilization differs from actual capacity utilization, then material and labor pricing coefficients are different from material and labor production coefficients (more on this below). This clearly suggests a disjuncture between price and actual output-costs.

3 There is, contrary to some Sraffian claims (Pivetti 1985), little evidence that a component of product costs is interest costs, say, on working capital; if such costs arise, they are generally dealt with in the profit and loss accounts of the product.

4 There is an upper limit to the values for R_{d1} and Z_{d1} above which the price model becomes structurally incoherent. This occurs when the maximum eigenvalue of $R_{d1}Z_{d1}M_{11}$ is greater than one. In this case, $[I - R_{d1}Z_{d1}M_{11}]^{-1}$ ceases to be a strictly positive matrix and hence will have negative elements. This means that some prices will be negative.

5 The point here is that heterogeneous labor power cannot be reduced to some multiple of a universal 'simple labor power,' just as heterogeneous commodities cannot be reduced to some multiple of a universal 'simple commodity' and heterogeneous social activities cannot be reduced to some multiple of a universal 'simple social activity.'

6 For further discussion of the convergence issue, see Caminati (1990), Roncaglia (1996), Lee (1996), and D'Olando (2005).

7 In terms of empirical evidence, neither of the variables appears very important by themselves in the investment decision-making process. In an uncertain, transmutable world, these variables are overwhelmed in importance by other variables – for example, see Andrews and Brunner (1951), Barna (1962), Mackintosh (1963), Petty, Scott, and Bird (1975), Bromiley (1986), and Scheibl and Wood (2005). Moreover, the unimportance of the rate of interest is due to its state money foundation and the absence of the 'productivity' of fixed investment goods – see Nell (2003). Finally, the use of historical costs, state-mandated rates of depreciation, and cost accounting difficulties of measuring the value of fixed investment goods, makes any measurement of the rate of profit for an enterprise-specific product line highly dubious and most certainly quite different from the 'rate of profit' used in heterodox (and mainstream) theory.

8   Households can be differentiated by other characteristics as well, but household income is the primary factor that differentiates consumption patterns. The fact that households have different consumption patterns that involve purchasing different goods and services (as opposed to greater or lesser amounts of the same goods while keeping the proportions constant) means that households are truly different.

9   Editor's note: For other notations, see Equation 2.10.

10 The output-employment multiplier is not the same as the Keynesian multiplier in that the finite value of the latter is dependent on leakages such as imports or savings, while the finite value of the former is dependent not on leakages but that the basic technology produces a surplus which means $0 < \lambda_{m11} < 1$. Still, they are similar. The latter is a relationship between nominal investment and national income mediated by the propensity to save, with prices assumed to be stabled (Trigg 2006; 2008). This suggests that the 'real' variables of investment goods, output, and the capacity to produce investment goods lie at its heart. Moreover, since consumption goods (along with government goods) are part of the social surplus, the multiplier is altered from 'savings' to fertility of production. The outcome is that a demand for an investment (or other surplus) good will generate a demand for material and labor inputs that are in addition to those directly used in its production.

11 This is in slight contrast to the classical-Sraffian view of physical real costs as the amount of $\mathbf{Q}_1$ destroyed or used up in the production of the surplus (Kurz 2006; 2011; Kurz and Salvadori 2005; Roncaglia 2010).

12 For the theory of production that is the foundation for this claim, see Chapter 3 of this volume.

13 It might be argued that because basic goods are not part of the social surplus, basic goods industries do not produce a surplus and hence are sterile. However, this Physiocratic issue is not relevant because the whole system of production as represented by the output-employment multiplier is responsible for producing the surplus, not any one industry or section of the economy.

14 Because agency of the ruling class determines how the state and the business enterprise react to changes in capacity utilization and employment, it is not possible to articulate a structural 'accelerator' component of the output-employment multiplier, as for example in the case of the Sraffian supermultiplier. For the Sraffian multiplier, dependent and working class households have no agency with regard to their consumption patterns and enterprises have no agency regarding their capacity-enhancing decisions. Thus, autonomous or agency-based decisions are restricted to capitalist (or ruling class) consumption, non-capacity enhancing investment, and state demand for government goods and services (Bortis 1997; 2003; 2008; Serrano 1995a; 1995b). However, no explanation is given why enterprises do not have agency regarding capacity-enhancing investment decisions or why working class households do not have at least some agency to determine consumption patterns that would enhance their particular lifestyles.

15 This core component and some of its implications are accepted by Sraffians, but others are not – see Bortis (1997; 2003; 2011), Kurz (2006), Roncaglia (1996; 2009; 2010), Lee and Jo (2011), and Chapter 3 of this volume.

16 An implication of going enterprise prices is that prices are not only sector, industry, or market related in that they are creatures just of them – that is, of structures and institutions outside of agency.

17 This suggests that workers are exploited in a Marxian sense, but without being articulated through the labor theory of value (Mongiovi 2010).

18 This implication is found in classical political economy and was clearly established by Sraffa (1960, 6). Its significance is that the existence of the profit mark-up is a non-price phenomenon and hence is not dependent on whether markets are competitive or not (Pasinetti 2007, 198; Bortis 2003). So, in contrast to various Kaleckian statements,

imperfect competition is not the basis for the existence of the profit mark-up. Moreover, profit mark-ups are not profit rates or rates of return. These latter concepts are synthetic concepts constructed by enterprises to help in making strategic business decisions with regard to discretionary expenditures, such as fixed investment goods and research and development. Hence, they are not fundamental 'properties' of capitalism. Rather, it can be plausibly argued that profit rates are not dominant in these decision-making processes, but rather are one of many other important variables, such as internal rate of return based on an administratively determined 'interest rate,' pay-off period, net present value, discounted cash flow, nature of the investment project (growing markets, replacement investment, product change, or new technology to reduce production costs), the level of management that proposed the investment project, type of funding for the investment project (internal vs. external), and management judgment which may be reflective or in the form of animal spirits (Lee 2012; 2013b).

19 The production of the surplus qua profits is in contrast to the Marxian argument that profits emerge via the exploitation of labor. The difference between the two accounts arises from whether the total social product is driven by agency decisions concerning the surplus or whether it is given and profits appear as a residual (Lee and Jo 2011).

20 Editor's note: For the notations used here, refer to Equations 2.17, 2.19, 2.20, and 2.23.

21 This implies that the greater the government expenditures are, the greater amount of financial assets in existence. Thus the question of financialization of the economy arises. However, the assumption of a state banking system essentially sterilizes this concern.

22 A subsistence household income is not a social right under capitalism but a political concession obtained from the ruling class.

23 Because profit mark-ups are not rates of profit, there is no reason for them to be uniform. Moreover, it is not clear what a competitive vs. non-competitive profit mark-up is since competition does not have a fundamental role in the economy (Lee 2012). Finally, very little empirical work has been done on the determination of the profit mark-up, so there is little that can be said about it. In particular, there is no evidence that enterprises are influenced by interest rates when determining/setting their profit mark-ups.

8 The role of microeconomics in heterodox economics

A view of a heterodox micro theorist[1]

Introduction

I don't believe in a distinction between micro and macro. It's a system as a whole that we analyze, and we do it from various perspectives. Most economists believe that micro and macro are separate, and that, from one's perspective, one is better than the other. And mostly it's macro from heterodox economists' perspective, because the only micro they get as undergraduates is neoclassical micro. And rightly so; students in the heterodox economics programs condemning neoclassical micro as pure nonsense, or 'incoherency,' is a reasonable position. Therefore, they think that why would anybody want to study microeconomics; the only real stuff happens in macroeconomics. And I can understand that. But, it's just absolutely wrong; there is a different way of doing economics as a whole.

The neoclassical approach to the micro-macro relationship is to make micro and macro coherent with each other. They do it by reducing macroeconomics to microeconomics. That's not a fault, that's certainly a way they can make it coherent. Many heterodox economists believe that micro and macro are unrelated. So their understanding of the economy as a whole is incoherent. They believe this fervently and try to push it. To me, it's either weak minds, or people are incapable of thinking. If you're an urban economist, you want to be able to talk about things that happen in the city that in a sense ties in with the economy as a whole. So doing micro has a simultaneous connection with the economy as a whole or the macro. The notion that things can be totally isolated in an interdependent economy is nonsense. So this is why I rant and rave about getting people not only to study and to look at micro seriously, but also, in fact, discard the concepts of micro and macro. We are just interested in different areas of the economy and how they relate to each other.

Obviously, when you go out into the world and have to teach, you'll have to teach micro and macro. That doesn't make it right; that's the way things are set up. So you'll need to be able to do some things you think of in those terms, and some things you think of as the economy as a whole. You always have to know a lot of wrong stuff as well as right stuff. Because knowing wrong stuff can help you understand how thinking gets done and what's going on. So this is why I always insist that if you want to do stuff that is heterodox micro, you have to know neoclassical micro that is relevant to the areas that you are interested in. And if you're interested in heterodox macro, you should study neoclassical macro areas, which are relevant to what you're interested in. Unfortunately, you have to know twice as much, or more, than any mainstream economist. And you have to know twice as much as heterodox economists, so that equates to four, or maybe six or ten. But the point is that that's what you have to do. You basically have to be twice as good as any neoclassical economist, even to teach in a heterodox program. If you want to do economics, you give your students the best opportunities and know what various viewpoints are out there in a coherent manner.[2]

The economy as a whole, as a conceptual and theoretical foundation

I want to start with the economy as a whole, as a conceptual and theoretical foundation. You can't talk about any microeconomic issue unless you know what the economy as a whole is. The way I deal with the economy as a whole – that is, framing the economy – is in a disaggregated framework. I am not referring to $C + I + G$. Those are just letters. There's no causal relationship, actually, to any of the items that we're dealing with. And they're not actually referring to any real industries or production, so most of the macro actually has no production in it whatsoever. And production is 45–50 percent of all economic activity in the American economy. So basically, if you do macro in such a way, you actually don't deal with anything important; you just deal with the surplus, as if it magically appeared. And you don't deal with any industries and markets, and such. A disaggregated framework, however, not only does everything an aggregated framework does, but also it does better. So framing of the economy is what we have to go through.

You're in economics. If you think that you can do anything in economics and not have any recourse to schemas or models, I suggest that you look elsewhere for an occupation. Whether you're a heterodox or mainstream economist, schemas and models form a method from which we engage in analytical reasoning to make points. When you deal with the economy as a whole, this kind of a disaggregated framework is the only way to go. You have to provide a schema as well as a model of the economy as a whole. We can talk about models later and what they should be like, but not at this point.

Now see Table 2.1 Stock-flow social accounting schema of the productive structure of the social provisioning process (p. 50). Here we have the productive structures of the economy. First of all, we have a set of basic goods structure – basically these are the inputs that are needed to produce a surplus in the economy. This is represented by G_{11} and L_{11} – these are matrices, and represent different kinds of intermediate inputs and labor inputs, respectively. Next, we shall deal with homogeneous labor and heterogeneous inputs. Many economists assume that labor is homogeneous, but at the same time we have to have heterogeneous capital. Consider Veblen's 'joint-stock of knowledge.' We can't have a joint-stock of knowledge at a differentiated set of inputs or produced goods without having differentiated sets of labor skills to go along with it. Homogeneity makes absolutely no sense. But people do it. The point is that a disaggregated framework is what we have to have. There is no getting around that.

Remember, we're dealing with a level of theory, the conceptual foundations. And we have a set of resource reserves (**RR**), these resources 'become' from the institutionalist perspective (see De Gregori 1987). That is to say, resources are socially constructed. I'm not saying that they're not finite, but we socially construct our resources. The joint-stock of knowledge can make resources appear or not appear. Unfortunately, this is an under-theorized area. Heterodox economists should be able to come in and work on this stuff. This is an area of research that needs to be developed. The ecological economists don't seem to recognize it. I can't say much more than that. But what does it mean? It means that there are investment goods, which are produced in the system. So, all the inputs are produced – that is, the intermediate outputs (Q_1), which go into the production of surplus goods and services (Q_2) – all are produced; in a sense, socially constructed and reproducible. So the notion of scarcity has no foundation in the system.

Let us talk about the surplus goods sector. What I have in Table 2.1 is that all the output of the intermediate goods sector – that is, basic goods sector – is utilized in the surplus producing goods sector, and the output of the surplus goods sector is the surplus of the system. So we have the same setup here. The production of the government (Q_{2G}), consumption (Q_{2C}), and investment goods (Q_{2I}) constitute surplus goods. What do we call those goods as a collective whole? What term would you utilize there? *Effective demand* – the demand for those goods by the state or the capitalists, drives the entire system. Of course, here we have the state. The state also has some investment goods (K_{S4}), resources (RR_{S4}), and a set of goods (Q_{2G}^T) from the surplus goods sector. In addition, there is a whole set of government people out there (L_{41}) who get paid from the state and government payment (GP). Don't ever call them 'transfer payments.' Why? The government doesn't spend your tax money. So it's not transfer money from somebody else. In the Chartalist modern monetary theory framework, governments create money. So it's not a transfer payment. In the modern monetary theory framework it's simply government payments. Of course, government payments always go to government services (GS). And government payments create goods, which are now back in use. What would be such a good? Tanks! Things like that: those are investment goods. I would have said lighthouses, but governments don't do those anymore. Governments actually create resources – for example, Uranium-235. Is that a resource or not? It becomes a resource only when the government decides to produce atomic bombs or nuclear power. If governments don't want to do that, then it's not a resource. So they create it as a resource. There's a lot of debate about how one can do this. This is a simple, institutionalist kind of story. And that requires theorizing.

What do households do? Households get consumption goods (Q_{2C}) and they generate household services and activities (HSA). Does anybody want to go out to dinner with their favorite partner? That would be household services. These are the kinds of things that people buy.

Investment goods (Q_{2I}) go into the stock investment goods (K_{S1-2}) that are used with resources (RR_{1-2}). That is, Q_{2I} is connected as a flow of basic sector fixed investment goods (K_{S1}) and as a flow of surplus sector fixed investment goods (K_{F2}) to the stock of surplus sector fixed investment goods (K_{S2}). That's the productive structure of the economy. One thing you should notice is that this is what really happens. This is how we live our lives. These are physical relationships. When we talk about finance, that is something different, but it has an impact on the productive sector. But we don't live on finance. We live on production of goods and services. And sometimes this obvious point gets lost.

You will also note that these schemas show sectors, industries, or markets depending on how we disaggregate the economy. Which means that what happens in any one industry has an impact on the economy. So when you do micro and want to study a particular area, industry, location, or whatever, it's not isolated within itself; it's related to the economy as a whole. However, when lots of economists analyze the financial sector, they tend to ignore other sectors as if the rest is irrelevant. That's certainly not the case.

See Table 2.2 SFSA schema of the productive and financial structure of the social provisioning process (p. 55). There must be a way you think about, in a sense, commodities and the financial structure of the economy. There is a lot of stuff one can deal with. First of all, I'll just simply state, straightforwardly, 'classes' – the capitalist class, the state, and those who have to work for a living, the working class, and their dependents. So it's a class system. And in this class system, certain classes have more say than others, such as the capitalist class, which can determine the production of investment goods and consumption goods. The state, in conjunction with the capitalist class, determines state demand for goods, and the state can finance expenditures with state money.

Do we want to start an economy in which there's no state? I've done that many, many times in early years, even though I had read Keynes's *Treatise on Money*, which I've always read as the state creates money, though it never filtered it into my work, because I got stuck around it. If you ever start modeling and start talking about the economy without the state, for example, a model with banks but no state, that's not the world we live in. So if you want to do that, fine. Go write fairy tales, if they're much more interesting.

The bottom line is that you have to start with classes, the state, and state money. Once we have government expenditures with state money, what do we end up with? Financial assets! As long as we don't have a balanced budget, we create financial assets in the system. I'd like to say that the state gets into trouble with financial assets, but that would make a lot of other people upset. So we'll have a financial/banking sector. But it's all predicated on the fact that the state creates these financial assets – that is, the debt. This means in this particular case we have to have a banking sector, which uses a set of inputs, and banks produce loans – that is, a set of financial assets for various sectors, such as loans for the basic goods sector, for the household sector, and for the business enterprise sector. It creates loans for those sectors, which are deposited back to the banking sector as financial assets. That's about far as I can go on this thing. The building block is that through state expenditures we have a set of financial assets and liabilities throughout the system, as shown in Table 2.2.

What we have now is a statement of the economy in which there is both a productive structure and a financial structure, integrated with each other. And most importantly, we have a disaggregated framework, which is totally consistent with the modern monetary theory of Chartalism. Where does this bring us? In this framework, where are profits going to come from? They've got to come from someplace. They're from the surplus. Profits are somehow attached to the surplus. All the intermediate stuff is just cost. So we have to have connection of profits to some form of the surplus and wages to some form of the surplus. It's government expenditures that filter into the system as profits.

See Table 2.3 SFSA model of the monetary structure of the social provisioning process (p. 59). I'm going to talk about the financial structure of the system. How about the current financial balances? We have government expenditures (GOV_E) minus taxes. And total profits after taxes (Π^*), consisting of investment goods ($Q_{21}^T p_2$), and the liabilities (LB_{BE}) and assets of the system ($FA_{BE} + FA_{SRC}$). Profits are connected to investment goods and government expenditures. That's how the system creates profits. We don't create profits by exploiting labor in this model. We create profits by investments and government expenditures. Creation of profits requires people to work beyond what they need to be producing for themselves. But it's not the same thing as exploitation of labor. Because even if you have a total cooperative system, everybody would still be producing investment goods, which means that investment goods have to be set up for the production of consumption goods. Some people are producing goods and services, and some people are producing savings when they support others. That's what we call 'exploitation,' but not the sort of exploitation under capitalism. You have a different way of talking about the margin of profits, but, clearly, profits are produced. There is no shortage of profits in the system. You either produce more investment goods, or you get the government to run up a bigger deficit. Every time you reduce that deficit, you're simply reducing profits in the system. This is modern monetary theory. So we have an explanation of profit that does not involve a labor theory of value, although it has resemblance to aspects of what they're trying to get at in terms of the labor theory of value. We should go beyond it. If you can't go beyond an economist, any economist, then I suggest that you have an occupation in which the final word was written a thousand years ago, two thousand, five hundred years, or fifty years. There's no final word in economics. If you're going to do science, there's no final word said by any one economist. If you're not good enough to go beyond that, you're not a very good economist.

Where do wages come from? Production of the consumption goods. We can't have wages before the production of consumption goods, because we produce consumption goods for people to buy. Production of consumption goods creates wages. So we have this kind of system. Then, we'll have an issue about distribution in a particular way. We'll get back to that. But the point is that it's still disaggregated. I have profit and income taxes in the system. This makes things complex, what do taxes do? Reflux! Taxes bring money back.

Let's briefly talk about agency. There are five forms of agency in the system – the business enterprise, the state, the household, market governance organizations, and class-based organizations (see Table 2.4. Agency and core decisions, p. 69. All are predicated on the acting person. The concept of agency comes right out of social economics. If you think you are a heterodox economist of any sort and you don't have this kind of stuff coming out of social economics, think again. Not very many people want to go into social economics. When it comes to people or agency as real things, Marxists do a much better job than Post Keynesians. There's actually almost no agency in Post Keynesian economics. So we have five major acting organizations/institutions. And they make a whole bunch of decisions about the surplus, bank loans, employment, prices, wages, salaries, mark-ups, dividends, government payments, interest rates, and taxes. Anytime we want to talk about these issues, we have to have agency, for example, the state as a form of agency. What do Post Keynesians talk about when they get to the state? Nothing, except assuming that the state must be nice. And they don't talk about the state in conjunction with the business community. Post Keynesians are essentially ideologically in favor of the status quo. Otherwise they would talk about the state. I've been having this argument with Post Keynesians for decades. They make presumptions about what the state is and also at the same time talk about 'bad' workers who want higher wages. They pass it off as Post Keynesian theory qua policy. I object to it, and they say "okay," but they never change it. It still occurs today. ELR (employer of last resort) is not designed to change the system – it never has been. It's designed to maintain the status quo in the system. It would be better to have change through social uprising. Not that the state can't carry out ELR through their monetary policy. They can do it. It's not designed to change the system. And these are core decisions made in the economy.

Basically what I've done here in Table 2.5 Economic model of the social provisioning process (p. 70) is to simply add acting organizations to the rest of the structures in Table 2.3. And so far, I've only had structures. You can structure the economy easily, but that doesn't tell you what the economy does. You have to have agency. Marxians and Post Keynesians do the primary modeling in heterodox economics. Which is fine; I don't have any problem with that. But they don't talk much about agency. They set up the model, and simply have it lying around. They actually don't talk about people making decisions. What happens when you have people make decisions? Your parameters change. So there's no equilibrium; no long-run scenarios that are definite in their position. There's only cumulative causation without an end. The system changes when people make decisions. Some heterodox economists want to stay in some kind of equilibrium framework so that they can change parameters. But that's not about agency. I did that ten or twenty years ago. I remember that I stopped thinking about this kind of theoretical stuff around that time – for example, agency really isn't working if I do this and the other; let's make it systematic and frame it; let's be consistent. I'm not a pot calling the kettle black. I did that stuff in the past. The problem is that heterodox economists do it now. They simply change parameters and talk about how a system works, with no agency whatsoever. You can't talk about modeling the economy as a whole in a disaggregated way as if there is no agency. The only way things do happen is when agents make decisions. We have to think more historically, as opposed to simply changing the parameters of the model.[3]

We should be able to think how things work in some abstract analytical way. For example, suppose that in this framework (see Table 2.5) we want to change wage rates. What would be the kind of impact we could be looking for? So we should explore it to see how the actual world works. We can't say the parameters remain unchanged as we change things through agency. The other important implication in this framework is that I have a trade union. It doesn't exist as anything important as an agent in heterodox models. Except for Marxists. If you don't know what comes out of radical political economy, then you don't know what are the important things that are happening in heterodox economics. Of course, there are other forces that we should be exploring as well.

That was a model of our economy. This economy now gets placed into a social fabric matrix, developed by F. Gregory Hayden and others, in which we have norms and institutions, a joint-stock of knowledge (or technology), and ecological systems. Table 2.6 Historically grounded model of the economy as a whole (p. 72) shows that each social fabric has an influence on how the agents of the system – acting organization and institutions – make decisions. So the agents make decisions about the social provisioning process – that is, the production of the social surplus. Agents don't think of the economy; they are independent in themselves. And agents act within a socially embedded framework. If we don't know what the socially embedded framework is, then we have an incomplete picture about what things are going on. Greg Hayden's work, and he is a pioneer in this, is very important. I don't mean that you will spend a lot of time on the social fabric matrix, but it will give you a way to help ground your framework, whether it's a very narrow one – looking at banking or a city or something – or a broad one. The point is that the economic activities are not generated simply inside the economy. They come from a much broader framework, basically a socially embedded economy. That's a truism. An economy has always been socially embedded. How could it not be true, unless you believe neoclassical economics. We have a set of ideas out there, which says that the economy is not socially embedded. The trouble is that people believing this very silly idea might as well believe in Hobbits, which are actually much more interesting than a non-socially embedded economy.

The last part is that we are in a historical context. This is a particular way in which we view things. History and the social fabric of the socially embedded economy mean that every economic analysis is a historical one. If you believe that you can do an economic analysis outside of history, then every variable that you use has no meaning. Every variable that we have in economics is historically grounded and historically contextualized. If you take them out of history or of historical time, they have no meaning. In other words, the socially embedded economy in historical context is in contrast to the equilibrium framework, which is not what you are going to look at; you want to look at or develop an articulated historical, theoretical framework. I've only worked on it briefly. I have a lot more to work out.

The last thing that I want to really have time for is the framework of the economy as a whole. There's also an output-employment model in it and a price model in it. Maybe we'll come back to the output-employment model where agency makes decisions about what to produce and who gets employed. The price model is designed to explain how prices get set and generate an income for business enterprises.

Effective demand, income distribution, and the social provisioning process

Our next topic is "effective demand, income distribution, and the social provisioning process." This is at the level of the economy as a whole. It's almost like macro in the way people think about micro and macro. To me this almost looks like micro. You might say I have a bizarre view of the world. You should simply see it as the economy as a whole.

What does effective demand do? Effective demand is the production of the surplus. So when you talk about effective demand, you're talking about producing the surplus of the system. It's a unique constraint to the production of the surplus. Remember we have all the inputs, either reproducible or socially constructed inputs. In that context there is no given input that is relatively scarce. As noted above, resources are made available by the joint-stock of knowledge and socially created in the sense that the enterprise's and state's decision to produce a good or service requires a particular input qua resource. That is, resources are socially produced means of production. So there is no productive constraint to the system. The system can produce whatever it wants to produce. Clearly if there is a shortage of a particular kind of labor power, what does the system do? Change technology, use different kinds of labor power, or set up an educational system that produces that kind of labor power or skill. That's what we do. So there's no constraint of labor. Not to mention that there are a number of people outside of the border of the United States, who are capable of working and learning. So anyone can come here and learn, and do whatever. So there's no shortage of labor. Full employment as a constraint to the system is a bogus notion. You can employ as many people as possible, but there's no notion of full employment, unless you want to believe that there exists such a notion. We keep changing. So that's not a constraint to the system. There may be shortages while you work through it, but that's not a fundamental constraint.

What are fundamental constraints to the system supposed to do? If we have relative scarcity, there's a constraint on what can be produced. What does that generate in neoclassical economics? Exchange and prices. That's what relative scarcity does. If the system had no constraint, there simply would be no prices; everything would be free. That's what constraints do. If you want to put in a constraint into the system, then what you're saying is that the system is organized through a price mechanism. And if you say that, then throw out effective demand. The system is not constrained in that way. There may be shortages. You may say some things that were resources are no longer resources. Get rid of whaling, for example, and make your perfume out of some chemicals. The point is that you can tell some resources shouldn't be resources and you can create others. You have shortages, you may say well that we want to put a whole bunch of wind farms out there in Kansas and eliminate coal production. It's hard for me as an ex-labor historian to say this. But if you want to get rid of coal production, you can do that.

The point is that this is what we do. These are socially constructed decisions dealing with issues of shortages. So you can as an ecological economist argue that the system has no productive constraints. And then you simply argue how we carry out production, which resources we want to use or not. But it's not an inherent constraint that rules the system through the price mechanism, which is what many people don't get.

Is there a savings-profits constraint in the system? If we have a savings constraint in the system, you're organizing the system through the price mechanism. Remember since things are producible and reproducible, there's no constraint on the production of investment goods. In fact, it's the production of investment goods, which creates profits, that is savings, to buy investment goods. So there's no savings constraint in the system. People talk about that in heterodox economics. But some heterodox economists talk about savings through the price mechanism – that is, savings are regulated by interest rates. So if you are going to say that investment is regulated though interest rates, you are talking about investment being regulated through the price mechanism. So you have to be very clear. Again, the only thing you are dealing with is a constraint in the system, which generates in some fashion a set of prices to regulate the system. You've got to be very careful. If you want to be really radical, you attack the price mechanism. That's what radical stuff does. That's the core.[4]

Do government expenditures somehow constrain savings, profits, and investment? The answer is "no." There's no constraint on government expenditures. In fact, government expenditures help generate a surplus and profits in the system through deficit spending. The wage rates and wages or the production of consumption goods make an impact on profits. How many people think that the distribution of income is a constraint to the system? In other words, if you have a more equal distribution of income, we have a better economic system? Well, first of all, can the economy produce as many consumption goods as it wants? Remember, we aren't constrained in terms of production. So it could, right? It could also produce as many investment goods as it wants. It would appear that the production of consumption goods is not a constraint on investment goods. If you think otherwise, then you are in a production possibility frontier theory – that is, neoclassical economics with constraints. The system is not constrained in that way.

Producing more consumption goods versus investment goods or government goods is non-constrainable. Recall the model of the social provisioning process (see Table 2.5). To increase the production of the consumption goods in this case you have to increase wages or wage-rates to purchase them. Remember, wages equals consumption. That doesn't have any impact on profit-squeeze. These are a bunch of claptrap arguments that are bad analyses. Some would argue that they think in terms of a price mechanism. Theoretically, that's what they seem to do.

They never claim that too much profit has a negative impact upon the system. What do prices do? Price is a way that the going concerns generate their income flows to remain going concerns. That's a different proposition from coordinating economic activity.

Clearly, income distribution is not between households and business enterprises. Business enterprises get their profits from investment goods and getting basically profits from governments in an indirect way with savings and financial assets, which they distribute to households. The notion that enterprises make so much profit or workers make so much wages is an irrelevant scenario. The distribution of income is a question inside the household sector, and who gets what. Households are separated into different classes – for example, households that have access to dividends because maybe they are part of the management class, or they inherited dividends from grandmothers who have a whole bunch of financial assets and didn't worry about lifestyle that would not normally be accompanied with an ordinary professor. So if you have access to those, then your income would be great, whether you get paid more or not. If you work at much lower paying jobs, then what do we have? We have a set of consumption goods, which are designed for certain kinds of people. Remember, you're going to spend your income on different kinds of consumption goods. The production of cheap consumption goods is designed for those with low income. So the issue of income distribution is related to the kind of consumption goods the business enterprises produce. The construction or development of Wal-Mart – they're cheap goods made by bloody labor elsewhere – is simply the desire of, or have the impact on, lowering workers' wages. Workers aren't designed to save anything; you're designed to spend their entire income. That's how we model it.

So, the distribution of income may be a problem, but it's not the income distribution between business enterprises and households. It's the production of a whole set of cheap goods and services for particular classes. You don't see these cheap goods being produced for the wealthy. They have a different set of goods. So in this production system, the enterprises in conjunction with the state demand a certain kind of goods to be produced and construct a set of wages for the working class to buy goods and services. That's the issue. That's a social issue. It's not the issue of income distribution that just simply falls out of it. So when you complain about income distribution, you are complaining about the wrong thing. You should be complaining about the production of a set of consumption goods for certain classes. Why should the poor live in crap housing? We have a system that can produce excellent housing for them, but we don't. That's the issue. The wages simply fall out of that. So I'm never a big fan of all the demand about income distribution. I see a much more fundamental problem. It exhibits itself as an income distribution problem, but that's a secondary, ephemeral outcome of a more fundamental problem. If you deal with the question about what an enterprise or government is going to produce for various segments of society, then you're fundamentally questioning the nature of this capitalist system. That's clearly what people don't want to have.

Microeconomics in heterodox economics

What is meant by 'micro' in the context of the economy as a whole? I've already mentioned that we should eliminate the micro *versus* macro framework. I don't want to hear it, I don't want to see it; I want to use it jokingly to get people to think about this traditional way of thinking about micro and macro issues. I know it can be very odd coming from a person like myself who's a microeconomist, because I'm actually objecting to how people call me and how I identify myself. I hope the future is different from what I've lived through in the past. We have an inter-dependent, disaggregated economy in which there are agency-specific issues. You can examine specific issues such as households and trade unions. That would be what is thought of as micro; that's a tradition. Agents in the system are particular areas to study. And this becomes interesting in many kinds of ways. But it doesn't mean that you are not doing micro and macro at the same time. Traditionally, peo-ple have treated this as a micro question. I just see it as an issue of agency within a whole interdependent economy.

So we have agency-specific issues. Of course, we could have market-, indus-try-, sector-, and location-specific issues. Urban economics, for example, is rel-evant if we study the computer industry. It's simply a different way of looking at a particular sector that can be examined in the context of the economy as a whole. So the micro and the macro are connected. So we have agency- or market- or whatever-specific analysis, which deals with how each specific analysis is inter-dependent with other specific analyses. So when you talk about urban issues, you cannot help but also talk about markets in your urban area, and then decisions by enterprises or governments either to produce or not produce there. So there's no possible way a study in any one specific analysis can have it be isolated from any-thing else. This means that you've backed into the economy as a whole.

The reason people think they could do an isolated analysis is that they rely on a partial equilibrium framework. In order to make it work, individuals, sub-sectors, or parts of the economy are to be isolated. Clearly, what I've rejected outright is any form of partial equilibrium. It's an economy as a whole. We look at interde-pendent parts of it. This is a fundamental critique of neoclassical economics. In fact, however, many heterodox economists are using a sort of partial equilibrium analysis.

Heterodox microeconomic topics and future research

I'd like to suggest microeconomic topics for a dissertation and future research. Note that I'm a theorist. I know people will say that I may be an applied or empiri-cal economist, simply because I think the only way to do theory is to actually know something about the economy. Such a work requires not only qualitative research, interviews, and/or archival studies, but also a whole range of statistical analysis. If you think that you can get out and become a good economist without some basic, good knowledge of econometrics, social network analysis, or a range of other forms of statistical analysis, then you're wrong. As a graduate student

I took a course in econometrics. I didn't believe there's a random distribution of variables, which underlined conventional econometrics. So I didn't take a second semester. Instead, I was into history in which everything is causally related and causally created. That I did not study econometrics enough was the worst mistake of my academic life. I would have learned a whole bunch of Bayesian stuff. That's what the second semester of econometrics would have been back in the late 1970s or early 1980s, not that that wouldn't have been useful. But I never took the time to really learn the econometrics. And that has been a drag on my work in my entire career. So if you think that you can become a decent economist without thoroughly knowing econometric-statistical methods, then you are wrong. The way I do econometrics now is to get friends to help. I ask them about different ways of doing things because I didn't take the time to learn the stuff. You don't want to be as bad as me. You should be able to know how to write and how to ask the right kind of questions when you come to econometrics or to statistical analysis. So you can figure out what you need to do and who to help you out with it. Don't make the same mistake I made as a graduate student. I still believe in a causally created world. That doesn't mean that I shouldn't have learned econometrics.

Now let's talk about some topics in terms of theory. If you're going to do a dissertation or future research, my position is that the only sensible research to do is one that helps develop heterodox economic theory. So there has to be something in that research that drives at developing heterodox economic theory in some fashion. So you don't want to simply do a study that is self-contained without having an impact upon economic theory that would be developed. It means that people like myself who would read, say, more of applied work do so because they want to know what they're actually working on. It would be helpful if such an applied work is designed to develop a particular theory or point. For me, that particular theoretical point happens to be in cartels and in prices. It means that I'm interested in these issues. If it happens to be in futures or derivatives markets, I might not be interested in it; but other people would be interested in it. Because people will be working outside your area, if that work has an impact on the theoretical developments relevant to their area. So you want to make that kind of connection.

I would also argue, because I'm a micro theorist, that research must engage with the price mechanism, and refute it. I know people don't want to get along with neoclassical economics. But if you don't have anything to say about the price mechanism, and how economic activity is organized from the neoclassical perspective, you are truly the 1 percent. The only way to change is to actually and forcibly engage with the price mechanism. People want to say about the capital controversies – that's where the real competition between heterodoxy and mainstream takes place. What do the capital controversies do, fundamentally? It pushes the price mechanism. But there's been a long development of pushing the price mechanism called the marginalist controversy. This challenged the price mechanism; this is a much more direct challenge in that the price mechanism doesn't exist anymore. People who directly challenge the price mechanism at a fundamental level have a much more difficult time, even in the same profession (see, for example, Lee 1984). That's what you must do. Challenging the price mechanism

would mean that you are challenging the notion of markets working or not working – that's actually the wrong phrase. Markets are socially constructed, there's
no notion of them working or not. People work, not markets. When you reject
that notion – that is also rejecting the price mechanism – then you say that every
argument that any neoliberal has put out has no coherent theoretical foundation
on their own terms. That's what you have to do. If you don't question that, then
you might as well just not do anything. Because you are not questioning what is
the fundamental theoretical underpinnings of mainstream economics. That's what
you have to question. There are many different routes to tackle the core of mainstream economics, but it has to come back to the price mechanism if you want to
make an impact on and a change to the system of how we do economics.

I would argue that all dissertations must do both – that is, developing heterodox theory and challenging the core of mainstream economics. But that's certainly
up to the individual and dissertation advisor. My dissertation on full cost pricing
implied both, development of heterodox theory, and it was also a rejection of the
price mechanism (see Lee 1983). It wasn't well-articulated back then. I had 400
pages to do it, but I didn't make it that clear. It was there, but it took me a while to
really fully develop that. An example of a problem in which there is no attack on
the price mechanism is modern monetary theory (MMT) that deals with ELR. We
all know this. And we know that they make statements about inflation. Somehow
you run ELR and you run economy at full employment, and then there will be inflation. So the question is: why do we give a damn? Remember, how do I talk about
the economy being coordinated? Through effective demand! Not through prices.
Prices don't do that. Prices have another job to do. So, from this perspective, inflation is irrelevant. So why do modern monetary theorists talk about inflation? Is
it because some heterodox economists keep attacking them and they don't have
any explanation for inflation? And they give in to this, and try to come up with
something? My response is that those critics of MMT are neoclassical economists,
because they believe that somehow inflation, if it has any meaning, works through
the price mechanism. That directs in effect how economic activity is coordinated.
This is a theoretical issue; we're not talking about politics. We're talking about a
theoretical issue of rising prices because we run into a constraint in the system that
affects how the system works. That's what we're asking. People get tied up in all
the politics. It's a theoretical issue. If the system is not constrained in that way, then
there is no notion of running up to the full utilization of resources. And hence there
is no inflation in that particular way. I can give you inflation any time if you want
it. It's called increasing production coefficients in the production model. That gives
rising prices, while everything else remains constant. Nobody talks about inflation
that way. The point is that we can have rising prices in the heterodox world due
to declining productivity of inputs, which means rising production coefficients.
I've seen some heterodox works that talk about inflation with regard to ELR, then
they buy into the price mechanism. They're basically talking about neoclassical
economics, a constraint-based system in which the prices emerge and organize the
economy. You should stop talking about it all together and tell those neoclassically-
oriented heterodox economists that they're neoclassical economists.

Other areas of interest that I'm going to go through briefly are related with the business enterprise. You can do stuff on prices. But that's not a most fruitful area to look at. By enterprise I'm talking about investment. You can do an econometric study of investment, like Steve Fazzari. But nobody really looks at how actual enterprises make investment decisions from a heterodox perspective. You don't get research like that, or actually very little.

How are wage rates determined? Some Marxians set wages in the MELT (monetary expression of labor time) model and this is a way to defend the labor theory of value. But that's not actually how wage rates get set in the economy; why do we care about this model? The question is that some people defend it. This means that empirical evidence about how the actual world works is irrelevant. They didn't put enough work in this. I sent out a list of journals that people could buy. The one journal that wasn't bought dealt with labor. This means that heterodox economists in general don't care much about labor, wage rates, or anything along this line, whether it's a general area or related specifically to the business enterprise. If you don't do research on labor, then you might do something else. But as a collective whole there should be people who are interested in it.

We don't know anything about how profit mark-ups are set. That brings about too much work. We have to go into the actual individual businesses. How do they set mark-ups at the level of enterprise? This requires a lot of work. People make all kinds of generalized statements, and I can give you a kind of structural understanding of profit mark-ups. I've read an awful lot of stuff to give you some indication, but we don't really know much about profit mark-ups. It's easy to do easy work; much more difficult to do hard work. Unfortunately, the real advances come with the hard work.

I've already talked about the state. Work needs to be done on that. Households, all kinds of work need to be done on that. We get very little work about households for all kinds of reasons. Feminist economists do the work, some Marxists, and even social economists. And do we get anybody from a Post Keynesian kind of background doing this? The answer is no. In fact, when there was some effort, something on gender, *Journal of Post Keynesian Economics* turned it down. If you want to think that Post Keynesians are really open to this stuff, think again. That's why I say I'm a heterodox economist. I come from a Post Keynesian background. People have actually denied that I actually do Post Keynesian economics, and that I can be identified as a Post Keynesian. That's basically lying. It doesn't mean that it's an all-encompassing lie. I stopped calling myself a Post Keynesian back in the 1990s, when I realized that I'd been consciously gone to the institutionalist-Marxist-social economics approach. What I do is not Post Keynesian, although there are clearly defined components that can be seen as Post Keynesian. What I do is to start out with a system, which has class. I'm not a Post Keynesian, since Post Keynesians do not talk about class. I come from some engagements with other traditions, so I'll put them together as a heterodox economist. You shouldn't be ashamed that you come from a Post Keynesian background, but it's not the be-all and end-all of anything. If you think that it is, then you severely limit yourself from being a good, good economist.

Market governance is about how markets work and how they get constructed and organized. The neoclassical economists have gone to incredible lengths to talk about cartels in the past fifteen or twenty years. Almost no heterodox economist has worked on this issue. I've done some stuff and never had it published (see Lee 1999). On the surface, it indicates that there is no heterodox work on market governance. How can that possibly be the case that no heterodox economist is interested in how actual markets work? I've got to read a whole bunch of neoclassical works to get stories about how the markets work. And they infuse it with neoclassical theory to no end, as if it's truth. If you're not going to engage in how actual markets work, as opposed to some works on financial markets that are only one small form of markets in the entire economy, and if you don't do it through cartels, that's nonsense. I've actually asked heterodox economists and they've said there's no cartels out there, just collective agreements as to how financial markets work, *et cetera*. If you don't do this stuff, then you might as well just pack it up because you're not actually talking about the economy in which we live. There are cartels that determine the price of pharmaceuticals in third world countries, not to mention the United States. They run it through a cartel. There are various kinds of chemicals for agricultural production. My god, these are the things we live off of, and no heterodox economist seems interested in how these markets work. So, that's another area to work on. Not to mention, except for the Marxists out there, nobody has done a serious work about trade unions, worker organizations, and cooperatives.

In short, the financial sector is simply a sector of economy; it's not the economy. The state is simply one sector of the economy; it's not the economy. And of course there are a whole bunch of industrial and retail sectors. If you somehow think that you talk about the economy as a whole and just talk about the financial sector, then you're wrong. What we clearly need is a work with all these various sectors. And there's not that kind of work being done. If you start getting out to specific areas, as I've already mentioned this earlier, such as urban, region, and city, these are particular sectorial areas of the economy that need a lot of work being done on them.

That "resources are not; they become," to use De Gregori's (1987) words, is another topic. Personally, I think if you have to actually choose something that would be one, because it would be a way to integrate all the ecological movement people into a heterodox framework in a consistent manner. This is far beyond a dissertation – it's an agenda for a decade. But a dissertation can be a beginning point, just like my full cost pricing dissertation became a beginning point producing a heterodox microeconomic theory, which is still coming after thirty years. But don't let that discourage you.

We have a lot of gender and race stuff done by everybody outside of Post Keynesian economics. Which means if you want to integrate insights from all of those, you should do so. There have been a couple of works done by S. Charusheela, but not nearly enough to deal with that.

Development and international trade. People think that these are somehow different areas. I don't understand how development can be thought of as something that is separate from what we talk about in the United States. You talk about development of the third world, why don't you use the same kind of approach as what you talk about in the United States. I don't see the distinction. We're talking about different kinds of countries where there are different kinds of economies, and how they work. International trade is simply the difference between whether you import your inputs from Mexico or you create them here in the United States and you import them from another industry in another state. What's the difference? It's simply a legal system that you have to go through. I don't see any difference between international trade in one sense and the way we talk about how any inter-industrial flows in the United States. I would like to see a lot more innovation from those two research areas.

Let's just jump to what is not so good research for a dissertation: one that does not engage with core heterodox theory, and one that does not engage with the price mechanism. History of economic thought in isolation is not good. It should be history of economic thought tied with the development of heterodox theory and an attack on the price mechanism. So one can do history of economic thought but I'd be very careful. My dissertation on full cost pricing was a form of history of economic thought. Although I started in 1930 with pre-War history of economic thought, I designed it, on the one hand, to engage with a contemporary issue of how prices get set, which is a very controversial, and, on the other hand, of course to help develop heterodox theory.

I think I've run out of time. Thank you for my last lecture.

Notes

1 Editor's note: Fred Lee planned to conclude the book with a chapter on "Social Provisioning and Corporate Capitalism." However, he was unable to write such a concluding chapter, which would have not only extended his heterodox microeconomic approach to the analysis of corporate capitalism, but also provided readers, students of heterodox economics in particular, with future directions for developing microeconomic theory from a heterodox perspective. I find that Fred's last graduate microeconomics lecture delivered on April 24, 2014 at the University of Missouri-Kansas City most suitable for these purposes. As it was a lecture, and delivered hurriedly and passionately, I have taken the liberty to severely edit his remarks. Nothing substantial has been altered in these following remarks. The lecture remains true to Fred, in particular to his spirit, if not the letter. So this chapter is an edited (and abridged) transcript of the lecture. All the footnotes and references are added by the editor. I am grateful to Elizabeth Fides for transcribing the lecture video. I also thank John Henry for reading and editing an earlier version of this chapter. The full video of this lecture is available at Youtube (https:// youtu.be/6HncE6ApwgY) and at the Fred Lee memorial website (http://heterodoxnews. com/leefs).
2 Editor's note: Lee taught microeconomics courses following this pedagogical approach for his entire academic career. For a more detailed explanation of his teaching philosophy and method, see Lee (2005; 2010b) and the microeconomics course syllabi in Appendix I of this book. He had also developed neoclassical microeconomics lecture notes, "Neoclassical Microeconomics from a Heterodox Perspective," for his graduate students. He made these 'incomplete' lecture notes available online at http://heterodox news.com/leefs/nc-micro/.
3 Editor's note: On the issue of modeling in heterodox economics, see Lee (2016a; b).
4 Editor's note: For further discussion on the market price mechanism from a heterodox perspective, see Lee (2013c) and Jo (2016).

Appendix 1
Heterodox microeconomics course syllabus[*]

Required Textbooks

- Fligstein, N. 2001. *The Architecture of Markets*. Princeton: Princeton University Press.
- Morgan, M. 2012. *The World in the Model*. Cambridge: Cambridge University Press.
- Lee, F. S. 1998. *Post Keynesian Price Theory*. Cambridge: Cambridge University Press.
- Todorova, Z. 2009. *Money and Households in a Capitalist Economy: A Gendered Post Keynesian-Institutional Analysis*. Edward Elgar.
- Lee, F. S., ed. 2011. *Social, Methods, and Microeconomics: Contributions to Doing Economics Better*. Hoboken, NJ: Wiley-Blackwell.
- Lee, F. S., ed. 2011. *Social Provisioning, Embeddedness, and Modeling the Economy*. Hoboken, NJ: Wiley-Blackwell.
- Lee, F. S., ed. 2013. *Markets, Competitions, and the Economy as a Social System*. Hoboken, NJ: Wiley-Blackwell.

Optional texts

- Bortis, H. 1997. *Institutions, Behaviour and Economic Theory*. Cambridge: Cambridge University Press.
- Moudud, J. K., C. Bina, and P. L. Mason, eds. 2012. *Alternative Theories of Competition*. London: Routledge.

Support material

- Lee, F. S. *The Simple Mathematics of Linear Production Models*.
- Websites to help students build their mathematical skills

  - The Khan Academy: www.khanacademy.org/math/algebra
  - Geogrebra: www.geogebra.org/cms/

Assessment

- From Part I, a set essay of 3,000 words typed. It is due on September 10, 2013. It is worth 20 percent of your final grade.

- In-class Exam on September 24, 2013. It is worth 20 percent of your final grade.
- From Part II, a set essay of 6,000 words, typed. It is due on November 19, 2013. It is worth 30 percent of your final grade.
- Final exam worth 30 percent of your final grade. The exam is on Tuesday December 11, 2013, from 8:00–10:00pm.

Problem Set

It will be distributed and placed on Blackboard (see Appendix 2).

Course Description

The course covers heterodox microeconomic theory. It introduces the student to the historical background and methodology of the theory and then deals with the business enterprise, production and costs, pricing and prices, industry and market, reproduction of the business enterprise, consumer, industrial and government demand, market price and market governance, trade associations, price leadership, government regulation, and the microfoundations of heterodox macroeconomics. The course will also introduce the student to the heterodox disaggregated price-output model of the economy.

Lecture and Reading Outline

"Well, in *our* country, "said Alice, still panting a little, "you'd generally get somewhere else – if you ran very fast for a long time . . . ." "A slow sort of country!" said the Queen. "Now *here*, you see, it takes all the running *you* can do to keep in the same place. If you want to get somewhere else, you must run at least twice as fast as that!"

(Lewis Carroll, *Through the Looking-Glass*)

I The making of heterodox microeconomics

A. Heterodox economics

1 Lee, F. S. and T.-H. Jo. 2011. "Social Surplus Approach and Heterodox Economics." *Journal of Economic Issues* 45 (4): 857–875.
2 Lee, F. S. 1998. *Post Keynesian Price Theory*. Cambridge: Cambridge University Press, Chs. 1–10.
3 Lee, F. S. 2011. *Social, Methods, and Microeconomics: Contributions to Doing Economics Better*. Hoboken, NJ: Wiley-Blackwell, Chs. 1, 2, and 8.
4 Lee, F. S. 2013. *Markets, Competition, and the Economy as a Social System*. Hoboken, NJ: Wiley-Blackwell, Ch. 2.
5 Bortis, H. 1997. *Institutions, Behaviour and Economic Theory*. Cambridge: Cambridge University Press, Chs. 1, 2, and 5.

6 Polanyi, K. 1968. "The Economy as Instituted Process." In *Primitive, Archaic and Modern Economies: Essays of Karl Polanyi*, edited by G. Dalton, 139–174. New York: Doubleday and Co.
7 Dugger, W. M. 1996. "Redefining Economics: From Market Allocation to Social Provisioning." In *Political Economy for the 21st Century: Contemporary Views on the Trends of Economics*, edited by C. Whalen, 31–43. M. E. Sharpe.
8 Dobb, M. 1945. *Political Economy and Capitalism: Some Essays in Economic Tradition.* New York: International Publishers, Ch. 1.
9 Spash, C. L. 2012. "New Foundations for Ecological Economics." *Ecological Economics* 77: 36–47.

B. *Methodology of heterodox economics*

1 Lawson, T. 2003. *Reorienting Economics.* New York: Routledge, Chs. 1–4, 6, and 10.
2 Downward, P., ed. 2003. *Applied Economics and the Critical Realist Critique.* New York: Routledge, Chs. 5, 6, 7, and 9.
3 Downward, P. and A. Mearman. 2007. "Retroduction as Mixed-Methods Triangulation in Economic Research: Reorienting Economics into Social Science." *Cambridge Journal of Economics* 31 (1): 77–99.
4 Olsen, W. and J. Morgan. 2005. "A Critical Epistemology of Analytical Statistics: Addressing the Sceptical Realist." *Journal for the Theory of Social Behaviour* 35 (3): 255–284.
5 Emirbayer, M. and A. Mische. 1998. "What Is Agency?" *American Journal of Sociology* 103 (4): 962–1023.
6 Morgan, M. 2012. *The World in the Model.* Cambridge: Cambridge University Press, Chs. 1, 3, 4, 6, and 10.

II Structure, agency, and modeling the economy

1 Lee, F. S. 2012. *Social Provisioning, Embeddedness, and Modeling the Economy.* London: Wiley-Blackwell, Chs. 1, 5, 6, and 8.
2 Lee, F. S. 2011. *Social, Methods, and Microeconomics: Contributions to Doing Economics Better.* London: Wiley-Blackwell, Chs. 3 and 5.
3 De Gregori, T. R. 1987. "Resources Are Not; They Become: An Institutional Theory." *Journal of Economic Issues* 21 (3): 1241–1263.
4 O'Boyle, E. J. 2011. "The *Acting* Person: Social Capital and Sustainable Development." *Forum for Social Economics* 40 (1): 79–98.
5 Herman, E. S. 1981. *Corporate Control, Corporate Power.* Cambridge: Cambridge University Press, Chs. 1 and 2.
6 Todorova, Z. 2009. *Money and Households in a Capitalist Economy: A Gendered Post Keynesian-Institutional Analysis.* Edward Elgar, Chs. 2 and 3.
7 Dean, E. N. 2013. "Toward a Heterodox Theory of the Business Enterprise: The Going Concern Model and the US Computer Industry." PhD diss., University of Missouri-Kansas City, Ch. 2.

III The business enterprise: production, costs, and pricing

A. Decision-making and the acting enterprise

1 Moss, S. 1981. *An Economic Theory of Business Strategy*. John Wiley and Sons, Ch. 2.
2 Fligstein, N. 1990. *The Transformation of Corporate Control*. Cambridge, MA: Harvard University Press.

B. Structure of production and costs

1 Lee, F. 1986. "Post Keynesian View of Average Direct Costs: A Critical Evaluation of the Theory and the Empirical Evidence." *Journal of Post Keynesian Economics* 8 (3): 400–424.
2 Dean, J. 1976. *Statistical Cost Estimation*. Indiana University Press, "Introduction to Part I."
3 Scranton, P. 1991. "Diversity in Diversity: Flexible Production and American Industrialization, 1880–1930." *Business History Review* 64 (1): 27–90.
4 Abruzzi, A. 1965. "The Production Process: Operating Characteristics." *Management Science* 11 (6, Series B): B98–B118.
5 Scazzieri, R. 1983. "The Production Process: General Characteristics and Taxonomy." *Rivista Internazionale di Sciencze Economiche e Commerciali* 30 (7): 597–611.
6 Scazzieri, R. 1993. *A Theory of Production: Tasks, Processes, and Technical Practices*. Clarendon Press.
7 Morroni, M. 1992. *Production Process and Technical Change*. Cambridge: Cambridge University Press, parts I and II.
8 Mir-Artigues, P. and J. Gonzalez-Calvet. 2007. *Funds, Flows, and Time: An Alternative Approach to the Microeconomic Analysis of Productive Activities*. New York: Springer.

C. Pricing and prices

1 Lee, F. S. 1998. *Post Keynesian Price Theory*. Cambridge: Cambridge University Press, Ch. 11; Appendix A, B.
2 Downward, P. 2003. *Applied Economics and the Critical Realist Critique*. Routledge, Ch. 14.
3 Downward, P. 1999. *Pricing Theory in Post Keynesian Economics: A Realist Approach*. Edward Elgar, Chs. 3–8.
4 Hall, S., M. Walsh, and A. Yates. 2000. "Are UK Companies' Prices Sticky?" *Oxford Economic Papers* 52 (3): 425–446.
5 Downward, P. 2000. "A Realist Appraisal of Post Keynesian Pricing Theory." *Cambridge Journal of Economics* 24 (2): 211–224.
6 Fabiani, S., C. Loupias, F. Martins, and R. Sabbatini, eds. 2007. *Pricing Decisions in the Euro Area: How Firms set Prices and Why*. Oxford: Oxford University Press, parts I and II.

7   Gu, G. C. 2012. "Pricing, Price Stability, and Post Keynesian Price Theory." PhD diss., University of Missouri-Kansas City, Chs. 2 and 3.
8   Melmies, J. 2010. "New Keynesian Versus Post Keynesians on the Theory of Prices." *Journal of Post Keynesian Economics* 32 (3): 445–465.
9   Coutts, K. and N. Norman. 2013. "Post-Keynesian Approaches to Industrial Pricing: A Survey and Critique." In *The Oxford Handbook of Post-Keynesian Economics, Volume 1: Theory and Origins*, edited by G. C. Harcourt and P. Kriesler, 443–466. Oxford University Press.

IV The business enterprise: investment, output, and employment

A. Investment

1   Lavoie, M., L.-P. Rochon, and M. Seccareccia, eds. 2010. *Money and Macrodynamics: Alfred Eichner and Post-Keynesian Economics*. M.E. Sharpe, Chs. 3 and 4.
2   Moss, S. 1981. *An Economic Theory of Business Strategy*. John Wiley and Sons, Chs. 3 and 8.
3   Baddeley, M. C. 2003. *Investment: Theories and Analysis*. New York: Palgrave Macmillan.
4   Scheibl, F. and A. Wood. 2005. "Investment Sequencing in the Brick Industry: An Application of Grounded Theory." *Cambridge Journal of Economics* 29 (2): 223–247.

B. Production and employment

1   Spencer, D. A. 2011. "Work Is a Four-Letter Word: The Economics of Work in Historical and Critical Perspective." *American Journal of Economics and Sociology* 70 (3): 563–586.

C. Wages, salaries, and dividends

1   Bewley, T. F. 1999. *Why Wages Don't Fall During a Recession*. Cambridge, MA: Harvard University Press.
2   Bewley, T. F. 1998. "Why Not Cut Pay?" *European Economic Review* 42: 459–490.
3   Dickens, W. T. et al. 2007. "How Wages Change: Micro Evidence from the International Wage Flexibility Project." *Journal of Economic Perspectives* 21 (2): 195–214.

D. Theory of the business enterprise

1   Dean, E. N. 2013. "Toward a Heterodox Theory of the Business Enterprise: The Going Concern Model and the US Computer Industry." PhD diss., University of Missouri-Kansas City, Chs. 3 and 4.
2   Jo, T.-H. and J. F. Henry. 2015. "The Business Enterprise in the Age of Money Manager Capitalism." *Journal of Economic Issues* 49 (1): 23–46.

V Markets and demand for the social product

A. Market, industry, and the social provisioning process

1   Fligstein, N. 1996. "Markets as Politics: A Political-Cultural Approach to Market Institutions." *American Sociological Review* 61 (4): 656–673.
2   Granovetter, M. 1985. "Economic Action and Social Structure: The Problem of Embeddedness." *American Journal of Sociology* 91 (3): 481–510.
3   Smelser, N. J. and R. Swedberg, eds. 1994. *The Handbook of Economic Sociology*. Princeton: Princeton University Press, Chs. 11 and 15.
4   Fligstein, N. 2001. *The Architecture of Markets*. Princeton: Princeton University Press, Chs. 1, 2, 3, and 4.
5   Hermann, A. 2008. "The Institutional Analysis of the Market." *International Journal of Green Economics* 2 (4): 379–391.
6   Lee, F. S., ed. 2013. *Markets, Competition, and the Economy as a Social System*. Hoboken, NJ: Wiley-Blackwell, Chs. 5 and 6.

B. Demand for the social product

1   Fuller, C. G. 1996. "Elements of a Post Keynesian Alternative to 'Household Production'." *Journal of Post Keynesian Economics* 18 (4): 595–607.
2   Lavoie, M. 1994. "A Post Keynesian Approach to Consumer Choice." *Journal of Post Keynesian Economics* 16 (4): 539–562.
3   Lavoie, M. 1992. *Foundations of Post-Keynesian Economic Analysis*. Edward Elgar, Ch. 2.
4   Devetag, M. G. 1999. "From Utilities to Mental Models: A Critical Survey on Decision Rules and Cognition in Consumer Choice." *Industrial and Corporate Change* 8 (2): 289–351.

C. Structure of market demand and the market price

D. Competition, market power, and the going market price

VI Competition, the market price, and market governance

A. Market Governance: controlling instability through regulating markets

1   Richardson, G. B. 1965. "The Theory of Restrictive Trade Practices." *Oxford Economic Papers* 17 (3): 432–449.
2   Moss, S. 1981. *An Economic Theory of Business Strategy*. John Wiley and Sons, Chs. 5, 6, 7, and 8.
3   Clifton, J. A. 1987. "Competitive Market Process." In *The New Palgrave Dictionary of Economics*, Vol. I, A to D, edited by J. Eatwell, M. Milgate, and P. Newman, 553–556. Stockton Press.

4 Grabher, G., ed. 1993. *The Embedded Firm*. Routledge, Chs. 1 and 2.
5 Campbell, J., J. Hollingsworth, and L. Lindberg, eds. 1991. *Governance of the American Economy*. Cambridge: Cambridge University Press, Chs. 1, 2, 11, and 12.
6 Lee, F. S., ed. 2013. *Markets, Competition, and the Economy as a Social System*. Wiley-Blackwell, Chs. 7 and 8.
7 Moudud, J. K., C. Bina, and P. L. Mason, eds. 2012. *Alternative Theories of Competition*. Routledge, Chs. 2, 3, and 12.

B. Private market governance and the market price: trade associations, price leadership, and other forms of private collective activities

1 Howe, M. 1972–1973. "A Study of Trade Association Price Fixing." *Journal of Industrial Economics* 21 (3): 236–256.
2 Smelser, N. J. and R. Swedberg, eds. 1994. *The Handbook of Economic Sociology*. Princeton: Princeton University Press, Ch. 18.
3 Lee, F. S., ed. 2013. *Markets, Competition, and the Economy as a Social System*. Hoboken, NJ: Wiley-Blackwell, Ch. 9.
4 Levenstein, M. C. and V. Y. Suslow. 2003. "What Determines Cartel Success?" *Journal of Economic Literature* 44 (1): 43–95.

C. Public market governance and the market price: laws and government regulation

VII Microeconomics and the social provisioning process

A. Microeconomics and modeling the going economy

1 Lee, F. S. 2011. "Heterodox Surplus Approach: Production, Prices and Value Theory." *Bulletin of Political Economy* 6 (2): 65–105.
2 Lee, F. S. 1996. "Pricing, the Pricing Model and Post-Keynesian Price Theory." *Review of Political Economy* 8 (1): 87–99.
3 Miller, R. E. and P. D. Blair. 2009. *Input-Output Analysis: Foundations and Extensions*, 2nd edn. Cambridge: Cambridge University Press, Chs. 1–2, 4–5, and 11.
4 Bortis, H. 1997. *Institutions, Behaviour and Economic Theory*. Cambridge: Cambridge University Press, Ch. 4.
5 Bortis, H. 2003. "Keynes and the Classics: Notes on the Monetary Theory of Production." In *Modern Theories of Money*, edited by L.-P. Rochon and S. Rossi, 411–474. Edward Elgar.
6 Lavoie, M., L.-P. Rochon, and M. Seccareccia, eds. 2010. *Money and Macrodynamics: Alfred Eichner and Post-Keynesian Economics*. M.E. Sharpe, Chs. 1 and 2.

B. *Model of the going economy and the social provisioning process*

1   Moudud, J. K., C. Bina, and P. L. Mason, eds. 2013. *Alternative Theories of Competition*. New York: Routledge, Ch. 7.
2   Lee, F. S. 2013. "Post-Keynesian Price Theory: From Pricing to Market Governance to the Economy as a Whole." In *The Oxford Handbook of Post-Keynesian Economics, Vol. I: Theory and Origins*, edited by G. C. Harcourt and P. Kriesler, 467–484. Oxford: Oxford University Press.
3   Lee, F. S. 2011. "Heterodox Microeconomics and the Foundation of Heterodox Macroeconomics." *Economia Informa* 367: 6–20.
4   Lavoie, M., L.-P. Rochon, and M. Seccareccia, eds. 2010. *Money and Macrodynamics: Alfred Eichner and Post-Keynesian Economics*. M.E. Sharpe, Chs. 3 and 4.
5   Shapiro, N. 1988. "Market Structure and Economic Growth: Steindl's Contribution." *Social Concept* 4 (2): 72–83.
6   Jo, T.-H. 2007. "Microfoundations of Effective Demand." PhD diss., University of Missouri-Kansas City, Chs. 2–6.
7   Todorova, Z. 2009. *Money and Households in a Capitalist Economy: A Gendered Post Keynesian-Institutional Analysis*. Edward Elgar, Chs. 4, 5, and 6.

VIII Social provisioning and corporate capitalism

1   Bortis, H. 1997. *Institutions, Behaviour and Economic Theory*. Cambridge: Cambridge University Press, Chs. 6 and 7.
2   Wisman, J. D. and K. W. Capehart. 2010. "Creative Destruction, Economic Insecurity, Stress, and Epidemic Obesity." *American Journal of Economics and Sociology* 69 (3): 936–982.

Note

*   Editor's note: This is a doctoral level microeconomics course, "Colloquium in Advanced Microeconomics," offered in the Fall 2013 semester at the University of Missouri-Kansas City. Fred Lee had developed and updated this course since Fall 2000.

Appendix 2

Narrative-qualitative-analytical problem sets[*]

Problem set I

Introduction to heterodox microeconomic theory

I The scope and historical framework of heterodox microeconomics

1   What contributions did Gardiner Means, Philip Andrews, and Harry Edwards make towards a heterodox understanding of the business enterprise?
2   The visible hand of management is an important feature of the heterodox view of prices and markets. Who first articulated the view? Discuss its development.
3   What significant contributions did Joan Robinson, Nicholas Kaldor, Luigi Pasinetti, and Piero Sraffa make to the development of heterodox price theory from 1950 to 1971?
4   To what extent is Steindl's analysis of stagnation dependent on the pre-Keynesian assumption that savings determine investment?
5   Describe how the clash of administered prices and market prices directly affect the utilization of economic resources over the business cycle.
6   What is administrative inflation? What are the causes of administrative inflation and how does it affect the rate of growth of economic activity?
7   What are Kalecki's contributions to heterodox microeconomics?
8   Discuss the historical emergence of the notion of non-equilibrium.
9   Familiarity with the real economy is the basis of heterodox microeconomics. Discuss.
10 The Great Depression provided the background for the emergence of heterodox microeconomics. Discuss.
11 What theoretical differences for microeconomic theory emerge when economics is defined as the science of social provisioning as opposed to the allocation of scarce resources between competing ends?
12 If enterprises do not set their profit maximizing prices by equating MC = MR, then according to P.W.S. Andrews how do they do it?
13 What contributions do the doctrines of administered prices and normal cost prices make to the development of a non-equilibrium microeconomic theory?

14 The emergence of heterodox economics in the 1960s and 1970s was due solely to outside social movements since mainstream economic theory was perfectly sound and had no theoretical problems. Discuss.

15 Compare a Kaleckian determination of the mark up to a Sylos-Labini and H. R. Edwards analysis of the determination of the mark up.

II Methodology of heterodox microeconomics

1 What are the philosophical foundations of heterodox economics?

2 What are causal mechanisms? Why are they important for heterodox theorizing?

3 What are structures? Why do structures evolve?

4 What is epistemological relativism? What is its significance for heterodox theorizing?

5 What is the method of grounded theory?

6 What role does pre-existing ideas and concepts play in grounded theory?

7 Why is it important for heterodox economists that their theories explain, are historical narratives, and are not universal laws?

8 Why is logical coherence not a feature of heterodox theories?

9 What are the following: holism, pattern models, and the participant-observer approach?

10 How are grounded theories evaluated?

11 What is a case study? Why are they important for the creation of heterodox theories?

12 How is a grounded theory translated into mathematics and an economic model?

13 What is meant by a rigorous, non-deductive economic model?

14 What contributions does econometrics make towards creating heterodox theories?

15 How do critical realism and the method of grounded theory affect the development of heterodox microeconomic theory?

16 Heterodox theories are analytical narratives. What does this mean and are such theories "scientific"?

17 How do critical realism and the method of grounded theory affect the development of heterodox microeconomic theory?

18 Agency is both a structure and embedded in a causal mechanism. Discuss.

19 Heterodox microeconomics is not, like neoclassical economics, a "positive" science. Discuss

III Structural organization of economic activity: an overview

1 What is meant by "production as a circular flow"? What are the advantages of this production schema relative to a classical production schema for heterodox microeconomic theory?

2 What are the structural linkages for income flows relative to goods for social provisioning?

3 What are the structural linkages for income flows relative to goods for social provisioning?

4 What would be the possible impact on social provisioning if there was a disruption in the flow of wage income?

5 Production as a circular process, cumulative causation, and the economy as a social organism and a class society ensure that economic activity and the social provisioning process are affected by political activity. Discuss.

Problem set II

Heterodox production theory

I Classical production models

1 Describe the one-way production schema. How are capital goods placed in the schema?

2 In a linear view of the production process, intermediate products move steadily towards their final goal, consumption, down a strictly one-way path. What does this mean? Discuss.

3 What was the Kiel Group's response to the linear view of the production process?

4 What is a 'numeraire'?

5 What is the labor theory of value?

6 In Pasinetti's pure labor economy, why is there no mark-up for profit or a rate of profit?

7 In Pasinetti's pure labor economy, how does technical change affect relative prices?

8 In Pasinetti's pure labor economy, what determines relative prices? What is meant when it is said that prices represent embodied labor or prices represent commanded labor?

9 What is the difference between wages advanced and wages taken from the surplus?

10 What is a real wage? If the real wage is given why is it possible to obtain a physical rate of profit?

11 For Ricardo what is wealth? Also what is, for Ricardo, value? Finally, for Ricardo, what is the source of value? What is the measure of value? And what is the creator of wealth?

12 What did Ricardo mean by the value of labor?

13 What did Ricardo mean by the rise and fall in the value of labor?

14 "The proportions in which capital that is to support labour, and the capital that is invested in tools, machinery and buildings, may be variously combined. This difference in the degree of durability of fixed capital, and this

variety in the proportions in which the two sort of capital may be combined, introduce another cause, besides the greater or less quantity of labour necessary to produce commodities, for the variations in their relative value – this cause is the rise or fall in the value of labour" (Ricardo, *On the Principles of Political Economy and Taxation*, Sraffa edition, p. 30). What is Ricardo talking about?

15   "If men employed no machinery in production but labour only, and were all the same length of time before they brought their commodities to market, the exchangeable value of their goods would be precisely in proportion to the quantity of labour employed" (Ricardo, *On the Principles of Political Economy and Taxation*, Sraffa edition, p. 32). Develop a production-price model to illustrate Ricardo's statement.

16   "There can be no rise in the value of labour without a fall of profits. If the corn is to be divided between the farmer and the labour, the larger the proportion that is given to the latter, the less will remain for the former" (Ricardo, *On the Principles of Political Economy and Taxation*, Sraffa edition, p. 35). Construct a model to demonstrate this statement.

17   Define "integrated unit of capacity."

18   Show that the rate of profit and the growth rate are determined in the consumption good sector and that the production of luxury goods reduces the growth rate of the economy.

II Burchardt production model

1   Investment determines output and savings, and profit mark-ups determine prices; but this is not so when the mark-up is determined by investment needs. In this case, there is no flexibility in the economy and its change depends on technical change. Explain.

2   Answer the following questions.

   a   What are the differences between a one-stage and a two-stage classical production model?

   b   What are the differences between a classical production model and a Burchardt production model?

3   Describe the interdependencies of the 2-sector Burchardt model.

4   "the self-reproduction of capital is an elementary 'technological' fact of capitalistic production" (Nurkse 1935, 238). Explain.

5   What is Marx's contribution to the Burchardt model?

6   What is the difference between fixed capital and working capital?

7   Describe Lowe's description of the Burchardt model.

8   What is Kalecki's degree of monopoly?

9   "Workers spend what they get and capitalists get what they spend." What did Kalecki mean by this?

10   Why does a higher profit mark-up (or degree of monopoly) produce a lower degree of capacity utilization (or output) and a higher profit share in national income?

11 What determines profits and savings in the Burchardt models?
12 What determines the distribution of income between wages and profits in the Burchardt models?
13 Why in the Burchardt models do wages and profits constitute all of the net national income and gross national income, so that net national income equals gross national income?
14 What drives output and the expansion of output in the Burchardt models?
15 Is it possible to derive a wage-profit line in a two-sector Burchardt model? Why or why not?
16 What is the relationship between the wage rate and the rate of profit or profit mark-up in a one-sector and two-sector Burchardt model?

III Circular production: Corn models

1 Why does David Ricardo make the following statement?

"If the interests of the landlords be of sufficient consequence, to determine us not to avail ourselves of all the benefits which would follow from importing corn at a cheap price, they should also influence us in rejecting all improvements in agriculture, and in the implements of husbandry." (Ricardo, "An Essay on the Influence of a Low Price of Corn on the profit of Stocks," Sraffa edition, Vol. IV, p. 41)

2 What is the difference between a productive worker and an unproductive worker?
3 "It follows then, that the interest of the landlord is always opposed to the interest of every other class in the community. His situation is never so prosperous, as when food is scarce and dear: whereas, all other persons are greatly benefited by procuring food cheap" (Ricardo, "An Essay on the Influence of a Low Price of Corn on the profit of Stocks," Sraffa edition, Vol. IV, p. 21). Explain.
4 "Profits then depend on the price, or rather on the value of food. Everything which gives facility to the production of food, however scare, or however abundant commodities may become, will raise the rate of profits, whilst on the contrary, everything which shall augment the cost of production without augmenting the quantity of food, will, under every circumstance, lower the general rate of profit" (Ricardo, "An Essay on the Influence of a Low Price of Corn on the profit of Stocks," Sraffa edition, Vol. IV, p. 26). Explain.

IV Circular production: Leontief models

1 Construct your own transaction table and identify the value added and the household industry. How did Leontief alter the transaction table in order to analysis economic events over time?
2 Describe a closed input-output model. What are the differences between a closed and an open input-output model?
3 Describe the relationship between the quantity model and the price model with respect to the level of employment and net national income.

4   Discuss the relationship between Leontief's production coefficients and the marginal productivity theory of distribution.

5   In the closed Leontief model, the solution price vector consists of relative prices. Why is this the case? The choice of the *numeraire* good is important; what properties should a good have in order to be the *numeraire* good? Can this *numeraire* good be called money? Why or why not?

V Circular production: Sraffian models

1   Compare and contrast the classical production model, the two-sector Burchardt production model, and the circular production model with regard to the nature of production, the origin of profits, and the relationship between wages and profits.

2   Compare and contrast the nature of interdependency in the two-sector Burchardt model and the circular production model.

3   Why does production as a circular process (flow) mean that the maximum rate of profit is finite?

4   Why does production as a circular process (flow) mean that prices cannot be resolved completely into direct and indirect multiplied by wage rates and rate of profit? What does this mean for the labor theory of value?

5   What is the commodity residual? What does it represent? What are its implications for the determination of prices?

6   Why does a surplus producing economy have a maximum eigenvalue less than one and greater than zero?

7   If the maximum eigenvalue was equal to zero, what would this mean about the schema of production, commodity residual, the maximum rate of profits, the labor theory of value?

8   What are the determinants of prices in a circular production model?

9   Why is Sraffa's analysis of prices, wage rates, and rates of profit not predicated on constant returns to scale?

10 Why does the production of a surplus necessitate the introduction of distributional variables? What does this imply about the origins of profits? What is the mathematical explanation for why the production of a surplus necessitates the introduction of distribution variables into a Sraffian (and Leontief) production model?

11 What is a non-basic 'commodity own rate of return' and what importance does it have for prices in a decomposable economic system?

12 In what manner does the choice of commodity *numeraire* affect prices in a decomposable economic system?

13 Utilizing mathematical and literary discourse, critically compare the Ricardian one-good economy with the Sraffian multi-good economy in the following areas:

   •   Origin of profits
   •   Origin of value

- The notion of the surplus
- Determination of prices
- The role of prices
- Distribution of wages and profits
- The quantity of capital
- Relationship between the K/L ratio and the rate of profit.

Problem set III

The business enterprise

I Nature of the business enterprise

1 Delineate the heterodox view of the business enterprise, focusing on its ownership and control, its managerial and administrative structure, and its motivation. Is this view 'realistic'? Explain.
2 What are the essential features of the large business enterprise? Why is it not possible to say that the large business enterprise simply tries to maximize profits?
3 What implication does the separation of ownership from control have for the operation of the business enterprise?
4 Why do managerial resources drive the business enterprise to grow and change? Are there any limits or constraints on managerial resources?
5 In what ways can the business enterprise be seen as a capitalist institution?
6 What is the managerial thesis regarding the business enterprise? Is it compatible with the heterodox view of the nature of the business enterprise? Explain.
7 Describe the three ways business enterprises are legally organized and owned.
8 Explain why individuals who legally own the business enterprises do not necessarily control the business enterprise.
9 Describe the different kinds of control.
10 Describe a functional managerial structure and a centralized administrative structure.
11 Describe a divisional managerial structure and a decentralized administrative structure.
12 What is long range planning? What are the two general types of long range planning?
13 Price setting is one aspect of long range planning. Discuss.

II The structure of production and costs of the business enterprise

1 Define the following terms:

- Direct costs
- Plant segment
- Technical coefficients

- Production coefficients
- Shop expenses
- Managerial technique of production
- Shop technique of production
- Business enterprise expenses
- Indirect costs
- Depreciation
- Business enterprise technique of production
- Factory costs
- Total costs of production
- Plant segment cost of production
- Production period
- Enterprise average direct costs
- Plant segment average direct costs
- Enterprise average direct costs
- Cost of shop technique of production
- Average shop expenses
- Accounting period
- Average enterprise expenses
- Cost of enterprise technique of production
- Bench-mark output

2   Describe the cost structure of the business enterprise.
3   What is the difference between the production period and the accounting period?
4   What are technical and managerial innovations and how do they affect the production and cost structure of the business enterprise?
5   Describe the structure of production of the business enterprise and critically evaluate its implications for the issues of the constancy of average direct costs and the size of the business enterprise.
6   Over time as an enterprise expands its production and sales, it will reach a point where its average total costs start to increase. What will the enterprise do?
7   It is the fertility rather than the niggardliness of technology that dominates and the production and cost structure of the business enterprise. Discuss and relate the discussion to the theoretical issues of constant average direct costs and the size of the business enterprise.
8   Heterodox production and cost theory is not dependent on the marginal product of labor. Why is this the case and what implications does this have for using equilibrium analysis to explain the economic decisions of the business enterprise?

III Costing, pricing, and prices

1   Define the following terms:

- Costing
- Normal output/capacity utilization

- Costing margin
- Pricing
- Estimated costing
- Standard costing
- Mark up pricing
- Normal cost pricing
- Target rate of return pricing
- Administered price
- Gross costing margin
- Profit margin
- Exchange-specific price

2   Define administered prices and describe their essential features and properties.
3   Assuming increasing average direct costs and decreasing average total costs, explain the role of normal volume of output (or normal capacity utilization) in establishing stable and common prices.
4   What is the difference between the mark-up for profit and the actual profit mark-up? Under what conditions will the latter differ from the former?
5   Define common price and exchange-specific price. Why does the exchange-specific price undermine the business enterprise's ability to reproduce itself?
6   What is the difference between costing and pricing?
7   Compare the costing and pricing procedures of normal cost pricing to the procedures used in neoclassical price theory to set the price. In what ways are normal cost prices different from neoclassical prices? Explain why, from a heterodox perspective, business enterprises would use such pricing procedures.
8   Compare and contrast mark up, normal cost, and target rate of return pricing procedures.
9   Draw on the enterprise's cost structure and the structure of market demand to explain why the management of a business enterprise would utilize mark-up, normal cost, and target rate of return pricing procedures when setting prices.

IV Investment, employment, and production

1   Discuss the relationship between the financing of a business enterprise's investment activities and the determination of the costing margin or the profit mark-up.
2   What are the uses of business income? What are the demands for business income?
3   What are the determinants of dividend payments? Why does Eichner view them as a cost to the megacorp?
4   What are the determinants of investment in plant and equipment?
5   How does the business enterprise select its investment projects?
6   What are the sources of funds for financing investment projects?
7   In the Eichner, Harcourt, and Wood models, what determines the amount of funds the business enterprise will raise from internal sources and from external sources?

8 What is the distinction between Eichner's corporate levy and the costing margin?

9 Define the degree of monopoly. What are the determinants of the degree of monopoly?

10 Critically evaluate the investment explanation and the competition-barriers to entry explanation of the magnitude of the profit mark-up. Which of the explanations is best supported by the empirical evidence?

11 From a heterodox view, what are the determinants of the wage rate? Describe the empirical evidence.

12 The business enterprise bases its hiring decisions on expected production. Discuss.

13 The business enterprise bases its production decisions on expectations and not prices or profits. Discuss.

14 What are the possible structural constraints on the determination of the profit mark-up? Do these constraints allow for agency in the determination of the profit mark-up as such by Eichner, Harcourt, and Wood? Discuss.

15 Post Keynesians and Marxists have different explanations for the origin of profits. This means they have different explanations for the profit mark-up. Discuss comparatively and critically.

16 The business enterprise can finance its working and fixed capital expenditures through its price policy and hence is independent of the financial system. Discuss.

Problem set IV

The market and the business enterprise

I Industry and market

1 Define the concept of industry.

2 Define the market, and discuss the relationship between its two dimensions – i.e., income class and social use-value – and competition, especially with respect to the number of enterprises in the market and the determination of the market price.

3 Why is a market non-clearable and what does this imply about prices?

4 Markets are social institutions that are non-clearable; hence price do not clear markets and do not allocate resources and coordinate economic activity. Discuss.

5 The market is a social structure. Discuss.

6 What is the difference between industry and market? Why is the distinction important to the heterodox view of competition, the competitive process, and the relative pervasiveness of competition in a capitalist economy?

II Structure of market demand

1 What are the determinants of market demand for consumer goods and investment goods?

2 The structure of consumer, industrial, and government demand means that prices have little impact on market sales. Discuss.

3 Describe the heterodox theory of consumer choice. In what ways is it incompatible with neoclassical theory of consumer choice?

4 How do households make choices when purchasing consumer goods?

5 What role does household income play in the purchasing of consumer goods?

6 What role do prices play in the purchasing of consumer goods by households?

7 The structures and causal mechanisms that constitute consumer markets separate market price from market sales. Discuss and delineate the implications for the determination of the market price.

8 The existence of agency enables the household to overcome the advertising of corporations and determine their own patterns of consumption. Discuss.

9 While many believe and argue that there is a functional relationship between a good's price and the quantity of sales of that good, the argument is in fact incoherent and without empirical support and the belief is irrational. Discuss from a heterodox perspective.

10 It is because heterodox microeconomics does not have a theory of individual choice that it cannot have a coherent theory of consumer demand. Discuss.

11 Heterodox microeconomics does not have a theory of consumer choice between work and leisure, but it can still discuss employment decisions by business enterprises and workers. Discuss.

III Structure of market demand, the business enterprise, and the market price

1 Outline the forces that make the enterprises in a market set the same price. (Be sure to discuss the role of 'goodwill' in dividing up the market.)

2 Outline the relationship between the price the enterprise sets and its ability to engage in sequential production. What implication does this relationship have for stable prices?

3 Why do fluctuating, non-uniform market prices inhibit the enterprise's ability to undertake investment and grow?

4 Why do differential prices produce a rapid shifting of market shares? What impact does a rapidly declining market share have on the enterprise's ability to reproduce itself?

5 Why does destructive price competition drive enterprises to establish market institutions that would eliminate price competition?

6 Discuss the fluidity of market shares and its impact on the enterprise's ability to engage in sequential production.

7 Why are variations in the market price not connected with variations in market sales?

8 Why do business enterprises prefer administered prices as opposed to auction or highly flexible prices?

9 The structure of the market, non-uniform market prices, and declining market share undermines the enterprise's ability to engage in sequential production and to grow. Discuss.

10 It is 'rational' for enterprises to use cost-plus pricing procedures whereas it is 'irrational' for them to use MC=MR profit maximizing procedures. Discuss.
11 Administered prices, restrictive trade practices, and big business are fundamental components of heterodox microeconomics. Why?

Problem set V

Competition, the market price, and market governance

I Business enterprise, competition, and the market price

1 Define market power and what is the basis of market power?
2 Why does market depression destabilize the market price and reduce profits?
3 Why does a significant and permanent drop in the market growth rate destabilize the market price and reduce profits?
4 Identify two differences between enterprises in the same market that create the problem of establishing a single market price. Why do these problems push enterprises to set up market institutions and other arrangements whose purpose is to establish a single market price?
5 Describe the forces that determine the strength of market competition.
6 Discuss the extent that the severity of competition can differ between markets.
7 What is the relationship between market organization, concentration, and the business enterprise? Be sure to discuss the following points:

a   Measures of business enterprise size and market concentration.
b   Relationship between the multi-plant business enterprise and concentration.

8 Define potential competition.
9 Define the following terms:

- Gini coefficient
- Lorenz Curve
- Hirshman-Herfindahl Index

10 What role do restrictive trade practices have in market governance and setting the market price?
11 Why is market governance and market power necessary for capitalist's markets to work from the perspective of the business enterprise?
12 Define market governance and describe the forms that it takes.
13 Why do cost differentials between enterprises and the decline in the secular growth of market sales precipitate bouts of destructive price competition and thereby drive business enterprises to establish market institutions that would eliminate such price competition?
14 Under what conditions would a business enterprise decide to grow through vertical integration and through market expansion?
15 Using the notion of a product cycle, describe how business enterprise growth can alter market concentration as well as market organization.

II Market governance and the market price: trade associations, price leadership, government regulation, and laws

1   What are trade associations? What are the legal forms they take?
2   Describe the general activities of trade associations.
3   What practices do trade associations use to regulate market activities?
4   Describe the following terms: quota system, resale price maintenance, collective boycott, exclusive dealings, and discriminatory rebates.
5   Under what conditions will a business enterprise become a price leader? Will a price leader provide greater control over competition than a trade association? Explain.
6   What are the reasons for the poor performance of trade associations in stabilizing market prices?
7   Describe the internal evolution of an administered price market.
8   Assume that the market is growing over time, then if

   a   the price leader is growing relatively faster than the price-following business enterprises, what will be the impact on the price followers' profit mark-up and on the organization of the market; and

   b   the price leader is growing relatively slower than the price followers, what will be the impact on their profit mark up and on the organization of the market (be sure to give a detailed description of the shift in market power)?

9   Assume that a dominant enterprise emerges in a market following a merger. Discuss the following points:

   a   What will be its impact on the market price with respect to its stability during the accounting period?

   b   What will be its impact on the level of the market price if destructive price competition occurred in the market prior to the merger?

   c   Assume that the market is growing. Prove, given a constant profit mark up, that the market price will fall over time.

10   What economic factors contribute to the economic stability of the dominant enterprise?
11   What legal factors contribute to the legal stability of the dominant enterprise?
12   Under what conditions will business enterprise form a cartel to govern market competition?
13   Business enterprises that become dominant in their industries and markets and hence become the price leaders are usually the first movers. What activities must business enterprises undertake to become a first mover and to retain its dominant position over time?
14   What is regulation and why is it usually associated with government regulation?
15   What are some of the 'private' interest explanations of government regulation?
16   What are some of the 'public' interest explanations of government regulation?
17   Why is it hard to define the public interest?

18   What are the differences (if any) between private and public interest explanations of government regulation?

19   Are there any real differences between the outcomes of government regulation in the name of private interests vs. government regulation in the name of the public interest?

20   What is regulatory capture? Does it really exist?

21   In what way are laws a form of government regulation of market activity?

22   The governance and hence the regulation of market activity by laws and other means of government are competitive strategies often adopted by business enterprises. Explain.

23   Explain and discuss from a heterodox perspective why restrictive trade practices, government and legal restrictions, trade associations, and price leaders are necessary for competitive, stable, and dynamic capitalism to exist.

24   Market governance consists of institutionalized patterns of behavior that constrain decision making of the business enterprise. Discuss.

25   Since markets are social institutions, market governance with restrictions on competition is the norm under capitalism. Discuss.

Problem set VI

Microfoundations of heterodox macroeconomics

I Disaggregated price-output model of the economy

1   Describe the heterodox price and output disaggregated model of the economy. What implications does the model have for effective demand in coordinating economic activity and for the role of prices in determining aggregate output and employment?

2   Using the heterodox price-quantity model, show that price-fixing by cartels, restrictive trade practices, and economic concentration do not necessarily affect the economic performance of the economy.

3   Using a heterodox price-quantity model, show that the demand for consumption and investment goods is determined by investment decisions and not by prices.

II Mark-ups, investment, and economic activity

1   The economic stagnation thesis is grounded in heterodox price theory. Explain.

2   From a heterodox perspective, should the emergence of large business enterprises and the ensuing rise in market concentration produce a tendency towards economic stagnation? Explain your answer.

3   If business enterprises vary the mark ups for profit in line with their needs for investment funds for plant and equipment, would increasing mark ups necessarily result in stagnation?

4 How would you answer change if it were investment funds for financial investments?

5 In a general way describe the way the micro-behavior of business enterprises affect the aggregate level of economic activity and the evolution of the economy.

6 The coordination of economic activity is effectuated only by the investment decisions of business enterprises and expenditure decisions of government. Discuss.

7 Using a circular production model, explain the iron law of wages.

8 Why is net national income not equal to gross national income; or the other way around, why is net national product not equal to gross national product?

9 What are the differences between a Burchardt model and a heterodox price-quantity model?

10 Foreign wars, paying workers so little that they cannot save, and monopoly is the 'optimal' environment for capitalism. Discuss in terms of the heterodox disaggregated price-quantity model.

11 If stagnation of a capitalist economy is brought about by the emergence of large business enterprises and ensuing concentration, then from a heterodox perspective what remedial actions could be undertaken by a social democratic government to correct the situation?

12 Use heterodox price and production models to critically evaluate the following statement: "The reduction of the profit mark up increases economic activity by increasing the wage share in net national income."

III Micro theorizing and macroeconomic activity

1 Neoclassical economics view the market and market prices as natural phenomena whereas in this course they are viewed as social phenomena. Which view do you think is correct, and why?

2 Restrictive trade practices, government and legal restrictions, cartels, and megacorps are necessary for a competitive and dynamic capitalism to exist. This is a paradox from a neoclassical perspective, but clearly understandable from a heterodox perspective. Explain.

3 The microfoundations of heterodox economics is grounded in society and social conventions. Discuss.

4 What is social economics?

5 In the absence of the traditional distinction between micro and macro, evaluate the following statement: "Macroeconomic outcomes have their microfoundations in social relationships and social conventions."

6 Critically analyze the following comments: "Profit is the driving force of the capitalist economy."

7 Given the existence of institutions, structures, and agency, is it possible to theorize about macroeconomic economic outcomes? Discuss.

8 Markets as institutions and the coordination of economic activity by market prices are theoretically incompatible. Discuss.

9   Unlike in neoclassical economics, heterodox economists need not distinguish between a competitive price and a monopolistic price; therefore, heterodox economists do not view cartels, collusion, oligopoly, or large industrial and financial business enterprises as disrupters to the smooth working of a capitalist economy. Evaluate this statement.

10 For heterodox economists, pricing, business enterprise reproduction, and growth are different facets of the same activity; however, for neoclassical economists, they are separate activities that do not have any necessary connection at all. What impact do these different views – pricing, reproduction, and growth – have on how heterodox and neoclassical economists view the microfoundations of macroeconomics?

11 The profit mark-up is affected by the realization of effective demand, the micro problem of competition, and the political economy problem of government regulation, and the institutional problem of custom and tradition. This makes a theory of the mark-up impossible, so it is best that heterodox economists just assume the profit mark-up is given or say that it is determined by the price elasticity of demand. Discuss.

12 It might be argued that a dynamic, viable industrial enterprise is only possible if its managers and directors adopt growth as their most important objective. Briefly outline the heterodox view on growth and the industrial enterprise, and then describe what happens to an enterprise, which does not have growth as its most important objective, and what happens to a capitalist economy whose industrial enterprises are not interested in growth.

13 What constraints does the business enterprise face on its ability to grow? Do these same constraints affect the growth of the economy as a whole? Explain why or why not.

14 Delineate the pricing and production foundations of heterodox microeconomics.

15 Discuss the extent to which the foundations make heterodox microeconomics incompatible with equilibrium and long-period price theories.

16 State intervention into markets is necessary for market governance and in fact is demanded by enterprises. Discuss.

Note

* Editor's note: This is one of two-part problem sets handed out to students in Fred Lee's doctoral level microeconomics course, "Colloquium in Advanced Microeconomics" (last updated in the Fall 2013 semester). The other part is "Mathematical-Quantitative Problem set" that is not included in the present book, but can be downloaded from http://heterodox news.com/leefs/wp-content/uploads/2017/06/Lee-2013-5602-math-problems.pdf.

Bibliography

Abraham-Frois, G. and E. Lendjel. 2006. "Father Potron's Early Contributions to Input-Output Analysis." *Economic Systems Research* 18 (4): 357–372.

Abruzzi, A. 1965. "The Production Process: Operating Characteristics." *Management Science* 11 (6): B98–B118.

Ackerman, F. and A. Nadal. 2004. *The Flawed Foundations of General Equilibrium: Critical Essays on Economic Theory.* London: Routledge.

Alnestig, P. and A. Segerstedt. 1996. "Product Costing in Ten Swedish Manufacturing Companies." *International Journal of Production Economics* 46 (December): 441–457.

Al-Omiri, M. and C. Drury. 2007. "A Survey of Factors Influencing the Choice of Product Costing Systems in UK Organizations." *Management Accounting Research* 18 (4): 399–424.

Álvarez, L. J., E. Dhyne, M. Hoeberchts, C. Kwapil, H. Le Bihan, P. Lünnemann, F. Martins, R. Sabbatini, H. Stahl, P. Vermeulen, and J. Vilmunen. 2006. "Sticky Prices in the Euro Area: A Summary of New Micro-Evidence." *Journal of the European Economic Association* 4 (2–3): 575–584.

Anderson, S. W. 1995. "A Framework for Assessing Cost Management System Changes: The Case of Activity Based Costing Implementation at General Motors, 1986–1993." *Journal of Management Accounting Research* 7: 1–51.

Andrews, P. W. S. and E. Brunner. 1951. *Capital Development in Steel: A Study of the United Steel Companies, Ltd.* New York: Augustus M. Kelley.

Annells, M. 1996. "Grounded Theory Method: Philosophical Perspectives, Paradigm of Inquiry, and Postmodernism." *Qualitative Health Research* 6 (3): 379–393.

Appleby, J., L. Hunt, and M. Jacob. 1994. *Telling the Truth About History.* New York: W. W. Norton and Company.

Arestis, P. 1996. "Post-Keynesian Economics: Towards Coherence." *Cambridge Journal of Economics* 20 (1): 111–135.

Armstrong, E. G. A. 1984. "Employers Associations in Great Britain." In *Employers Association and Industrial Relations: A Comparative Study*, edited by J. P. Windmuller and A. Gladstone, 44–78. Oxford: Clarendon Press.

Aspromourgos, T. 2004. "Sraffian Research Programs and Unorthodox Economics." *Review of Political Economy* 16 (2): 179–206.

Atkinson, G. W. and T. Oleson. 1996. "Institutional Inquiry: The Search for Similarities and Differences." *Journal of Economic Issues* 30 (3): 701–718.

Ball, R. J. 1964. *Inflation and the Theory of Money.* London: George Allen & Unwin.

Baran, P. and P. Sweezy. 1966. *Monopoly Capital: An Essay on the American Economic and Social Order*. New York: Monthly Review Press.

Barna, Y. 1962. *Investment and Growth Policies in British Industrial Firms*. Cambridge: Cambridge University Press.

Becker, W. H. 1971. "American Wholesale Hardware Trade Associations, 1870–1900." *Business History Review* 45 (2): 179–200.

Bell, S. 2001. "The Role of the State and the Hierarchy of Money." *Cambridge Journal of Economics* 25 (2): 149–163.

Berle, A. A. and G. C. Means. 1933. *The Modern Corporation and Private Property*. New York: Palgrave Macmillan.

Betz, H. K. 1988. "How Does the German Historical School Fit?" *History of Political Economy* 20 (3): 409–430.

Bidard, C. and G. Erreygers, eds. 2010. *The Analysis of Linear Economic Systems: Father Maurice Potron's Pioneering Works*. London: Routledge.

Bidard, C., G. Erreygers, and W. Parys. 2009. " 'Our Daily Bread': Maurice Potron, from Catholicism to Mathematical Economics." *European Journal of Economic Thought* 16 (1): 123–154.

Bigus, O. E., S. C. Hadden, and B. G. Glaser. 1994. "The Study of Basic Social Processes." In *More Grounded Theory Methodology: A Reader*, edited by B. G. Glaser, 38–64. Mill Valley: Sociology Press.

Blinder, A. S., E. R. D. Canetti, D. E. Lebow, and J. G. Rudd, eds. 1998. *Asking About Prices: A New Approach to Understanding Price Stickiness*. New York: Russell Sage Foundation.

Bonnett, C. E. 1956. *History of Employers' Associations in the United States*. New York: Vantage Press.

Bortis, H. 1997. *Institutions, Behaviour and Economics Theory: A Contribution to Classical-Keynesian Political Economy*. Cambridge: Cambridge University Press.

Bortis, H. 2003. "Keynes and the Classics: Notes on the Monetary Theory of Production." In *Modern Theories of Money: The Nature and Role of Money in Capitalist Economies*, edited by L.-P. Rochon and S. Rossi, 411–474. Cheltenham: Edward Elgar.

Bortis, H. 2008. "The Multiplier Relation as the Pure Theory of Output and Employment in a Monetary Production Economy." In *The Keynesian Multiplier*, edited by C. Gnos and L.-P. Rochon, 58–84. London: Routledge.

Bortis, H. 2011. "Toward a Synthesis in Post-Keynesian Economics in Luigi Pasinetti's Contribution." In *Structural Dynamics and Economic Growth*, edited by R. Arena and P. L. Porta, 145–180. Cambridge: Cambridge University Press.

Boumans, M. 2005. *How Economists Model the World into Numbers*. London: Routledge.

Boylan, T. and P. O'Gorman. 1995. *Beyond Rhetoric and Realism in Economics: Towards a Reformulation of Economic Methodology*. London: Routledge.

Boyns, T. and J. R. Edwards. 1995. "Accounting Systems and Decision-Making in the Mid-Victorian Period: The Case of the Consett Iron Company." *Business History* 37 (3): 28–51.

Boyns, T. and J. R. Edwards. 1997. "The Construction of Cost Accounting Systems in Britain to 1900: The Case of the Coal, Iron and Steel Industries." *Business History* 39 (3): 1–29.

Boyns, T., J. R. Edwards, and M. Nikitin. 1997. *The Birth of Industrial Accounting in France and Britain*. New York: Garland Publishing.

Bradley, R. L. 2007. "Resourceship: An Austrian Theory of Mineral Resources." *The Review of Austrian Economics* 20 (1): 63–90.

Brierley, J. A., C. J. Cowton, and C. Drury. 2006a. "A Note on the Importance of Product Costs in Decision-Making." *Advances in Management Accounting* 15: 249–265.

Brierley, J. A., C. J. Cowton, and C. Drury. 2006b. "Reasons for Adopting Different Capacity Levels in the Denominator of Overhead Rates: A Research Note." *Journal of Applied Management Accounting Research* 4 (2): 53–62.

Bright. J., R. E. Davies, C. A. Downes, and R. C. Sweeting. 1992. "The Deployment of Costing Techniques and Practices: A UK Study." *Management Accounting Research* 3 (3): 201–211.

Bromiley, P. 1986. *Corporate Capital Investment: A Behavioral Approach.* Cambridge: Cambridge University Press.

Brown, H. I. 2001. "Incommensurability and Reality." In *Incommensurability and Related Matters*, edited by P. Hoyningen-Huene and H. Sankey, 123–143. Dordrecht: Kluwer Academic Publisher.

Bunge, M. 1983. *Epistemology and Methodology II: Understanding the World.* Boston: D. Reidel Publishing Company.

Bunge, M. 1985. *Epistemology and Methodology III: Philosophy of Science and Technology, Part II Life Science, Social Science and Technology.* Boston: D. Reidel Publishing Company.

Bunge, M. 1998. *Social Science Under Debate: A Philosophical Perspective.* Toronto: University of Toronto Press.

Burchardt, F. 1931. "Die schemata des stationaren kreislaufs bei Böhm-Bawerk und Marx (Part I)." *Weltwirtschaftliches Archiv* 34: 525–564.

Burchardt, F. 1932. "Die schemats des stationaren kreislaufs bei Böhm-Bawerk und Marx (Part II)." *Weltwirtschaftliches Archiv* 35: 116–176.

Burchardt, F. [1931, 1932] 2013. "The Schemata of the Stationary Circuit in Böhm-Bawerk and Marx." Translated by C. Spanberger and F. S. Lee. Unpublished.

Burns, J. and R. W. Scapens. 2000. "Conceptualizing Management Accounting Change: An Institutional Framework." *Management Accounting Research* 11 (1): 3–25.

Caminati, M. 1990. "Gravitation: An Introduction." *Political Economy: Studies in the Surplus Approach* 6 (1–2): 11–44.

Campbell, J. L. and L. N. Lindberg. 1991. "The Evolution of Governance Regimes." In *Governance of the American Economy*, edited by J. L. Campbell, J. R. Hollingsworth, and L. N. Linberg, 319–355. Cambridge: Cambridge University Press.

Çapoğlu, G. 1991. *Prices, Profits and Financial Structures: A Post Keynesian Approach to Competition.* Aldershot: Edward Elgar.

Carr, D. 1986. "Narrative and the Real World: An Argument for Continuity." *History and Theory: Studies in the Philosophy of History* 25 (2): 117–131.

Carroll, L. 1902. *Through the Looking-Glass and What Alice Found There.* New York: Harper and Brothers.

Carter, A. P. and P. A. Petri. 1989. "Leontief's Contribution to Economics." *Journal of Policy Modeling* 11 (1): 7–30.

Cartwright, N. 1995. "*Ceteris Paribus* Laws and Socio-Economic Machines." *The Monist* 78 (3): 276–294.

Chandler, A. D. 1977. *The Visible Hand: The Managerial Revolution in American Business.* Cambridge: Harvard University Press.

Chandler, A. D. 1990. *Scale and Scope: The Dynamics of Industrial Capitalism.* Cambridge: Harvard University Press.

Channon, D. F. 1973. *The Strategy and Structure of British Enterprise.* Cambridge: Harvard University Press.

Charmaz, K. 1983. "The Grounded Theory Method: An Explication and Interpretation." In *Contemporary Field Research: A Collection of Readings*, edited by R. M. Emerson, 109–126. Boston: Little, Brown & Company.

Charusheela, S. and C. Danby. 2006. "A Through-Time Framework for Producer House-holds." *Review of Political Economy* 18 (1): 29–48.

Chatfield, M. 1974. *A History of Accounting Thought*. Hinsdale, IL: Dryden Press.

Chenery, H. B. and P. G. Clark. 1959. *Interindustry Economics*. New York: John Wiley and Sons.

Chiodi, G. 1992. "On Sraffa's Notion of Viability." *Studi Economici* 46 (1): 5–23.

Chiodi, G. 1998. "On Non-Self-Replacing States." *Metroeconomica* 49 (1): 97–107.

Chiodi, G. 2008. "Beyond Capitalism: Sraffa's Economic Theory." In *Sraffa or an Alter-native Economics*, edited by G. Chiodi and L. Ditta, 187–198. New York: Palgrave Macmillan.

Chiodi, G. 2010. "The Meaning of Subsistence and the Notion of Viability in Sraffa's Sur-plus Approach." In *Computable, Constructive and Behavioural Economic Dynamics: Essays in Honour of Kumaraswamy (Vela) Velupillai*, edited by S. Zambelli, 318–330. London: Routledge.

Chiodi, G. and L. Ditta. 2008. "Introduction." In *Sraffa or an Alternative Economics*, edited by G. Chiodi and L. Ditta, 1–19. New York: Palgrave Macmillan.

Ciccarone, G. 1998. "Prices and Distribution in a Sraffian Credit Economy." *Review of Political Economy* 10 (4): 399–413.

Clark, C. L. and L. A. Baglione. 1998. "Men of Steel Meet the Market: Interpreting Firm Behavior in Russia's Metallurgy Industry." *Journal of Economic Issues* 32 (4): 925–963.

Clark, D. 1984. "Planning and the Real Origins of Input-Output Analysis." *Journal of Contemporary Asia* 14 (4): 408–429.

Coase, R. H. 1937. "The Nature of the Firm." *Economica* 4 (16): 386–405.

Coates, J. 1996. *The Claims of Common Sense: Moore, Wittgenstein, Keynes and the Social Sciences*. Cambridge: Cambridge University Press.

Commons, J. R. 1957. *Legal Foundations of Capitalism*. Madison, WI: University of Wis-consin Press.

Connor, J. M. 2008. *Global Price Fixing*, 2nd edn. Berlin: Springer-Verlag.

Conrad, C. F. 1978. "A Grounded Theory of Academic Change." *Sociology of Education* 51 (2): 101–112.

Cooper, G. A. 1953. "Trade Associations in the United States Before 1900." Unpublished.

Corbin, J. and A. Strauss. 1990. "Grounded Theory Research: Procedures, Canons, and Evaluative Criteria." *Qualitative Sociology* 13 (1): 3–21.

Coutts, K. and N. Norman. 2013. "Post-Keynesian Approaches to Industrial Pricing." In *Oxford Handbook of Post-Keynesian Economics*, Vol. 1, edited by G. C. Harcourt and P. Kriesler, 443–466. Oxford: Oxford University Press.

Cox, J. H. 1950. "Trade Associations in the Lumber Industry of the Pacific Northwest, 1899–1914." *Pacific Northwest Quarterly* 41 (4): 285–311.

D'Olando, F. 2005. "Will the Classical-Type Approach Survive Sraffian Theory?" *Journal of Post Keynesian Economics* 27 (4): 633–654.

Dale, G. 2010. *Karl Polanyi: The Limits of the Market*. Cambridge: Polity Press.

Danby, C. 2010. "Interdependence Through Time: Relationships in Post-Keynesian Thought and the Care Literature." *Cambridge Journal of Economics* 34 (6): 1157–1171.

Davidson, P. 1996. "Reality and Economic Theory." *Journal of Post Keynesian Economics* 18 (4): 479–508.

Davis, J. B., ed. 1992. *The Economic Surplus in Advanced Economy*. Aldershot: Edward Elgar.

Davis, J. B. 2011. *Individuals and Identity in Economics*. Cambridge: Cambridge University Press.

De Gregori, T. R. 1985. *A Theory of Technology: Continuity and Changes in Human Development*. Ames: Iowa State University Press.

De Gregori, T. R. 1987. "Resources are Not: They Become: An Institutional Theory." *Journal of Economic Issues* 21 (3): 1241–1263.

Dean, E. 2013. "Toward a Heterodox Theory of the Business Enterprise: The Going Concern Model and the US Computer Industry." PhD diss., University of Missouri-Kansas City.

Dean, J. 1976. *Statistical Cost Estimation*. Bloomington: Indiana University Press.

Derber, M. 1984. "Employers Associations in United States." In *Employers Association and Industrial Relations: A Comparative Study*, edited by J. P. Windmuller and A. Gladstone, 79–114. Oxford: Clarendon Press.

Dey, I. 1999. *Grounding Grounded Theory: Guidelines for Qualitative Inquiry*. San Diego: Academic Press.

Dey, I. 2007. "Grounding Categories." In *The Sage Handbook of Grounded Theory*, edited by A. Bryant and K. Charmaz, 167–190. Los Angeles: Sage.

Diesing, P. 1971. *Patterns of Discovery in the Social Sciences*. New York: Aldine.

Dobb, M. 1945. *Political Economy and Capitalism: Some Essays in Economic Tradition*. New York: International Publishers.

Dopfer, K. and J. Potts. 2008. *The General Theory of Economic Evolution*. London: Routledge.

Dow, S. C. 1999. "Post Keynesianism and Critical Realism: What Is the Connection?" *Journal of Post Keynesian Economics* 22 (1): 15–34.

Dow, S. C. 2001. "Post Keynesian Methodology." In *A New Guide to Post Keynesian Economics*, edited by R. F. Holt and S. Pressman, 11–20. London: Routledge.

Downward, P. 1999. *Pricing Theory in Post Keynesian Economics: A Realist Approach*. Cheltenham: Edward Elgar.

Downward, P., ed. 2003. *Applied Economics and the Critical Realist Critique*. London: Routledge.

Downward, P. and A. Mearman. 2002. "Critical Realism and Econometrics: Constructive Dialogue with Post Keynesian Economics." *Metroeconomica* 53 (4): 391–415.

Downward, P. and A. Mearman. 2007. "Retroduction as Mixed-Methods Triangulation in Economic Research: Reorienting Economics into Social Science." *Cambridge Journal of Economics* 31 (1): 77–99.

Downward, P. and P. Reynolds. 1996. "Alternative Perspectives on Post-Keynesian Price Theory." *Review of Political Economy* 8 (1): 67–78.

Drury, C. and M. Tayles. 1994. "Product Costing in UK Manufacturing Organizations." *The European Accounting Review* 3 (3): 443–469.

Dugger, W. M. 1996. "Redefining Economics: From Market Allocation to Social Provisioning." In *Political Economy for the 21st Century: Contemporary Views on the Trends of Economics*, edited by C. Whalen, 31–43. Armonk, NY: M. E. Sharpe.

Dupré, J. 2001. "Economics Without Mechanism." In *The Economic World View: Studies in the Ontology of Economics*, edited by U. Mäki, 308–332. Cambridge: Cambridge University Press.

Dzarasov, R. 2015. "Post Keynesian Investment and Pricing Theory: Contributions of Alfred S. Eichner and Frederic S. Lee." In *Advancing the Frontiers of Heterodox*

Economics: Essays in Honor of Frederic S. Lee, edited by T.-H. Jo and Z. Todorova, 135–153. London: Routledge.

Edwards, J. R. 1980. "British Capital Accounting Practices and Business Finance 1852–1919: An Exemplification." *Accounting and Business Research* 10 (38): 241–258.

Edwards, J. R. 1986. "Depreciation and Fixed Asset Valuation in British Railway Company Accounts to 1911." *Accounting and Business Research* 16 (63): 251–263.

Edwards, J. R. 1989. "Industrial Cost Accounting Developments in Britain to 1830: A Review Article." *Accounting and Business Research* 19 (76): 305–317.

Edwards, J. R. and C. Baber. 1979. "Dowlais Iron Company: Accounting Policies and Procedures for Profit Measurement and Reporting Purposes." *Accounting and Business Research* 9 (34): 139–151.

Eichner, A. S. 1976. *The Megacorp and Oligopoly: Micro Foundations of Macro Dynamics*. New York: Cambridge University Press.

Eichner, A. S. 1979. "An Anthropogenic Model of the Labor Market." *Eastern Economic Journal* 5 (4): 349–366.

Eichner, A. S. 1987a. *The Macrodynamics of Advanced Market Economies*. Armonk, NY: M. E. Sharpe.

Eichner, A. S. 1987b. "Prices and Pricing." *Journal of Economic Issues* 21 (4): 1555–1584.

Eisenhardt, K. M. 1989. "Building Theories from Case Study Research." *Academy of Management Review* 14 (4): 532–550.

Ellis, B. 1985. "What Science Aims to Do." In *Images of Science*, edited by P. M. Churchland and C. A. Hooker, 48–74. Chicago: University of Chicago Press.

Emigh, R. J. 1997. "The Power of Negative Thinking: The Use of Negative Case Methodology in the Development of Sociological Thinking." *Theory and Society* 26 (5): 649–684.

Emirbayer, M. and A. Mische. 1998. "What Is Agency?" *American Journal of Sociology* 103 (4): 962–1023.

Emore, J. R. and J. A. Ness. 1991. "The Slow Pace of Meaningful Change in Cost Systems." *Journal of Cost Management* 5 (4): 36–45.

Erdos, P. and F. Molnar. 1980. "Profit and Paper Profit: Some Kaleckian Evolution." *Journal of Post Keynesian Economics* 3 (1): 3–18.

Erdos, P. and F. Molnar. 1983. "An Answer to Asimakopulos's Comment." *Journal of Post Keynesian Economics* 6 (1): 133–139.

Erdos, P. and F. Molnar. 1990. *Inflation and Recessions in the U.S. Economy in the 1970s: Price, Profit, and Business Cycles in Theory and Practice*. Budapest: Akademiai.

Fabiani, S., C. Loupias, F. Martins, and R. Sabbatini, eds. 2007. *Pricing Decisions in the Euro Area: How Firms Set Prices and Why*. Oxford: Oxford University Press.

Fickle, J. E. 1980. *The New South and the 'New Competition': Trade Association Development in the Southern Pine Industry*. Urbana: University of Illinois Press.

Finch, J. H. 1999. "The Methodological Implications of Post Marshallian Economics." In *Contingency, Complexity and the Theory of the Firm: Essays in Honour of Brian J. Loasby*, edited by S. C. Dow and P. E. Earl, 156–177. Cheltenham: Edward Elgar.

Finch, J. H. 2002. "The Role of Grounded Theory in Developing Economic Theory." *Journal of Economic Methodology* 9 (2): 213–234.

Fleetwood, S. 2001a. "Causal Laws, Functional Relations and Tendencies." *Review of Political Economy* 13 (2): 201–220.

Fleetwood, S. 2001b. "Conceptualizing Unemployment in a Period of Atypical Employment: A Critical Realist Perspective." *Review of Social Economy* 59 (1): 45–69.

Fleischman, R. K. 2009. "Management Accounting: Theory and Practice." In *The Routledge Companion to Accounting History*, edited by J. R. Edwards and S. P. Walker, 189–223. London: Routledge.

Fleischman, R. K. and L. D. Parker. 1997. *What Is Past Is Prologue: Cost Accounting in the British Industrial Revolution, 1760–1850*. New York: Garland Publishing.

Fligstein, N. 1996. "Markets as Politics: A Political-Cultural Approach to Market Institutions." *American Sociological Review* 61 (4): 656–673.

Foley, D. K. 1998. "An Interview with Wassily Leontief." *Macroeconomic Dynamics* 2 (1): 116–140.

Forman, H. and R. Lancioni. 2002. "The Determinants of Pricing Strategies for Industrial Products in International Markets." *Journal of Business-to-Business Marketing* 9 (2): 29–64.

Foster, J. F. 1981. "The Relation Between the Theory of Value and Economic Analysis." *Journal of Economic Issues* 15 (4): 899–905.

Fujimura, D. 2012. "The Old DuPont Company's Accounting System Lasting a Hundred Years: An Overlooked Accounting System." *Accounting Historians Journal* 39 (1): 53–88.

Fusfeld, D. R. 1980. "The Conceptual Framework of Modern Economics." *Journal of Economic Issues* 14 (1): 1–52.

Galambos, L. 1966. *Competition and Cooperation: The Emergence of a National Trade Association*. Baltimore: The Johns Hopkins Press.

Garner, S. P. 1954. *Evolution of Cost Accounting to 1925*. Tuscaloosa: The University of Alabama Press.

George, A. L. 1979. "Case Studies and Theory Development: The Method of Structured, Focused Comparison." In *Diplomacy: New Approaches in History, Theory, and Policy*, edited by P. G. Lauren, 43–68. New York: The Free Press.

Georgescu-Roegen, N. 1970. "The Economics of Production." *American Economic Review* 60 (2): 1–9.

Georgescu-Roegen, N. 1971. *The Entropy Law and the Economic Process*. Cambridge: Harvard University Press.

Georgescu-Roegen, N. 1986. "Man and Production." In *Foundations of Economics: Structures of Inquiry and Economic Theory*, edited by M. Baranzini and R. Scazzieri, 247–280. Oxford: Basil Blackwell.

Gioia, D. A. and E. Pitre. 1990. "Multiparadigm Perspectives on Theory Building." *The Academy of Management Review* 15 (4): 584–602.

Gladstone, A. 1984. "Employers Associations in Comparative Perspective: Functions and Activities." In *Employers Association and Industrial Relations: A Comparative Study*, edited by J. P. Windmuller and A. Gladstone, 24–43. Oxford: Clarendon Press.

Glaser, B. G. 1992. *Emergence vs Forcing: Basics of Grounded Theory Analysis*. Mill Valley: Sociology Press.

Glaser, B. G. 2007. "Doing Formal Theory." In *The Sage Handbook of Grounded Theory*, edited by A. Bryant and K. Charmaz, 97–113. Los Angeles: Sage.

Glaser, B. G. and A. L. Strauss. 1967. *The Discovery of Grounded Theory: Strategies for Qualitative Research*. New York: Aldine Publishing Company.

Godley, W. and M. Lavoie. 2007. *Monetary Economics: An Integrated Approach to Credit, Money, Income, Production and Wealth*. New York: Palgrave Macmillan.

Gold, B. 1981. "Changing Perspectives on Size, Scale, and Returns: An Interpretive Survey." *Journal of Economic Literature* 19 (1): 5–33.

Goulding, C. 2002. *Grounded Theory: A Practical Guide for Management, Business and Market Researchers*. London: Sage.

Grabher, G. 1993. "Rediscovering the Social in the Economics of Interfirm Relations." In *The Embedded Firm: On the Socioeconomics of Industrial Networks*, edited by G. Grabher, 1–31. London: Routledge.

Granlund, M. 2001. "Towards Explaining Stability in and Around Management Accounting Systems." *Management Accounting Research* 12 (2): 141–166.

Granlund, M. and T. Malmi. 2002. "Moderate Impact of ERPS on Management Accounting: A Lag or Permanent Outcome?" *Management Accounting Research* 13 (3): 299–321.

Granovetter, M. 1985. "Economic Action and Social Structure: The Problem of Embeddedness." *American Journal of Sociology* 91 (3): 481–510.

Graziani, A. 2003. *The Monetary Theory of Production*. Cambridge: Cambridge University Press.

Gruchy, A. G. 1987. *The Reconstruction of Economics: An Analysis of the Fundamentals of Institutional Economics*. New York: Greenwood Press.

Gu, G. C. and F. S. Lee. 2012. "Pricing and Prices." In *Elgar Companion to Post Keynesian Economics*, edited by J. E. King, 456–462. Cheltenham: Edward Elgar.

Hakansson, H. and J. Johanson. 1993. "The Network as a Governance Structure: Interfirm Cooperation Beyond Markets and Hierarchies." In *The Embedded Firm: On the Socioeconomics of Industrial Networks*, edited by G. Grabher, 35–51. London: Routledge.

Hall, S., M. Walsh, and A. Yates. 2000. "Are UK Companies' Prices Sticky?" *Oxford Economic Papers* 52 (3): 425–446.

Hamilton, D. B. 1973. "What Has Evolutionary Economics to Contribute to Consumption Theory?" *Journal of Economic Issues* 7 (2): 197–207.

Hamilton, D. B. 1987. "Institutional Economics and Consumption." *Journal of Economic Issues* 41 (4): 1531–1554.

Harcourt, G. C. and P. Kenyon. 1976. "Pricing and the Investment Decision." *Kyklos* 29 (3): 449–477.

Hayden, F. G. 1982. "Social Fabric Matrix: From Perspective to Analytical Tool." *Journal of Economic Issues* 16 (3): 637–662.

Hayden, F. G. 1986. "Values, Beliefs, and Attitudes in a Sociotechnical Setting." *Journal of Economic Issues* 22 (2): 415–426.

Hayden, F. G. 2006. *Policymaking for a Good Society: The Social Fabric Matrix Approach to Policy Analysis and Program Evaluation*. New York: Springer.

Hayden, F. G. 2011. "Assessment of the Possibility of Integrating the Social Structure of Accumulation and Social Accounting Matrix with the Social Fabric Matrix Approach." *American Journal of Economics and Sociology* 70 (5): 1208–1233.

Herman, E. S. 1981. *Corporate Control, Corporate Power*. New York: Cambridge University Press.

Hertenstein, J. H., L. Polutnik, and C. J. McNair. 2006. "Capacity Cost Measures and Decisions: Two Field Studies." *The Journal of Corporate Accounting and Finance* 17 (3): 63–78.

Hirshleifer, J. 1985. "The Expanding Domain of Economics." *American Economic Review* 75 (6): 53–68.

Hodgson, G. M. 1998. "Emergence." In *The Handbook of Economic Methodology*, edited by J. B. Davis, D. W. Hands, and U. Mäki, 156–160. Cheltenham: Edward Elgar.

Hodgson, G. M. 2000. "From Micro to Macro: The Concept of Emergence and the Role of Institutions." In *Institutions and the Role of the State*, edited by L. Burlamaquiun, A. C. Castro, and H.-J. Chang, 103–126. Cheltenham: Edward Elgar.

Hodgson, G. M. 2001. *How Economics Forgot History: The Problem of Historical Specificity in Social Science*. London: Routledge.

Hoover, K. D. 2012. "Microfoundational Programs." In *Microfoundations Reconsidered: The Relationship of Micro and Macroeconomics in Historical Perspective*, edited by P. G. Duarte and G. T. Lima, 19–61. Cheltenham: Edward Elgar.

Hounshell, D. A. 1984. *From the American System to Mass Production, 1800–1932*. Baltimore: The Johns Hopkins University Press.

Hudson, P. 1977. "Some Aspects of 19th Century Accounting Development in the West Riding Textile Industry." *Accounting History* 2 (2): 4–22.

Hunt, S. D. 1994. "A Realist Theory of Empirical Testing: Resolving the Theory-Ladenness/ Objectivity Debate." *Philosophy of the Social Sciences* 24 (2): 133–158.

Indounas, K. 2009. "Successful Industrial Service Pricing." *Journal of Business and Industrial Marketing* 24 (2): 86–97.

Ingham, G. 1996. "Money is a Social Relation." *Review of Social Economy* 54 (4): 507–529.

Innes, J., F. Mitchell, and D. Sinclair. 2000. "Activity-Based Costing in the U.K. Largest Companies: A Comparison of 1994 and 1999 Survey Results." *Management Accounting Research* 11 (3): 349–362.

Israel, G. 1981. "'Rigor' and 'Axiomatics' in Modern Mathematics." *Fundamenta Scientiae* 2 (2): 205–219.

Israel, G. 1991. "Volterra's 'Analytical Mechanics' of Biological Associations." *Archives Internationales d'Histoire des Sciences* 41 (127): 306–351.

Jo, T.-H. 2015. "Financing Investment Under Fundamental Uncertainty and Instability: A Heterodox Microeconomic View." *Bulletin of Political Economy* 9 (1): 33–54.

Jo, T.-H. 2016. "What If There are No Conventional Price Mechanisms?" *Journal of Economic Issues* 50 (2): 327–344.

Jo, T.-H. 2017. "A Heterodox Theory of the Business Enterprise." In *The Routledge Handbook of Heterodox Economics*, edited by T.-H. Jo, L. Chester, and C. D'Ippoliti, 199–212. London: Routledge.

Jones, H. 1985. *Accounting, Costing and Cost Estimation: Welsh Industry 1700–1830*. Cardiff: University of Wales Press.

Joseph, J. 1998. "In Defense of Critical Realism." *Capital and Class* 65: 73–106.

Kalecki, M. [1954] 1990. "Theory of Economic Dynamics." In *Collected Works of Michał Kalecki*, Vol. II, *Capitalism: Economic Dynamics*, edited by J. Osiatyński, 205–348. Oxford: Clarendon Press.

Kanth, R. 1992. "Economics and Epistemology: A Realist Critique." *Capital and Class* 47: 93–112.

Kaufman, B. E. 2006. "The Institutional Economics of John R. Commons: Complement and Substitute for Neoclassical Economic Theory." *Socio-Economic Review* 5 (1): 3–45.

Keen, S. 2001. *Debunking Economics: The Naked Emperor of the Social Sciences*. New York: St. Martin's Press.

Kesting, S. 1998. "A Potential for Understanding and the Interference of Power: Discourse as an Economic Mechanism of Coordination." *Journal of Economic Issues* 32 (4): 1053–1078.

Kling, R. W. 1988. "Trucking Deregulation: Evolution of a New Power Structure." *Journal of Economic Issues* 22 (4): 1201–1211.

Kohli, M. C. 2001. "Leontief and the U.S. Bureau of Labor Statistics, 1941–1954: Developing a Framework for Measurement." In *The Age of Economic Measurement*, edited by J. L. Klein and M. S. Morgan, 190–212. Durham: Duke University Press.

Konecki, K. 1989. "The Methodology of Grounded Theory in the Research of the Situation of Work." *The Polish Sociological Bulletin* 2: 59–74.

Kregel, J. A. 1975. *The Reconstruction of Political Economy: An Introduction to Post-Keynesian Economics*, 2nd edn. London: Palgrave Macmillan.

Kuhbach, P. D. and M. A. Planting. 2001. "Annual Input-Output Accounts of the U.S. Economy, 1997." *Survey of Current Business* 81 (1): 9–43.

Kurz, H. D. 2006. "The Agents of Production are the Commodities Themselves: On the Classical Theory of Production, Distribution and Value." *Structural Change and Economic Dynamics* 17 (1): 367–662.

Kurz, H. D. 2011. "Who is Going to Kiss Sleeping Beauty? On the 'Classical' Analytical Origins and Perspectives of Input-Output Analysis." *Review of Political Economy* 23 (1): 153–179.

Kurz, H. D. and N. Salvadori. 1995. *Theory of Production: A Long-Period Analysis*. Cambridge: Cambridge University Press.

Kurz, H. D. and N. Salvadori. 2000. "Classical Roots of Input-Output Analysis: A Short Account of Its Long Prehistory." *Economic Systems Research* 12 (2): 153–179.

Kurz, H. D. and N. Salvadori. 2005. "Representing the Production and Circulation of Commodities in Material Terms: On Sraffa's Objectivism." *Review of Political Economy* 17 (3): 413–441.

Kurz, H. D. and N. Salvadori. 2006. "Input-Output Analysis from a Wider Perspective: A Comparison of the Early Works of Leontief and Sraffa." *Economic Systems Research* 18 (4): 373–390.

Lager, C. 2006. "The Treatment of Fixed Capital in the Long Period." *Economic Systems Research* 18 (4): 411–426.

Lamminmaki, D. and C. Drury. 2001. "Budgeting and Standard Costing Practices in New Zealand and the United Kingdom." *The International Journal of Accounting* 33 (5): 569–588.

Larson, A. 1992. "Network Dyads in Entrepreneurial Settings: A Study of the Governance of Exchange Relationships." *Administrative Science Quarterly* 37 (1): 76–104.

Lavoie, M. 1994. "A Post Keynesian Approach to Consumer Choice." *Journal of Post Keynesian Economics* 16 (2): 539–562.

Lavoie, M. 2004. "Post-Keynesian Consumer Theory: Potential Synergies with Consumer Research and Economic Psychology." *Journal of Economic Psychology* 25 (5): 639–649.

Lavoie, M. 2011. "Should Sraffians Be Dropped Out of the Post-Keynesian School?" *Économies et Société* 44 (7): 1027–1059.

Lawson, C., M. Peacock, and S. Pratten. 1996. "Realism, Underlabouring and Institutions." *Cambridge Journal of Economics* 20 (1): 137–151.

Lawson, T. 1989. "Abstraction, Tendencies and Stylised Facts: A Realist Approach to Economic Analysis." *Cambridge Journal of Economics* 13 (1): 59–78.

Lawson, T. 1994. "The Nature of Post Keynesianism and Its Links to Other Traditions: A Realist Perspective." *Journal of Post Keynesian Economics* 16 (4): 503–538.

Lawson, T. 1997a. *Economics and Reality*. London: Routledge.

Lawson, T. 1997b. "On Criticizing the Practices of Economists: A Case for Interventionist Methodology." In *Pluralism in Economics: New Perspectives in History and Methodology*, edited by A. Salanti and E. Screpanti, 13–36. Cheltenham: Edward Elgar.

Lawson, T. 1998a. "Tendencies." In *The Handbook of Economic Methodology*, edited by J. B. Davis, D. W. Hands, and U. Mäki, 493–498. Cheltenham: Edward Elgar.

Lawson, T. 1998b. "Transcendental Realism." In *The Handbook of Economic Methodology*, edited by J. B. Davis, D. W. Hands, and U. Mäki, 504–510. Cheltenham: Edward Elgar.

Lawson, T. 1998c. "Social Relations, Social Reproduction and Stylized Facts." In *Method, Theory and Policy in Keynes: Essays in Honour of Paul Davidson*, Vol. 3, edited by P. Arestis, 17–43. Cheltenham: Edward Elgar.

Lawson, T. 1999. "Connections and Distinctions: Post Keynesianism and Critical Realism." *Journal of Post Keynesian Economics* 22 (1): 3–14.

Lee, F. S. 1983. "Full Cost Pricing: An Historical and Theoretical Analysis." PhD diss., Rutgers University.

Lee, F. S. 1984. "Full Cost Pricing: A New Wine in a New Bottle." *Australian Economic Papers* 23 (42): 151–166.

Lee, F. S. 1985. "Full Cost Prices, Classical Price Theory, and Long Period Method Analysis: A Critical Evaluation." *Metroeconomica* 37 (2): 199–219.

Lee, F. S. 1986. "Post Keynesian View of Average Direct Costs: A Critical Evaluation of the Theory and the Empirical Evidence." *Journal of Post Keynesian Economics* 8 (3): 400–424.

Lee, F. S., ed. 1991. "Tributes in Memory of Alfred S. Eichner." http://facstaff.buffalostate.edu/joth/eichner/1991-eichner-tributes.pdf [Accessed June 1, 2017].

Lee, F. S. 1994. "From Post-Keynesian to Historical Price Theory, Part I: Facts, Theory and Empirically Grounded Pricing Model." *Review of Political Economy* 6 (3): 303–336.

Lee, F. S. 1996. "Pricing, the Pricing Model and Post-Keynesian Price Theory." *Review of Political Economy* 8 (1): 87–99.

Lee, F. S. 1998. *Post Keynesian Price Theory*. Cambridge: Cambridge University Press.

Lee, F. S. 1999. "Market Governance in the American Gunpowder Industry, 1865–1880." Unpublished working paper.

Lee, F. S. 2005. "Teaching Heterodox Microeconomics." *Post-Autistic Economics Review* 31: 26–39.

Lee, F. S. 2009a. *A History of Heterodox Economics: Challenging the Mainstream in the Twentieth Century*. London: Routledge.

Lee, F. S. 2009b. "The Economics of the Industrial Workers of the World: Job Control and Revolution." In *Radical Economics and Labor: Essays Inspired by the IWW Centennial*, edited by F. S. Lee and J. Bekken, 55–77. London: Routledge.

Lee, F. S. 2010a. "Pluralism in Heterodox Economics." In *Economic Pluralism*, edited by R. F. Garnett, E. K. Olsen, and M. Starr, 19–35. London: Routledge.

Lee, F. S. 2010b. "A Heterodox Teaching of Neoclassical Microeconomic Theory." *International Journal of Pluralism and Economics Education* 1 (3): 203–235.

Lee, F. S. 2011a. "Modeling the Economy as a Whole: An Integrative Approach." *American Journal of Economics and Sociology* 70 (5): 1282–1314.

Lee, F. S. 2011b. "The Pluralism Debate in Heterodox Economics." *Review of Radical Political Economics* 43 (4): 540–551.

Lee, F. S. 2011c. "Heterodox Economics, Tolerance and Pluralism: A Reply to Garnett and Mearman." *Review of Radical Political Economics* 43 (4): 573–577.

Lee, F. S. 2011d. "Heterodox Microeconomics and the Foundations of Heterodox Macroeconomics." *Economia Informa* 367: 6–20.

Lee, F. S. 2012. "Competition, Going Enterprise, and Economic Activity." In *Alternative Theories of Competition: Challenges to the Orthodoxy*, edited by J. K. Moudud, C. Bina, and P. L. Mason, 160–173. London: Routledge.

Lee, F. S. 2013a. "Heterodox Economics and Its Critics." In *In Defense of Post-Keynesian and Heterodox Economics: Responses to Their Critics*, edited by F. S. Lee and M. Lavoie, 104–131. London: Routledge.

Lee, F. S. 2013b. "Post-Keynesian Price Theory: From Pricing to Market Governance to the Economy as a Whole." In *The Oxford Handbook of Post-Keynesian Economics*, Vol. 1, edited by G. C. Harcourt and P. Kriesler, 467–484. Oxford: Oxford University Press.

Lee, F. S. 2013c. "What If There are No Conventional Price Mechanisms?" *New Economics Perspectives Blog*, November 26.

Lee, F. S. 2014. "Heterodox Theory of Production and the Mythology of Capital: A Critical Inquiry into the Circuit of Production." Unpublished.

Lee, F. S. 2015. "Predestined to Heterodoxy and How I Became a Heterodox Economist." In *Advancing the Frontiers of Heterodox Economics: Essays in Honor of Frederic S. Lee*, edited by T.-H. Jo and Z. Todorova, 316–319. London: Routledge.

Lee, F. S. 2016a. "Critical Realism, Method of Grounded Theory, and Theory Construction." In *Handbook of Research Methods and Applications in Heterodox Economics*, edited by F. S. Lee and B. Cronin, 35–53. Cheltenham: Edward Elgar.

Lee, F. S. 2016b. "Modeling as a Research Method in Heterodox Economics." In *Handbook of Research Methods and Applications in Heterodox Economics*, edited by F. S. Lee and B. Cronin, 272–285. Cheltenham: Edward Elgar.

Lee, F. S. and B. Cronin, eds. 2016. *Handbook of Research Methods and Applications in Heterodox Economics*. Cheltenham: Edward Elgar.

Lee, F. S. and T.-H. Jo. 2011. "Social Surplus Approach and Heterodox Economics." *Journal of Economic Issues* 45 (4): 857–875.

Lee, F. S. and S. Keen. 2004. "The Incoherent Emperor: A Heterodox Critique of Neoclassical Microeconomic Theory." *Review of Social Economy* 62 (2): 169–199.

Lee, F. S., X. Pham, and G. Gu. 2013. "The UK Research Assessment Exercise and the Narrowing of UK Economics." *Cambridge Journal of Economics* 37 (4): 693–717.

Levine, D. P. 1977. *Economic Studies: Contributions to the Critique of Economic Theory.* London: Routledge & Kegan Paul.

Levine, D. P. 1978. *Economic Theory: The Elementary Relations of Economic Life*, Vol. 1. London: Routledge & Kegan Paul.

Levine, D. P. 1998. *Subjectivity in Political Economy: Essays on Wanting and Choosing.* London: Routledge.

Levrini, E. 1988. "Joint Production: Review of Some Studies on Sraffa's System." *Political Economy: Studies in the Surplus Approach* 4 (2): 159–175.

Lewis, M. W. and A. J. Grimes. 1999. "Metatriangulation: Building Theory from Multiple Paradigms." *The Academy of Management Review* 24 (4): 672–690.

Lewis, P. A. 2005. "Structure, Agency and Causality in Post-Revival Austrian Economics: Tensions and Resolutions." *Review of Political Economy* 17 (2): 291–316.

Lindberg, L. N., J. L. Campbell, and J. R. Hollingsworth. 1991. "Economic Governance and the Analysis of Structural Change in the American Economy." In *Governance of the American Economy*, edited by J. L. Campbell, J. R. Hollingsworth, and L. N. Linberg, 3–34. Cambridge: Cambridge University Press.

Litherland, D. A. 1951. "Fixed Asset Replacement a Half Century Ago." *The Accounting Review* 26 (4): 475–480.

Lloyd, C. 1993. *The Structures of History*. Oxford: Basil Blackwell.

Lovering, J. 1990. "Neither Fundamentalism Nor 'New Realism': A Critical Realist Perspective on Current Divisions in Socialist Theory." *Capital and Class* 42: 30–54.

Lower, M. D. 1987. "The Concept of Technology Within the Institutionalist Perspective." *Journal of Economic Issues* 21 (3): 1147–1176.

Lukka, K. 2007. "Management Accounting Change and Stability: Loosely Coupled Rules and Routines in Action." *Management Accounting Research* 18 (1): 76–103.

Mackintosh, A. S. 1963. *The Development of Firms*. Cambridge: Cambridge University Press.

Mahner, M. 2007. "Demarcating Science from Non-Science." In *General Philosophy of Science: Focal Issues*, edited by T. A. F. Kuipers, 515–575. Amsterdam: Elsevier.

Major, M. and T. Hopper. 2005. "Managers Divided: Implementing ABC in a Portuguese Telecommunications Company." *Management Accounting Research* 16 (2): 205–229.

Mäki, U. 1989. "On the Problem of Realism in Economics." *Ricerche Economiche* 43 (1–2): 176–198.

Mäki, U. 1990. "Scientific Realism and Austrian Explanation." *Review of Political Economy* 2 (3): 310–344.

Mäki, U. 1992a. "The Market as an Isolated Causal Process: A Metaphysical Ground for Realism." In *Austrian Economics: Tensions and New Directions*, edited by B. J. Caldwell and S. Boehm, 35–59. Boston: Kluwer Academic Publishers.

Mäki, U. 1992b. "On the Method of Isolation in Economics." *Poznan Studies in the Philosophy of the Sciences and the Humanities* 26: 317–351.

Mäki, U. 1996. "Scientific Realism and Some Peculiarities of Economics." In *Realism and Anti-Realism in the Philosophy of Science*, edited by R. S. Cohen, R. Hilpinen, and Q. Renzong, 427–447. Dordrecht: Kluwer Academic Publishers.

Mäki, U. 1998a. "Realism." In *The Handbook of Economic Methodology*, edited by J. B. Davis, D. W. Hand, and U. Mäki, 404–409. Cheltenham: Edward Elgar.

Mäki, U. 1998b. "Aspects of Realism About Economics." *Theoria* 13 (2): 310–319.

Mäki, U. 2001. "The Way the World Works (www): Towards an Ontology of Theory Choice." In *The Economic World View: Studies in the Ontology of Economics*, edited by U. Mäki, 369–389. Cambridge: Cambridge University Press.

Malmi, T. 1997. "Towards Explaining Activity-Based Costing Failure: Accounting and Control in a Decentralized Organization." *Management Accounting Research* 8 (4): 459–480.

Martins, N. O. 2014. *The Cambridge Revival of Political Economy*. London: Routledge.

Martinson, O. B. and G. R. Campbell. 1979. "Social Network Analysis: Suggested Applications to Economic Control." *Journal of Economic Issues* 13 (2): 471–487.

Matthaei, J. 1984. "Rethinking Scarcity: Neoclassicism, NeoMalthusianism, and Neo-Marxism." *Review of Radical Political Economics* 16 (2/3): 81–94.

McCormick, K. 2002. "Veblen and the New Growth Theory: Community as the Source of Capital's Productivity." *Review of Social Economy* 60 (2): 263–277.

McCullagh, C. B. 1984. *Justifying Historical Descriptions*. Cambridge: Cambridge University Press.

McCullagh, C. B. 2000. "Bias in Historical Description, Interpretation, and Explanation." *History and Theory: Studies in the Philosophy of History* 39 (1): 39–66.

McDonough, T. 2010. "The State of the Art of the Social Structures of Accumulation Theory." In *Contemporary Capitalism and its Crisis*, edited by T. McDonough, M. Reich, and D. M. Kotz, 23–44. Cambridge: Cambridge University Press.

McDonough, T. 2011. "Social Structures of Accumulation: A Punctuated View of Embeddedness." *American Journal of Economics and Sociology* 70 (5): 1234–1247.

Means, G. C. 1939. *The Structure of the American Economy, Part I: Basic Characteristics*. Washington, DC: US Government Printing Office.

Megill, A. 1989. "Recounting the Past: 'Description', Explanation, and Narrative in Historiography." *American Historical Review* 94: 627–653.

Millard, D., ed. 1995. *Input-Output for the United Kingdom 1990*, 10th edn. London: HMSO.

Miller, E. S. 1985. "Controlling Power in the Social Economy: The Regulatory Approach." *Review of Social Economy* 43 (3): 129–139.

Miller, E. S. 1996. "Economic Regulation and New Technology in the Telecommunications Industry." *Journal of Economic Issues* 30 (3): 719–735.

Miller, R. A. 1967. "Marginal Concentration Ratios and Industrial Profit Rates: Some Empirical Results of Oligopoly Behavior." *Southern Economic Journal* 34 (2): 259–267.

Miller, R. A. 1971. "Marginal Concentration Ratios as Market Structure Variables." *Review of Economics and Statistics* 53 (3): 289–293.

Miller, R. E. and P. D. Blair. 2009. *Input-Output Analysis: Foundations and Extensions*, 2nd edn. Cambridge: Cambridge University Press.

Mir-Artigues, P. and J. Gonzalez-Calvert. 2007. *Funds, Flows and Time: An Alternative Approach to the Microeconomic Analysis of Production Activities*. Berlin: Springer Verlag.

Molnar, F. 1981. "Consumers' Investment Versus Capital Investment: A Contribution to Contemporary Business Fluctuations." *Acta Oeconomica* 26 (1–2): 133–155.

Mongiovi, G. 2010. "Notes on Exploitation and the Theory of Value in Marxian Economics." Paper presented at the conference on Sraffa's *Production of Commodities by Means of Commodities*, 1960–2010, Rome, Italy.

Morgan, M. S. 2012. *The World in the Model: How Economists Work and Think*. Cambridge: Cambridge University Press.

Morris, W. 1995. *News from Nowhere*, edited by K. Kumar. Cambridge: Cambridge University Press.

Morroni, M. 1992. *Production Process and Technical Change*. Cambridge: Cambridge University Press.

Mosler, W. 1997–1998. "Full Employment and Price Stability." *Journal of Post Keynesian Economics* 20 (2): 167–182.

Napier, C. J. 1990. "Fixed Asset Accounting in the Shipping Industry: P&O 1840–1914." *Accounting, Business and Financial History* 1 (1): 23–50.

Natarajan, T., W. Elsner, and S. Fullwiler, eds. 2009. *Institutional Analysis and Praxis: The Social Fabric Matrix Approach*. New York: Springer.

Nell, E. J. 2003. "Nominal Money, Real Money and Stabilization." In *The State, the Market and the Euro*, edited by S. Bell and E. J. Nell, 111–137. Cheltenham: Edward Elgar.

Nix, J. and D. Gabel. 1996. "The Introduction of Automatic Switching into the Bell System: Market Versus Institutional Influences." *Journal of Economic Issues* 30 (3): 737–753.

Norman, A. P. 1991. "Telling It Like It Was: Historical Narratives on Their Own Terms." *History and Theory: Studies in the Philosophy of History* 30 (2): 119–135.

Nurkse, R. 1935. "The Schematic Representation of the Structure of Production." *The Review of Economic Studies* 2 (3): 232–244.

O'Boyle, E. J. 2010. "From Individual to Person: An Evolutionary Process Grounded in Human Communication." In *Looking Beyond the Individualism and Homo Economicus of Neoclassical Economics*, edited by E. J. O'Boyle, 91–119. Milwaukee: Marquette University Press.

O'Boyle, E. J. 2011. "The *Acting* Person: Social Capital and Sustainable Development." *Forum for Social Economics* 40 (1): 79–98.

O'Brien, W. F. 1972. "Practices Relating to Corporate Objectives." *Managerial Planning* 20: 16–20.

O'Connor, J. 1973. *The Fiscal Crisis of the State*. New York: St. Martin's Press.

O'Hara, P. A. 2002. "The Role of Institutions and the Current Crises of Capitalism: A Reply to Howard Sherman and John Henry." *Review of Social Economy* 60 (4): 609–618.

O'Hara, P. A. 2008. "Exploitation and Surplus." In *The Elgar Companion to Social Economics*, edited by J. B. Davis and W. Dolfsma, 649–665. Cheltenham: Edward Elgar.

Olsen, W. 2003. "Triangulation, Time and the Social Objects of Econometrics." In *Applied Economics and the Critical Realist Critique*, edited by P. Downward, 153–169. London: Routledge.

Olsen, W. 2012. *Data Collection: Key Debates and Methods in Social Research*. Los Angeles: Sage.

Olsen, W. and J. Morgan. 2005. "A Critical Epistemology of Analytical Statistics: Addressing the Skeptical Realist." *Journal for the Theory of Social Behavior* 35 (3): 255–284.

Orum, A. M., J. R. Feagin, and G. Sjoberg. 1991. "Introduction: The Nature of the Case Study." In *A Case for the Case Study*, edited by J. R. Feagin, A. M. Orum, and G. Sjoberg, 1–26. Chapel Hill: University of North Carolina Press.

Palacio-Vera, A. 2005. "The 'Modern' View of Macroeconomics: Some Critical Reflections." *Cambridge Journal of Economics* 29 (5): 747–767.

Panico, C. 1985. "Market Forces and the Relation Between the Rates of Interest and Profits." *Contributions to Political Economy* 4 (1): 37–60.

Panico, C. 1988. *Interest and Profit in the Theories of Value and Distribution*. London: Palgrave Macmillan.

Pasinetti, L. L. 1981. *Structural Change and Economic Growth: A Theoretical Essay on the Dynamics of the Wealth of Nations*. Cambridge: Cambridge University Press.

Pasinetti, L. L. 1986a. "Theory of Value – A Source of Alternative Paradigms in Economic Analysis." In *Foundations of Economics*, edited by M. Baranzini and R. Scazzieri, 409–431. Oxford: Basil Blackwell.

Pasinetti, L. L. 1986b. "Sraffa's Circular Process and the Concept of Vertical Integration." *Political Economy: Studies in the Surplus Approach* 2 (1): 3–16.

Pasinetti, L. L. 1993. *Structural Economic Dynamics: A Theory of the Economic Consequences of Human Learning*. Cambridge: Cambridge University Press.

Pasinetti, L. L. 1997. "The Principle of Effective Demand." In *A 'Second Edition' of the General Theory*, Vol. 1, edited by G. C. Harcourt and P. Kriesler, 93–104. London: Routledge.

Pasinetti, L. L. 2001. "The Principle of Effective Demand and Its Relevance in the Long Run." *Journal of Post Keynesian Economics* 23 (3): 383–390.

Pasinetti, L. L. 2005. "From Pure Theory to Full Economic Analysis: A Place for the Economic Agent." *Cahiers d'économie politique* 49: 211–216.

Pasinetti, L. L. 2007. *Keynes and the Cambridge Keynesians*. Cambridge: Cambridge University Press.

Pentland, B. T. 1999. "Building Process Theory with Narrative: From Description to Explanation." *Academy of Management Review* 24 (4): 711–724.

Petri, F. 2004. *General Equilibrium, Capital and Macroeconomics: A Key to Recent Controversies in Equilibrium Theory*. Cheltenham: Edward Elgar.

Petty, J. W., D. F. Scott, and M. M. Bird. 1975. "The Capital Expenditure Decision-Making Process of Large Corporations." *The Engineering Economist* 20 (3): 159–172.

Pivetti, M. 1985. "On the Monetary Explanation of Distribution." *Political Economy: Studies in the Surplus Approach* 1: 73–103.

Polanyi, K. 1944. *The Great Transformation*. Boston: Beacon Press.

Polanyi, K. 1968. "The Economy as Instituted Process." In *Primitive, Archaic and Modern Economies: Essays of Karl Polanyi*, edited by G. Dalton, 139–174. Garden City: Doubleday and Company.

Ponsot, J.-F. and S. Rossi, eds. 2009. *The Political Economy of Monetary Circuits: Tradition and Change on Post-Keynesian Economics*. New York: Palgrave Macmillan.

Powell, W. W. 1990. "Neither Market Nor Hierarchy: Network Forms of Organization." *Research in Organizational Behavior* 12: 295–336.

Powell, W. W. and L. Smith-Doerr. 1994. "Networks and Economic Life." In *The Handbook of Economic Sociology*, edited by N. J. Smelser and R. Swedberg, 368–402. Princeton: Princeton University Press.

Power, M. 2004. "Social Provisioning as a Starting Point for Feminist Economics." *Feminist Economics* 10 (3): 3–19.

Pratt, A. C. 1995. "Putting Critical Realism to Work: The Practical Implications for Geographical Research." *Progress in Human Geography* 19 (1): 61–74.

Quinn, M. 2014. "Stability and Change in Management Accounting Over Time – A Century or So of Evidence from Guinness." *Management Accounting Research* 25 (1): 76–92.

Ramstad, Y. 2001. "John R. Commons's Reasonable Value and the Problem of Just Price." *Journal of Economic Issues* 35 (2): 253–277.

Ranson, B. 1987. "The Institutionalist Theory of Capital Formation." *Journal of Economic Issues* 21 (3): 1265–1278.

Rao, V. R. and B. Kartono. 2009. "Pricing Objectives and Strategies: A Cross-Country Survey." In *Handbook of Pricing Research in Marketing*, edited by V. R. Rao, 9–36. Cheltenham: Edward Elgar.

Rizvi, S. A. T. 1994. "The Microfoundations Project in General Equilibrium Theory." *Cambridge Journal of Economics* 18 (4): 357–377.

Robinson, J. and J. Eatwell. 1973. *An Introduction to Modern Economics*. Maidenhead: McGraw-Hill.

Robinson, M. N. 1926. "The Gary Dinner System: An Experiment in Cooperative Price Stabilization." *Southwestern Political and Social Science Quarterly* 7 (2): 137–161.

Rochon, L.-P. and S. Rossi. 2003. *Modern Theories of Money: The Nature and Role of Money in Capitalist Economies*. Cheltenham: Edward Elgar.

Roncaglia, A. 1989. "A Reappraisal of Classical Political Economy." *Political Economy: Studies in the Surplus Approach* 5: 169–180.

Roncaglia, A. 1996. "The Classical Approach and Long-Period Positions: A Comment on Cesaratto." *Review of Political Economy* 8 (4): 403–408.

Roncaglia, A. 2005. *The Wealth of Ideas: A History of Economic Thought*. Cambridge: Cambridge University Press.

Roncaglia, A. 2009. *Piero Sraffa*. New York: Palgrave Macmillan.

Roncaglia, A. 2010. "Some Notes on the Notion of Production Process." In *Economic Theory and Economic Thought: Essays in Honour of Ian Steedman*, edited by J. Vint, J. S. Metcalfe, H. D. Kurz, N. Salvadori, and P. Samuelson, 174–188, 299–320. London: Routledge.

Rothschild, K. W. 1947. "Price Theory and Oligopoly." *The Economic Journal* 57 (227): 299–320.

Rotheim, R. J. 1999. "Post Keynesian Economics and Realist Philosophy." *Journal of Post Keynesian Economics* 22 (1): 71–104.

Runde, J. 1998. "Assessing Causal Economic Explanations." *Oxford Economic Papers* 50 (2): 151–172.

Salter, W. E. G. 1966. *Productivity and Technical Change*, 2nd edn. Cambridge: Cambridge University Press.

Sarre, P. 1987. "Realism in Practice." *Area* 19 (1): 3–10.

Sawyer, M. C. 1995. *Unemployment, Imperfect Competition and Macroeconomics*. Aldershot: Edward Elgar.

Sayer, A. 1992. *Method in Social Science: A Realist Approach*, 2nd edn. London: Routledge.

Scapens, R. W. 1994. "Never Mind the Gap: Towards an Institutional Perspective on Management Accounting Practices." *Management Accounting Research* 5 (3–4): 301–321.

Scazzieri, R. 1983. "The Production Process: General Characteristics and Taxonomy." *Rivista Internazionale di Scienze Economiche e Commerciali* 30 (7): 597–611.

Scazzieri, R. 1993. *A Theory of Production: Tasks, Processes, and Technical Practices.* Oxford: Clarendon Press.

Schaede, U. 2000. *Cooperative Capitalism: Self-Regulation, Trade Associations, and the Antimonopoly Law in Japan.* Oxford: Oxford University Press.

Scheibl, F. and A. Wood. 2005. "Investment Sequencing in the Brick Industry: An Application of Grounded Theory." *Cambridge Journal of Economics* 29 (2): 223–247.

Schumpeter, J. 1969. *The Theory of Economic Development.* Oxford: Oxford University Press.

Scranton, P. 1991. "Diversity in Diversity: Flexible Production and American Industrialization, 1880–1930." *Business History Review* 65 (1): 27–90.

Serrano, F. 1995a. "The Sraffian Supermultiplier." PhD diss., St. Edmund's College, University of Cambridge.

Serrano, F. 1995b. "Long Period Effective Demand and the Sraffian Supermultiplier." *Contributions to Political Economy* 14 (1): 67–90.

Setterfield, M. 2003. "Critical Realism and Formal Modelling: Incompatible Bedfellows?" In *Applied Economics and the Critical Realist Critique*, edited by P. Downward, 71–88. London: Routledge.

Sheehan, M. F. 1988. "Institutionalists Before Regulatory Commissions: The Value of Doing in Thinking, Teaching, and Writing." *Journal of Economic Issues* 22 (4): 1169–1178.

Sinha, A. 2010. *Theories of Value from Adam Smith to Piero Sraffa.* London: Routledge.

Smith, L. M. 1998. "Biographical Method." In *Strategies of Qualitative Inquiry*, edited by N. K. Denzin and Y. S. Lincoln, 184–224. Thousand Oaks: Sage.

Spiethoff, A. 1952. "The 'Historical' Character of Economic Theories." *Journal of Economic History* 12 (2): 131–139.

Spiethoff, A. 1953. "Pure Theory and Economic Gestalt Theory: Ideal Types and Real Types." In *Enterprise and Secular Change: Readings in Economic History*, edited by F. C. Lane and J. C. Riemersma, 444–463. Homewood: Richard D. Irwin.

Sraffa, P. 1960. *Production of Commodities by Means of Commodities.* Cambridge: Cambridge University Press.

Stake, R. E. 1998. "Case Studies." In *Strategies of Qualitative Inquiry*, edited by N. K. Denzin and Y. S. Lincoln, 86–109. Thousand Oaks: Sage.

Stanfield, J. R. 1995. *Economics, Power and Culture.* London: Palgrave Macmillan.

Staubus, G. J. 1990. "Activity Costing: Twenty Years On." *Management Accounting Research* 1 (4): 249–264.

Sterling, R. R. 1968. "The Going Concern: An Examination." *The Accounting Review* 43 (3): 481–502.

Stevenson, R. E. 1987. "Institutional Economics and the Theory of Production." *Journal of Economic Issues* 21 (4): 1471–1493.

Stewart, R. L., J. B. Stone, and M. L. Streitwieser. 2007. "U.S. Benchmark Input-Output Accounts, 2002." *Survey of Current Business* 87 (10): 19–48.

Stone, W. E. 1973–1974. "An Early English Cotton Mill Cost Accounting System: Charlton Mills, 1810–1889." *Accounting and Business Research* 4 (13): 71–78.

Storey, R. K. 1959. "Revenue Realization, Going Concern, and Measurement of Income." *The Accounting Review* 34 (2): 232–238.

Stratton, W., R. Lawson, and T. Hatch. 2009. "Activity-Based Costing: Is It Still Relevant?" *Management Accounting Quarterly* 10 (3): 31–40.

Strauss, A. L. 1987. *Qualitative Analysis for Social Scientists*. Cambridge: Cambridge University Press.

Strauss, A. L. and J. Corbin. 1990. *Basics of Qualitative Research: Grounded Theory Procedures and Techniques*. Newbury Park: Sage.

Strauss, A. L. and J. Corbin. 1994. "Grounded Theory Methodology: An Overview." In *Handbook of Qualitative Research*, edited by N. K. Denzin and Y. S. Lincoln, 273–285. Thousand Oaks: Sage.

Swedberg, R. 1994. "Markets as Social Structures." In *The Handbook of Economic Sociology*, edited by N. J. Smelser and R. Swedberg, 255–282. Princeton: Princeton University Press.

Taras, D. G. 1997. "Managerial Intentions and Wage Determination in the Canadian Petroleum Industry." *Industrial Relations* 36 (2): 178–205.

Thurmond, V. A. 2001. "The Point of Triangulation." *Journal of Nursing Scholarship* 33 (3): 253–258.

Todorova, Z. 2009. *Money and Households in a Capitalist Economy: A Gendered Post Keynesian-Institutional Analysis*. Cheltenham: Edward Elgar.

Tool, M. R. 2001. *The Discretionary Economy: A Normative Theory of Political Economy*. New Brunswick: Transaction Publishers.

Tosh, J. 1991. *The Pursuit of History*, 2nd edn. London: Longman.

Trigg, A. B. 2006. *Marxian Reproduction Schema: Money and Aggregate Demand in a Capitalist Economy*. Abingdon: Routledge.

Trigg, A. B. 2008. "Quantity and Price Systems: Toward a Framework for Coherence Between Post-Keynesians and Sraffian Economics." In *Future Directions for Heterodox Economics*, edited by J. T. Harvey and R. F. Garnett, 127–141. Ann Arbor: University of Michigan Press.

Tsang, E. and K.-M. Kwan. 1999. "Replication and Theory Development in Organization Science: A Critical Realist Perspective." *Academy of Management Review* 24 (4): 759–780.

Turner, B. A. 1981. "Some Practical Aspects of Qualitative Data Analysis: One Way of Organising the Cognitive Processes Associated with the Generation of Grounded Theory." *Quality and Quantity* 15 (3): 225–247.

Turner, B. A. 1983. "The Use of Grounded Theory for the Qualitative Analysis of Organizational Behaviour." *Journal of Management Studies* 20 (3): 333–348.

Tyson, T. 1992. "The Nature and Environment of Cost Management Among Early Nineteenth Century U. S. Textile Manufacturers." *The Accounting Historians Journal* 19 (2): 1–24.

Uzzi, B. 1996. "The Sources and Consequences of Embeddedness for the Economic Performance of Organizations: The Network Effect." *American Sociological Review* 61 (4): 674–698.

Vaughan, D. 1992. "Theory Elaboration: The Heuristics of Case Analysis." In *What is a Case? Exploring the Foundations of Social Inquiry*, edited by C. C. Ragin and H. S. Becker, 173–202. Cambridge: Cambridge University Press.

Veblen, T. 1904. *The Theory of Business Enterprise*. New York: Charles Scribner's Sons.

Veblen, T. 1908. "On the Nature of Capital." *Quarterly Journal of Economics* 22 (4): 517–542.

Veblen, T. 1914. *The Instinct of Workmanship and the State of the Industrial Arts*. New York: Palgrave Macmillan.

Viton, A. 2004. *The International Sugar Agreements: Promise and Reality*. West Lafayette: Purdue University Press.

Wale, J. 1989a. "The Griff Colliery Company Limited, Warwickshire, 1882–1914: A Case Study in Business History." *Midland History* 14 (1): 95–119.

Wale, J. 1989b. "The Cramlington Coal Company, Northumberland, 1824–1914: A Case Study in Business History." *Business Archives* 58: 1–21.

Wale, J. 1990. "The Reliability of Reported Profits and Asset Values, 1890–1914: Case Studies from the British Coal Industry." *Accounting and Business Research* 20 (79): 253–267.

Weintraub, E. R. 1998a. "From Rigor to Axiomatics: The Marginalization of Griffith C. Evans." In *From Interwar Pluralism to Postwar Neoclassicism*, edited by M. Morgan and M. Rutherford, 227–259. Durham: Duke University Press.

Weintraub, E. R. 1998b. "Controversy: Axiomatisches Mißverstandis." *The Economic Journal* 108 (451): 1837–1847.

Weintraub, E. R. 2001. "Measurement, and Changing Images of Mathematical Knowledge." In *The Age of Economic Measurement*, edited by J. L. Klein and M. S. Morgan, 303–312. Durham: Duke University Press.

Weintraub, E. R. 2002. *How Economics Became a Mathematical Science*. Durham: Duke University Press.

Weisberg, M. 2007. "Who is a Modeler?" *British Journal for the Philosophy of Science* 58 (2): 207–233.

Wellman, B. and S. D. Berkowitz, eds. 1997. *Social Structures: A Network Approach*. Greenwich: JAI Press.

Westfield, F. M. 1955. "Marginal Analysis, Multi-Plant Firms, and Business Practice: An Example." *The Quarterly Journal of Economics* 69 (2): 253–268.

White, G. 2004. "Capital, Distribution and Macroeconomics: 'Core' Beliefs and Theoretical Foundations." *Cambridge Journal of Economics* 28 (4): 527–547.

White, H. C. 1997. "Varieties of Markets." In *Social Structures: A Network Approach*, edited by B. Wellman and S. D. Berkowitz, 226–260. Greenwich: JAI Press.

Wieviorka, M. 1992. "Case Studies: History or Sociology?" In *What is a Case? Exploring the Foundations of Social Inquiry*, edited by C. C. Ragin and H. S. Becker, 159–172. Cambridge: Cambridge University Press.

Wilber, C. K. and R. S. Harrison. 1978. "The Methodological Basis of Institutional Economics: Pattern Model, Storytelling, and Holism." *Journal of Economic Issues* 12 (3): 61–89.

Williamson, O. E. 1975. *Markets and Hierarchies: Analysis and Antitrust Implications*. New York: The Free Press.

Windmuller, J. P. 1984. "Employers Associations in Comparative Perspective: Organization, Structure, Administration." In *Employers Association and Industrial Relations: A Comparative Study*, edited by J. P. Windmuller and A. Gladstone, 1–23. Oxford: Clarendon Press.

Wisman, J. D. and J. Rozansky. 1991. "The Methodology of Institutionalism Revisited." *Journal of Economic Issues* 25 (3): 709–737.

Wood, A. 1975. *A Theory of Profits*. Cambridge: Cambridge University Press.

Wray, L. R. 1998. *Understanding Modern Money: The Key to Full Employment and Price Stability*. Cheltenham: Edward Elgar.

Wray, L. R. 2003. "Seigniorage or Sovereignty?" In *Modern Theories of Money: The Nature and Role of Money in Capitalist Economies*, edited by L.-P. Rochon and S. Rossi, 84–102. Cheltenham: Edward Elgar.

Yanagisako, S. J. 1979. "Family and Household: The Analysis of Domestic Groups." *Annual Review of Anthropology* 8: 161–205.

Yeung, H. 1997. "Critical Realism and Realist Research in Human Geography: A Method or a Philosophy in Search of a Method?" *Progress in Human Geography* 21 (1): 51–74.

Yin, R. K. 1981a. "The Case Study Crisis: Some Answers." *Administrative Science Quarterly* 26 (1): 58–65.

Yin, R. K. 1981b. "The Case Study as a Serious Research Strategy." *Knowledge: Creation, Diffusion, Utilization* 3 (1): 97–114.

Yin, R. K. 1994. *Case Study Research: Design and Methods*, 2nd edn. London: Sage.

Zimmermann, E. W. 1951. *World Resources and Industries: A Functional Appraisal of the Availability of Agricultural and Industrial Materials*, Revised edn. New York: Harper and Brothers.

Index

Page numbers in *italic* indicate a figure and page numbers in **bold** indicate a table on the corresponding page.

Printed in the United States
by Baker & Taylor Publisher Services